DICTIONARY OF
COMPUTING

Other titles in the series

English Law Dictionary
ISBN 0-948549-01-7

English Business Dictionary
ISBN 0-948549-00-9

Dictionary of Government and Politics
ISBN 0-948549-05-X

English Medical Dictionary
ISBN 0-948549-02-5

Dictionary of Information Technology
ISBN 0-948549-03-3

DICTIONARY OF
COMPUTING

S.M.H. Collin

PETER COLLIN PUBLISHING

First published in Great Britain 1988
by Peter Collin Publishing Ltd
31 Teddington Park, Teddington, Middlesex

British Library Cataloguing in Publication Data

Collin, S. M. H., *1966–*
Dictionary of computing.
1. Computer system. Encyclopaedias
I. Title
004′.03′21

ISBN 0-948549-04-1

Text computer typeset in Geneva, Times, Stymie and Souvenir by
Systemset, Stotfold, Hertfordshire
Printed in Great Britain by
Richard Clay Ltd, Bungay, Suffolk

PREFACE

This dictionary provides the user with a comprehensive vocabulary used in the field of computing. It covers all aspects of computing, including hardware, software, peripherals, networks, programming, as well as many applications in which computers are used, such as desktop publishing.

The 5,000 main words are each explained in simple English, using a limited vocabulary of about 500 words, over and above those words which appear in the dictionary as main words. Many examples are given to show how the words and phrases can be used in context. Words which pose particular problems of grammar have short grammatical notes attached.

General comments about particular items of interest, complex ideas, or hardware or software applications are given in separate boxes. Quotations from a wide range of magazines and journals are given to show how the words are used in real text. The supplement at the back of the book describes the architecture of single and multi-user computer systems, and a central processing unit; the ASCII and EBCDIC codes are listed and the RS232 interface is described along with examples of different programming languages.

We would like to thank many people who helped with this dictionary, by reading the text and making useful comments. The cover design is by Peter Cartwright.

Aa

A = AMPERE base SI unit of electrical current; defined as the current flowing through an impedance of one ohm which has a voltage of one volt across it

A hexadecimal equivalent to decimal number 10

A-bus *noun* main internal bus in a microprocessor

A programming language (APL) *noun* high-level programming language used for scientific and mathematical work

A to D *or* **A/D** = ANALOG TO DIGITAL changing a signal from an analog form to a digitally coded form; **A to D converter** = (analog to digital converter) device used to convert an analog input to a digital output form which can be understood by a computer; *the speech signal was first passed through an A to D converter before being analysed; opposite is* DIGITAL TO ANALOG

abbreviation *noun* short form of a word *or* command *or* instruction; *within the text, the abbreviation proc is used instead of processor;* **abbreviated addressing** *or* **abb. add.** = use of a smaller computer address word than normal which provides faster address decoding operations

abend *noun* = ABNORMAL END unexpected stoppage of a program being run, due to a fault *or* error *or* power failure; *an interrupt from a faulty printer caused an abend;* **abend recovery program** = software that will reload a program (or system software) and restart it at the point where the abend occurred; *if a fault occurs, data loss will be minimized due to the improved abend recovery program*

abnormal *adjective* not normal; *its abnormal for two consecutive disk drives to break down; abnormal error;* **abnormal end** *or* **abend** *or* **abnormal termination** = unexpected stoppage of a program being run, caused by a fault *or* error *or* power failure

◊ **abnormally** *adverb* not as normal *or* not as usual; *the signal is abnormally weak; the error rate with this disk is abnormally high*

abort *verb* to end a process (when a malfunction occurs), by switching the computer off manually *or* by an internal feature; *the program was aborted by pressing the red button; abort the program before it erases any more files; see also* RESET

absolute address *or* **actual address** *or* **machine address** *noun* **(a)** computer storage address that directly, without any modification, accesses a location *or* device; *compare* INDEXED ADDRESS *program execution is slightly faster if you code only with absolute addresses* **(b)** computer storage address that can only access one location; **absolute addressing** = locating a data word in memory by the use of its absolute address; **absolute assembler** = type of assembly language program designed to produce code which uses only absolute addresses and values; **absolute code** = binary code which directly operates the central processing unit, using only absolute addresses and values (this is the final form of a program after a compiler *or* assembler pass); *see also* OBJECT CODE; **absolute instruction** = instruction which completely describes the operation to be performed (no other data is required); **absolute loader** = program that loads a section of code into main memory; **absolute maximum rating** = maximum values or limits of a system; **absolute program** = computer program written in absolute code; **absolute value** = size *or* value of a number, regardless of its sign; *the absolute value of -62.34 is 62.34; an absolute value of the input is generated*

AC = ALTERNATING CURRENT electric current whose value varies with time in a regular, sinusoidal way

COMMENT: the mains electricity supply uses alternating current to minimize transmission power loss, with a frequency of 50Hz in U.K., 60Hz in the USA

ACC *noun* = ACCUMULATOR most important internal CPU storage register, containing the data word that is to be processed

acceleration time *noun* **(a)** time taken for a disk drive to spin a disk at the correct speed, from rest; *allow for acceleration time in the access time* (b) total time between an access instruction being issued (to a peripheral) and the data being is transferred

accept *verb* (a) to agree to do something; *he accepted the quoted price for printing; she has accepted our terms; he did not accept the programming job he was offered* (b) to take something which is being offered; *the laser printer will accept a card as small as a business card; the multi-disk reader will accept 3.5 inch disks as well as 5.25 inch formats;* call accept signal = signal sent by a device showing that it is willing to accept (caller's) data

◇ **acceptable** *adjective* which can be accepted; *the error rate was very low, and is acceptable; for the price, the scratched case is acceptable*

◇ **acceptance** *noun* action of accepting something; acceptance sampling = testing a small random part of a batch to see if the whole batch is up to standard; acceptance test *or* testing = method of checking that a piece of equipment will perform as required *or* will reach required standards

access 1 *noun* being allowed to use a computer and read *or* alter files stored in it (this is usually controlled by a security device such as a password); to have access to something = to be able to get *or* examine *or* reach something; *to have access to a file of data; he has access to numerous sensitive files;* to bar access to a system = to prevent a person from using a system; *after he was discovered hacking, he was barred access to the system;* access arm = mechanical device in a disk drive used to position the read/write head over the correct track on a disk; *the access arm moves to the parking region during transport;* access charge = cost due when logging onto a system *or* viewing special pages on a bulletin board; access code = series of characters *or* symbols that must be entered to identify a user before access to a computer is permitted; *see also* PASSWORD; access line = permanently connected communications line between a terminal and a computer; access method = means used for the internal transfer of data between memory and display *or* peripheral devices (differences in the methods used is often the cause of compatibility problems); access point = test point on a circuit board *or* in software, allowing an engineer to check signals *or* data; direct access storage device (DASD) = storage medium whose memory locations can be directly read *or* written to; disk access = operations

required to read from or write to a magnetic disk, including device selection, sector and track address, movement of read/write head to the correct location and access the location on disk; disk access management = regulating the users who can access stored data; direct memory access (DMA) = direct, rapid link between a peripheral and a computer's main memory which avoids the use of accessing routines for each item of data required; public access terminal = terminal which can be used by anyone to access a computer; instantaneous access = storage that has virtually no access time delay, such as access to RAM; *the instantaneous access of the RAM disk was welcome;* parallel access = data transfer between two devices with a number of bits (usually one byte wide) being sent simultaneously; random access = ability to access immediately memory locations in any order; sequential access = method of retrieving data from a storage device by starting at the beginning of the medium (such as tape) and reading each record until the required data is found; serial access = one item of data accessed by reading through all the data in a list until the correct one is found **2** *verb* to call up (data) which is stored in a computer; to obtain data from a storage device; *she accessed the employee's file stored on the computer*

◇ **access control** *noun* security device (such as a password) that only allows selected users to use a computer system *or* read files

> COMMENT: a good access control system should allow valid users to gain access and operate the computer easily with the minimum of checks, whilst barring entry to hackers *or* unauthorized users

◇ **accessible** *adjective* which can be reached *or* accessed; *details of customers are easily accessible from the main computer files*

◇ **access time** *noun* (a) total time which a storage device takes between the moment the data is requested and the data being returned; *the access time of this dynamic RAM chip is around 200nS - we have faster versions if your system clock is running faster* (b) length of time required to find a file *or* program, either in main memory *or* a secondary memory source

accessory *noun* useful device which is attached to *or* used with another; *the printer comes with several accessories, such as a soundproof hood; this popular home computer has a large range of accessories*

accidental *adjective* which happens by accident; *always keep backup copies in case of accidental damage to the master file*

accordion fold *or* **fanfold** *noun* method of folding continuous paper, one sheet in one direction, the next sheet in the opposite direction, allowing the paper to be fed into a printer continuously with no action on the part of the user

accumulate *verb* to gather several things together over a period of time; *we have gradually accumulated a large databank of names and addresses*

◊ **accumulator** *or* **ACC (register)** *noun* most important internal CPU storage register, containing the data word that is to be processed; **accumulator shift instruction** = command to shift the contents of an accumulator left *or* right by one bit

accurate *adjective* correct; without any errors; *the printed bar code has to be accurate to within a thousandth of a micron*

◊ **accurately** *adverb* correctly *or* with no errors; *the OCR had difficulty in reading the new font accurately; the error was caused because the data had not been accurately keyed*

◊ **accuracy** *noun* total number of bits used to define a number in a computer, the more bits allocated the more accurate the definition

COMMENT: most high level languages allow numbers to be represented in a more accurate form by using two or more words to store the number

achieve *verb* to succeed in doing something; *the hardware designers are trying to achieve compatibility between all the components of the system*

ACIA = ASYNCHRONOUS COMMUNICATIONS INTERFACE ADAPTER circuit that allows a computer to transmit and receive serial data using asynchronous access

ACK = ACKNOWLEDGE signal that is sent from a receiver to indicate that a transmitted message has been received and that it is ready for the next one; *the printer generates an ACK signal when it has received data*

Ackerman's function *noun* recursive function used to test the ability of a compiler to cope with recursion

acknowledge 1 *noun* signal that is sent from a receiver to indicate that a transmitted message has been received and that it is ready for the next one **2** *verb* (i) to tell a sender that a message *or* letter has been received; (ii) to send a signal from a receiver to show that a transmitted message has been received; **acknowledge character** = special code sent by a receiver to indicate to the transmitter that the message has been correctly received

acoustic *adjective* referring to sound; **acoustic hood** = soundproof hood placed over a printer to reduce the noise; *the acoustic hood allows us to speak and print in the same room;* **acoustic delay line** = original data storage method that delays data (in the form of sound pulses) as it travels across a medium; **acoustic store** *or* **acoustic memory** = (old) regenerative memory that uses an acoustic delay line

◊ **acoustic coupler** *noun* device that connects to a telephone handset, converting binary computer data into sound signals to allow data to be transmitted down a telephone line; *I use an acoustic coupler with my lap-top computer*

COMMENT: the acoustic coupler also converts back from sound signals to digital signals when receiving messages; it is basically the same as a modem but uses a handset on which a loudspeaker is placed to send the signals rather than direct connection to the phone line. It is portable, and clips over both ends of a normal telephone handset; it can be used even in a public phone booth

acquisition *noun* accepting *or* capturing *or* collecting information; **data acquisition** = gathering data about a subject

ACR = AUDIO CASSETTE RECORDER; **ACR interface** = interface which allows a cassette recorder to be linked to a computer

acronym *noun* abbreviation, formed from various letters, which makes up a word which can be pronounced; *the acronym FORTRAN means Formula Translator; the acronym RAM means Random Access Memory*

action *noun* thing which has been done; *action has been taken to repair the fault;* **to take action** = to do something; **action cycle** = complete set of actions involved in one operation (including reading data, processing, storing results, etc.); **action message** = prompt given to inform the user that an action *or* input is required

◊ **activate** *verb* to start a process *or* to make a device start working; *pressing CR activates the printer*

◊ **active** *adjective* busy *or* working *or* being used; **active device** = electronic component that requires electrical power to operate and provides gain *or* a logical function; *compare with* PASSIVE DEVICE; **active file** = file which is being worked on; **active star** = network consisting of a central point with nodes branching out, in which a central processor controls and routes all messages between devices; **active state** = electronic state in which an action occurs; **active window** = area of display screen in which you are currently working; *see also* WINDOW

◊ **activity** *noun* **(a)** being active *or* busy; **activity loading** = method of organizing disk contents so that the most often accessed files *or* programs can be loaded quickly; **activity ratio** = number of files currently in use compared to the total stored **(b) activities** = jobs *or* tasks which are being performed on a computer

actual address *or* **absolute address** *noun* computer storage address that directly, without any modification, accesses a location *or* device; *compare with* INDEXED ADDRESS; **actual code** = binary code which directly operates the central processing unit, using only absolute addresses and values (this is the final form of a program after a compiler *or* assembler pass); **actual instruction** = the resulting instruction executed after the modification of an original instruction

actuator *noun* mechanical device that can be controlled by an external signal (such as the read/write head in a disk drive)

ACU = AUTOMATIC CALLING UNIT device which allows a computer to call stations *or* dial telephone numbers automatically

A/D *or* **A to D** = ANALOG TO DIGITAL change a signal from an analog form to a digitally coded form

ADA *noun* high-level programming language that is used mainly in military, industrial and scientific fields of computing

adapt *verb* to change to fit; *can this computer be adapted to take 5.25 inch disks ?*

◊ **adapter** *or* **adaptor** *noun* device that allows two *or* more incompatible devices to be connected together; *the cable adapter allows attachment of the scanner to the SCSI interface; the cable to connect the scanner to the adapter is included in the package;* **adapter card** = add on interface board that allows incompatible devices to communicate; **adapter plug** = plug which allows devices with different plugs (two-pin, three-pin, etc.) to be fitted into the same socket; **data adapter unit** = device that interfaces a CPU to one or more communications channels

◊ **adaptation** *noun* ability of a device to adjust its sensitivity range according to various situations; *the adaptation of the eye to respond to different levels of brightness*

◊ **adaptive channel allocation** *noun* providing communications channels according to demand rather than a fixed allocation; **adaptive routing** = ability of a system to change its communications routes according to various events *or* situations such as line failure; **adaptive systems** = ability of a system to alter its responses and processes according to inputs *or* events *or* situations

adaptor *see* ADAPTER

ADC *noun* = ANALOG TO DIGITAL CONVERTER device used to convert analog input to a digital output form, that can be understood by a computer

add *verb* **(a)** to put figures together to make a total; *in the spreadsheet each column should be added to make a subtotal;* **add time** = period of time taken to perform one addition operation (either of a CPU *or* adder); **add register** = register which is an adder **(b)** to put things together to form a larger group; *the software house has added a new management package to its range of products; adding or deleting material from the text is easy using function keys*

◊ **addend** *noun* number added to the augend in an addition

◊ **adder** *noun* device *or* routine that provides the sum of two *or* more (digital *or* analog) inputs; **adder-subtractor** = device that can either add or subtract; **full adder** *or* **three input adder** = binary addition circuit which can produce the sum of two inputs, and can also accept a carry input, producing a carry output if necessary; **half adder** *or* **two input adder** = binary addition circuit which can produce the sum of two inputs and a carry output if necessary, but will not accept a carry input; **parallel adder** = a number of full adders arranged in parallel to add two words at once; **serial adder** = one bit full adder used to add two words one bit at a time

> COMMENT: a parallel adder takes one clock cycle to add two words, a serial adder takes a time equal to the number of bits in a word to add

◊ **add-in** *noun & adjective* (something) which is added; *the first method is to use a page description language, the second is to use an add-in processor card; can you explain the add-in card method? processing is much faster with add-in cards*

◊ **addition** *adjective* arithmetic operation that produces the sum of an addend and augend; **addition record** = record with changes used to update a master record *or* file; **addition time** = time an adder takes to carry out an add operation; **addition without carry** = addition operation without any carry bits *or* words; *same as* EXOR FUNCTION; **destructive addition** = addition operation in which the result is stored in the location of one of the operands used in the sum, so overwriting it

◊ **additional** *adjective* which is added *or* which is extra; *can we add three additional workstations to the network ?*

◊ **add-on** *noun & adjective* piece of software *or* hardware that is added to a computer system to improve its performance; *the add-on hard disk will boost the computer's storage capabilities; the new add-on board allows colour graphics to be displayed*

address 1 *noun* number allowing a central processing unit to reference a physical location in a storage medium in a computer system; *each separate memory word has its own unique address; this is the address at which the data starts;* **absolute address** *or* **actual address** *or* **direct address** = (i) computer storage address (within a CPU's address range) that directly, without any modification, accesses a location *or* device; (ii) computer storage address that can only access one location; **address access time** = total time which a storage device takes between the moment the data is requested and the data being returned; **address bus** = physical connection that carries the address data in parallel form from the central processing unit to external devices; **address computation** = operation on address data (in an instruction); **address decoder** = logical circuit that will produce a signal when a certain address *or* range is placed on the address bus; **address field** *or* **operand field** = part of a computer instruction that contains the location of the operand; **address format** = rules defining the way the operands, data and addresses are arranged in an instruction; **address mapping** =

virtual address translated to an absolute real address; **address mark** = special code on a disk that indicates the start of sector location data; **address modification** = changing the address field, so that it can refer to a different location; **address register** = register in a computer that is able to store all the bits that make up an address which can then be processed as a single unit (in small micros, the address register is usually made up of two data bytes); *see also* MAR; **address space** = total number of possible locations that can be directly addressed by the program *or* CPU; **address strobe** = signal (pulse) that indicates that a valid address is on the address bus; **address track** = track on a magnetic disk containing the addresses of files, etc., stored on other tracks; **address word** = computer word, usually made up, in a small micro, of two data words that contain the address data; **base address** = initial address in a program used as a reference for others; **initial address** = address at which the first location of a program is stored; **machine address** = storage address that directly, without any modification, accesses a location *or* device; **relative address** = location specified in relation to a reference (address) **2** *verb* to put the location data onto an address bus to identify which word in memory *or* storage device is to be accessed; *a larger address word increases the amount of memory a computer can address*

◊ **addressability** *noun* the control available over pixels on screen

◊ **addressable** *adjective* which can be addressed; *all the 5Mb of RAM is addressable;* **addressable cursor** = cursor which can be programmed to be placed in a certain position; **addressable terminal** = terminal that will only accept data if it has the correct address and identification number in the message header

◊ **addressing** *noun* process of accessing a location in memory; **absolute addressing** = locating a data word stored in memory, by the use of its absolute address; **abbreviated addressing** = use of a smaller address word than normal, which provides faster address decoding operations; **bit addressing** = selecting a register and examing one bit within it; **deferred addressing** = indirect addressing where the location accessed contains the address of the operand to be processed; **direct addressing** = method of addressing where the storage location address given in the instruction is the location to be used; **immediate addressing** = accessing data immediately because it is held in the address field itself; **indexed addressing** = addressing mode, in which the storage location to be accessed is made up of a start (base) address and an offset (index) word, which is then added to it to give the address to be used; **indirect addressing** = way of addressing data, where the first instruction refers to an address which contains a second address; **addressing capacity** = largest location that a certain program *or* CPU can directly address, without special features (such as virtual memory *or* memory banks); **addressing level** = zero-level: operand is the address part of the instruction; first-level: operand stored at the address of the instruction; second-level: operand stored at the address given in the instruction; **addressing method** = manner in which a section of memory is located; **addressing mode** = way in which a location is addressed, either sequential, indexed, direct, etc.

adjacent *adjective* which is near *or* next to something; *the address is stored adjacent to the customer name field*

adjust *verb* to change something to fit new conditions *or* so that it works better; *you can adjust the brightness and contrast by turning a knob*
◊ **adjustment** *noun* slight change made to something so that it works better; *the brightness needs adjustment; I think the joystick needs adjustment as it sometimes gets stuck*

administrator *noun* control *or* supervisor *or* executive software *or* person; **data administrator** = control section of a database management system; **database administrator (DBA)** = person in charge of running and maintaining a database system

ADP = AUTOMATIC DATA PROCESSING data processing done by a computer

advance *verb* to move forward; to make something move forward; *the paper is advanced by turning this knob; advance the cursor two spaces along the line*
◊ **advanced** *adjective* more complicated *or* more difficult to learn; **advanced version** = program with more complex features for use by an experienced user

adventure game *noun* game played on a computer, where the user pretends to be a hero in an imaginary land and has to get through various dangerous situations, fight monsters, etc.

affect *verb* to touch *or* to influence *or* to change something; *changes in voltage will affect the way the computer functions*

affirmative *adjective* meaning "yes"; **the answer was in the affirmative** = the answer was "yes"; **affirmative acknowledgement** = acknowledge signal from the receiver that it has accepted the message and is ready for the next one

afterglow *see* PERSISTENCE

aggregate *noun* **data aggregate** = collection of items of data that are related

AI = ARTIFICIAL INTELLIGENCE the design and development of computer programs that attempt to imitate human intelligence and decision-making functions, providing basic reasoning and other human characteristics; *see also* EXPERT SYSTEM, IKBS

aid 1 *noun* help; *the computer is a great aid to rapid processing of large amounts of information;* **diagnostic aid** = hardware *or* software device that helps find faults **2** *verb* to help; *industrial design is aided by computers; see also* COMPUTER-AIDED

air gap *noun* narrow gap between a recording *or* playback head and the magnetic medium

alarm *noun* ringing or other sound which warns of a danger; *all staff must leave the building if the alarm sounds; an alarm rings when the printer has run out of paper*

algebra *noun* use of letters in certain mathematical operations to represent unknown numbers *or* a range of possible numbers; **Boolean algebra** = rules set down to define, simplify and manipulate logical functions, based on statements that are true or false

ALGOL = ALGORITHMIC LANGUAGE high level programming language using algorithmic methods for mathematical and technical applications

algorithm *noun* rules used to define *or* perform a specific task *or* to solve a specific problem
◊ **algorithmic** *adjective* expressed using algorithms; **algorithmic language** = computer language designed to process and express algorithms, such as ALGOL

QUOTE image processing algorithms are step by step procedures for performing image processing operations
Byte

QUOTE the steps are: acquiring a digitized image, developing an algorithm to process it, processing the image, modifying the algorithm until you are satisfied with the result
Byte

QUOTE the complex algorithms needed for geometrical calculations make heavy demands on the processor
PC Business World

alien *adjective* different *or* not fitting the usual system; **alien disk =** disk formatted on another system *or* containing data in a format which is in a form that cannot be read *or* understood; **alien disk reader =** add-on device which allows a computer to access data on disks from other computers *or* systems; *when you have an alien disk select the multi-disk option to allow you to turn the disk drive into an alien disk reader*

align *verb* **(a)** to make sure that the characters to be printed are spaced and levelled correctly **(b)** to ensure that a read/write head is correctly positioned over the recording medium
◊ **aligner** *noun* device used to make sure that the paper is straight in a printer
◊ **aligning edge** *noun* edge of an optical character recognition system used to position a document
◊ **alignment** *noun* correct spacing and levelling of printed characters; **in alignment =** correctly aligned; **out of alignment =** not aligned correctly; **alignment pin =** peg that fits in a hole to ensure that two devices are correctly aligned

allocate *verb* to divide (a period of time *or* a piece of work) in various ways and share it out between users; *the operating system allocated most of main memory to the spreadsheet program*
◊ **allocation** *noun* dividing something in various ways; *allocation of time or capital to a project;* **allocation routine =** short program that divides the memory resources of a system between the different peripherals that use it; **dynamic allocation =** system where resources are allocated during a program run, rather than being determined in advance

alpha beta technique *noun* (free structure) technique used in artificial intelligence for solving game and strategy problems

alpha radiation *noun* naturally occurring radiation; **alpha-particle =** emitted alpha radiation particle; **alpha-particle sensitivity =** problem experienced by certain (MOS) memory devices exposed to alpha radiation, causing loss of stored charge (data)

alphabet *noun* the 26 letters used to make words
◊ **alphabetic character (set)** *noun* characters (capitals and small letters) that make up the alphabet; **alphabetic string =** string that only contains alphabetic characters
◊ **alphabetical order** *noun* arrangement of records (such as files, index cards) in the order of the letters of the alphabet (A,B,C,D, etc.)
◊ **alphabetically** *adverb* in alphabetical order; *the files are arranged alphabetically under the customer's name*
◊ **alphabetize** *verb* to put into alphabetical order; *enter the bibliographical information and alphabetize it*

alphageometric *adjective* (set of codes) that instruct a teletext terminal to display various graphics patterns *or* characters

alphameric *US* = ALPHANUMERIC

alphamosaic *adjective* (character set) used in teletext to provide alphanumeric and graphics characters

alphanumeric *adjective* **alphanumeric characters** *or* **alphanumerics =** roman letters and arabic numerals (and other signs such as punctuation marks); **alphanumeric data =** data that represents the letters of the alphabet and the arabic numerals; **alphanumeric display =** display device able to show characters as well as numbers; **alphanumeric keyboard =** keyboard containing character keys as well as numerical keys; **alphanumeric operand =** operand which can contain alphanumeric characters, such as a string; **alphanumeric string =** series of alphanumeric characters that are manipulated and treated as a single unit

QUOTE geometrical data takes up more storage space than alphanumeric data
PC Business World

alphaphotographic *adjective* which represents pictures using predefined graphics characters, for teletext services
◊ **alphasort** *verb* to sort data into alphabetical order

alter *verb* to change; *to alter the terms of a contract; the program specifications have just been altered*

◊ **alterable** *adjective* which can be altered; *see* EAPROM, EAROM

◊ **alteration** *noun* change which has been made; *the agreement was signed without any alterations; the new version of the software has many alterations and improvements*

alternate 1 *verb* to change from one state to another and back, over and over again **2** *adjective* which change from one to another; **alternate mode** = application for multi-user use, where two operators can access and share a single file at the same time; **alternate route** = backup path in a communications system, used in case of a fault *or* breakdown

◊ **alternately** *adverb* switching from one to the other

◊ **alternation** *noun* logical function that produces a true output if any input is true

◊ **alternating current** *or* **AC** *noun* electric current whose value varies with time in a regular, sinusoidal way (changing direction of flow each half cycle)

alternative 1 *noun* thing which can be done instead of another; *what is the alternative to re-keying all the data?;* we have no alternative = there is nothing else we can do **2** *adjective* other *or* which can take the place of something; **alternative denial** = logical function whose output is false if all inputs are true and true if any input is false

ALU = ARITHMETIC LOGIC UNIT section of the CPU that performs all arithmetic and logical functions

ambient *adjective* normal background (conditions); **ambient temperature** = normal average temperature of the air around a device

ambiguous *adjective* which has two possible meanings; **ambiguous filename** = filename which is not unique to a single file, making it difficult to locate the file

◊ **ambiguity** *noun* something which is not clearly defined; **ambiguity error** = error due to incorrect selection of ambiguous data

amendment record *noun* record containing new information used to update a master record *or* file

American National Standards Institute (ANSI) organization which specifies computer and software standards including those of high-level programming languages

American Standard Code for Information Interchange (ASCII) code which represents alphanumeric characters as binary codes

amount 1 *noun* quantity of data *or* paper, etc.; *what is the largest amount of data which can be processed in one hour?* **2** *verb* to **amount to** = to make a total of; *the total keyboarded characters amount to ten million*

amp *or* **ampere (A)** *noun* base SI unit of electrical current; defined as the current flowing through an impedance of one ohm which has a voltage of one volt across it NOTE: used with figures: **a 13-amp fuse**

ampersand *noun* printing sign (&) which means "and"

amplifier *noun* electronic circuit that magnifies the power of a signal

◊ **amplification** *noun* the output-to-input signal strength ratio; *increase the amplification of the input signal; the amplification is so high, the signal is distorting*

◊ **amplify** *verb* to magnify a signal power *or* amplitude; *the received signal needs to be amplified before it can be processed*

amplitude *noun* strength *or* size of a signal; **amplitude quantization** = conversion of an analog signal to a numerical representation

analog *or* **analogue** *noun* representation and measurement of numerical data by continuously variable physical quantities, such as the size of electrical voltages; *compare with* DIGITAL; **analog channel** = communications line that carries analog signals such as speech; **analog computer** = computer which processes data in analog form (that is, data which is represented by a continuously varying signal - as opposed to digital data); **analog gate** = logic gate whose output is proportional to an input signal; **analog input card** = all circuitry on one PCB required for amplifying and converting analog input signals to a digital form; **analog output card** = all circuitry on one PCB required to convert digital output data from a computer to an analog form; **analog recording** = storing signals in their natural form without conversion to digital form; **analog representation** = value *or* variable in analog form; **analog signal** =

continuously varying signal; **analog to digital (A to D** or **A/D) =** change a signal from an analog form to a digitally coded form; **analog to digital converter (ADC** or **A to D converter) =** device used to convert an analog input signal to a digital output form, that can be understood by a computer; **digital to analog converter (DAC** or **D to A converter) =** circuit that outputs an analog signal that is proportional to the input digital number, and so converts a digital input to an analog form

COMMENT: a DAC allows the computer to work outside the computer's enviroment, controlling machines, producing sound or speech, etc.; an ADC allows real-world signals to be processed by a computer

analyse or **analyze** verb to examine in detail; *to analyse a computer printout; to analyse the market potential for a new computer*
◊ **analysis** noun detailed examination and report; *market analysis; sales analysis; to carry out an analysis of the market potential; to write an analysis of the sales position;* **cost analysis =** examination in advance of the costs of a new product; **data analysis =** to extract information and results from data; **systems analysis =** analysing a process or system to see if it could be more efficiently carried out by computer NOTE: plural is **analyses**
◊ **analyst** noun person who carries out an analysis of a problem; **systems analyst =** person who specializes in systems analysis
◊ **analyzer** noun electronic test equipment that displays various features of a signal

ancestral file noun system of backing up files (son to father to grandfather file), where the son is the current working file

ancillary equipment noun equipment which is used to make a task easier, but which is not absolutely necessary

AND or **coincidence function** noun logical function whose output is true if both its inputs are true; **AND** or **coincidence gate** or **circuit** or **element =** electronic gate that performs a logical AND function on electrical signals; **AND** or **coincidence operation =** processing two or more input signals, outputting their AND function

COMMENT: if both inputs are 1, results of the AND will be 1; if one of the input digits is 0, then AND will produce a 0

angstrom noun unit of measurement equal to one thousand millionth of a metre

angle noun measure of the change in direction, usually as the distance turned from a reference line

annotation noun comment or note in a program which explains how the program is to be used; **annotation symbol =** symbol used when making flowcharts, to allow comments to be added

annunciator noun & adjective signal that can be heard or seen that is used to attract attention

anode noun positive electrical terminal of a device

ANSI US = AMERICAN NATIONAL STANDARDS INSTITUTE organization which specifies computer and software standards, including those of high-level programming languages

answer 1 noun reply or solution to a question **2** verb **(a)** to reply or provide the solution to a question **(b)** to reply to a signal and set up a communications link; *the first modem originates the call and the second answers it;* **answer back =** signal sent by a receiving computer to identify itself; **answer time =** time taken for a receiving device to respond to a signal

anti- prefix meaning against; **anticoincidence circuit** or **function =** logical function whose output is true if either (of 2) inputs is true, and false if both inputs are the same
◊ **anti-tinkle suppression** noun (in a modem) switch which prevents other telephones on a line ringing when a modem dials out

aperture card noun method of storing microfilmed information with a card surround, that can contain punched information
◊ **aperture mask** noun mask used in colour monitors, used to keep separate the red, green and blue beams

APL = A PROGRAMMING LANGUAGE high-level programming language used in scientific and mathematical work

append verb to add data to an existing file or record
◊ **appendix** noun section at the back of a book, containing additional information; *for further details see the appendices; a complete list is printed in the appendix*

NOTE: plural is **appendices**

appliance *noun* machine, especially one used in the home; *all electrical appliances should be properly earthed*

◊ **appliance computer** *noun* ready to run computer system that can be bought in a shop, taken home and used immediately for a particular purpose; *see also* TURNKEY

application *noun* **(a)** asking for something, usually in writing; *application for an account on the system;* **application form** = form to be filled in when applying; *to fill in an application (form) for an account on the system* **(b)** task which a computer performs *or* problem which a computer solves (as opposed to an operating system which is the way in which a computer works); **application layer** = top layer in an ISO/OSI network, which requests a transmission (from a users program); **application orientated language** = programming language that provides functions that allow the user to solve certain application problems; **applications package** = set of computer programs and manuals that cover all aspects of a particular task (such as payroll, stock control, tax, etc.); **applications software** *or* **applications program** = programs which are used by a user to make the computer do what is required, designed to allow a particular task to be performed; *the multi-window editor is used to create and edit applications programs;* **applications specific integrated circuits (ASIC)** = specially designed ICs for one particular function *or* to special specifications; **applications terminal** = terminal (such as at a sales desk) which is specially configured to carry out certain tasks

QUOTE they have announced a fourth generation application development tool which allows users of PCs and PC networks to exchange data with mainframe databases
Minicomputer News

apply *verb* **(a)** to ask for something, usually in writing **(b)** to affect *or* to touch; *this formula applies only to data received after the interrupt signal*

approve *verb* **(a) to approve of** = to think something is good; *the new graphics monitor was approved by the safety council before being sold; I approve of the new editor - much easier to use* **(b)** to agree to something; *to approve the terms of a contract; the software has to be approved by the board; an approved modem should carry a label with a green circle and the words "Approved by ...."*

◊ **approval** *noun* **(a)** agreement that something can be used; *a BABT approval is needed for modems;* **certificate of approval** = document showing that an item has been approved officially **(b) on approval** = sale where the buyer only pays for goods if they are satisfactory
NOTE: no plural

approximate *adjective* not exact, but almost correct; *we have made an approximate calculation of the time needed for keyboarding*

◊ **approximately** *adverb* almost correctly; *processing time is approximately 10% lower than during the previous quarter*

◊ **approximating** *adjective* which is nearly correct; *the figures for running costs are only approximate*

◊ **approximation** *noun* rough calculation; *approximation of keyboarding time; the final figure is only an approximation;* **approximation error** = error caused by rounding off a real number

APT = AUTOMATICALLY PROGRAMMED TOOLS programming language used to control numerically controlled machines

Arabic *adjective* **Arabic numbers** *or* **figures** = figures such as 1, 2, 3, 4, etc. (as opposed to the Roman numerals I, II, III. IV, etc.); *the page numbers are written in Arabic figures*

arbitration *noun* **bus arbitration** = protocol and control of transmission over a bus that ensures fair usage by several users

arcade game *noun* adventure game played on a machine in a public place

architecture *noun* layout and interconnection of a computer's internal hardware and the logical relationships between CPU, memory and I/O devices; **onion skin architecture** = design of a computer system in layers, according to function *or* priority; *the onion skin architecture of this computer is made up of a kernel at the centre, an operating system, a low-level language and then the user's programs*

archive 1 *noun* storage of data over a long period; **archive file** = file containing data which is out of date, but which is kept for future reference **2** *verb* to put data in storage; **archived copy** = copy kept in storage

◊ **archival quality** *noun* length of time that a copy can be stored before it becomes illegible

QUOTE on-line archiving is also used to keep down the interruption needed for archiving to seconds

Computer News

area *noun* **(a)** measurement of the space taken up by something (calculated by multiplying the length by the width); *the area of this office is 3,400 square feet; we are looking for a shop with a sales area of about 100 square metres* **(b)** section of memory *or* code that is reserved for a certain purpose; **area search** = search for specific data within a certain section of memory *or* files; **image area** = region of a display screen in which characters can be displayed; **input area** = section of main memory that holds data transferred from backing store until it is processed

argue *verb* to discuss something about which you do not agree; *they argued over or about the design of the cover; we spent hours arguing with the managing director about the layout of the new factory* NOTE: you argue **with** someone **about** *or* **over** something

◊ **argument** *noun* **(a)** discussing something without agreeing; *they got into an argument with the customs officials over the documents; he was sacked after an argument with the managing director* **(b)** variable acted upon by an operator *or* function; *see also* OPERAND

arithmetic *noun* concerned with mathematical functions such as addition, subtraction, division and multiplication; **arithmetic capability** = ability of a device to perform mathematical functions; **arithmetic check** = further arithmetic operation carried out to ensure that a result is correct; **arithmetic functions** = calculations carried out on numbers, such as addition, subtraction, multiplication, division; **arithmetic instruction** = program instruction in which the operator defines the arithmetic operation to be carried out; *compare with* LOGICAL INSTRUCTION; **arithmetic logic unit (ALU)** *or* **arithmetic unit** = hardware section of a CPU that performs all the mathematical and logical functions; **arithmetic operation** = mathematical function carried out on data; **arithmetic operators** = symbol which indicates an arithmetic function (such as + for addition, x for multiplication); **arithmetic register** = memory location which stores operands; **arithmetic shift** = word *or* data moved one bit to the left *or* right inside a register, losing the bit shifted

off the end; *compare with* LOGICAL SHIFT; **external arithmetic** = arithmetic performed by a coprocessor; **internal arithmetic** = arithmetic performed by the ALU

arm 1 *noun* **access arm** = mechanical device in a disk drive used to position the read/write head over the correct track on a disk **2** *verb* (i) to prepare a device *or* machine *or* routine for action *or* inputs; (ii) to define which interrupt lines are active; **armed interrupt** = interrupt line which has been made active (using an interrupt mask)

array *noun* ordered structure containing individually accessible elements referenced by numbers, used to store tables *or* sets of related data; **alphanumeric array** = array whose elements are letters and numbers; **array bounds** = limits to the number of elements which can be given in an array; **array dimension** = number of elements in an array, given as rows and columns; **array element** = one individual piece of data within an array; **array processor** = computer that can act upon several arrays of data simultaneously, for very fast mathematical applications; *the array processor allows the array that contains the screen image to be rotated with one simple command;* **string array** = array whose elements can be strings (of alphanumeric characters); **three-dimensional array** = array made up of a number of two dimensional arrays, arranged in parallel, giving rows, columns and depth; **two-dimensional array** = ordered structure whose elements are arranged as a table (of rows and columns)

arsenide *see* GALLIUM ARSENIDE

artificial intelligence (AI) *noun* the design and device of computer programs that attempt to imitate human intelligence and decision making functions, providing basic reasoning and other human characteristics

artwork *noun* graphical work *or* images NOTE: no plural

ascender *noun* part of a character that rises above the main line of printed characters (as the 'tail' of a 'b', 'd', etc.)

ASCII = AMERICAN STANDARD CODE FOR INFORMATION INTERCHANGE code which represents alphanumeric characters in binary code; **ASCII character** = character which is in the ASCII list of codes; **ASCII file** = stored file containing only ASCII coded character data; *use a word processor or other program that generates a standard ASCII file;* **ASCII keyboard** = keyboard which gives all the ASCII characters NOTE: when speaking say "as-key"

ASIC = APPLICATION SPECIFIC INTEGRATED CIRCUITS specially designed ICs for one particular function *or* to special specifications

aspect *noun* way in which something appears; **aspect card** = card containing information on documents in an information retrieval system; **aspect ratio** = ratio of the width to the height of pixel shapes; **aspect system** = method of storing and indexing documents in a retrieval system

ASR = AUTOMATIC SEND/RECEIVE device *or* terminal that can transmit *or* receive information; *compare* KSR

COMMENT: an ASR terminal can input information via a keyboard or via a tape cassette or paper tape. It can receive information and store it in internal memory or on tape

assemble *verb* (a) to put a hardware *or* software product together from various smaller parts; *the parts for the disk drive are made in Japan and assembled in France* (b) to translate assembly code into machine code; *there is a short wait during which time the program is assembled into object code; syntax errors spotted whilst the source program is being assembled* (c) to insert specific library routines *or* macros *or* parameters into a program

◇ **assembler (program)** *noun* assembly program *or* program which converts a program written in assembly language into machine code; **absolute assembler** = type of assembly language program designed to produce code which uses only absolute addresses and values; **assembler error messages** = messages produced by an assembler program that indicate that errors have been found in the source code; **cross-assembler** = assembler that produces machine-code code for one computer while running on another; **single-pass assembler** = object code produced in one run through the assembler of the source program; **two-pass assembler** = assembler that converts an assembly language program into machine code in two passes, the first pass stores symbolic addresses, the second converts them to absolute addresses

◇ **assembly** *noun* (a) putting an item together from various parts; *there are no assembly instructions to show you how to put the computer together;* **assembly plant** = factory where units are put together from parts made in other factories (b) converting a program into machine code; **assembly code** = mnemonics which are used to represent machine code instructions in an assembler program; **assembly language** *or* **assembler language** = programming language used to code information which will then be converted to machine code; **assembly listing** = display of an assembly program ordered according to memory location; **assembly (language) program** = number of assembly code instructions which perform a task; **assembly routine** *or* **system** = *see* ASSEMBLER; **assembly time** = (i) time taken by an assembler program to translate a program; (ii) period during which an assembler is converting a program from assembly language into machine code

assertion *noun* (i) program statement of a fact *or* rule; (ii) fact that is true *or* defined as being true

assign *verb* (a) to give a computer *or* someone a job of work; *he was assigned the job of checking the sales figures; two PCs have been assigned to outputting the labels* (b) (i) to set a variable equal to a string of characters *or* numbers; (ii) to reserve part of a computer system for use while a program is running

◇ **assignment** *noun* (a) particular job of work (b) setting a variable equal to a value *or* string *or* character; **assignment statement** = basic programming command that sets a variable equal to a value *or* string *or* character

associative addressing *or* **content-addressable addressing** *noun* location addressed by its contents rather than its address; **associative processor** = processor that uses associative storage; **associative memory** *or* **storage** *or* **content-addressable storage** = method of data retrieval that uses part of the data rather than an address to locate the data; **associative storage register** = register that is located by its contents rather than a name *or* address

asterisk *noun* graphical symbol (*) used as a sign for multiplication

async *(informal)* = ASYNCHRONOUS

asynchronous *adjective* serial data *or* equipment which does not depend on being synchronized with another piece of equipment; **asynchronous access =** communications using handshaking to synchronize data transmission; **asynchronous communications =** data transmission between devices that is not synchronized to a clock, but is transmitted when ready; **asynchronous communications interface adapter (ACIA) =** circuit that allows a computer to transmit and receive serial data using asynchronous access; **asynchronous computer =** (i) computer that changes from one operation to the next according to signals received when the process is finished; (ii) computer in which a process starts on the arrival of signals *or* data, rather than on a clock pulse; **asynchronous mode =** linking a terminal linked to another piece of equipment in a way where the two need not be synchronized; **asynchronous port =** connection to a computer allowing asynchronous data access; *since asynchronous ports are used no special hardware is required;* **asynchronous transmission =** data transmission that uses handshaking signals rather than clock signals to synchronize data pulses

---

QUOTE each channel handles two forms of communication: asynchronous communication is mainly for transferring data between computers and peripheral devices, while character communication is for data transfer between computers

Electronics & Power

ATC = AUTHORIZATION TO COPY software publisher granting the user the permission to make a certain number of copies of a program

ATE = AUTOMATIC TEST EQUIPMENT computer controlled testing facilities, that can check a complex circuit *or* PCB for faults *or* problems

atom *noun* **(a)** smallest particle of an element that has the same properties as the element **(b)** value *or* string that cannot be reduced to a simpler form
◊ **atomic** *adjective* referring to atoms; **atomic clock =** very accurate clock which uses changes in energy of atoms as a reference

attach *verb* to fasten *or* to link; **attached processor =** separate microprocessor in a system that performs certain functions under the control of a central processor
◊ **attachment** *noun* device which is attached to a machine for a special

purpose; *there is a special single sheet feed attachment*

attend *verb* to be present at
◊ **attend to** *verb* to give careful thought to (something) and deal with it; *attend to this fault first - its the worst*
◊ **attended operation** *noun* process which has an operator standing by in case of problems
◊ **attention** *noun* giving careful thought, especially to processing a particular section of a program; *this routine requires the attention of the processor every minute;* **attention interruption =** interrupt signal that requests the attention of the processor; **attention key =** key on a terminal that sends an interrupt signal to the processor

attribute *noun* (i) field entry in a file; (ii) information concerning the display *or* presentation of information; *this attribute controls the colour of the screen;* **screen attributes =** variables defining the shape, size and colour of text *or* graphics displayed

auctioneering device *noun* device that will select the maximum *or* minimum signal from a number of input signals

audible *adjective* which can be heard; *the printer makes an audible signal when it runs out of paper*

audio *adjective & noun* referring to sound *or* to things which can be heard; **audio cassette =** reel of magnetic recording tape in a small protective casing inserted into a cassette recorder (for data storage), usually in home computers; **audio response unit =** speech synthesizer that allows a computer to speak responses to requests

audit *noun* noting tasks carried out by a computer; **audit trail =** recording details of use of a system by noting transactions carried out (used for checking on illegal use *or* to trace a malfunction)

augend *noun (in an addition)* the number to which another number, the addend, is added to produce the sum

augment *verb* to increase; **augmented addressing =** producing a usable address word from two shorter words
◊ **augmenter** *noun* value added to another

authentic *adjective* which is true
◊ **authenticate** *verb* to say that something is true *or* genuine

◊ **authentication** *noun* making sure that something is authentic; **authentication of messages** = using special codes to identify the sender of messages, so that the messages can be recognized as being genuine

author *noun* person who wrote a program; **author language** = programming language used to write CAL and training programs; **authoring system** = computer system that is able to run an author language

authority *noun* power to do something; *he has no authority to delete your account;* **authority file** *or* **list** = list of special terms used by people compiling a database and also by the users of the database

authorize *verb* **(a)** to give permission for something to be done; *to authorize the purchase of a new computer system* **(b)** to give someone the authority to do something

◊ **authorization** *noun* **(a)** permission *or* power to do something; **authorization to copy (ATC)** = software publisher granting the user the permission to make a certain number of copies of a program

> COMMENT: some companies have introduced ATC schemes which allow users of certain software to make duplicates of the companies' programs for a fee

(b) giving a user permission to access a system; **authorization code** = code used to restrict access to a computer system to authorized users only NOTE: no plural

◊ **authorized** *adjective* permitted; **authorized user** = person who is allowed to access a system

auto *adjective & prefix* automatic *or* which works without the user needing to act; **auto advance** = paper in a printer that is automatically moved forward to the next line at the end of a line; **auto-answer** = (modem) that will automatically answer a telephone when called; **auto-baud scanning** circuit that can automatically sense and select the correct baud rate for a line; **auto boot** = computer system that will initiate a boot-up procedure when it is switched on; **auto-dial** = to dial a number automatically using stored data; **auto-login** *or* **auto-logon** = phone number, password and user's number transmitted when requested by a remote system to automate logon; *see also* LOGIN, LOGON; **auto-redial** = (modem) that dials a telephone number again if engaged, until it replies; **auto repeat** = facility where a character is automatically

repeated if the key is kept pressed down; **auto restart** = computer that can initialize and reload its operating system if there is a fault *or* power failure *or* at switch on; **auto start** = facility to load a program automatically when the computer is switched on; **auto stop** = feature of a tape player which stops when it has reached the end of a tape; **auto verify** = verification procedure carried out automatically, as soon as the data has been saved

> QUOTE expansion accessories include auto-dial and auto-answer
> *Electronic & Wireless World*

automate *verb* to install machines to do work previously done by people

◊ **automation** *noun* use of machines to do work with very little supervision by people NOTE: no plural

automatic *noun* which works by itself, without being worked by an operator; **automatic calling unit (ACU)** = device which allows a computer to call telephone numbers automatically; **automatic carriage return** = system where the cursor automatically returns to the beginning of a new line when it reaches the end of the previous one; **automatic checking** = error detection and validation check carried out automatically on received data; **automatic data capture** = system where data is automatically recorded in a computer system, as it is input; **automatic data processing (ADP)** = data processing done by a computer; **automatic decimal adjustment** = process of lining up all the decimal points in a column of figures; **automatic error correction** = correction of received data, using error detection and correction codes; **automatic error detection** = use of an (alphanumeric) code, such as a gray code, that will allow any errors to be detected; **automatic letter writing** = writing form letters (using a wordprocessor); **automatic loader** = short program (usually in ROM) that will boot up a system and load a program; **automatic programming** = process of producing an optimum (operating) system for a particular process; **automatic repeat** = facility where a character is automatically repeated if the key is kept pressed down; **automatic sequencing** = ability of a computer to execute a number of programs *or* tasks without extra commands; **automatic test equipment (ATE)** = computer controlled testing facilities, that can check a complex circuit *or* PCB for faults *or* problems

◊ **automatically** *adverb* (machine) working without a person giving instructions; *the compiler automatically* *corrected the syntax errors; a SBC automatically limits the movement of the machine; the program is run automatically when the computer is switched on*

automation *see* AUTOMATE

auxiliary *adjective* which helps; *the computer room has an auxiliary power supply in case there is a mains failure;* **auxiliary equipment** = backup *or* secondary equipment in case of a breakdown; **auxiliary processor** = extra, specialized processor, such as an array *or* numerical processor that can work with a main CPU to increase execution speed; **auxiliary storage** *or* **memory** *or* **store** = any data storage medium (such a magnetic tape *or* floppy disk) that is not the main high speed computer storage (RAM); *disk drives and magnetic tape are auxiliary storage on this machine*

available *adjective* which can be obtained *or* bought; *available in all branches; item no longer available; items available to order only;* **available list** = list of unallocated memory and resources in a system; **available point** = smallest single unit *or* point of a display whose colour and brightness can be controlled; **available power** = maximum electrical *or* processing power that a system can deliver; **available time** = time during which a system may be used
◊ **availability** *noun* being easily obtained; *the availability of the latest software package is very good*
NOTE: no plural

avalanche *noun* one action starting a number of other actions; *there was an avalanche of errors after I pressed the wrong key*

average 1 *noun* number calculated by adding together several figures and dividing by the number of figures added; *the average for the last three months or the last three months' average; sales average or average of sales;* weighted average = average which is calculated taking several factors into account, giving some more value than others; **on an average** = in general; *we sell, on an average, five computers a day* **2** *adjective* middle (figure); **average cost per unit;** *average price; average sales per representative;* **average access time** = the average time taken between a request being sent and data being returned from a memory device; **average delay** = average time that a user must wait when trying to access a communication network; *see also* MEAN *the average delay increases at nine-thirty when everyone tries to log-in* **3** *verb* to produce as an average figure

◊ **average out** *verb* to come to a figure as an average; *it averages out at 120 dpi*

axis *noun* (i) line around which something turns; (ii) reference line which is the basis for coordinates on a graph; *the CAD package allows an axis to be placed anywhere;* **horizontal axis** = reference line used for horizontal coordinates on a graph; **vertical axis** = reference line used for vertical coordinates on a graph
NOTE: plural is **axes**

azerty keyboard *noun* method of arranging the keys on a keyboard where the first line begins AZERTY (used mainly in Europe); *compare* QWERTY

azimuth *noun* angle of a tape head to a reference (such as a tape plane); **azimuth alignment** = correct horizontal angle of a tape head to the magnetic tape; *azimuth alignment is adjusted with this small screw; azimuth alignment might not be correct for tape recorded on a different machine*

Bb

B hexadecimal equivalent to decimal number 11

babble *noun* crosstalk *or* noise from other sources which interferes with a signal

back 1 *noun* opposite side to the front; *there is a wide range of connectors at the back of the main unit* **2** *verb* to help; **battery backed** = (volatile storage device) that has a battery backup; *the RAM disk card has the option to be battery-backed; battery-backed CMOS memory replaces a disk drive in this portable*

back-end processor *noun* special purpose auxiliary processor

background *noun* **(a)** past work *or* experience; *his background is in the computer industry; the company is looking for someone with a background of success in the electronics industry; what is his background or do you know anything about his background?* **(b)** part of a picture which is behind the main object of interest; *the new graphics processor chip can handle background, foreground and sprite movement independently;* **background colour** = colour of a computer screen display (characters and graphics are normally displayed in a different foreground colour); *white background colour with black characters is less stressful for the eyes;* **background noise** = noise which is present along with the required signal; *the other machines around this device will produce a lot of background noise; the modem is sensitive to background noise* **(c)** system in a computer where low-priority work can be done in the intervals when very important work is not being done; **background job** = low priority task; **background printing** = printing from a computer while it is processing another task; *background printing can be carried out whilst you are editing another document;* **background program** = computer program with a very low priority; **background task** = process executed at any time by the computer system, not normally noticed by the user

◊ **background processing** *noun* **(a)** low priority job which is executed when there are no higher priority activities for the computer to attend to **(b)** process which does not use the on-line capabilities of a system
NOTE: opposite is **foreground**

backing *noun* **backing store** *or* **storage** *or* **memory** = permanent storage medium onto which data can be recorded before being processed by the computer *or* after processing for later retrieval; *by adding another disk drive, I will increase the backing store capabilities; paper tape is one of the slowest access backing stores; compare with* MAIN MEMORY

backlog *noun* work *or* tasks that have yet to be processed; *the programmers can't deal with the backlog of programming work; the queue was too short for the backlog of tasks waiting to be processed*
NOTE: no plural

backplane *noun* part of the body of a computer which holds the circuit boards, buses and expansion connectors (the backplane does not provide any processing functions); *see* MOTHERBOARD, RACK

backspace *noun* movement of a cursor *or* printhead back by one character; **backspace character** = code that causes a backspace action in a display device; **backspace key** = key which moves the cursor back one space; *if you make a mistake entering data, use the backspace key to correct it*

backtrack *verb* to carry out list processing in reverse, starting with the goal and working towards the proofs

back up *verb* **(a)** to make a copy of a file *or* data *or* disk; *the company accounts were backed up on disk as a protection against fire damage; the program enables users to back up hard disk files with a single command* **(b)** to help; *he brought along a file of documents to back up his claim; the printout backed up his argument for a new system*

◇ **backup** *adjective & noun* **(a)** helping; *we offer a free backup service to customers;* **battery backup** = use of a battery to provide power to a volatile device (RAM chip) to retain data after a computer has been switched off **(b) backup** *or* **backup file** *or* **backup copy** = copy of a file *or* set of data kept for security against errors in the original *or* master copy; **backup copy** = copy of a computer disk to be kept in case the original disk is damaged; *the most recent backup copy is kept in the safe;* **backup procedure** = method of making backup copies of files; **memory backup capacitor** = very high capacitance (small) device that can provide power for volatile RAM chips for up to two weeks (used instead of a battery)

QUOTE the system backs up at the rate of 2.5Mb per minute
Microcomputer News
QUOTE the previous version is retained, but its extension is changed to .BAK indicating that it's a back-up
Personal Computer World

Backus-Naur-Form (BNF) system of writing and expressing the syntax of a programming language

backward *or* **backwards** *adjective & adverb* towards the back *or* in the opposite direction; **backward channel** = channel from the receiver to transmitter allowing the receiver to send control and handshaking signals; **backward error correction** = correction of errors which are detected by the receiver and a signal is sent to the transmitter to request a re-transmission of the data; **backward mode** = negative displacement from an origin; **backward recovery** = data retrieval from a system that has crashed; **backwards supervision** = data transmission controlled by the receiver

COMMENT: backward recovery is carried out by passing the semi-processed data from the crashed computer through a routine that reverses the effects of the main program to return the original data

bad sector *noun* sector which has been wrongly formatted *or* which contains an error *or* fault and is unable to be correctly written to or read from; *you will probably receive error messages when you copy files that are stored on bad sectors on a disk*

badge reader *noun* machine that reads data from an identification badge; *a badge reader makes sure that only authorized personnel can gain access to a computer room*

bag *noun* number of elements in no particular order

balance 1 *noun* placing of text and graphics on a page in an attractive way; *the dtp package allows the user to see if the overall page balance is correct* **2** *verb* to plan something so that two parts are equal; **balanced circuit** = electronic circuit that presents a correct load to a communications line (the correct load is usually equal to the impedance of a line element); **balanced error** = the probability of any error occurring (from a number of errors) is the same for all errors; **balanced line** = communications line that is terminated at each end with a balanced circuit, preventing signal reflections

band *noun* **(a)** range of frequencies between two limits; **base band** = frequency range of a signal before it is processed *or* transmitted; *voice base band ranges from 20Hz to 15KHz;* **base band modem** = communications circuit that transmits an unmodulated (base band) signal over a short distance; *do not use a base band modem with a normal phone line;* **base band local area network** = LAN using unmodulated signals transmitted over coaxial cable, often using a CSMA/CD protocol **(b)** group of tracks on a magnetic disk

◇ **band printer** *noun* printer in which the characters are located along a movable steel belt

◇ **banding** *noun* **elastic banding** = method of defining the limits of an image on the computer screen by stretching a boundary round it; *elastic banding is much easier to control with a mouse*

bank *noun* collection of similar devices; *a bank of minicomputers process all the raw data;* **bank switching** = selection of a particular memory bank from a group; **memory bank** = collection of electronic memory devices connected together to form one large area of memory; *an add-on card has a 128KB memory bank made up of 16 chips; see also* DATABANK

COMMENT: memory banks are used to expand the main memory of a CPU (often above the addressing range of the CPU) by having a number of memory chips arranged into banks. Each bank operates over the same address range but is selected independently by a special code

bar 1 *noun* thick line *or* block of colour **2** *verb* to stop someone from doing something; **to bar entry to a file** = to stop someone accessing a file

◊ **bar chart** or **bar graph** noun graph on which values are represented as vertical or horizontal bars

◊ **bar code** or US **bar graphics** noun data represented as a series of printed stripes of varying widths; **bar-code reader** or **optical scanner** = optical device that reads data from a bar code

COMMENT: bar codes are found on most goods and their packages; the width and position of the stripes is sensed by a light pen or optical wand and provides information about the goods, such as price, stock quantities, etc.

◊ **bar printer** noun printer in which the characters are on arms which strike the paper to print characters; see also DAISY WHEEL

barrel noun conducting post in a terminal

◊ **barrel printer** noun type of printer where characters are located around a rotating barrel

base 1 noun (a) lowest or first position (b) collection of files used as a reference; see DATABASE (c) place where a company has its main office or factory or place where a businessman has his office; *the company has its base in London and branches in all European countries* (d) initial or original position; **base address** = initial address in a program used as a reference for others; **base addressing** = relative addressing; **base band** = frequency range of a signal before it is processed or transmitted; **base band modem** = communications circuit that transmits an unmodulated (base band) signal over a short range; **base band local area network** = LAN for very short distances, in which devices use a base band modem; **base language** = assembly language; **base register** = register in a CPU (not usually in small computers) that contains the address of the start of a program (e) (notation) referring to a number system; **base 2** = binary number system (using the two digits 0 and 1); **base 8** = octal number system (using the eight digits 0 - 7); **base 10** = decimal number system (using the ten digits 0 - 9); **base 16** = hexadecimal number system (using the ten digits 0 - 9 and six letters A - F) **2** verb (a) to start to calculate from a position; *we based our calculations on the basic keyboarding rate;* **based on** = calculating from; *based on last year's figures; the price is based on estimates of keyboarding costs* (b) to set up a company or a person in a place; *the European manager is based in our London*

office; *a London-based system serves the whole country*

BASIC = BEGINNER'S ALL-PURPOSE SYMBOLIC INSTRUCTION CODE high-level programming language for developing programs in a conversational way, providing an easy introduction to computer programming

◊ **basic** adjective normal or from which everything starts; *the basic architechture is the same for all models in this range;* **basic code** = binary code which directly operates the CPU, using only absolute addresses and values (this is the final form of a program after a compiler or assembler pass); **basic control system satellite (BCS)** = system that runs dedicated programs or tasks for a central computer, controlled using interrupt signals; **basic input/output operating system (BIOS)** = system routines that interface between high-level program instructions and the system peripherals to control the input and output to various standard devices, this often includes controlling the screen, keyboard and disk drives; **basic instruction** = unmodified program instruction which is processed to obtain the instruction to be executed; **basic mode link control** = standardized control of transmission links using special codes; **basic operating system (BOS)** = software that controls the basic, low-level running of the hardware and file management; **basic telecommunications access method (BTAM)** = method to provide access (read or write operations) to a remote device

◊ **basically** adverb seen from the point from which everything starts; *the acoustic coupler is basically the same as a modem*

◊ **basis** noun point or number from which calculations are made; *we calculated keyboarding costs on the basis of 5,500 keystrokes per hour*

batch 1 noun (a) group of items which are made at one time; *the last batch of disk drives are faulty* (b) (i) group of documents which are processed at the same time; (ii) group of tasks or amount of data to be processed as a single unit; *today's batch of orders; we deal with the orders in batches of fifty;* **batch file** = stored file containing a sequence of system commands, used instead of typing them in; *this batch file is used to save time and effort when carrying out a routine task;* **(processing data in) batch mode** = (processing the data) in related groups in one machine run; **batch region** = memory area where the operating system executes batch programs; **batch system** = system that executes batch files; **batch total** = sum of a number of batches of data, used for error checking, validation or to provide useful information **2** *verb* **(a)** to put data *or* tasks together in groups; **batched communication** = high-speed transmission of large blocks of data without requiring an acknowledgement from the receiver for each data item **(b)** to put items together in groups

◊ **batch number** *noun* reference number attached to a batch

◊ **batch processing** *noun* system of data processing where information is collected into batches before being processed by the computer in one machine run

> COMMENT: batch processing is the opposite to interactive processing (where the user gives instructions and receives an immediate response)

battery *noun* chemical device that produces electrical current; **battery backup** = use of a battery to provide power to volatile storage devices (RAM chips) to retain data after a computer has been switched off; **battery-backed** = (volatile storage device) that has a battery backup

baud *or* **baud rate** *noun* measure of the number of signal changes transmitted per second; *the baud rate of the binary signal was 300 bits per second; a modem with auto-baud scanner can automatically sense at which baud rate it should operate;* **baud rate generator** = device that produces various timing signals to synchronize data at different baud rates; **split baud rate** = modem which receives data at one baud rate but transmits data at another; *the viewdata modem uses a 1200/75 split baud rate; see also* SCANNING

> COMMENT: baud rate is often considered the same as bits per second, but in fact it depends on the protocol used and the error checking (300 baud is roughly equivalent to 30 characters per second using standard error checking)

baudot code *noun* five-bit character transmission code, used mainly in teletypewriters

B box *noun* register in a CPU (not usually in small computers) that contains the address of the start of a program

BBS = BULLETIN BOARD SYSTEM information and message database accessible by modem and computer link

BCC = BLOCK CHARACTER CHECK error detection method for blocks of transmitted data

BCD = BINARY CODED DECIMAL representation of single decimal digits as a pattern of four binary digits; *the BCD representation of decimal 8 is 1000;* **BCD adder** = full adder able to add two four-bit BCD words

BCH code = BOSE-CHANDHURI-HOCQUENGHEM CODE

BCPL *noun* high level programming language

BCS (a) = BRITISH COMPUTER SOCIETY **(b)** = BASIC CONTROL SYSTEM (SATELLITE)

bead *noun* small section of a program that is used for a single task

beep 1 *noun* audible warning noise; *the printer will make a beep when it runs out of paper* **2** *verb* to make a beep; *the computer beeped when the wrong key was hit; see also* BLEEP

beginning *noun* first part; **beginning of file (bof)** = character *or* symbol that shows the start of a valid section of data; **beginning of information mark (bim)** = symbol indicating the start of a data stream stored on a disk drive *or* tape; **beginning of tape (bot) marker** = section of material that marks the start of the recording area of a reel of magnetic tape

Beginner's All-Purpose Symbolic Instruction Code (BASIC) *noun* high-level programming language for developing programs in a conversational way, providing an easy introduction to computer programming

bell character *noun* control code which causes a machine to produce an audible signal

benchmark *noun* **(a)** point in an index which is important, and can be used to compare with other figures **(b)** program used to test the performance of software *or* hardware *or* a system; *the magazine gave the new program's benchmark test results*

◊ **benchmark problem** *noun* task *or* problem used to test and evaluate the performance of hardware *or* software

◊ **benchmarking** *noun* testing a system *or* program with a benchmark

COMMENT: the same task *or* program is given to different systems and their results and speeds of working are compared

Bernoulli box *noun* high capacity storage system using exchangeable 20MB cartridges

QUOTE I use a pair of Bernoulli boxes for back up and simply do a disk-to-disk copy
PC Business World

best fit *noun* (i) (something) which is the nearest match to a requirement; (ii) function that selects the smallest free space in main memory for a requested virtual page

bias *noun* **(a)** electrical reference level **(b)** deviation of statistical results from a reference level

◊ **biased** *adjective* which has a bias; **biased data** = data *or* records which point to one conclusion; **biased exponent** = value of the exponent in a floating point number

bid *verb (of a computer)* to gain control of a network in order to transmit data; *the terminal had to bid three times before there was a gap in transmissions on the network*

bi-directional *adjective* (operation *or* process) that can occur in forward *or* reverse directions; *bi-directional file transfer;* **bi-directional bus** = data *or* control lines that can carry signals travelling in two directions; **bi-directional printer** = printer which is able to print characters from left to right and from right to left as the head is moving forward *or* backward across the paper (speeding up the printing operation); *compare* OMNIDIRECTIONAL

bifurcation *noun* system where there are only two possible results

Big Blue *informal name for* IBM

billion number equal to one thousand million *or* one million million
NOTE: in the US it means one thousand million, but in GB it usually means one million million. With figures it is usually written **bn: $5bn** (say 'five billion dollars')

BIM = BEGINNING OF INFORMATION MARK symbol indicating the start of a data stream stored on a disk drive *or* tape

binary *adjective & noun* base 2 *or* number notation system which uses only the digits 0 and 1; **binary adder** = device that provides the sum of two *or* more binary digits; **binary arithmetic** = rules and functions governing arithmetic operations in base 2; **binary bit** = smallest single unit in (base 2) binary notation, either a 0 or a 1; **binary cell** = storage element for one bit; **binary chop** *see* BINARY SEARCH; **binary code** = using different patterns of binary digits to represent various symbols, elements, etc.; **binary coded characters** = alphanumeric characters represented as patterns of binary digits; **binary coded decimal (BCD)** = representation of single decimal digits as a pattern of four binary digits; **binary counter** = circuit that will divide a binary input signal by two (producing one output pulse for two input pulses); **binary digit** *or* **bit** = smallest single unit in (base 2) binary notation, either a 0 or a 1; **binary dump** = display of a section of memory in binary form; **binary encoding** = representing a character *or* element with a unique combination *or* pattern of bits in a word; **binary exponent** = one word that contains the sign and exponent of a binary number (expressed in exponent and mantissa form); **binary fraction** = representation of a decimal fraction in binary form; *the binary fraction 0.011 is equal to one quarter plus one eighth (i.e. three eighths);* **binary half adder** = binary adder that can produce the sum of two inputs, producing a carry output if necessary, but cannot accept a carry input; **binary loader** = short section of program code that allows programs in binary form (such as object code from a linker *or* assembler) to be loaded into memory; **binary mantissa** = fractional part of a number (in binary form); **binary notation** *or* **representation** = base 2 numerical system using only the digits 0 and 1; **binary number** = quantity represented in base 2; **binary operation** = (i) operation on two operands; (ii) operation on an operand in binary form; **binary point** = dot which indicates the division between the whole unit bits and the fractional part of a binary number; **binary scale** = power of two associated with each bit position in a word; *in a four bit word, the binary scale is 1,2,4,8;* **binary search** *or* **chop** = fast search method for use on ordered lists of data (the search key is compared with the data in the middle of the list and one half is discarded, this is repeated with the remaining half until only the required data item is left); **binary sequence** = series of binary digits; **binary signalling** = transmission using positive and zero voltage levels to represent binary data; **binary synchronous communications**

(BSC) = (old) standard for medium/high speed data communication links; **binary system** = use of binary numbers *or* operating with binary numbers; **binary-to-decimal conversion** = process to convert a binary number into its equivalent decimal value; **binary tree** = tree structure for data, where each item of data can have only two branches; **binary variable** = variable that can contain either a one or zero

QUOTE with this type of compression you can only retrieve words by scanning the list sequentially, rather than by faster means such as a binary search
Practical Computing

bind *verb* to link and convert one or more object code programs into a form that can be executed; **binding time** = time taken to produce actual addresses from an object code program; *see also* LINKER

BIOS = BASIC INPUT/OUTPUT SYSTEM system routines that interface between high-level program instructions and the system peripherals to control the input and output to various standard devices, this often includes controlling the screen, keyboard and disk drives

bipolar *adjective* with two levels; **bipolar coding** = transmission method which uses alternate positive and negative voltage levels to represent a binary one, with binary zero represented by zero level; **bipolar signal** = use of positive and negative voltage levels to represent the binary digits; **bipolar transistor** = transistor constructed of three layers of alternating types of doped semiconductor (p-n-p or n-p-n)

COMMENT: each layer has a terminal labelled emitter, base and collector, usually the base signal controls the current flow between the emitter and collector

biquinary code *noun* decimal digits represented as two digits added together (for decimal digits less than 5, represented as 0 + the digit, for decimal digits greater than 4, represented as 5 + the digit minus 5)

bistable *adjective* (device *or* circuit) that has two possible states, on and off; **bistable circuit** *or* **multivibrator** = circuit which can be switched between two states

bit *noun* **(a)** = BINARY DIGIT smallest unit in binary number notation, which can have the value 0 or 1 **(b)** smallest unit of data that a system can handle; **bit addressing** = selecting a register *or* word and examining

one bit of it; **bit density** = number of bits that can be recorded per unit of storage medium; **bit handling** = CPU commands and processes that allow bit manipulation, changing, etc.; **bit manipulation** = various instructions that provide functions such as examine a bit, change *or* set *or* move a bit within a word; **bit pattern** = certain arrangement of bits within a word, that represents a certain character *or* action; **bit position** = place of a bit of data in a computer word; **bit rate** = measure of the number of bits transmitted per second; **bit slice design** = construction of a large word size CPU by joining a number of smaller word size blocks; *the bit slice design uses four four-bit word processors to construct a sixteen-bit processor;* **most significant bit (MSB)** = bit in a computer word that represents the greatest power of two (in an eight-bit word the MSB is in bit position eight and represents a decimal number of two to the power eight, or 128); **bit stream** = binary data sequence that does not consist of separate, distinct character codes *or* groups; **bit stuffing** = addition of extra bits to a group of data to make up a certain length required for transmission; **bit track** = track on a magnetic disk along which bits can be recorded *or* read back; *compare* LOGICAL TRACK; **bits per inch (bpi)** = number of bits that can be recorded per inch of recording medium; **bits per second (bps)** = measure of the number of binary digits transmitted every second; **check bit** = one bit of a binary word that is used to provide a parity check; **mask bit** = one bit (in a mask) used to select the required bit from a word *or* string; **sign bit** = single bit that indicates if a binary number is positive or negative (usually 0 = positive, 1 = negative); *see also* BYTE

◊ **bit-map** *verb* to define events *or* data using an array of single bits; (this can be an image *or* graphics *or* a table of devices in use, etc.); **bit-mapped graphics** = image whose individual pixels can be controlled by changing the value of its stored bit (one is on, zero is off; in colour displays, more than one bit is used to provide control for the three colours - Red, Green, Blue)

QUOTE it became possible to store more than one bit per pixel
Practical Computing
QUOTE the expansion cards fit into the PC's expansion slot and convert bit-mapped screen images to video signals
Publish
QUOTE it is easy to turn any page into a bit-mapped graphic
PC Business World
QUOTE microcomputers invariably use raster-scan cathode ray tube displays, and frequently use a bit-map to store graphic images
Soft

black *adjective* with no colour; **black and white** = use of shades of grey to represent colours on a monitor *or* display; **black box** = device that performs a function without the user knowing how

◊ **blackout** *or* **black-out** *noun* complete loss of electrical power; *compare with* BROWN-OUT

◊ **black writer** *noun* printer where toner sticks to the points hit by the laser beam when the image drum is scanned; *compare* WHITE WRITER

COMMENT: a black writer produces sharp edges and graphics, but large areas of black are muddy

blank 1 *adjective* empty *or* with nothing written on it; **blank character** = character code that prints a space; **blank instruction** = program instruction which does nothing; **blank tape** *or* **blank disk** = magnetic tape *or* disk that does not have data stored on it; **blank string** = (i) empty string; (ii) string containing spaces **2** *noun* space on a form which has to be completed; *fill in the blanks and insert the form into the OCR*

blast *verb* **(a)** to write data into a programmable ROM device **(b)** to free sections of previously allocated memory *or* resources

◊ **blast-through alphanumerics** *noun* characters that can be displayed on a videotext terminal when it is in graphics mode

bleed *noun* line of printing that runs off the edge of the paper

bleep 1 *noun* audible warning noise; *the printer will make a bleep when it runs out of paper* **2** *verb* to make a bleep; *see also* BEEP

blind *adjective* which will not respond to certain codes

◊ **blind dialling** *noun* ability of a modem to dial out even if the line appears dead, used on certain private lines; **blind keyboard** = keyboard whose output is not displayed but is stored directly on magnetic tape *or* disk

B-line counter *noun* address register that is added to a reference address to provide the location to be accessed

blinking *noun* flashing effect caused by varying the intensity of a displayed character

block 1 *noun* **(a)** (i) series of items grouped together; (ii) number of stored records treated as a single unit; **block character check (BCC)** = error detection method for blocks of transmitted data; **block code** = error detection and correction code for block data transmission; **block compaction** = *see* COMPRESS, COMPACT; **block copy** = to duplicate a block of data to another section of memory; **block error rate** = number of blocks of data that contain errors compared with the total number transmitted; **block header** = information at the start of a file describing content organization or characteristics; **block ignore character** = symbol at the start of a block indicating that it contains corrupt data; **block input processing** = input system that requires a whole error-free block to be received before it is processed; **block length** = number of bytes of data in a block; **block list** = list of the blocks and records as they are organized in a file; **block mark** = code that indicates the end of a block; **block operation** = process carried out on a block of data; **block parity** = parity error check on a block of data; **block retrieval** = accessing blocks of data stored in memory; **block synchronization** = correct timing of start, stop and message bits according to a predefined protocol; **block transfer** = moving large numbers of records around in memory; **building block** = self-contained unit that can be joined to others to form a system; **data block** = all the data required for *or* from a process; **end of block (EOB)** = code which indicates that the last byte of a block of a data has been sent; **interblock gap (IBG)** = space between two blocks of stored data **(b)** wide printed bar; **block diagram** = graphical representation of a system *or* program operation **(c)** block capitals *or* block letters = capital letters (such as A,B,C); *write your name and address in block letters* **2** *verb* to stop something taking place; *the system manager blocked his request for more CPU time*

◊ **blocking factor** *noun* number of records in a block

bloop *verb* to pass a magnet over a tape to erase signals which are not needed

blow *verb* to program a PROM device with data

blueprint *noun* copy of an original set of specifications *or* design in graphical form

◊ **blue-ribbon program** *noun* perfect program that runs first time, with no errors *or* bugs

blur 1 *noun* image where the edges *or* colours are not clear **2** *verb* to make the edges *or* colours of an image fuzzy; *the image becomes blurred when you turn the focus knob*

bn = BILLION

BNF = BACKUS-NAUR-FORM system of writing and expressing the syntax of a programming language

board *noun* flat insulation material on which electronic components are mounted and connected; **bus board** = PCB containing conducting paths for all the computer signals (for the address, data and control buses); **daughter board** = add-on board that connects to a system motherboard; **expansion board** *or* **add on board** = printed circuit board that is connected to a system to increase its functions *or* performance; **motherboard** = main printed circuit board of a system, containing most of the components and connectors for expansion boards, etc.; **printed circuit board (PCB)** = flat insulating material that has conducting tracks of metal printed *or* etched onto its surface, which complete a circuit when components are mounted on it

◇ **bulletin board system (BBS)** *noun* information and message database accessible by modem and computer link

> QUOTE both models can be expanded to the current maximum of the terminals by adding further serial interface boards
> *Micro Decision*

body *noun* main section of text in a document

bof = BEGINNING OF FILE character *or* symbol that shows the start of a valid section of data

boilerplate *noun* final document that has been put together using standard sections of text held in a word processor

◇ **boilerplating** *noun* putting together a final document out of various standard sections of text

bold *adjective & noun* **bold face** = thicker and darker form of a typeface

bomb 1 *verb* *(of software) informal* to fail; *the program bombed, and we lost all the data; the system can bomb if you set up several desk accessories or memory-resident programs at the same time* **2** *noun* logic

bomb = section of code that performs various unpleasant functions such as system crash when a number of conditions are true (the logic bomb is installed by unpleasant hackers *or* very annoyed programmers); *the system programmer installed a logic bomb when they made him redundant*

Boolean algebra *or* **logic** *noun* rules set down to define, simplify and manipulate logical functions, based on statements which are true or false; *see* AND, NOT, OR

◇ **Boolean connective** *noun* symbol *or* character in a Boolean operation that describes the action to be performed on the operands

◇ **Boolean operation** *noun* logical operation on a number of operands, conforming to Boolean algebra rules; **Boolean operation table** = table showing two binary words (operands), the operation and the result; **Boolean operator** = logical operator such as AND, OR etc.; **monadic Boolean operation** = logical operation on only one word, such as NOT; **dyadic Boolean operation** = logical operation producing a result from two words, such as AND; **Boolean value** = one of two values, either true or false; **Boolean variable** = binary word in which each bit represents true or false, using the digits 1 or 0

boost 1 *noun* help received; *the prize was a real boost; the new model gave a boost to the sales figures* **2** *verb* to make something increase; *the extra hard disk will boost our storage capacity by 25Mb*

boot *verb* to execute a set of instructions automatically in order to reach a required state

◇ **boot up** *or* **booting** *noun* automatic execution of a set of instructions usually held in ROM when a computer is switched on

◇ **bootleg** *noun* illegal copy of recorded material

◇ **bootstrap (loader)** *noun* set of instructions that are executed by the computer before a program is loaded, usually to load the operating system once the computer is switched on; *compare* LOADER

> QUOTE the digital signal processor includes special on-chip bootstrap hardware to allow easy loading of user programs into the program RAM
> *Electronics & Wireless World*

border *noun* area around printed *or* displayed text

borrow *verb* operation in certain arithmetic processes, such as subtraction from a smaller number

BOS = BASIC OPERATING SYSTEM software that controls the basic, low-level running of the hardware and file management

Bose-Chandhuri-Hocquenghem code (BCH) *noun* error correcting code

bot *or* **BOT** = BEGINNING OF TAPE; **BOT marker** = section of material that marks the start of the recording area of magnetic tape

bottom up method *noun* combining low-level instructions to form a high-level instruction (which can then be further combined)

bounce *noun* (error) multiple key contact caused by a faulty switch; **de-bounce** = preventing a single touch on a key producing multiple key contact

boundary *noun* limits of something; **boundary protection** = preventing any program writing into a reserved area of memory; **boundary punctuation** = punctuation which marks the beginning *or* end of a file; **boundary register** = register in a multi-user system that contains the addresses for the limits of one user's memory allocation

bounds *noun* limits *or* area in which one can operate; **array bounds** = limits to the number of elements which can be given in an array

box *noun* cardboard *or* wood *or* plastic container; *the goods were sent in thin cardboard boxes; the keyboard is packed in plastic foam before being put into the box;* **black box** = device that performs a function without the user knowing how
◊ **boxed** *adjective* put in a box *or* sold in a box; **boxed set** = set of items sold together in a box

BPI *or* **bpi** = BITS PER INCH number of bits that can be recorded per inch of recording medium

BPS *or* **bps** = BITS PER SECOND number of bits that can be transmitted per second; *their transmission rate is 60,000 bits per second (bps) through a parallel connection*

bracket 1 *noun* printing sign to show that an instruction *or* operations are to be separated; **round brackets** *or* **square brackets** = different types of bracket (( ), [ ]) **2** *verb* **to bracket together** = to print brackets round several items to show that they are treated in the same way and separated from the rest of the text

branch 1 *noun* **(a)** possible path *or* jump from one instruction to another; **branch instruction** = conditional program instruction that provides the location of the next instruction in the program (if a condition is met); **program branch** = one or more paths that can be followed after a conditional statement **(b)** line linking one or more devices to the main network; *the faulty station is on this branch* **2** *verb* to jump from one section of a program to another
◊ **branchpoint** *noun* point in a program where a branch can take place

COMMENT: in BASIC, the instruction GOTO makes the system jump to the line indicated; this is an unconditional branch. The instruction IF...THEN is a conditional branch, because the jump will only take place if the condition is met

brand *noun* make of product, which can be recognized by a name *or* by a design; *the number one brand of magnetic tape; the company is developing a new brand of screen cleaner;* **brand name** = name of a brand

breach *noun* failure to carry out the terms of an agreement; **breach of warranty** = supplying goods which do not meet the standards of the warranty applied to them

break 1 *noun* action *or* key pressed to stop a program execution **2** *verb* **(a)** to fail to carry out the duties of an agreement; *the company has broken the agreement* **(b)** to decipher a difficult code; *he finally broke the cipher system* NOTE: **breaking - broke - has broken**
◊ **break down** *verb* to stop working because of mechanical failure; *the modem has broken down; what do you do when your line printer breaks down?*
◊ **breakdown** *noun* stopping work because of mechanical failure; *we cannot communicate with our New York office because of the breakdown of the telex lines*
◊ **breaker** *noun* **circuit breaker** = device which protects equipment by cutting off the electrical supply
◊ **breakpoint** *noun* symbol inserted into a program which stops its execution at that point to allow registers, variables and

memory locations to be examined (used when debugging a program); **breakpoint instruction** *or* **halt** = halt command inserted in a program to stop execution temporarily, allowing the programmer to examine data and registers while debugging a program; **breakpoint symbol** = special character used to provide a breakpoint in a program (the debugging program allows breakpoint symbols to be inserted, it then executes the program until it reaches one, then halts)

◊ **breakup** *noun* loss *or* distortion of a signal

B register *noun* (i) address register that is added to a reference address to provide the location to be accessed; (ii) register used to extend the accumulator in multiplication and division operations

bridge *or* **bridging product** *noun* **(a)** matching communications equipment that makes sure that power losses are kept to a minimum **(b)** hardware *or* software that allows parts of an old system to be used on a new system; *a bridging product is available for companies with both generations of machines*

◊ **bridgeware** *noun* hardware *or* software used to make the transfer from one computer system to another easier (by changing file format, translation etc.)

◊ **bridging** *noun* using bridgeware to help transfer programs, data files etc., to another system

brightness *noun* luminance of an object which can be seen; *a control knob allows you to adjust brightness and contrast; the brightness of the monitor can hurt the eyes;* **brightness range** = variation of reflected light intensity

QUOTE there is a brightness control on the front panel
Micro Decision

brilliant *adjective* very bright and shining (light *or* colour)

British Standards Institute (BSI) *UK* organization that monitors design and safety standards in the UK

broadcast 1 *noun* data transmission to many receivers; **broadcast network** = network for sending data to a number of receivers **2** *verb* to distribute information over a wide area *or* audience; *he broadcast the latest news over the WAN*

brown-out *noun* power failure (low voltage level rather than no voltage level); *see also* BLACK-OUT

browse *verb* to search through and access database material without permission

brute force method *noun* problem-solving method which depends on computer power rather than elegant programming techniques

BSC = BINARY SYNCHRONOUS COMMUNICATIONS (old) standard for medium/high speed data communication links

BSI = BRITISH STANDARDS INSTITUTE organization that monitors design and safety standards in the UK

BTAM = BASIC TELECOMMUNICATIONS ACCESS METHOD method to provide access (read *or* write operations) to a remote device

bubble memory *noun* method of storing binary data using the magnetic properties of certain materials, allowing very large amounts of data to be stored in primary memory; **bubble memory cassette** = bubble memory device on a removable cartridge that can be inserted into a controller card (like an audio cassette) to provide high capacity, high speed, removable memory

◊ **bubble sort** *noun* sorting method which repeatedly exchanges various pairs of data items until they are in order

bucket *noun* storage area containing data for an application

buffer 1 *noun* **(a)** (circuit) that isolates and protects a system from damaging inputs from circuits *or* peripherals; *see also* DRIVER **(b)** temporary storage area for data waiting to be processed; **buffer register** = temporary storage for data read from *or* being written to main memory; **buffer size** = total number of characters that can be held in a buffer; **data buffer** = temporary storage location for data received by a device that is not yet ready to process it; **dynamic** *or* **elastic buffer** = buffer whose size varies with demand; **I/O buffer** = temporary storage area for data waiting to be input *or* output **2** *verb* using a temporary storage area to hold data until the processor *or* device is ready to deal with it; **buffered input/output** = use of a temporary storage area on input *or* output ports to allow slow peripherals to operate with a fast CPU; **buffered memory** = device that allows instructions *or* data to be entered before it has completed its present ones; **buffering** = using buffers to provide a link between slow and fast devices; **double buffering** = two buffers working together so that one can be read while the other is accepting data

COMMENT: buffers allow two parts of a computer system to work at different speeds (i.e. a high-speed central processing unit and a slower line printer)

QUOTE the speed is enhanced by the 8K RAM printer buffer included
QUOTE the software allocates a portion of cache as a print buffer to restore program control faster after sending data to the printer
Which PC?

bug *noun informal* error in a computer program which makes it run incorrectly; **bug patches** = (temporary) correction made to a program; small correction made to software by a user on the instructions of the software publisher; *see also* DEBUG

◊ **buggy** *noun* small computer-controlled vehicle

building block *noun* self-contained unit that can be joined to others to form a system

built-in *adjective* (special feature) that is already included in a system; *the built-in adapter card makes it fully IBM compatible; the computer has a built-in hard disk;* **built-in check** = error detection and validation check carried out automatically on received data; **built-in function** = special function already implemented in a program

◊ **built into** *adjective* feature that is already a physical part of a system; *there are communications ports built into all modems* NOTE: opposite is **add on**

bulk *noun* large quantity of something; **in bulk** = in large quantities; **bulk erase** = to erase a complete magnetic disk *or* tape in one action; **bulk storage medium** = medium that is able to store large amounts of data in a convenient size and form; *magnetic tape is a reliable bulk storage medium;* **bulk update terminal** = device used by an information provider to prepare videotext pages off-line, then transmit them rapidly to the main computer

bulletin board system (BBS) *noun* information and message database accessible by modem and computer link

bundle *noun* number of optic fibres gathered together

◊ **bundled software** *noun* programs included in the price of a computer hardware package

bureau *noun* office which specializes in keyboarding data *or* processing batches of data for other small companies; *the company offers a number of bureau services, such as printing and data collection; our data manipulation is handled by a bureau;* **information bureau** = office which gives information; **word-processing bureau** = office which specializes in word-processing; *we farm out the office typing to a local bureau* NOTE: the plural is **bureaux**

burner *noun* device which burns in programs onto PROM chips

◊ **burn-in** *noun* heat test for electronic components

◊ **burn in** *verb* **(a)** to mark a (television *or* monitor) screen after displaying a high brightness image for too long **(b)** to write data into a PROM chip

◊ **burn out** *noun* excess heat *or* incorrect use that causes an electronic circuit *or* device to fail

burst *noun* short isolated sequence of transmitted signals; **burst mode** = data transmission using intermittent bursts of data; **error burst** = group of several consecutive errors (in a transmission)

burster *noun* machine used to separate the sheets of continuous fanfold paper

bus *noun* **(a)** communication link consisting of a set of leads *or* wires which connects different parts of a computer hardware system, and over which data is transmitted and received by various circuits in the system; **address bus** = bus carrying address data between a CPU and a memory device; **bi-directional bus** = data *or* control lines that can carry signals travelling in two directions; **bus address lines** = wires, each of which carries one bit of an address word; **bus arbitration** = protocol and control of transmission over a bus that ensures fair usage by several users; **bus board** = PCB containing conducting paths for all the computer signals; **bus control lines** = wires, each of which carries one bit of a control word; **bus data lines** = wires, each of which carries one bit of a data word; **bus driver** = high power transistors *or* amplifier that can provide enough power to transmit signals to a number of devices; **bus master** = data source that controls the bus whilst transmitting (bus master status moves between sending stations); **bus network** = network of computers where the machines are connected to a central bus unit which transmits the messages it receives; **bus slave** = data sink which receives data from a bus master; **bus structure** = way in which buses are organized, whether serial, parallel, bidirectional, etc.; **control bus** = bus carrying control signals between a CPU and other circuits; **daisy chain bus** = one communications bus that joins one device to the next, each device being able to receive *or* transmit *or* modify data as it passes through to the next device in line; **data bus** = bus carrying data between a CPU and memory and peripheral devices; **dual bus system** = way for linking different parts of a system which keeps the memory bus separate from the input/output bus; **input/output bus (I/O bus)** = links allowing data and control transfer between a CPU and external peripherals; **memory bus** = bus carrying address data between a CPU and memory devices **(b)** central source of information which supplies several devices

business *noun* **(a)** work in buying *or* selling; *business is expanding; business is slow; he does a good business in repairing computers; what's your line of business?;* **business computer** = powerful small computer which is programmed for special business tasks; **business efficiency exhibition** = exhibition which shows products (computers, word-processors) which help a business to be efficient; **business system** *or* **business package** = set of programs adapted for business use (such as payroll, invoicing, customers file, etc.) **(b)** commercial company; *he owns a small computer repair business; she runs a business from her home; he set up in business as an computer consultant;* **business equipment** = machines used in an office

NOTE: no plural for (a); (b) has the plural **businesses**

busy *adjective* (i) occupied in doing something *or* in working; (ii) electrical signal indicating that a device is not ready to receive data; *when the busy line goes low, the printer will accept more data;* **the line is busy** = the telephone line is being used

buzz 1 *noun* sound like a loud hum **2** *verb* to make a loud hum

◇ **buzzer** *noun* electrical device which makes a loud hum

◇ **buzzword** *noun informal* word which is popular among a certain group of people

bypass *noun* alternative route around a component *or* device, so that it is not used; *there is an automatic bypass around any faulty equipment*

byte *noun* group of bits *or* binary digits (usually eight) which a computer operates on as a single unit; **byte addresses** = location of data bytes in memory; **byte machine** = variable word length computer; **byte manipulation** = moving, editing and changing the contents of a byte; **byte serial transmission** *or* **mode** = transmission of bytes of data sequentially; the individual bits of which can be sent in a serial *or* parallel way

Cc

C high level programming language developed mainly for writing structured systems programs

QUOTE these days a lot of commercial software is written in C
PC Business World

C hexadecimal number equivalent to decimal 12

cable *noun* flexible conducting electrical *or* optical link; *the cable has the wrong connector for this printer*

◊ **cabling** *noun* cable (as a material); *using high-quality cabling will allow the user to achieve very high data transfer rates; cabling costs up to £1 a foot*
NOTE: no plural

cache 1 *noun* **cache memory** = section of high-speed memory which stores data that the computer can access quickly; *file access time is much quicker if the most frequently used data is stored in cache memory;* **instruction cache** = section of high-speed memory which stores the next few instructions to be executed by a processor (to speed up operation) **2** *verb* to file *or* store in a cache; *this program can cache any size font*

QUOTE the first range of 5.25 inch Winchester disk drives to feature inbuilt cache
Minicomputer News
QUOTE a serious user might also want a tape streamer and cache memory
PC Business World

CAD = COMPUTER AIDED DESIGN *or* COMPUTER ASSISTED DESIGN the use of a computer and graphics terminal to help a designer in his work; *all our engineers design on CAD workstations;* **CAD/CAM** = CAD/COMPUTER AIDED MANUFACTURE interaction between computers used for designing and those for manufacturing a product

QUOTE CAD software is memory-intensive
PC Business World

CAI = COMPUTER AIDED INSTRUCTION *or* COMPUTER ASSISTED INSTRUCTION use

of a computer to assist pupils in learning a subject

CAL = COMPUTER AIDED LEARNING *or* COMPUTER ASSISTED LEARNING use of a computer to assist pupils in learning a subject

calculate *verb* **(a)** to find the answer to a problem using numbers; *the DP manager calculated the rate for keyboarding; you need to calculate the remaining disk space* **(b)** to estimate; *I calculate that we have six months' stock left*

◊ **calculation** *noun* answer to a problem in mathematics; **rough calculation** = approximate answer; *I made some rough calculations on the back of an envelope; according to my calculations, we have six months' stock left*

◊ **calculator** *noun* electronic machine which works out the answers to numerical problems; *my pocket calculator needs a new battery; he worked out the discount on his calculator*

calibration *noun* comparing the signal from an input with a known scale to provide a standardized reading

call 1 *noun* conversation (between people or machines) on the telephone; **to log calls** = to note all details of telephone calls made **2** *verb* **(a)** to transfer control to a separate program *or* routine from a main program; *after an input is received, the first function is called up; the subroutine call instruction should be at this point;* **call instruction** = programming instruction that directs control to a routine (after saving the program counter contents to show the return instruction where to return to in the main program) **(b) call accepted signal** = signal sent by a device showing that it is willing to accept (caller's) data; **call control signal** = signal necessary to establish and end a call; **call duration** = length of time spent between starting and ending a call; *call duration depends on the complexity of the transaction; charges are related to call duration;* **called party** = person *or* station to which a call is made

◊ **caller** *noun* person who telephones *or* requests a call

◊ **calling** *noun* signal to request attention, sent from a terminal *or* device to the main computer; **calling sequence** = series of program commands required to direct execution to or back from a subroutine

◊ **call up** *verb* to ask for information from a backing store to be displayed; *all the customers addresses were called up; call up the previous file*

CAM **(a)** = COMPUTER AIDED MANUFACTURE *or* COMPUTER ASSISTED MANUFACTURING use of a computer to control machinery *or* assist in a manufacturing process **(b)** = CONTENT ADDRESSABLE MEMORY memory that is addressed and accessed by its contents rather than a location

Cambridge ring *noun* local area networking standard used for connecting several devices and computers together in a ring with simple cable links

cancel *verb* to stop a process *or* instruction before it has been fully executed; **cancel character** = control code used to indicate that the last data transmitted was incorrect; *the software automatically sends a cancel character after any error*

◊ **cancellation** *noun* action of stopping a process which has been started

canonical schema *noun* model of a database that is independent of hardware *or* software available

capability *noun* being able to do something; *resolution capabilities; electronic mail capabilities;* **capability list** = list of operations that can be carried out

◊ **capable** *adjective* able to do something; *that is the highest speed that this printer is capable of; the software is capable of far more complex functions*
NOTE: a device is capable **of** something

capacitance *noun* ability of a component to store electrical charge

◊ **capacitative** *or* **capacititive** *adjective* something which has capacitance

◊ **capacitor** *noun* electronic component that can store charge; **capacitor storage** = device using capacititive properties of a material to store data; **memory backup capacitor** = very high-capacitance, small device that can provide power for volatile RAM chips for up to two weeks (used instead of a battery); *see also* BATTERY BACKUP

capacity *noun* **(a)** amount which can be produced *or* amount of work which can be done; *industrial* *or* *manufacturing* *or* *production capacity;* **channel capacity** = maximum rate for data transmission over a channel; **to work at full capacity** = to do as much work as possible; **to use up spare** *or* **excess capacity** = to make use of time *or* space which is not fully used **(b)** amount of storage space available in a system *or* on a disk; **storage capacity** = space available for storage; *total storage capacity is now 3Mb*

capitals *or informal* **caps** *noun* large form of letters (A,B,C,D, etc.) as opposed to lower case (a,b,c,d, etc.); *the word BASIC is always written in caps;* **caps lock** = key on a keyboard *or* typewriter that allows all characters to be entered as capitals; *the LED lights up when caps lock is pressed*

capture 1 *noun* **data capture** = action of obtaining data (either by keyboarding *or* by scanning or often automatically from a recording device *or* peripheral); *data capture starts when an interrupt is received* **2** *verb* to take data into a computer system; *the software allows captured images to be edited; scanners usually capture images at a resolution of 300 dots per inch (dpi)*

QUOTE images can then be captured, stored, manipulated and displayed
Electronics & Wireless World

carbon ribbon *noun* thin plastic ribbon, coated with black ink, used in printers; *compare* FIBRE RIBBON

card *noun* **(a)** small piece of stiff paper *or* plastic; **punched card** = card with holes punched in it that represent data; **smart card** = plastic card with a memory and microprocessor device embedded in it, so that it can be used for electronic funds transfer *or* for identification of the user; *smart cards reduce fraud; future smart cards could contain an image of the users fingerprint for identification* **(b)** a punched card; **card code** = combination of punched holes that represent characters on a punched card; **card column** = line of punched information about one character, parallel to the shorter side of the card; **card feed** = device which draws punched cards into a reader automatically; **card field** = part of a card column reserved for one type of data; **card format** = way in which columns and rows are arranged to represent data fields *or* characters in a punched card; **card image** = section of memory that contains an exact representation of the information on a card; **card loader** = short program that transfers data from a punched card into main memory; **card punch (CP)** = machine that punches the holes in punched cards; **card reader** *or* **punched card reader** = device that transforms data on a punched card to a form that can be recognized by the computer; **card row** = punch positions parallel to the longer edge of a card **(c)** sheet of insulating material on which electronic components can be mounted; **card cage** = metal supporting frame for circuit boards; **card edge connector** = series of metal tracks ending at the edge and on the surface of a card, allowing it to be plugged into an edge connector to provide electrical contact (for data transmission, etc.); **card extender** = card containing only conducting tracks, inserted between a motherboard connector and an expansion card, allowing the expansion card to be worked on and examined easily, outside the card cage; **expansion card** *or* **expansion board** = printed circuit board that is connected to a system (expansion connector) to increase its functions *or* performance; **hard card** = board containing a hard disk drive and the required interfacing electronics, which can be slotted into a system (expansion connector); **card frame** *or* **card chassis** = frame containing a motherboard into which printed circuit boards can be plugged to provide a flexible system

QUOTE this card does not occupy system memory space and provides fifty functions including programmable character sets
Computing Today

carriage *noun* mechanical section of a typewriter *or* printer that correctly feeds *or* moves the paper that is being printed; **carriage control** = codes that control the movements of a printer carriage; *carriage control codes can be used to move the paper forward two lines between each line of text;* **carriage return (CR)** = signal *or* key to move to the beginning of the next line of print *or* display; *the carriage return key is badly placed for touch-typists*

carrier *noun* **(a)** device that holds a section of microfilm **(b)** continuous high frequency waveform that can be modulated by a signal; *he's not using a modem - there's no carrier signal on the line;* **carrier sense multiple access - collision detection (CSMA-CD)** = network communications protocol that prevents two sources transmitting at the same time by waiting for a quiet moment, then attempting to transmit; **carrier signalling** = simple data transmission (by switching on and off a carrier signal according to binary

data); **carrier system** = method of transmitting several different signals on one channel by using different carrier frequencies; **carrier wave** = waveform used as a carrier; **data carrier** = (i) any device *or* medium capable of storing data; (ii) a waveform used as a carrier for data signals; **data carrier detect (DCD)** = RS232C signal from a modem to a computer, indicating a carrier wave is being received; *the call is stopped if the software does not receive a DCD signal from the modem*

carry 1 *noun* (extra) digit due to an addition result being greater than the number base used; *when 5 and 7 are added, there is an answer of 2 and a carry which is put in the next column, giving 12;* **carry bit** *or* **flag** = indicator that a carry has occurred; **carry complete signal** = signal from an adder circuit indicating that all carry operations have been completed; **carry look ahead** = high speed adder that can predict if a carry will be generated by a sum and add it in, removing the delay found in an adder with ripple-through carry; **carry time** = period of time taken to transfer a carry digit to the next higher digit position; **cascade carry** = carry generated in an adder from an input carry signal; **end-around carry** = most significant digit (the carry) is added into the least significant place (used in BCD arithmetic); **high speed carry** = when a carry into an adder results in a carry out, all produced in one operation; **partial carry** = temporary storage of all carries generated in parallel adders, rather than a direct transfer; **ripple-through carry** = carry generated by a carry in to an adder **2** *verb* to move (something) from one place to another; *the fibre optic link carried all the data; the information-carrying abilities of this link are very good*

cartesian coordinates *noun* positional system that uses two axes at right angles to represent a point which is located with two numbers, giving a position on each

◊ **cartesian structure** *noun* data structure whose size is fixed and the elements are in (a linear) order; *compare with* AXIS, POLAR COORDINATES

cartridge *noun* removable cassette, containing a disk *or* tape *or* program *or* data (usually stored in ROM); **data cartridge** = cartridge that contains stored data; **disk cartridge** = removable hard disk; **ROM cartridge** = sealed module (with electrical connections) which can be plugged into a computer and contains data *or* extra programs stored in a ROM chip; *the portable computer has no disk drives, but has* *a slot for ROM cartridges;* **tape cartridge =** cassette box containing magnetic tape; **cartridge drive =** drive which uses a disk *or* tape in a cartridge; **cartridge fonts =** ROM cartridge which can be plugged into a printer, providing a choice of new typefaces, but still limited to the typefaces and styles included in the cartridge; *compare* RESIDENT FONTS; **cartridge ribbon =** printer ribbon in a closed cartridge

cascade carry *noun* carry generated in an adder from an input carry signal
◊ **cascade connection** *noun* number of devices *or* circuits arranged in series, the output of one driving the input of the next
◊ **cascade control** *noun* multiple control units, each controlling the next

case 1 *noun* **(a)** protective container for a device *or* circuit **(b) upper case** *or* **lower case =** capital letters *or* ordinary letters; *he corrected the word "coMputer", replacing the upper case M with a lower case letter;* **case change =** key used to change from upper to lower case on a keyboard

casing *noun* solid protective box in which a computer *or* delicate equipment is housed

cassette *noun* hard container used to store and protect magnetic tape; *you must back up the information from the computer onto a cassette;* **audio cassette =** small cassette containing a reel of narrow magnetic tape on which audio signal can be recorded (used to store data in small home computers); **data cassette =** special high-quality tape for storing data; **cassette recorder =** machine to transfer audio signals onto magnetic tape; **cassette tape =** narrow reel of magnetic tape housed in a solid case for protection

COMMENT: using cassette tape allows data to be stored for future retrieval; it is used instead of a disk system on small computers or as a slow, serial access, high-capacity back-up medium for large systems

CAT (a) = COMPUTER AIDED *or* ASSISTED TRAINING use of a computer to demonstrate to and assist pupils in learning a skill **(b) =** COMPUTER AIDED *or* ASSISTED TESTING use of a computer to test equipment *or* programs to find any faults

catalogue 1 *noun* list of contents *or* items in order; **disk catalogue** *or* **directory =** list of files stored on a magnetic disk; *the entry in the disk catalogue is removed when the file is deleted* **2** *verb* to make a catalogue of items

stored; *all the terminals were catalogued, with their location, call sign and attribute table*

catastrophe *noun* serious fault, error *or* breakdown of equipment, usually leading to serious damage and shutdown of a system
◊ **catastrophic error** *noun* error that causes a program to crash *or* files to be accidentally erased; **catastrophic failure =** complete system failure *or* crash

catena *noun* (i) number of items in a chained list; (ii) series of characters in a word
◊ **catenate** *verb* to join together two or more sets of data

cathode *noun* negative electrical terminal of a device *or* battery NOTE: opposite is **anode**
◊ **cathode ray tube (CRT)** *noun* device used for displaying characters *or* figures *or* graphical information, similar to a TV set; **cathode ray tube storage =** a cathode ray tube with a long persistence phosphor screen coating that retains an image for a long time NOTE: CRT is now often used to mean 'monitor'

COMMENT: cathode ray tubes are used in television sets, computer monitors and VDUs; a CRT consists of a vacuum tube, one end of which is flat and coated with phosphor, the other end containing an electron beam source. Characters *or* graphics are visible when the controllable electron beam strikes the phosphor causing it to glow

CBL = COMPUTER BASED LEARNING learning mainly using a computer

CBMS = COMPUTER BASED MESSAGE SYSTEM use of a computer system to allow users to send and receive messages from other users (usually in-house); *see also* BBS

CBT = COMPUTER BASED TRAINING use of a computer system to train students

CCD = CHARGE COUPLED DEVICE; **CCD memory =** capacitors used (with MOS transistors) to store data, allowing either serial or random access

CCP = COMMAND CONSOLE PROCESSOR software which interfaces between a user's terminal and system BIOS

CD = COMPACT DISK; **CD-ROM =** COMPACT DISK-READ ONLY MEMORY small plastic disk that is used as a high capacity ROM device, data is stored in binary form as holes etched on the surface which are then read by a laser

cell *noun* **(a)** single function *or* number in a spreadsheet program; **cell reference variable =** register that contains the reference locating a certain cell that is being operated on **(b)** single memory location, capable of storing a data word, accessed by an individual address

cellar *noun* temporary storage for data *or* registers *or* tasks, in which items are added and retrieved from the same end of the list in a LIFO order

central *adjective* in the middle; **central computer =** HOST COMPUTER; **central memory (CM) =** area of memory whose locations can be directly and immediately addressed by the CPU; **central processing element (CPE) =** short (2, 4 or 8 bit) word length module that can be used to produce large word CPUs using bit slice techniques; **central processing unit (CPU)** *or* **central processor =** group of circuits which perform the basic functions of a computer, made up of three parts: the control unit, the arithmetic and logic unit and the input/output unit; **central terminal =** terminal which controls the communications between a central *or* host computer and remote terminals

◊ **centralized** *adjective* which is located in a central position; **centralized data processing =** data processing facilities located in a centralized place that can be accessed by other users; **centralized computer network =** network with processing power provided by a central computer

centre *or US* **center 1** *noun* point in the middle of something; **centre holes =** location holes punched along the centre of paper tape; **centre operator =** person who looks after central computer operations; **centre sprocket feed =** centre (sprocket) holes that line up with coding hole positions on punched tape **2** *verb* **(a)** to align the read/write head correctly on a magnetic disk *or* tape **(b)** to place a piece of text in the centre of the paper *or* display screen; *which key do you press to centre the heading?*

◊ **centering** *noun* action of putting text in the centre of the screen; *centering of headings is easily done, using this function key*

Centronics interface *noun* parallel printer interface devised by Centronics Inc

CGA = COLOUR GRAPHICS ADAPTER popular microcomputer medium-resolution colour display system; *see also* EGA

chad *noun* waste material produced from holes punched in tape *or* card; **chadded** *or* **chadless tape =** punched tape that retains chad by not punching holes through fully

chain 1 *noun* (i) series of files *or* data items linked sequentially; (ii) series of instructions to be executed sequentially; **chain code =** series of words, each word being derived (usually shifted by one bit) from the previous word; **chain list =** list of data with each piece of information providing an address for the next consecutive item in the list; **chain printer =** printer whose characters are located on a continuous belt; **command chain =** list of commands (in a file) executed sequentially by a batch mode system; **daisy chain =** method of connecting equipment with a single cable passing from one machine *or* device to the next (rather than separate cables to each device); **daisy chain bus =** one communications bus that joins one device to the next, each device being able to receive *or* transmit *or* modify data as it passes through to the next device in line **2** *verb* to link files *or* data items in series by storing a pointer to the next file *or* item at each entry; *more than 1,000 articles or chapters can be chained together when printing; see also* CATENA; **chained** *or* **threaded file =** file in which an entry will contain data and an address to the next entry that has the same data content (allowing rapid retrieval of all identical data records); **chained list =** list in which each element contains data and an address to the next element in the list; **chained record =** data record in a chained file; **daisy-chain =** to connect equipment using the daisy chain method; *daisy-chaining saves a lot of cable*

◊ **chaining** *noun* execution of a very large program by executing small segments of it at a time, this allows programs larger than memory capacity to be run; **chaining search =** search of a file of elements arranged in a chained list; **data chaining =** storing one record that holds the address of the next in the list

change *verb* to make something different; to use one thing instead of another; **change dump =** printout of locations where data has been changed; **change file =** file containing records that are to be used to update a master file; **change record** = record containing new data which is to be used to update a master record; **change tape** = (magnetic) tape containing recent changes *or* transactions to records which is used to update a master file

◇ **change-over** *verb* to switch from one computer system to another

◇ **changer** *noun* device which changes one thing for another; **gender changer** = two connectors, used to change a female connector to a male one (or vice-versa); *you can interconnect all these peripherals with just two cables and a gender changer*

channel 1 *noun* physical connection between two points that allows data to be transmitted (such as a link between a CPU and a peripheral); **channel adapter** = interfacing device allowing different channels to be inter-connected; **channel bank** = collection of a number of channels, and circuits to switch between them; **channel capacity** = maximum rate of data transmission over a channel; **channel command** = instruction to a channel *or* control unit, providing control information such as data selection *or* routes; **channel isolation** = separation of channels measured as the amount of crosstalk between two channels (low crosstalk is due to good channel isolation); **channel overload** = transmission of data at a rate greater than the channel capacity; **channel synchronizer** = interface between a central computer and peripherals, providing a channel, channel command interpretation and status signals from the peripherals; **channel queue** = (i) queue of requests to use a channel; (ii) queue of data that has yet to be sent over a channel; **channel-to-channel connection** = direct link between the main I/O channels of two computers, allowing high speed data transfer; **data channel** = communications link able to carry data signals; **dedicated channel** = communications channel reserved for a special purpose; **I/O channel** = link between a processor and peripheral allowing data transfer **2** *verb* to send signals *or* data via a particular path

◇ **channelling** *noun* protective pipe containing cables *or* wires

chapter *noun* section of a main program that can be executed in its own right, without the rest of the main program being required

character *noun* graphical symbol which appears as a printed *or* displayed mark, such as one of the letters of the alphabet, a number or a punctuation mark; **alphanumeric characters** = roman letters and arabic numerals (and other signs such as punctuation marks); **cancel character** = control code used to indicate that the last data transmitted was incorrect; **character assembly** = method of designing characters with pixels on a computer screen; **character blink** = character whose intensity is switched on and off (as an indicator); **character block** = the pattern of dots that will make up a character on a screen *or* printer; **character byte** = byte of data containing the character code and any error check bits; **character check** = check to ensure that a character code protocol and format are correct; **character code** = system where each character is represented by a unique number; *the ASCII code is the most frequently used character coding system;* **character density** = number of characters that can be stored *or* displayed per unit area; **character display** = device that displays data in alphanumeric form; **character fill** = writing one character to every location within an area of memory (for clearing and resetting the memory); **character generator** = ROM that provides the display circuits with a pattern of dots which represent the character (block); *the ROM used as a character generator can be changed to provide different fonts;* **character key** = word processor control used to process text one character at a time; **character machine** = computer in which the number of bits which make up a word is variable, and varies according to the type of data; **character orientated** = computer that addresses character locations rather than words; **character printer** = device that prints characters one at a time; *a daisy wheel printer is a character printer;* **character recognition** = system that optically reads written *or* printed characters into a computer, using various algorithms to ensure that characters are correctly recognized; *see also* OCR; **character repertoire** = list of all the characters that can be displayed *or* printed; **character representation** = combination of bits used for each character code; **character rounding** = making a displayed character more pleasant to look at (within the limits of pixel size) by making sharp corners and edges smooth; **character set** = list of all the characters that can be displayed *or* printed; **character string** = storage allocated for a series of alphanumeric characters; *compare with* NUMERIC STRING; **characters per inch (cpi)** = number of printed characters which fit within the space of one inch; *you can select 10 or 12 cpi with the green button;* **characters per second (cps)** = number of characters which are transmitted *or* printed per second; **character stuffing** = addition of blank characters to a file to increase its length to a preset size; **check character** = additional character inserted into transmitted data to serve as an error detection check, its value is dependent on the text; **device control character** = special code sent in a transmission to a device to instruct it to perform a special function

◊ **characteristic 1** *noun* **(a)** value of exponent in a floating point number; *the floating point number 1.345 x 10³ , has a characteristic of 3;* **characteristic overflow** = exponent value of a floating point number that is greater than the maximum allowable **(b)** measurements *or* properties of a component **2** *adjective* which is typical *or* special; *this fault is characteristic of this make and model of personal computer*

> QUOTE the screen displays very sharp and stable characters, each cell occupying an 8 by 11 dot matrix
>
> *Computing Today*

charge *noun* (i) a quantity of electricity; (ii) the number of *or* excess of *or* lack of electrons in a material *or* component; **charge-coupled device (CCD)** = electronic device operated by charge; **charge-coupled device memory** = capacitors used (with MOS transistors) to store data, allowing serial and random access; **electric charge** = a number of atoms that are charged (due to an excess *or* deficiency of electrons) **2** *verb* to supply a device with an electric charge; **battery charging** = to replenish the charge stored in a re-chargeable battery

◊ **chargeable** *adjective* which can be charged; **re-chargeable battery** = battery that can be used to supply power, and then have its charge replenished; *a re-chargeable battery is used for RAM back-up when the system is switched off*

chart *noun* diagram showing information as a series of lines *or* blocks, etc.; **bar chart** = graph on which values are represented as vertical *or* horizontal bars of different heights *or* lengths; **flowchart** = diagram showing the arrangement of various work processes as a series of stages; *a flowchart is the first step to a well designed program;* **logical chart** = graphical representation of logic elements, steps, decisions and interconnections in a system; **pie chart** = diagram where ratios are shown as slices of a circle; *the memory allocation is shown on this pie chart*

chassis *noun* metal frame that houses the circuit boards together with the wiring and sockets required in a computer system *or* other equipment; *see also* RACK

check 1 *noun* **(a)** act of making sure that something is correct; **character check** = check to ensure that a character code protocol and format are correct; **check bit** = one bit of a binary word that is used to provide a parity check; **check character** = additional character inserted into transmitted text to serve as an (error detection) check for the text, its value is dependent on the text; **check digit** *or* **number** = additional digit inserted into transmitted text to monitor and correct errors; **check indicator** = hardware *or* software device that shows that received text is not correct and a check has failed; **check key** = series of characters derived from a text used to check for and correct errors; **check point** = point in a program where data and program status can be recorded *or* displayed; **check point dump** = printout of data and program status at a check point; **check register** = temporary storage for received data before it is checked against the same data received via another path *or* method; **check total** = CHECKSUM; **desk check** = dry run of a program **(b)** short fault *or* pause in a process (that does not stop the process); **data check** = error in reading data due to a fault with the magnetic medium **2** *verb* to examine *or* to make sure than something is in good working order; *the separate parts of the system were all checked for faults before being packaged;* **he checked the computer printout against the invoices** = he examined the printout and the invoices to see if the figures were the same

◊ **checkerboarding** *noun* (virtual page) memory organization that has resulted in odd pages *or* spread-out pages *or* segments of memory being filled, wasting memory by leaving unusable gaps inbetween

◊ **checking** *noun* examination; *the maintenance engineer found some defects whilst checking the equipment;* **checking program** = software that finds errors in program *or* data syntax, format and coding; **self-checking code** = error detection code NOTE: no plural

◊ **checksum** *or* **check total** *noun* program which checks that data (retrieved from memory) is correct, summing it and comparing the sum with a stored value; *the data must be corrupted if the checksum is different*

chip *noun* device consisting of a small piece of a crystal of a semiconductor onto which are etched *or* manufactured (by doping) a number of components such as transistors, resistors and capacitors, which together perform a function; **chip architecture** = design and layout of components on a chip; **chip card** = plastic card with a memory and microprocessor device embedded in it, so that it can be used for electronic funds transfer *or* identification of a user; **chip count** = number of chips on a PCB *or* in a device; *it's no good, the chip count is still too high;* **chip select line** = connection to a chip that will enable it to function when a signal is present; *the data strobe line is connected to the latch chip select line;* **chip set** = chips which together will carry out a function; **diagnostic chip** = chip that contains circuits to carry out tests on circuits *or* other chips; *they are carrying out research on diagnostic chips to test computers that contain processors;* **single chip computer** = complete simple computer including CPU, memory and input/output ports on one chip; **sound chip** = device that will generate a sound *or* tune

chop *see* BINARY

chord keying *noun* action of pressing two *or* more keys at the same time to perform a function; *to access the second window, press control and F2; shift and character delete keys will delete a line of text*

chroma *noun* measure of colour hue and saturation

◇ **chromatic** *adjective* referring to colours

◇ **chrominance signal** *noun* section of a colour monitor signal containing colour hue and saturation information

chronological order *noun* arrangement of records *or* files according to their dates

CIM (a) = COMPUTER INPUT FROM MICROFILM coordinated use of microfilm for computer data storage and the method of reading the data **(b)** = COMPUTER INTEGRATED MANUFACTURE use of computers in every aspect of design and manufacturing

cipher *noun* system of transforming a message into an unreadable form with a secret key (the message can be read normally after it has passed through the cipher a second time); *always use a secure cipher when sending data over a telephone line;* **cipher key** = secret sequence of characters used with a cipher system to provide a unique ciphertext; **cipher system** = formula used to transform text into a secret form; **public key cipher** = cipher that uses a public key to encrypt messages and a secret key to decrypt them (conventional ciphers use one secret key to encrypt and

decrypt messages); **ciphertext** = data output from a cipher NOTE: opposite is **plaintext**

CIR = CURRENT INSTRUCTION REGISTER CPU register that stores the instruction that is currently being executed

circuit *noun* connection between electronic components that perform a function; **circuit board** *or* **card** = insulating board used to hold components which are then connected together (electrically) to form a circuit; **circuit breaker** = device which protects equipment by cutting off the electrical supply when conditions are abnormal; **circuit capacity** = information carrying capacity of a particular circuit; **circuit diagram** = graphical description of a circuit; *the CAD program will plot the circuit diagram rapidly;* **data circuit** = circuit which allows bi-directional data communications; **decision circuit** = logical circuit that operates on binary inputs, producing an output according to the function set in hardware; **digital circuit** = electronic circuit that operates on digital information providing logical functions *or* switching; **logic circuit** = electronic circuit made up of various logical gates, such as AND, OR and EXOR; **printed circuit board (PCB)** = flat insulating material that has conducting tracks of metal printed *or* etched onto its surface, which complete a circuit when components are mounted on it

◇ **circuitry** *noun* collection of circuits; *the circuitry is still too complex* NOTE: no plural

circular 1 *adjective* which goes round in a circle; **circular buffer** = computer-based queue that uses two markers, for top and bottom of the line of stored items (the markers move as items are read from *or* written to the stack); **circular file** = a data file that has no visible beginning *or* end, each item points to the location of the next item with the last pointing back to the first; **circular list** = list in which each element contains data and an address to the next element in the list with the last item pointing back to the first; **circular shift** = rotation of bits in a word with the previous last bit inserted in the first bit position

◇ **circulate** *verb* to go round in a circle, and return to the first point

◇ **circulating** *adjective* which is moving about freely; **circulating register** = shift register whose output is fed back to its input to form a closed loop; **circulating storage** = storage device that maintains stored data as a series of pulses, that move along the length of the medium, being regenerated and re-input when they reach the end

> COMMENT: circulating storage devices are not often used now, being slow (serial access) and bulky: typical devices are acoustic or mercury delay lines

◇ **circulation** *noun* movement; *the company is trying to improve the circulation of information between departments*

CISC COMPLEX INSTRUCTION SET COMPUTER CPU design whose instruction set contains a number of long, complex instructions, that makes program writing easier, but reduces execution speed; *compare with* RISC

cladding *noun* protective material surrounding a conducting core; *if the cladding is chipped, the fibre-optic cable will not functon well*

clapper *noun* mechanical part of a dot matrix printer that drives the printing needles onto the ribbon to print a character on the paper

classify *verb* to put into classes *or* under various headings; *the diagnostic printouts have been classified under T for test results*
◇ **classification** *noun* way of putting into classes

clean 1 *adjective* not dirty *or* with no errors *or* with no programs; *I'll have to start again - I just erased the only clean file;* **clean copy** = copy which is ready for keyboarding, and does not have many changes on it; **clean machine** = computer that contains only the minimum of ROM based code to boot its system from disk, any languages required must be loaded in; **clean page** = page (of memory) that has not been changed since it was read 2 *verb* to make something clean; **data cleaning** = to remove errors from data; **head cleaning disk** = special disk which will clean dirt from the read/write head; *use a head cleaning disk every week; write errors occur if you do not use a head cleaning kit regularly;* **screen cleaning kit** = liquids and cloth which remove any static and dirt from a VDU screen

clear 1 *adjective* easily understood; *the program manual is not clear on copying files; the booklet gives clear instructions how to connect the different parts of the system; he made it clear that the system will only work on IBM-compatible hardware* 2 *verb* (a) to wipe out *or* erase *or* set to zero a computer

file *or* variable *or* section of memory; *type CLS to clear the screen; all arrays are cleared each time the program is run; to clear an area of memory; to clear the data register* (b) to release a communications link when transmissions have finished; **clear to send (CTS)** = RS232C signal that a line *or* device is ready for data transmission
◇ **clearance** *noun* authority to access a file; *you do not have the required clearance for this processor*

click 1 *noun* (a) short duration sound, often used to indicate that a key has been pressed (b) pressing a key *or* button on a keyboard; *you move through text and graphics with a click of the button* 2 *verb* to press a key *or* a button on a keyboard *or* the mouse; *use the mouse to enlarge a frame by clicking inside its border*

clock *noun* (a) machine which shows the time; *the micro has a built-in clock; the time is shown by the clock in the corner of the screen;* **digital clock** = clock which shows the time using numbers (as 12:05) (b) circuit that generates pulses used to synchronize equipment; **clock cycle** = time period between two consecutive clock pulses; **clock pulse** = regular pulse used for timing *or* synchronizing purposes; **clock rate** = number of pulses that a clock generates every second; **clock track** = line of marks on a disk *or* tape which provides data about the read head location; **main clock** = clock signal that synchronizes all the components in a system; **programmable clock** = circuit whose frequency can be set by the user 2 *verb* to synchronize signals *or* circuits with a clock pulse; **clocked signals** = signals that are synchronized with a clock pulse

clone *noun* computer *or* circuit that behaves in the same way as the original it was copied from; *they have copied our new personal computer and brought out a cheaper clone; higher performance clones are available for all the models in our range*

close *verb* to shut down access to a file *or* disk drive; **close file** = to execute a computer instruction to shut down access to a stored file; **closed loop** = number of computer instructions that are repeated; **closed subroutine** = number of computer instructions in a program that can be called at any time, with control being returned on completion to the next instruction in the main program; **closed user group (CUG)** = to restrict the entry to a database *or* bulletin board *or* system (about or on a certain topic *or* subject) to certain known and registered users, usually by means of a password; *see also* USER GROUP

cluster *noun* number of terminals *or* stations *or* devices *or* memory locations grouped together in one place, controlled by a cluster controller; **cluster controller** = central computer that controls communications to a cluster of devices *or* memory locations

◊ **clustering** *noun* series of elements, occurring in a sequential line within a hash table

QUOTE cluster controllers are available with 8 or 16 channels
Microcomputer News
QUOTE these include IBM networking and clustering hardware and software
Personal Computer World

CM = CENTRAL MEMORY area of memory whose locations can be directly and immediately addressed by the CPU

CMI = COMPUTER MANAGED INSTRUCTION

CML = COMPUTER MANAGED LEARNING

CMOS = COMPLEMENTARY METAL OXIDE SEMICONDUCTOR integrated circuit design and construction method (using a pair of complementary p- and n-type transistors)

COMMENT: the final package uses very low power but is relatively slow and sensitive to static electricity as compared to TTL integrated circuits; their main use is in portable computers where battery power is being used

CNC = COMPUTER NUMERIC CONTROL machine operated automatically by computer; *see also* NUMERICAL CONTROL

coalesce *verb* to merge two or more files

co-axial cable *noun* cable made up of a central core, surrounded by an insulating layer then a second shielding conductor

COMMENT: co-axial cable is used for high frequency, low loss applications such as TV aerials

COBOL = COMMON ORDINARY BUSINESS ORIENTED LANGUAGE programming language mainly used in business applications

code 1 *noun* **(a)** rules used to convert instructions *or* data from one form to another; **code conversion** = rules used to change characters coded in one form, to another **(b)** sequence of computer instructions; **chain code** = series of words, each word being derived (usually shifted by one bit) from the previous word; **code area** = section of main memory in which program instructions are stored; **code line** = one written *or* displayed computer program instruction; **computer** *or* **machine code** = programming language that consists of commands in binary code that can be directly understood by the central processing unit, without the need for translation; **direct** *or* **one-level** *or* **specific code** = binary code which directly operates the central processing unit, using only absolute addresses and values (this is the final form of a program after a compiler *or* assembler pass); **macro code** = one word that is used to represent a number of instructions, simplifying program writing; **object code** = (i) binary code which directly operates a CPU; (ii) program code after it has been translated, compiled or assembled (into machine code); **optimum code** = coding system that provides the fastest access and retrieval time for stored data items; **source code** = set of codes (as a program) written by the programmer which cannot be directly executed by the computer, but have to be translated into an object code program by a compiler *or* assembler *or* interpreter; **symbolic code** = instruction that is in mnemonic form rather than machine code **(c)** system of signs *or* numbers *or* letters which mean something; **bar code** = data represented as a series of printed stripes of varying widths; **bar-code reader** = optical device that reads data from a bar code; **code element** = voltage *or* signal used to represent binary digits; **cyclic code** = coding system in which the binary representation of decimal numbers changes by only one bit at a time from one number to the next; **device code** = unique identification and selection code for a peripheral; **error code** = code that indicates that a particular type of error has occurred; **error correcting code** = coding system that allows bit errors occurring during transmission to be rapidly corrected by logical deduction methods; **error detecting code** = coding system that allows bit errors occurring during transmission to be detected, but is not complex enough to correct them; **escape codes** = transmitted code sequence which informs the receiver that all following characters represent control actions; **machine-readable codes** = sets of signs *or* letters (such as bar codes *or* post codes) which can be read by computers; **punched code** = combination of holes that represent characters in a punched card; **self-checking code** = error detecting code **2** *verb* **(a)** to convert instructions *or* data into another form **(b)** to write a program in a programming language

◇ **coder** *noun* device which encodes a signal

◇ **coding** *noun* act of putting a code on something; **coding sheet** *or* **coding form** = special printed sheet used by programmers to write instructions for coding a certain type of program

CODEC = CODER/DECODER device which encodes a signal being sent *or* decodes a signal received (used in many advanced PABX systems)

coincidence circuit *or* **element** *noun* electronic circuit that produces an output signal when two inputs occur simultaneously *or* two binary words are equal; *see also* AND

cold *adjective* **(a)** not hot; *the machines work badly in cold weather* **(b)** without being prepared; **cold fault** = computer fault *or* error that occurs as soon as it is switched on; **cold standby** = backup system that will allow the equipment to continue running, but with the loss of any volatile data; *compare with* HOT, WARM STANDBY; **cold start** = switching on a computer *or* to run a program from its original start point; *compare* WARM START

collate *verb* to compare and put items in order; **collating sequence** = characters ordered according to their codes

◇ **collator** *noun* (i) software that collates data; (ii) device that collates punched cards

collect *verb* to receive *or* capture data; **data collection** = act of receiving data from various sources (either directly from a data capture device *or* from a cartridge) and inserting correctly in order into a database; **data collection platform** = station that transmits collected data to a central point (usually via satellite)

◇ **collect transfer** *verb* to load a register with bits from a number of different locations

collision detection *noun* the detecting and reporting of the coincidence of two actions *or* events; **carrier sense multiple access-collision detection (CSMA-CD)** = network communications protocol that prevents two sources transmitting at the

same time by waiting for a quiet moment on the channel, then attempting to transmit

colon *noun* printing sign (:), which shows a break in a string of words; **semi-colon** = printed sign (;) which marks the end of a program line *or* statement in some languages (such as C and Pascal)

colour *noun* sensation sensed by the eye, due to its response to various frequencies of light; **colour cell** = smallest area on a CRT screen that can display colour information; **colour display** = display device able to represent characters *or* graphics in colour; **colour graphics adapter (CGA)** = popular microcomputer colour display system; *see also* EGA; **colour monitor** = screen that has a demodulator which shows information in colour; *the colour monitor is great for games;* **colour saturation** = purity of a colour signal

> QUOTE as a minimum, a colour graphics adapter (CGA) is necessary, but for best quality of graphic presentation an enhanced graphics adapter (EGA) should be considered
> *Micro Decision*

column *noun* series of characters, printed one under the other; *to add up a column of figures; put the total at the bottom of the column;* **card column** = line of punched information about one character, parallel to the shorter side of the card; **column parity** = parity check on every punched card *or* tape column; **80-column printer** = printer which has a maximum line width of 80 characters; *an 80-column printer is included in the price*

◇ **columnar** *adjective* in columns; **columnar graph** = graph on which values are shown as vertical *or* horizontal bars; **columnar working** = showing information in columns

COM = COMPUTER OUTPUT ON MICROFILM recording the output from a computer directly onto microfilm

COMAL = COMMON ALGORITHMIC LANGUAGE structured programming language similar to BASIC

combine *verb* to join together; **combined head** = transducer that can read and write data from the surface of a magnetic storage medium, such as a floppy disk; **combined station** = high-level data link control station that processes commands and responses; **combined symbol matching**

(CSM) = efficient optical character recognition system

◊ **combination** *noun* several things which are joined together; series of numbers which open a lock

◊ **combinational** *adjective* which combines a number of separate elements; **combinational circuit** = electronic circuit consisting of a number of connected components; **combinational logic** = logic function made up from a number of separate logic gates

command *noun* **(a)** electrical pulse *or* signal that will start *or* stop a process **(b)** word *or* phrase which is recognized by a computer system and starts *or* terminates an action; *interrupt command; the command to execute the program is RUN;* **channel command** = instruction to a channel *or* control unit, providing control actions such as data filtering *or* routes; **command code** = binary code that starts *or* stops an instruction *or* action in a CPU; **command console processor (CCP)** = software interface between a user's terminal and the BIOS; **command control language** = programming language that allows equipment to be easily controlled; **command-driven program** = program which requires the user to enter instructions at every stage; **command file** = sequence of frequently used commands stored in a file; **command file processor** = execution of a user's command file, allowing the user to create a customized simple operating environment *or* to carry out a series of frequently used commands; **command interface** = cue and prompts used by a program to inform and accept from a user required inputs (this can be user-friendly such as a WIMP environment, or not so friendly, such as a question mark); **command language** = programming language made up of procedures for various tasks, that can be called up by a series of commands; **command line** = program line that contains a command instruction; **command prompt** = symbol displayed to indicate a command is expected; **command register** = register that stores the instruction to be carried out *or* that is being processed; **command window** = area of a screen where commands are entered; *the user can define the size of the command window;* **dot command** = method of writing instructions, with a full stop followed by the command, used mainly for embedded commands in a word-processing system; **embedded command** = printer control command, such as indicating that text should be in italics, inserted into test

and used by a word-processor when formatting text

comment *noun* helpful notes in a program to guide the user; *the lack of comments is annoying; BASIC allows comments to be written after a REM instruction;* **comment field** = section of a command line in an assembly language program that is not executed but provides notes and comments

common *adjective* **(a)** which happens very often; *this is a common fault with this printer model* **(b)** belonging to several different people *or* programs *or* to everyone; **common channel signalling** = one channel used as a communications link to a number of devices *or* circuits; **common business orientated language (COBOL)** = programming language mainly used in business applications; **common hardware** = hardware items that can be used for a variety of tasks; **common language** = data *or* program instructions in a standardized form that can be understood by other processors *or* compilers/interpreters; **common software** = useful (routines) that can be used by any program; **common storage area** = memory *or* storage area used by more than one program; *the file server memory is mainly common storage area, with a section reserved for the operating system*

communicate *verb* to pass information to someone; *he finds it impossible to communicate with his staff; communicating with head office has been quicker since we installed the telex;* **communicating word processor** = word processor workstation which is able to transmit and receive data

communication *noun* **(a)** passing of information; *communication with the head office has been made easier by the telex* **(b)** **communications** = process by which data is transmitted and received, by means of telephones, satellites, radio or any medium capable of carrying signals; **communications buffer** = terminal *or* modem that is able to store transmitted data; **communications channel** = physical link over which data can be transmitted; **communications computer** = computer used to control data transmission in a network; **communications control unit** = electronic device that controls data transmission and routes in a network; **communications executive** = main set of programs that ensure that protocol, format and device and line handlers are correct for the type of device *or* line in use;

communications interface adapter = electronic circuit that allows a computer to communicate with a modem; **communications link** = physical path that joins a transmitter to a receiver; **communications link control** = processor that provides various handshaking and error detection functions for a number of links between devices; **communications network** = group of devices such as terminals and printers that are interconnected with a central computer, allowing the rapid and simple transfer of data; **communications network processor** = processor that provides various interfacing and management (buffering *or* code conversion) between a computer and communications link control; **communications port** = connection allowing a device to communicate; **communications scanner** = line monitoring equipment to check for data request signals; **data communications** = transmission and reception of data rather than speech *or* images; **data communications buffer** = buffer on a receiver that allows a slow peripheral to accept data from a fast peripheral, without slowing either down; **data communications equipment (DCE)** = equipment (such as a modem) which receives *or* transmits data

QUOTE it requires no additional hardware, other than a communications board in the PC
Electronics & Power

compact 1 *adjective* (thing) which does not take up much space; **compact cassette** = magnetic recording tape contained inside a standard plastic box, used in home personal computers for data storage; **compact code** = minimum number of program instructions required for a task; **compact disk (CD)** = small plastic disk that contains audio signals in digital form etched onto the surface; **compact disk player** = machine that reads the digital data from a CD and converts it back to its original form; **compact disk ROM** = small plastic disk that is used as a high capacity ROM device, data is stored in binary form as holes etched on the surface which are then read by a laser; *the compact disk ROM can store as much data as a dozen hard disks;* **compacting algorithm** = formula for reducing the amount of space required by text **2** *verb* to reduce the space taken by something; **data compacting** = reducing the storage space taken by data by coding it in a more efficient way

companding = COMPRESSING AND EXPANDING two processes which reduce *or* compact data before transmission *or*

storage then restore packed data to its original form

compare *verb* to check the differences between two pieces of information

◊ **compare with** *verb* to put two things together to see how they differ

◊ **comparable** *adjective* which can be compared; *the two sets of figures are not comparable*

◊ **comparator** *noun* logical device whose output is true if there is a difference between two inputs

◊ **comparison** *noun* way of comparing; *there is no comparison between speeds of the two processors* = one of the two is much faster than the other

compatible 1 *adjective* (two hardware *or* software devices) that function correctly together; *is the hardware IBM-compatible?* **2** *noun* hardware *or* software device that functions correctly with other equipment *or* is a clone; *this computer is much cheaper than the other compatibles*

◊ **compatibility** *noun* (of two hardware *or* software devices) ability to function together

COMMENT: by conforming to the standards of another manufacturer *or* organization, compatibility of hardware *or* software allows programs *or* hardware to be interchanged with no modifications

QUOTE the compatibles bring computing to the masses
PC Business World
QUOTE low-cost compatibles have begun to find homes as terminals on LANS
Minicomputer News
QUOTE it is a fairly standard feature on most low-cost PC compatibles
Which PC?
QUOTE check for software compatibility before choosing a display or graphics adapter
PC Business World
QUOTE this was the only piece of software I found that wouldn't work, but it does show that there is no such thing as a totally compatible PC clone
Personal Computer World

compile *verb* to convert a high level language program into a machine code program that can be executed by itself; *compiling takes a long time with this old version; debug your program, then compile it; compiled BASIC programs run much faster than the intrpretor version;* **compile and go** = computer program not requiring operator interaction that will load, compile and execute a high level language program; **compile phase** = the time during a program run, when the instructions are compiled

◇ **compilation** *noun* translation of an encoded source program into machine readable code; **compilation error** = syntax error found during compilation; *compilation errors result in the job being aborted;* **compilation time** = length of time it takes for a computer to compile a program; *compare with* DECOMPILATION

◇ **compiler (program)** *noun* piece of software that converts an encoded source program into a machine code program; *the new compiler has an in-built editor; this compiler produces a more efficient program;* **compiler diagnostics** = features in a compiler that help the programmer to find any faults; **compiler language** = high level language (such as C, Pascal) that will convert a source program that follows the language syntax into a machine code version, then run it; **cross-compiler** = assembler *or* compiler that compiles programs for one computer whilst running on another; *compare with* INTERPRETER *we can use the cross-compiler to develop the software before the new system arrives;* **language compiler** = software that converts an encoded source program into another (machine code) form

complement 1 *noun* (i) inversion of a binary digit; (ii) result after subtracting a number from one less than the radix; *the complement is found by changing the 1s to 0s and 0s to 1s;* **one's complement** = inversion of a binary digit; **nine's complement** = decimal complement (equivalent to binary one's complement) formed by subtracting each digit in the number from nine; **ten's complement** = formed by adding one to the nine's complement of the number; **two's complement** = formed by adding one to the one's complement of a number **2** *verb* to invert a binary digit; **complemented** = (binary digit) that has had a complement performed; **complementary operation** = logical operation that results in the logical NOT of a function

◇ **complementary metal oxide semiconductor (CMOS)** *noun* integrated circuit design and construction method (using a pair of complementary p- and n-type transistors)

◇ **complementation** *noun* number system used to represent positive and negative numbers

complete 1 *adjective* (a) finished *or* all ready; *the spelling check is complete; when this job is complete, the next in the queue is processed* (b) requiring nothing else (in order to function); **complete operation** = operation that retrieves the necessary operands from memory, performs the operation, returns the results and operands to memory and reads the next instruction to be processed **2** *verb* to finish a task; *when you have completed the keyboarding, pass the text through the spelling checker*

◇ **completion** *noun* time when something is complete; *completion date for the new software package is November 15th*

complex *adjective* very complicated *or* difficult to understand; *the complex mathematical formula was difficult to solve; the controller must work hard to operate this complex network;* **complex instruction set computer (CISC)** = CPU design whose instruction set contains a number of long, complex instructions, that makes programming easier, but reduces execution speed; *compare* REDUCED INSTRUCTION SET COMPUTER

◇ **complexity** *noun* being complicated; **complexity measure** = measure of the system resources used in an operation *or* job

complicated *adjective* with many different parts *or* difficult to understand; *this program is very complicated; the computer design is more complicated than necessary*

component *noun* (i) piece of machinery *or* section which will be put into a final product; (ii) electronic device that produces an electrical signal; **component density** = number of electronic components per unit area on a PCB; *component density increases with production expertise; component density is so high on this motherboard, that no expansion connectors could be fitted;* **component error** = error introduced by a malfunctioning device *or* component rather than incorrect programming

composite circuit *noun* electronic circuit made up of a number of smaller circuits and components

compound *adjective* **compound logical element** = logical circuit *or* function that produces an output from a number of inputs; **compound statement** = a number of program instructions in one line of program; *the debugger cannot handle compound statements*

compress *verb* to squeeze something to fit into a smaller space; *use the archiving program to compress the file*

◇ **compression** *noun* **data compression =** means of reducing the size of blocks of data by removing spaces, empty sections and unused material

◇ **compressor** *noun* (program *or* device) that provides data compression

compute *verb* to calculate *or* to do calculations; *connect charges were computed on an hourly rate*

◇ **computable** *adjective* which can be calculated

◇ **computation** *noun* calculation

◇ **computational** *adjective* referring to computation; **computational error =** mistake made in calculating

computer *noun* **(a)** machine that receives *or* stores *or* processes data very quickly according to a stored program; **analog computer =** computer which processes data in analog form (that is data which is represented by a continuously variable signal - as opposed to digital data); **business computer =** powerful small computer which is programmed for special business uses; **digital computer =** computer which processes data in digital form (that is data represented in discrete form); **mainframe computer =** large scale powerful computer system that can handle high capacity memory and backing storage devices as well as a number of operators simultaneously; **microcomputer** *or* **micro =** complete small-scale, cheap, low-power computer system based around a microprocessor chip and having limited memory capacity; **minicomputer** *or* **mini =** small computer with a greater range of instructions and processing power than a microcomputer, but not able to compete with the speed or data handling capacity of a mainframe computer; **personal computer (PC)** *or* **home computer =** small computer which can be used in the home, in which the various sections (screen, keyboard, disk drives, processing unit, memory etc.) are in one or two small compact cases; **single board computer (sbc) =** micro *or* mini computer whose components are all located on a single printed circuit board; **single chip computer =** complete simple computer, including CPU, memory and I/O ports on one chip; **supercomputer =** very powerful mainframe computer used for high speed mathematical tasks **(b) computer animation =** making a series of computer-generated images displayed in sequence to emulate motion; **computer applications =** the tasks and uses that a computer can carry out in a particular field *or* job; **computer architecture =** (i) layout and interconnection of a computer's internal hardware and the logical relationships between CPU, memory and I/O devices; (ii) way in which the CPU, terminals, printers and network connections are arranged; **computer bureau =** office which offers to do work on its computers for companies which do not have their own computers; **computer code =** programming language that consists of commands in binary code that can be directly understood by the central processing unit, without the need for translation; **computer conferencing =** connecting a number of computers *or* terminals together to allow a group of users to communicate; **computer crime =** theft, fraud or other crimes involving computers; **computer dating =** use of a computer to match single people who may want to get married; **computer department =** department in a company which manages the company's computers; **computer engineer =** person who maintains *or* programs *or* designs computer equipment; **computer error =** mistake made by a computer; **computer file =** section of information on a computer (such as the payroll, list of addresses, customer accounts); **computer graphics =** information represented graphically on a computer display; **computer image processing =** analysis of information in an image, usually by electronic means *or* using a computer, also used for recognition of objects in an image; **computer independent language =** programming language that will operate on any computer that has a correct compiler *or* interpreter; **computer input from microfilm (CIM) =** use of microfilm for computer data storage, and the method of reading the data; **computer language =** language (formed of figures *or* characters) used to communicate with a computer; **computer listing =** printout of a list of items taken from data stored in a computer; **computer literacy =** understanding the basic principles of computers, related expressions and concepts, and being able to use computers for programming *or* applications; **computer-literate =** (person) able to understand how to use a computer, the expressions and concepts used; *the managing director is simply not computer-literate;* **computer logic =** way in which the various sections of the CPU, memory and I/O are arranged (in hardware); **computer mail** *or* **electronic mail =** messages sent between users of a bulletin board *or* network; **computer manager =** person in charge of a computer department; **computer network =** number of computers, terminals and peripherals connected together to allow communications between each; **computer**

numeric control (CNC) = control of a machine by computer; **computer office system** = computer and related peripherals used for office tasks (filing, word processing, etc.); **computer operator** = person who operates a computer; **computer organization** *see* COMPUTER ARCHITECTURE; **computer output** = data *or* information produced after processing by a computer; **computer output on microfilm (COM)** = information output from a computer, stored directly onto microfilm; **computer power** = measure of speed and capacity of a computer (several tests exist, such as FLOPS *or* benchmark timings); **computer program** = series of instructions to a computer, telling it to do a particular piece of work; *the user cannot write a computer program with this system;* **computer programmer** = person who writes computer programs; **computer run** = action of processing instructions in a program by a computer; **computer science** = scientific study of computers, the organization of hardware and development of software; **computer services** = work using a computer, done by a computer bureau; **computer system** = a central processor with storage and associated peripherals that make up a working computer; **computer time** = time when a computer is being used (paid for at an hourly rate); *running all those sales reports costs a lot in computer time;* **computer word** = number of bits that make up a standard word within a CPU (usually 8,16 *or* 32 bits long)

◇ **computer generations** *noun* way of defining the advances in the field of computing

COMMENT: the development of computers has been divided into a series of "generations": *first generation:* computers constructed using valves having limited storage; *second generation:* computers where transistors were used in construction; *third generation:* use of integrated circuits in construction; *fourth generation:* most often used at present, using low cost memory and IC packages; *fifth generation:* future computers using very fast processors, large memory and allowing human input/output

computer- *prefix* referring to a computer; **computer-based learning (CBL)** = learning mainly using a computer; **computer-based message system (CBMS)** = use of a computer system to allow users to send and receive messages from other users (usually in-house); **computer-based training (CBT)** = use of a computer system to train students; **computer-generated** = which has been generated by a computer; *computer-*generated graphics; **computer-integrated manufacturing (CIM)** = coordinated use of computers in every aspect of design and manufacturing; **computer-integrated systems** = coordinated use of computers and other related equipment in a process; *this firm is a very well-known supplier of computer-integrated systems which allow both batch pagination of very long documents with alteration of individual pages;* **computer-managed instruction (CMI)** = using a computer to assist students in learning a subject; **computer-managed learning (CML)** = using a computer to teach students and assess their progress

◇ **computer-aided** *or* **computer-assisted** *adjective* which uses a computer to make the work easier; **computer-aided** *or* **assisted design (CAD)** = the use of computer and graphics terminal to help a designer in his work; **computer-aided** *or* **assisted engineering (CAE)** = use of a computer to help an engineer solve problems *or* calculate design *or* product specifications; **computer-aided** *or* **assisted instruction (CAI)** = use of a computer to assist pupils in learning a subject; **computer-aided** *or* **assisted learning (CAL)** = use of a computer to assist pupils to learn a subject; **computer-aided** *or* **assisted manufacture (CAM)** = use of a computer to control machinery *or* to assist in a manufacturing process; **computer-aided** *or* **assisted testing (CAT)** = use of a computer to test equipment *or* programs to find any faults; **computer-aided** *or* **assisted training (CAT)** = use of a computer to demonstrate to and assist pupils in learning a skill

◇ **computer-readable** *adjective* which can be read and understood by a computer; *computer-readable codes*

computerize *verb* to change from a manual system to one using computers; *our stock control has been completely computerized; they operate a computerized invoicing system*

◇ **computerization** *noun* action of introducing a computer system *or* of changing from a manual to a computer system; *computerization of the financial sector is proceeding very fast*

computing *adjective & noun* referring to computers *or* work done on computers; **computing power** = measure of speed and ability of a computer to perform calculations; **computing speed** = speed at which a computer calculates

concatenate *verb* to join together two or more sets of data; **concatenated data set** =

more than one file *or* set of data joined together to produce one set

conceal *verb* to hide *or* not display information *or* graphics from a user; *the hidden lines are concealed from view with this algorithm*

concentrate *verb* to combine a number of lines *or* circuits *or* data to take up less space; *the concentrated data was transmitted cheaply*

concertina fold *noun* accordion fold *or* method of folding continuous paper, one sheet in one direction, the next sheet in the opposite direction, allowing the paper to be fed into a printer continuously with no action on the part of the user

concurrent *adjective* almost simultaneous (actions *or* sets); *each concurrent process has its own window; three transputers provide concurrent processing cababilities for the entire department;* **concurrent operating system** = operating system software that allows several programs *or* activities to be processed at the same time; **concurrent programming** = running several programs apparently simultaneously, achieved by executing small sections from each program in turn

◇ **concurrently** *adverb* running at almost the same time; *see also the four categories for processors* SISD, SIMD, MISD, MIMD

condition 1 *noun* (i) state of a circuit *or* device *or* register; (ii) series of requirements that have to be met before an action can occur; **condition code register** = register that contains the state of the CPU after the execution of the last instruction; *see also* FLAG; **error condition** = state that is entered if an attempt is made to operate on data containing errors **2** *verb* to modify data that is to be transmitted so as to meet set parameters; *condition the raw data to a standard format*

◇ **conditional** *adjective* **(a)** provided that certain things take place **(b)** (process) which is dependent on the result of another; **conditional breakpoint** = breakpoint inserted, after which the programmer can jump to one of a number of sections, depending on data *or* program status; **conditional jump** *or* **branch** *or* **transfer** = programming instruction that

provides a jump to a section of a program if a certain condition is met; *the conditional branch will select routine one if the response is yes and routine two if no;* **conditional statement** = program instruction that will redirect program control according to the outcome of an event

conduct *verb* to allow an electrical current to flow through a material; *to conduct electricity; copper conducts well*

◇ **conduction** *noun* ability of a material to conduct; *the conduction of electricity by gold contacts*

◇ **conductive** *adjective* referring to the ability of a material to conduct

◇ **conductor** *noun* substance (such as a metal) which conducts electricity; *copper is a good conductor of electricity; see also* SEMICONDUCTOR

conduit *noun* protective pipe *or* channel for wires *or* cables; *the cables from each terminal are channelled to the computer centre by metal conduit*

conference *noun* meeting of people to discuss problems

◇ **conferencing** *noun* **computer conferencing** = connecting a number of computers *or* terminals together to allow a group of users to communicate; *the multi-user BBS has a computer conferencing facility*

confidence level *noun* likelihood that a number will lie to within a range of values

configure *verb* to select hardware, software and interconnections to make up a special system; *this terminal has been configured to display graphics; you only have to configure the PC once - when you first buy it*

◇ **configuration** *noun* way in which the hardware and software of a computer system are planned and set up; **configuration state** = state of a computer that allows it *or* the system *or* a program to be configured

◇ **configured-in** = device whose configuration state indicates it is ready and available for use; **configured-off** *or* **configured out** = device whose configuration state indicates it is not available for use

QUOTE the machine uses RAM to store system configuration information
PC Business World

QUOTE several configuration files are provided to assign memory to the program, depending on the available RAM on your system
PC Business World

QUOTE users can configure four of the eight ports to handle links at speeds of 64K bit/sec
Computer News

QUOTE if you modify a program with the editor, or with a word-processor specified in the configuration file, it will know that the program has changed and will execute the new one accordingly
PC Business World

conform *verb* to work according to set rules; *the software will not run if it does not conform to the operating system standards*

congestion *noun* state that occurs when communication *or* processing demands are greater than the capacity of a system

conjunct *noun* one of the variables in an logical AND function

◊ **conjunction** *noun* logical function whose output is true if all inputs are true

connect *verb* to link together two points in a circuit *or* communications network; **connect time** = length of time a user is logged onto an interactive system

◊ **connection** *noun* link *or* something which joins; **parallel connection** = connector on a computer allowing parallel data to be transferred; *their transmission rate is 60,000 bps through parallel connection*

◊ **connector** *noun* physical device with a number of metal contacts that allow devices to be easily linked together; *the connector at the end of the cable will fit any standard serial port;* **card edge connector** = series of metal tracks ending at the edge and on the surface of a circuit board, allowing it to be plugged into an edge connector to provide electrical path (for data transmission, etc.); *see also* FEMALE, MALE

connective *noun* symbol between two operands that describes the operation to be performed

conscious error *noun* operator error that is immediately spotted, but cannot be prevented in time

consecutive *adjective* following one after another; *the computer ran three consecutive files*

◊ **consecutively** *adverb* one after the other; *the sections of the program run consecutively*

console *noun* unit (keyboard and VDU, and usually a printer) which allows an operator to communicate with a computer system; *the console consists of input device such as a keyboard, and an output device such as a printer or CRT*

constant 1 *noun* item of data, whose value does not change (as opposed to a variable) **2** *adjective* which does not change; *the disk drive motor spins at a constant velocity;* **constant length field** = data field that always contains the same number of characters; **constant ratio code** = character representation code that has a constant number of binary ones per word length

construct *verb* to build *or* to make (a device *or* a system)

◊ **construction** *noun* building *or* making of a system; *construction of the prototype is advancing rapidly; construction techniques have changed over the past few years*

consult *verb* to ask an expert for advice; *he consulted the maintenance manager about the disk fault*

◊ **consultant** *noun* specialist who gives advice; *they called in a computer consultant to advise them on the system design*

◊ **consulting** *adjective* person who gives specialist advice; *a consulting engineer*

consumables *plural noun* small cheap extra items required in the day-to-day running of a computer system (such as paper and printer ribbons); *put all the printer leads and paper with the other consumables*

contact 1 *noun* section of a switch *or* connector that provides an electrical path when it touches another conductor; *the circuit is not working because the contact is dirty;* **contact bounce** = *see* BOUNCE, DE-BOUNCE **2** *verb* to try to call a user *or* device in a network

contain *verb* to hold something inside; *each carton contains two computers and their peripherals; we have lost a file containing important documents*

content *noun* the ideas inside a letter *or* other document

◊ **contents** *plural noun* **(a)** things contained *or* what is inside something; *the* *contents of the bottle poured out onto the computer keyboard; the customs officials inspected the contents of the box;* **the contents of the letter** = the words written in the letter **(b)** list of items in a file

◊ **content-addressable** *adjective* **content-addressable file** *or* **location** = method of storing data in which each item may be individually accessed; **content-addressable memory (CAM)** *or* **associative storage** = method of data retrieval which uses part of the data rather than an address to locate the data

contention *noun* situation that occurs when two or more devices are trying to communicate with the same piece of equipment; **contention bus** = communication control system in which a device must wait for a free moment before transmitting data; **contention delay** = length of time spent waiting for equipment to become free for use

contiguous *adjective* which touches the thing next to it; **contiguous file** = file stored in a series of adjacent disk sectors; **contiguous graphics** = graphic cells *or* characters that touch each other; *most display units do not provide contiguous graphics: their characters have a small space on each side to improve legibility*

contingency plan *noun* secondary plan *or* equipment that will be used if the first fails to work

continue *verb* to go on doing something *or* to do something which you were doing earlier

◊ **continual** *adjective* which happens again and again; *the continual system breakdowns have slowed down the processing*

◊ **continually** *adverb* again and again

◊ **continuation** *noun* act of continuing; **continuation page** = page *or* screen of text that follows on from a main page

◊ **continuity** *noun* clear conduction path between two points

◊ **continuous** *adjective* with no end *or* with no breaks; which goes on without stopping; **continuous data stream** = high speed serial data transmission, in which data words are not synchronized, but follow on immediately from each other; **continuous feed** = device which feeds continuous stationery into a printer; **continuous loop** = endless piece of recording *or* projection tape; **continuous signal** = analog (continuously variable) signal; **continuous stationery** = paper made as one long sheet, used in computer printers

◊ **continuously** *adverb* without stopping; *the printer overheated after working continuously for five hours*

contrast 1 *noun* **(a)** difference between black and white; *the control allows you to adjust brightness and contrast;* **contrast enhancement filter** = special filter put over a monitor to increase contrast and prevent eye-strain **(b)** control knob on a display that alters the difference between black and white tones **2** *verb* to examine the differences between two sets of information; *the old data was contrasted with the latest information*

control 1 *verb* to be in charge of something *or* to make sure that something is kept in check; **controlled vocabulary** = set of terms *or* words used in an indexing language NOTE: **controlling - controlled 2** *noun* **(a)** restricting *or* checking something *or* making sure that something is kept in check; **control computer** = dedicated computer used to control a process *or* piece of equipment; **control total** = result of summing certain fields in a computer file to provide error detection; **out of control** = not kept in check **(b)** (i) section of a computer *or* device that carries out instructions and processes signals, etc.; (ii) conditional program statements; **control statement** = program instruction that redirects a program (to another branch etc.); **control unit (CU)** = section of central processor that selects and executes instructions; **control word** = word that defines the actions (in a particular process) that are to be followed; **device control character** = special code sent in a transmission to a device to instruct it to perform a special function; **line control** = special code used to control a communications link **(c)** (i) key on a computer keyboard which sends a control character; (ii) data *or* a key which controls something; **control block** = reserved area of computer memory that contains control data; **control bus** = set of connections to a microcomputer that carry the control signals between CPU, memory and input/output devices; **control cards** = in a punched card system, the first cards which contain the processor control instructions; **control character** = special character that provides a control sequence rather than a alphanumeric character; **control cycle** = events required to retrieve, decode and execute an instruction stored in memory; **control data** = data that controls the actions of a device; **control driven** = computer architecture where instructions are executed once a control sequence has been received; **control field** = storage area for control instructions; **control instruction** = program instruction that controls the actions of a device; *the next control instruction will switch to italics;* **control language** = commands that describe the identification of and resources required by a job that a computer has to process; **control memory** or **ROM** = memory which decodes control instructions into microinstructions which operate the computer or microcontroller; **control mode** = state of a device in which control signals can be received to select options or functions; **control panel** = main computer system control switches and status indicators; **control program/monitor** or **control program for microcomputers (CP/M)** = old-fashioned but still popular operating system for microcomputers; **control register** = storage location only used for control data; **control signals** = electrical signals transmitted to control the actions of a circuit; **control sequence** = (series of) codes containing a control character and various arguments, used to carry out a process or change mode in a device; **control statement** = program instruction that directs a CPU to provide controlling actions or controls the operation of the CPU; **control token** = special sequence of bits transmitted over a LAN to provide control actions; **control transfer** = redirection of the CPU when a jump or call instruction is encountered **(d) control group** = small group which is used to check a sample group; **control systems** = systems used to check that a computer system is working correctly

◊ **controllable** *adjective* which can be controlled

◊ **controller** *noun* hardware or software device that controls a peripheral (such as a printer) or monitors and directs the data transmission over a local area network; **display controller** = device that accepts character or graphical codes and instructions, and converts them into dot-matrix patterns that are displayed on a screen; **printer's controller** = main device in a printer that translates output from the computer into printing instructions; *see also* DEVICE DRIVER

QUOTE a printer's controller is the brains of the machine. It translates the signals coming from your computer into printing instructions that result in a hard copy of your electronic document
Publish

QUOTE there are seven print control characters which can be placed in a document
Personal Computer World

convention *noun* well-known standards or rules which are followed, allowing hardware or software compatibility

conversational (mode) *noun* computer system that provides immediate responses to a user's input; *see also* INTERACTIVE MODE *compare with* BATCH MODE

conversion *noun* change from one system to another; **conversion equipment** = device that will convert data from one format to another (suitable for another system) without changing the content; **conversion tables** or **translation tables** = list of source codes or statements and their equivalent in another language or form; *conversion tables may be created and used in conjunction with the customer's data to convert it to our systems codes;* **conversion program** = (i) program that converts programs written for one computer into a suitable form for another; (ii) program that converts data format, coding, etc. for use in another program

◊ **convert** *verb* to change one thing into another

◊ **convertibility** *noun* ability to be changed

◊ **convertible** *adjective* which can be converted

◊ **converter** or **convertor** *noun* device or program that translates data from one form to another; *the convertor allowed the old data to be used on the new system;* **analog to digital converter (ADC)** = device used to convert an analog signal to a digital output form, that can be understood by a computer; **digital to analog converter (DAC)** = circuit that outputs an analog signal that is proportional to the input digital number

coordinate 1 *noun* **coordinates** = values used to locate a point on a graph or map; **coordinate graph** = means of displaying one point on a graph, using two values referring to axes which are usually at right angles to each other **2** *verb* to organize complex tasks, so that they fit together efficiently; *she has to coordinate the keyboarding of several parts of a file in six different locations*

◊ **coordination** *noun* organizing complex tasks; synchronizing two or more processes

coprocessor *noun* extra, specialized processor, such as an array or numerical processor that can work with a main CPU to increase execution speed; **graphics coprocessor** = high speed display adapter that is dedicated to graphics operations such as line drawing, plotting, etc.; **maths**

coprocessor = dedicated processor that provides results to mathematical operations much faster than the ALU section of a CPU

copy 1 *noun* **(a)** document which looks the same as another; duplicate of an original; **file copy** = copy of a document which is filed in an office for reference **(b)** document; **clean copy** = copy which is ready for keyboarding and does not have many changes to it; **fair copy** *or* **final copy** = document which is written *or* typed with no changes *or* mistakes; **hard copy** = printout of text *or* data which is stored in a computer; **rough copy** = draft of a program which, it is expected, will have changes made to it before it is complete **2** *verb* to make a second document which is like the first; to duplicate original data; *he copied all the personnel files at night and took them home; there is a memory resident utility which copies the latest files onto backing store every 40 minutes*

◇ **copy protect** *noun & verb* switch to prevent copies of a disk being made; *the program is not copy protected*

◇ **copy protection** *noun* preventing copies being made; *a hard disk may crash because of copy protection; the new program will come without copy protection*

copyright 1 *noun* legal right (lasting for fifty years after the death of an artist whose work has been published) which a writer *or* programmer has in his own work, allowing him not to have it copied without the payment of royalties; **Copyright Act** = Act of Parliament making copyright legal, and controlling the copying of copyright material; **work which is out of copyright** = work by a writer, etc., who has been dead for fifty years, and which anyone can publish; **work still in copyright** = work by a living writer, or by a writer who has not been dead for fifty years; **copyright owner** = person who owns the copyright in a work **2** *verb* to state the copyright of a written work by printing a copyright notice and publishing the work **3** *adjective* covered by the laws of copyright; *it is illegal to take copies of a copyright work*

◇ **copyrighted** *adjective* in copyright

CORAL = COMMON REAL-TIME APPLICATIONS LANGUAGE computer programming language used in a real-time system

cord *noun* wire used to connect a device to a socket

core *noun* **(a)** central conducting section of a cable **(b) core memory** *or* **store** = (i) central memory of a computer; (ii) non-volatile magnetic storage method used in old computers; **core program** = computer program stored in core memory

coresident *adjective* (two or more programs) stored in main memory at the same time

coroutine *noun* section of a program *or* procedure that can pass data and control to another coroutine then halt itself

correct 1 *adjective* accurate *or* right **2** *verb* to remove mistakes from something; **error correcting code** = coding system that allows bit errors occurring during transmission to be rapidly corrected by logical deduction methods rather than retransmission

◇ **correction** *noun* making something correct; change which makes something correct

◇ **corrective maintenance** *noun* actions to trace, find and repair a fault after it has occurred

corrupt 1 *adjective* data *or* program that contains errors **2** *verb* to introduce errors into data *or* a program; *power loss during disk access can corrupt the data*

◇ **corruption** *noun* **data corruption** = errors introduced into data, due to noise *or* faulty equipment; *acoustic couplers suffer from data corruption more than the direct connect form of modem; data corruption on the disk has made one file unreadable*

count *verb* to make a total of a number of items

counter *noun* (i) device which counts; (ii) register *or* variable whose contents are increased *or* decreased by a set amount every time an action occurs; *the loop will repeat itself until the counter reaches 100; the number of items changed are recorded with the counter;* **instruction** *or* **program counter** = register in a CPU that contains the location of the next instruction to be processed

couple *verb* to join together; *the two systems are coupled together*

◇ **coupler** *noun* mechanical device used to connect three or more conductors; **acoustic coupler** = device that connects to a telephone handset, converting binary computer data into sound signals to allow it to be transmitted down a telephone line

CP = CARD PUNCH

cpi = CHARACTERS PER INCH

CP/M = CONTROL PROGRAM/MONITOR popular operating system for microcomputers

CPM = CRITICAL PATH METHOD

cps = CHARACTERS PER SECOND number of characters printed *or* processed every second

CPU = CENTRAL PROCESSING UNIT group of circuits which perform the basic functions of a computer made up of three parts, the control unit, the arithmetic and logic unit and the input/output unit; **CPU cycle** = period of time taken to fetch and execute an instruction (usually a simple ADD instruction) used as a measure of computer speed; **CPU elements** = main sections that make up a CPU, including ALU, control unit, I/O bus, memory and various registers; **CPU handshaking** = interfacing signals between a CPU and a peripheral *or* I/O device; **CPU time** = total period of time that a CPU is used to actually process instructions

COMMENT: in a file handling program CPU time might be minimal, since data retrieval (from disk) would account for a large part of the program run; in a mathematical program, the CPU time could be much higher in proportion to the total run time

CR = CARRIAGE RETURN, CARD READER

crash 1 *noun* failure of a component *or* a bug in a program during a run, which halts and prevents further use of the system; **disk crash** = fault caused by the read/write head touching the surface of the disk **2** *verb* (*of a computer or program*) to come to an sudden stop; *the disk head has crashed and the data may have been lost*

◊ **crash-protected** *adjective* (disk) which uses a head protection *or* data corruption protection system; *if the disk is crash-protected, you will never lose your data*

COMMENT: it is sometimes possible to recover data from a crashed hard disk before reformatting, if the crash was caused by a bad sector on the disk rather than contact between the r/w head and disk surface

CRC = CYCLIC REDUNDANCY CHECK

create *verb* to make; *a new file was created on disk to store the document; move to the CREATE NEW FILE instruction on the menu*

crippled leapfrog test *noun* standard leapfrog test that uses a single memory location rather than a changing location

criterion *noun* specification that has to be met
NOTE: plural is **criteria**

critical path analysis *noun* the definition of tasks *or* jobs and the time each requires arranged in order to achieve certain goals NOTE: also called PERT (Program Evaluation and Review Techniques) **critical path method (CPM)** = use of analysis and projection of each critical step in a large project to help a management team; **critical resource** = resource that can only be used by one process at a time

CR/LF = CARRIAGE RETURN/LINE FEED

cross- *prefix* running from one side to another

◊ **cross-assembler** *noun* assembler that produces machine-code code for one computer whilst running on another

◊ **cross-compiler** assembler *or* compiler that compiles programs for one computer whilst running on another

COMMENT: cross-compilers and assemblers are used to compile programs for micros, but are run on larger computers to make the operation faster

◊ **cross-reference generator** *noun* section of an assembler *or* compiler *or* interpreter that provides a list of program labels, variables *or* constants with their location within the program

crossover *noun* change from one system to another; *the crossover to computerized file indexing was difficult*

CRT = CATHODE RAY TUBE device used for displaying characters *or* figures *or* graphical information, similar to a TV set

COMMENT: cathode ray tubes are used in television sets, computer monitors and VDUs; a CRT consists of a vacuum tube, one end of which is flat and coated with phosphor, the other end containing an electron beam source. Characters *or* graphics are visible when the controllable electron beam strikes the phosphor causing it to glow

cruncher, crunching *see* NUMBER

cryogenic memory *noun* storage medium operating at very low temperatures (4°K) to use the superconductive properties of a material

cryptanalysis *noun* study and methods of breaking ciphers

cryptography *noun* study of encryption and decryption methods and techniques
◇ **cryptographic** *adjective* referring to cryptography; **cryptographic algorithm =** rules used to encipher and decipher data; **cryptographic key =** number *or* code that is used with a cipher algorithm to personalize the encryption and decryption of data

crystal *noun* small slice of quartz crystal which vibrates at a certain frequency, used as a very accurate clock signal for computer *or* other high precision timing applications; **liquid crystal display (LCD) =** liquid crystals, that turn black when a voltage is applied, used in many watch, calculator and digital displays

CSM = COMBINED SYMBOL MATCHING effecient optical character recognition system

CSMA-CD = CARRIER SENSE MULTIPLE ACCESS-COLLISION DETECTION

CTR *or* **CTRL =** CONTROL control key *or* key on a computer terminal that sends a control character to the computer when pressed

CTS = CLEAR TO SEND RS232C signal that a line *or* device is ready for data transmission

CU = CONTROL UNIT

cue *noun* prompt *or* message displayed on a screen to remind the user that an input is expected

CUG = CLOSED USER GROUP to restrict the entry to a database *or* bulletin board system (on a certain topic *or* subject) to certain known and registered users usually by means of a password

current 1 *adjective* referring to the present time; **current address =** address being used (accessed) at this time; **current address register (CAR) =** CPU register that stores the address that is currently being accessed;

current instruction register (CIR) = CPU register that stores the instruction that is currently being executed **2** *noun* movement of charge-carrying particles in a conductor; **direct current (DC) =** constant value electrical current supply that flows in one direction; **alternating current (AC) =** electrical current whose value varies with time in a regular sinusoidal way (changing direction of flow each half cycle)

COMMENT: mains electricity provides a 240v AC supply at 50Hz in the U.K. and 110v at 60Hz in the USA

cursor *noun* marker on a display device which shows where the next character will appear; **cursor control keys =** keys on a keyboard that allow the cursor to be moved in different directions; **cursor home =** movement of the cursor to the top left hand corner of the screen; **cursor pad =** group of cursor control keys; **addressable cursor =** cursor whose position on the screen can be defined by a program

COMMENT: cursors can take several forms, such as a square of bright light, a bright underline or a flashing light

QUOTE above the cursor pad are the insert and delete keys, which when shifted produce clear and home respectively
Computing Today
QUOTE further quick cursor movements are available for editing by combining one of the arrow keys with the control function
Personal Computer World

customer *noun* person who buys *or* uses a computer system *or* any peripherals; **customer engineering =** maintenance and repair of a customer's equipment; **customer service department =** department which deals with customers and their complaints and orders
◇ **custom-built** *adjective* made specially for one customer
◇ **custom ROM (PROM)** *noun* ROM produced (usually in small numbers) by a manufacturer to suit a customer's requirements
◇ **customize** *verb* to modify a system to the customer's requirements; *we used customized computer terminals*

cut 1 *noun* removing a piece from a file; piece removed from a file **2** *verb* **(a)** cut sheet feeder mechanism that automatically feeds single sheets of paper into a printer **(b)** to remove pieces of text from a file to make it shorter NOTE: **cuts - cutting - has cut**
◇ **cut and paste** *noun* action of taking pieces of text from one point and inserting

them at another (often used in dtp packages for easy page editing)

CWP = COMMUNICATING WORD PROCESSOR

cybernetics *noun* study of the mechanics of human *or* electronic machine movements, and the way in which electronic devices can be made to work and imitate human actions

cycle 1 *noun* (i) period of time when something leaves its original position and then returns to it; (ii) one completed operation in a repeated process; **action cycle** = all the steps required to carry out a process *or* operation on data, (such as reading, processing, output and storage); **clock cycle** = period of time between two consecutive clock pulses; **cycle availability** = period of time in a cycle, during which data can be accessed *or* transmitted; **cycle count** = number of times a cycle has been repeated; **cycle index** = number of times a series of instructions have been *or* have to be repeated; **cycle shift** = to shift a pattern of bits within a word, with the bit(s) that are shifted off the end being inserted at the beginning of the word; **cycle stealing** =

memory access operation by a peripheral that halts a CPU for one *or* more clock cycles whilst data is being transferred from memory to the device; **cycle time** = time between start and stop of an operation, especially between addressing a memory location and receiving the data, and then ending the operation; *compare* ADDRESS TIME **2** *verb* to repeat an operation *or* series of instructions until instructed to stop

◇ **cyclic** *adjective* (operation) that is repeated regularly; **cyclic access** = access to stored information that can only occur at a certain point in a cycle; **cyclic check** = error detection method that uses *or* examines a bit of data every n bits (one bit examined then n bits transmitted, then another bit examined, etc.); **cyclic code** *see* GRAY CODE; **cyclic decimal code** = cyclic code that refers to decimal digits; **cyclic redundancy check (CRC)** = error detection code for transmitted data; **cyclic shift** = rotation of bits in a word with the previous last bit inserted in the first bit position

cylinder *noun* the tracks in a multi-disk device that can be accessed without moving the read/write head

cypher = CIPHER

Dd

D hexadecimal figure equivalent to decimal number 13

3D = THREE-DIMENSIONAL

> QUOTE the software can create 3D images using data from a scanner or photographs from an electronic microscope
> *PC Business World*

DAC *or* **d/a converter** = DIGITAL TO ANALOG CONVERTER circuit that outputs an analog number that is proportional to the input digital signal, and so converts a digital input to an analog form; *speech is output from the computer via a D/A converter; the D/A converter on the output port controls the analog machine*

> COMMENT: a d/a converter allows the computer to work outside the computer environment, by driving a machine, imitating speech, etc.

daisy chain *noun* method of connecting equipment with a single cable passing from one machine *or* device to the next (rather than separate cables to each device); **daisy chain bus** = communications bus that joins one device to the next, each device being able to receive *or* transmit *or* modify data as it passes through to the next device in line; **daisy chain interrupt** = line joining all the interrupt outputs of a number of devices to a CPU; **daisy chain recursion** = subroutines in a program that call another in the series, (the first routine calls the second routine which calls the third routine, etc.)

◊ **daisy-chain** *verb* to connect equipment using the daisy chain method

> QUOTE you can often daisy-chain cards or plug them into expansion boxes
> *Byte*

daisy-wheel *noun* wheel-shaped printing head, with characters on the end of spokes, used in a serial printer; **daisy-wheel printer** *or* **daisy-wheel typewriter** = serial character printer *or* typewriter with characters arranged on interchangeable wheels; *a daisy-wheel printer produces much better quality text than a dot-matrix, but is slower*

DAMA = DEMAND ASSIGNED MULTIPLE ACCESS

damage 1 *noun* harm done to things; **to suffer damage** = to be harmed; **to cause damage** = to harm something; *the breakdown of the electricity supply caused damage estimated at £100,000* NOTE: no plural **2** *verb* to harm; *the faulty read/write head appears to have damaged the disks; the hard disk was damaged when it was dropped*

◊ **damaged** *adjective* which has suffered damage *or* which has been harmed; *is it possible to repair the damaged files?*

D to A converter = DIGITAL TO ANALOG CONVERTER circuit that outputs an analog signal that is proportional to an input digital number

DASD = DIRECT ACCESS STORAGE DEVICE storage medium whose memory locations can be directly read *or* written to

data *noun* collection of facts made up of numbers, characters and symbols, stored on a computer in such a way that it can be processed by the computer; *programs act upon data files; data is input at one of several workstations; the company stores data on customers in its main computer file; a user needs a password to access data;* **raw data** = (i) pieces of information which have not been input into a computer system; (ii) data (in a databank) which has to be processed to provide information to the user; (iii) unprocessed data; **data access management** = regulating the users who can access stored data; **data acquisition** = gathering data about a subject; **data adapter unit** = device that interfaces a CPU to one or more communications channels; **data administrator** = control section of a database management system; **data aggregate** = collection of items of data that are related; **data analysis** = extracting information and results from data; **data area** = amount of storage space that contains data (rather than instructions); **databank** = collection of data (usually on one theme); **data block** = all the data required for *or* from a process; **data break** =

memory access operation by a peripheral that halts a CPU for one or more cycles whilst data is being transferred from memory to the device; **data buffer** = temporary storage location for data received by a device that is not yet ready to accept it; **data bus** = bus carrying the data between a CPU and memory and peripheral devices; **data capture** = act of obtaining data (either by keyboarding or by scanning, or often automatically from a recording device *or* peripheral); **data carrier** = (i) any device *or* medium capable of storing data; (ii) a waveform used as a carrier for data signals; **data carrier detect (DCD)** = RS232C signal from a modem to a computer indicating a carrier wave is being received; *the call is stopped if the software does not receive a DCD signal from the modem;* **data cartridge** = cartridge that contains stored data; **data chaining** = one stored record that holds the address of the next in the list; **data channel** = communication link able to carry data signals; **data check** = error in reading data due to a fault with the magnetic medium; **data circuit** = circuit which allows bi-directional data communications; **data cleaning** = removing errors from data; **data collection** = act of receiving data from various sources (either directly from a data capture device *or* from a cartridge) and inserting correctly in order into a database; **data collection platform** = station that transmits collected data to a central point (usually via satellite); **data communications** = transmission and reception of data rather than speech *or* images; **data communications buffer** = buffer on a receiver that allows a slow peripheral to accept data from a fast computer, without slowing either down; **data communications equipment (DCE)** = equipment (such as a modem) which receives *or* transmits data; **data communications network** = number of computers, terminals, operators and storage units connected together to allow data transmission between devices *or* files *or* users; **data compacting** = reducing the space taken by data by coding it in a more efficient way; *all the files were stored on one disk with this new data compacting routine;* **data compression** = means of reducing size of data by removing spaces, empty sections and unused material from the blocks of data; *scanners use a technique called data compression which manages to reduce, even by a third, the storage required;* **data concentrator** = data which combines intermittent data from various lines and sends it along a single line in one go; **data connection** = link which joins two devices and allows data transmission; **data control** = data management to and from a

database *or* processing system; **data corruption** = errors introduced into data due to noise *or* faulty equipment; *data corruption occurs each time the motor is switched on;* **data delimiter** = special symbol *or* character that marks the end of a file *or* data item; **data description language (DDL)** = part of database system software which describes the structure of the system and data; **data dictionary/directory (DD/D)** = software which gives a list of types and forms of data contained in a database; **data division** = part of a (COBOL) program giving full definitions of the data types and structures; **data-driven** = (computer architecture) in which instructions are executed, once the relevant data has been received; **data element** *see* DATA ITEM; **data element chain** = more than one data element treated as a single element; **data encryption** = encrypting data using a cipher system; **data encryption standard (DES)** = standard for a block data cipher system; **data entry** = method of entering data into a system (usually using a keyboard but also direct from disks after data preparation); **data error** = error due to incorrect *or* illegal data; **data field** = part of a computer instruction that contains the location of the data; **data file** = file with data in it (as opposed to a program file); *the data file has to be analysed;* **data flow** = movement of data through a system; **data flowchart** = diagram used to describe a computer *or* data processing system; *the data flowchart allowed us to improve throughput, by using a better structure;* **data flow diagram (DFD)** = diagram used to describe the movement of data through a system; **data format** = rules defining the way in which data is stored *or* transmitted; **data hierarchy** = data structure organized hierarchically; **data highway** = bus carrying data signals between a CPU and peripherals; *see also* BUS; **data independence** = structure of a database which can be changed without affecting what the user sees; **data input** = data transferred into a computer (from an I/O port *or* peripheral); **data input bus (DIB)** = bus used when transferring data from one section of a computer to another, such as between memory and CPU; **data integrity** = protection of data against damage *or* errors; **data item** = one unit of data such as the quantity of items in stock, a person's name, age or occupation; **data level** = position of a data item within a database structure; **data link** = connection between two devices to allow the transmission of data; **data link control** = protocol and rules used to define the way in which data is transmitted *or* received; **data link layer** = one layer in the ISO/OSI defined network that sends packets of data to the next link and deals with error correction; **data logging** = automatic data collection; **data management** = maintenance and upkeep of a database; **data manipulation language (DML)** = database software that allows the user to access, store and change data; **data medium** = medium which allows data to be stored *or* displayed (such as a VDU *or* magnetic disk *or* screen); **data migration** = data transfer (by a user's instruction) from an on-line device to an off-line device; **data name** = group of characters used to identify one item of data; *problems occur if an ambiguous data name is chosen;* **data network** = networking system which transmits data; **data origination** = conversion of data from its original form to one which can be read by a computer; **data path** = bus *or* connections over which data is transmitted; **data pointer** = register containing the location of the next item of data; **data preparation** = conversion of data into a machine-readable form (usually by keyboarding) before data entry; **data processing (DP** *or* **dp)** = selecting and operating on data to produce useful information; sorting *or* organizing data files; **data processing manager** = person who runs a computer department; **data protection** = means of making sure that data is private and secure; **data rate** = maximum rate at which data is processed *or* transmitted in a synchronous system, usually equal to the system clock rate; **data record** = one record containing data for use with a program; **data reduction** = producion of compact, useful data from raw data; **data register** = area within a CPU used to store data temporarily before it is processed; **data reliability** = measure of the number of data words with errors compared to the total number of words; **data retrieval** = process of searching, selecting and reading data from a stored file; **data routing** = defining the path to be taken by a message in a network; **data security** = protection of data against corruption *or* unauthorized users; **data set ready (DSR)** = signal from a device that is ready to accept data, this signal occurs after a DTR signal is received; **data signals** = electrical *or* optical pulses *or* waveforms that represent binary data; **data signalling rate** = total amount of data that is transmitted through a system per second; **data sink** = device in a data terminal which receives data; **data source** = device in a data terminal which sends data; **data station** = point that contains a data terminal and a data circuit; **data storage** = medium able to store large quantities of data; *see also* BACKING STORE; **data stream** = data transmitted serially one bit *or*

character at a time; **data strobe** = signal (in the control bus) that indicates that valid data is on the data bus; **data structure** = number of related items that are treated as one by the computer (in an address book record, the name, address and telephone number form separate entries which would be processed as one by the computer); **data switching exchange** = device used to direct and switch data between lines; **data tablet** *see* GRAPHICS TABLET; **data terminal** = device that is able to display and transmit *or* receive data; *a printer is a data terminal for computer output;* **data terminal equipment (DTE)** = device at which a communications path starts *or* finishes; **data terminal ready (DTR)** = signal from a device that indicates that it is ready to send data; **data transaction** = one complete operation on data; **data transfer rate** = rate at which data is moved from one point to another; **data translation** = conversion of data from one system format to another; **data transmission** = process of sending data from one location to another over a data link; **data type** = sort of data which can be stored in a register (such as string, number, etc.); **data validation** = process of checking data for errors and relevance in a situation; **data vetting** = process of checking data as it is input for errors and validity; **data word** = piece of data stored as a single word; **data word length** = number of bits that make up a word in a computer; **master data** = reference data which is stored in a master file; **optical data link** = connection between two devices to allow the transmission of data using light (either line-of-sight or using fibre optics); **variable data** = data which can be modified, and is not write protected

COMMENT: Data is different from information in that it is facts stored in machine-readable form. When the facts are processed by the computer into a form which can be understood by people, the data becomes information

◊ **databank** *noun* (i) large amount of data stored in a structured form; (ii) personal records stored in a computer

◊ **database** *noun* integrated collection of files of data stored in a structured form in a large memory, which can be accessed by one or more users at different terminals; **database administrator (DBA)** = person in charge of running and maintaining a database system; **database language** = series of languages, such as data description language, that make up a database management system; **database machine** = hardware and software combination designed for the rapid processing of database information;

database management system (DBMS) or **database manager** = series of programs that allow the user to create and modify databases easily; **database mapping** = description of the way in which the records and fields in a database are related; **database schema** = way in which a database is organized and structured; **database system** = series of programs that allows the user to create, modify, manage and use a database (often includes features such as a report writer or graphical output of data); **on-line database** = interactive search, retrieve and update of database records using an on-line terminal

◇ **datagram** *noun* packet of information in a packet switching system that contains its destination address and route

◇ **dataplex** *noun* multiplexing of data signals

◇ **dataset** *noun US* modem; **dataset ready (DSR)** = RS232C signal from a modem to a computer indicating it is ready for use

QUOTE data compression is the art of squeezing more and more information into fewer and fewer bytes
Practical Computing
QUOTE a database is a file of individual records of information which are stored in some kind of sequential order
Which PC?

date 1 *noun* **(a)** number of day, month and year; *I have received your message of yesterday's date; the date of creation for the file was the 10th of June* **(b)** up to date = current or recent or modern; *an up-to-date computer system;* to bring something up to date = to add the latest information to something; to keep something up to date = to keep adding information to something so that it is always up to date; *we spend a lot of time keeping our files up to date* **(c)** out of date = old-fashioned; *their computer system is years out of date; they are still using out-of-date equipment* **2** *verb* to put a date on a document

daughter board *noun* add-on board that connects to a system mother board

DBA = DATABASE ADMINISTRATOR person in charge of running and maintaining a database system

DBMS = DATABASE MANAGEMENT SYSTEM series of programs that allow the user to create and modify databases

DC = DIRECT CURRENT; **DC signalling** = method of communications using pulses of current over a wire circuit, like a telegraph system

DCD = DATA CARRIER DETECT RS232C signal from a modem to a computer indicating a carrier is being received

DCE = DATA COMMUNICATIONS EQUIPMENT

DD = DOUBLE DENSITY

DDC = DIRECT DIGITAL CONTROL machine operated automatically by machine

DD/D = DATA DICTIONARY/DIRECTORY software which gives a list of types and forms of data contained in a database

DDE = DIRECT DATA ENTRY keying in data directly onto magnetic tape or disk

DDL = DATA DESCRIPTION LANGUAGE *many of DDL's advantages come from the fact that it is a second generation language*

DDP = DISTRIBUTED DATA PROCESSING operations to derive information from data which is kept in different places

dead *adjective* not working; (computer or piece of equipment) that does not function; **dead halt** or **drop dead halt** = program instruction from the user or an error, that causes the program to stop without allowing recovery; *the manual does not say what to do if a dead halt occurs;* **dead keys** = keys on a keyboard that cause a function rather than a character to occur, such as the shift key; **dead time** = period of time between two events, in which nothing happens, to ensure that they do not interfere with each other; *efficient job management minimises dead time*

◇ **deaden** *verb* to make a sound or colour less sharp; *acoustic hoods are used to deaden the noise of printers*

◇ **deadlock** *noun* situation when two users want to access two resources at the same time, one resource is assigned to each user but neither can use the other

◇ **deadly embrace** *noun* = DEADLOCK

deal 1 *noun* business agreement or contract; **package deal** = agreement where several different items are agreed at the same time; *they agreed a package deal, which involves the development of software, customizing hardware and training of staff* **2** *verb* to deal with = to organize; *leave it to the DP manager - he'll deal with it*

◇ **dealer** *noun* person who buys and sells; *always buy hardware from a recognized dealer*

deallocate *verb* to free resources previously allocated to a job *or* process *or* peripheral; *when a reset button is pressed all resources are deallocated*

debit *noun* bit transmission rate that is twice the baud rate

deblock *verb* to return a stored block of data to its original form (of individual records)

de-bounce *noun* preventing a single touch on a key giving multiple key contact; **de-bounce circuit** = electronic circuit that prevents a key contact producing more than one signal when pressed

debug *verb* to test a program and locate and correct any faults *or* errors; *they spent weeks debugging the system; debugging takes up more time than construction;* **debugged program** = software that works correctly and in which all the mistakes have been removed *or* corrected

◇ **debugger** *noun* software that helps a programmer find faults *or* errors in a program

QUOTE the debug monitor makes development and testing very easy
Electronics & Wireless World

decade *noun* ten items *or* events

decentralized computer network *noun* network where the control is shared between several computers

◇ **decentralized data processing** *noun* data processing and storage carried out at each location rather than in one central location

deci- *prefix* meaning one tenth of a number

decimal (notation) *noun* arithmetic and number representation using the decimal system; **correct to three places of decimals** = correct to three figures after the decimal point (e.g. 3.485); **decimal point** = dot which indicates the division between the whole unit digits and the smaller (fractional) parts of a decimal number (such as 4.75); **decimal system** = number system using the digits 0 - 9; **decimal tabbing** = adjusting a column of numbers so that the decimal points are vertically aligned; **decimal tab key** = key for entering decimal numbers (using a word processor) so that the decimal points are automatically vertically aligned; **decimal-to-binary conversion** = converting a decimal (base ten) number into a binary (base two) number

◇ **decimalization** *noun* changing to a decimal system

◇ **decimalize** *verb* to change to a decimal system

decipher *verb* to convert an encrypted *or* encoded message (ciphertext) into the original message (plaintext)

decision *noun* making up one's mind to do something; *to come to a decision or to reach a decision;* **decision box** = graphical symbol used in a flowchart to indicate that a decision is to be made and a branch *or* path *or* action carried out according to the result; **decision circuit** *or* **element** = logical circuit that operates on binary inputs, providing an output according to the operation; **decision** *or* **descrimination instruction** = conditional program instruction that directs control by providing the location of the next instruction to be executed if a condition is met; **decision support system** = suite of programs that help a manager reach decisions using previous decisions, information and other databases; **decision table** = chart which shows the relationships between certain variables and actions available when various conditions are met; **decision tree** = graphical representation of a decision table showing possible paths and actions if different conditions are met

deck *noun* (a) **tape deck** = drive for magnetic tape (b) pile of punched cards

◇ **declare** *verb* to define a computer program variable *or* to set a variable equal to a number; *he declared at the start of the program that X was equal to nine*

◇ **declaration** *or* **declarative statement** *noun* statement within a program that informs the compiler *or* interpreter of the form, type and size of a particular element, constant or variable; **procedure declaration** = to write and declare the variable types used and (if any) the routine name and location

decode *verb* to translate encoded data back to its original form

◇ **decoder** *noun* program *or* device used to convert data into another form; **instruction decoder** = hardware that converts a machine-code code instruction (in binary form) into actions

◊ **decoding** *noun* converting encoded data back into its original form

decollate *verb* to separate continuous stationery into single sheets; to split two-part *or* three-part stationery into its separate parts (and remove the carbon paper)

◊ **decollator** *noun* machine used to separate continuous stationery into single sheets *or* to split 2-part or 3-part stationery into separate parts

decompilation *noun* conversion of a compiled program in object code into a source language; *fast incremental compilation and decompilation*

decrease 1 *noun* fall *or* reduction; *decrease in price; decrease in value; decrease in sales; sales show a 10% decrease on last year* **2** *verb* to fall *or* to become less; *sales are decreasing; the value of the pound has decreased by 5%*

decrement *verb* to subtract a set number from a variable; *the register contents were decremented until they reached zero*

decrypt *verb* to convert encrypted data back into its original form; *decryption is done using hardware to increase speed*

◊ **decryption** *noun* converting of encrypted data back into its original form

dedicated *adjective* (program *or* procedure *or* system) reserved for a particular use; *there's only one dedicated graphics workstation in this network;* **dedicated channel** = communications line reserved for a special purpose; **dedicated computer** = computer which is only used for a single special purpose; **dedicated logic** = logical function implemented in hardware designed (usually for only one task *or* circuit; *the person appointed should have a knowledge of micro-based hardware and dedicated logic; the dedicated logic cuts down the chip count;* **dedicated word processor** = computer which has been configured specially for word processing and which cannot run any other programs

deduct *verb* to remove something from a total

default *noun* predefined course of action *or* value that is assumed unless the operator alters it; **default drive** = disk drive that is accessed first in a multi-disk system (to try and load the operating system or a program); *the operating system allows the user to select the default drive;* **default option** = preset value *or* option that is to be used if no other value has been specified; **default rate** = baud rate (in a modem) that is used of no other is selected; **default response** = value which is used if the user does not enter new data; **default value** = value which is automatically used by the computer if no other value has been specified; *screen width has a default value of 80*

defect *noun* something which is wrong *or* which stops a machine from working properly; *a computer defect or a defect in the computer*

◊ **defective** *adjective* faulty *or* not working properly; *the machine broke down because of a defective cooling system*

◊ **defect skipping** *noun* means of identifying and labelling defective magnetic tracks during manufacture so that they will not be used, instead pointing to the next good track to be used

defensive computing *noun* method of programming that takes into account any problems *or* errors that might occur

deferred addressing *noun* indirect addressing, where the location accessed contains the address of the operand to be processed

define *verb* (i) to assign a value to a variable; (ii) to assign the characteristics of processes *or* data to something; *all the variables were defined at initialization*

◊ **definition** *noun* (i) ability of a screen to display fine detail; (ii) value *or* formula assigned to a variable *or* label; **macro definition** = description (in a program *or* to a system) of the structure, function and instructions that make up a macro operation

deflect *verb* to change the direction of an object *or* beam

◇ **deflection** *noun* **deflection yokes** = magnetic coils around a cathode ray tube used to control the position of the picture beam on the screen

degauss *verb* to remove unwanted magnetic fields and effects from magnetic tape, disks *or* read/write heads; *the r/w heads have to be degaussed each week to ensure optimum performance*

◇ **degausser** *noun* device used to remove unwanted magnetic fields from a disk *or* tape *or* recording head

degradation *noun* **(a)** loss of picture *or* signal quality; **image degradation** = loss of picture contrast and quality due to signal distortion *or* bad copying of a video signal **(b)** loss of processing capacity because of a malfunction; **graceful degradation** = allowing some parts of a system to continue to function after a part has broken down

delay 1 *noun* time when something is later than planned; *there was a delay of thirty seconds before the printer started printing; we are sorry for the delay in supplying your order, but the computer was not working;* **delay line** = device that causes a signal to take a certain time in crossing it; **delay line store** = (old) method of storing serial data as sound *or* pulses in a delay line, the data being constantly read, regenerated and fed back into the input; **delay vector** = time that a message will take to pass from one packet switching network node to another **2** *verb* to cause something to have a delay

delete *verb* **(a)** to cut out words in a document **(b)** to remove text *or* data from a storage device; *the word-processor allows us to delete the whole file by pressing this key;* **delete character** = special code used to indicate data *or* text to be removed

◇ **deletion** *noun* (i) making a cut in a document; (ii) text removed from a document; *the editors asked the author to make several deletions in the last chapter;* **deletion record** = record containing new data which is to be used to update *or* delete data in a master record

COMMENT: when you delete a file, you are not actually erasing it but you are making its space on disk available for another file by instructing the operating system to ignore the file by inserting a special code in the file header and deleting the entry from the directory

delimit *verb* to set up the size of data using delimiters

◇ **delimiter** *noun* (i) character *or* symbol used to indicate to a language *or* program the start *or* end of data *or* a record *or* information; (ii) the boundary between an instruction and its argument

delta clock *noun* clock that provides timing pulses to synchronize a system, and will restart (with an interrupt signal) a computer *or* circuit that has had an error *or* entered an endless loop *or* faulty state

demagnetize *verb* to remove stray *or* unwanted magnetic fields from a disk *or* tape *or* recording head

◇ **demagnetizer** *noun* device which demagnetizes something; *he used the demagnetizer to degauss the tape heads*

demand 1 *noun* asking for something to be done; **demand assigned multiple access (DAMA)** = means of switching in circuits as and when they are required; **demand paging** = system software that retrieves pages in a virtual memory system from backing store when it is required; **demand processing** = processing data when it appears, rather than waiting; **demand reading/writing** = direct data transfer between a processor and storage; **demand staging** = moving files *or* data from a secondary storage device to a fast access device when required by a database program **2** *verb* to ask for something and expect to get it; *she demanded her money back; the suppliers are demanding immediate payment*

demarcation *noun* showing the difference between two areas

democratic network *noun* synchronized network where each station has equal priority

demodulation *noun* recovery of the original signal from a received modulated carrier wave

demonstrate *verb* to show how something works; *he demonstrated the file management program*

◇ **demonstration** *noun* act of showing how something works; **demonstration model** = piece of equipment in a shop, used to show customers how the equipment works

denary notation *noun* number system in base ten, using the digits 0 to 9

denial *noun* **alternative denial** = logical function whose output is false if all inputs are true, and true if any input is false; **joint denial** = logical function whose output is false if any input is true

dense index *noun* database index containing an address *or* entry for every item *or* entry in the database; **dense list** = list that has no free space for new records

◇ **density** *noun* amount of data that can be packed into a space on a disk *or* tape; **double density** = system to double the storage capacity of a disk drive by doubling the number of bits which can be put on the disk surface; **double density disk (DD)** = disk that can store two bits of data per unit area compared to a standard disk, using a modified write process; **packing** *or* **recording density** = number of bits that can be stored in a unit area on a magnetic disk *or* tape; **single density disk (SD)** = standard magnetic disk able to store data

COMMENT: scanner software produces various shades of grey by using different densities *or* arrangements of black and white dots and/or different size dots

QUOTE diode lasers with shorter wavelengths will make doubling of the bit and track densities possible
Byte

deny access *verb* to refuse access to a circuit *or* system for reasons of workload *or* security

dependent *adjective* which is variable because of something; *a process which is dependent on the result of another process; the output is dependent on the physical state of the link;* **machine dependent** = not standardized *or* which cannot be used on hardware *or* software from a different manufacturer without modification

deposit 1 *noun* thin layer of a substance which is put on a surface **2** *verb* **(a)** to print out the contents of all *or* a selected area of memory **(b)** to coat a surface with a thin layer of a substance **(c)** to write data into a register *or* storage location

◇ **deposition** *noun* process by which a surface (of a semiconductor) is coated with a thin layer of a substance

deque *noun* = DOUBLE-ENDED QUEUE queue in which new items can be added to either end

derive *verb* to come from; *the results are derived from the raw data*

◇ **derivation graph** *noun* structure within a global database that provides information on the rules and paths used to reach any element *or* item of data

DES = DATA ENCRYPTION STANDARD standardized popular cipher system for data encryption

descender *noun* part of a printed letter that is below the line (such as the 'tail' of a 'g' or 'p')

de-scramble *verb* to reassemble an original message *or* signal from its scrambled form

◇ **de-scrambler** *noun* device which changes a scrambled message back to its original, clear form

describe *verb* to say what someone *or* something is like; *the leaflet describes the services the company can offer; the specifications are described in greater detail at the back of the manual*

◇ **description** *noun* words which show what something is like; **description list** = list of data items and their attributes; **data description language (DDL)** = part of a database system which describes the structure of the system and data; **page description programming language** = programming language that accepts commands to define the size, position and typestyle for text *or* graphics on a page

◇ **descriptor** *noun* code used to identify a filename *or* program name *or* pass code to a file

design 1 *noun* planning *or* drawing of a product before it is built *or* manufactured; **circuit design** = layout of components and interconnections in a circuit; **product design** = design of products; **design parameters** = specifications for the design of a product **2** *verb* to plan *or* to draw something before it is built *or* manufactured; *he designed a new chip factory; she designs typefaces*

◇ **designer** *noun* person who designs; *she is the designer of the new computer*

desk *noun* writing table in an office, usually with drawers for stationery; *desk diary; desk drawer; desk light;* **desk check** = dry run of a program

◇ **desktop** *adjective* which sits on top of a desk; which can be done on a desk; **desktop computer (system)** = small microcomputer system that can be placed on a desk; **desktop publishing (DTP)** = design, layout and printing of documents using special software, a small computer and a printer

despool *verb* to print out spooled files

despotic network *noun* network synchronized and controlled by one single clock

destination *noun* place to which something is sent *or* to which something is going; location to which a data is sent

destructive addition *noun* addition operation in which the result is stored in the location of one of the operands used in the sum, so overwriting it

◇ **destructive cursor** *noun* cursor that erases the text as it moves over it; *reading the screen becomes difficult without a destructive cursor;* **destructive read** = read operation in which the stored data is erased as it is retrieved; **destructive readout** = form of storage medium that loses its data after it has been read

detail 1 *noun* small part of a description; **detail file** = file containing records that are to be used to update a master file; **in detail** = giving many particulars; *the catalogue lists all the products in detail;* **detail paper** = thin transparent paper used for layouts and tracing **2** *verb* to list in detail; *the catalogue details the shipping arrangements for customers; the terms of the licence are detailed in the contract*

◇ **detailed** *adjective* in detail; **detailed account** = account which lists every item

detect *verb* to sense something (usually something very slight); *the equipment can detect faint signals from the transducer;* **detected error** = error noticed during a program run, but not corrected; **error detecting code** = coding system that allows errors occurring during transmission to be detected, but is not complex enough to correct the errors

◇ **detection** *noun* process of detecting something; *the detection of the cause of the fault is proving difficult*

◇ **detector** *noun* device which can detect

deterministic *adjective* (result of a process) that depends on the initial state and inputs

develop *verb* to plan and produce; *to develop a new product*

◇ **developer** *noun* **software developer** = person *or* company which writes software

◇ **development** *noun* planning the production of a new product; **research and development** = investigating new products and techniques; **development software** = suite of programs that help a programmer write, edit, compile and debug new software; **development time** = amount of time required to develop a new product

device *noun* small useful machine *or* piece of equipment; **device character control** = device control using various characters *or* special combinations to instruct the device; **device code** = unique identification and selection code for each peripheral; **device control (character)** = special code sent in a transmission to a device to instruct it to perform a special function; **device driver** = program *or* routine used to interface and manage an I/O device *or* peripheral; **device flag** = one bit in a device status word, used to show the state of one device; **device independent** = programming technique that results in a program that is able to run with any peripheral hardware; **device priority** = the importance of a peripheral device assigned by the user *or* central computer which dictates the order in which the CPU will serve an interrupt signal from it; *the master console has a higher device priority than the printers and other terminals;* **device queue** = list of requests from users *or* programs to use a device; **device status word (DSW)** = data word transmitted from the device that contains information about its current status; *this routine checks the device status word and will not transmit data if the busy bit is set;* **I/O device** = peripheral (such as a terminal) which can be used for inputting or outputting data to a processor; **output device** = device (such as a monitor *or* printer) which allows information to be displayed

devise *verb* to plan *or* build a system; *they devised a cheap method of avoid the problem*

DFD = DATA FLOW DIAGRAM diagram used to describe the movement of data through a system

diagnose *verb* to find the cause and effect of a fault in hardware or error in software

◇ **diagnosis** *noun* finding of a fault *or* discovering the cause of a fault (results of diagnosing faulty hardware or software)

diagnostic 1 *noun* **diagnostic aid** = hardware *or* software device that helps to find faults; **diagnostic chip** = chip that contains circuits to carry out tests on other circuits *or* chips; **diagnostic message** = message that appears to explain the type, location and probable cause of a software error *or* hardware failure; **diagnostic program** = software that helps find faults in a computer system; **diagnostic routine** = routine in a program which helps to find faults in a computer system; **diagnostic test** = means of locating faults in hardware and software by test circuits *or* programs; **self-diagnostic** = computer that runs a series of diagnostic programs (usually when the computer is switched on) to ensure that all circuits, memory and peripherals are working correctly

◊ **diagnostics** *noun* functions *or* tests that help a user find faults in hardware *or* software; **compiler diagnostics** = function in a compiler that helps a programmer find faults in the program code; *thorough compiler diagnostics make debugging easy;* **error diagnostics** = information and system messages displayed when an error is detected to help a user debug and correct it

QUOTE the implementation of on-line diagnostic devices that measure key observable parameters
Byte
QUOTE to check for any hardware problems, a diagnostic disk is provided
Personal Computer World

diagram *noun* drawing which shows something as a plan *or* a map; **flow diagram** = diagram showing the arrangement of work processes in a series

◊ **diagrammatic** *adjective* in diagrammatic form = in the form of a diagram; *the chart showed the sales pattern in diagrammatic form*

◊ **diagramatically** *adverb* using a diagram; *the chart shows the sales pattern diagramatically*

dial 1 *verb* to call a telephone number on a telephone; *to dial a number; to dial the computer centre;* **auto-dial** = modem that can automatically dial a number (under the control of a computer); **to dial into** = to call a telephone number, which has a modem and computer at the other end; *with the right access code it is possible to dial into a customer's computer to extract the files needed for the report* NOTE: GB English is **dialling - dialled,** but US spelling is **dialling - dialed 2** *noun* **dial-in modem** = auto-answer modem that can be called at any time to access a system

dialect *noun* slight variation of a standard language; *this manufacturer's dialect of BASIC is a little different to the one I'm used to*

dialogue *noun* speech *or* speaking to another person; communication between devices such as computers; **dialogue box** = on-screen message from a program to the user

DIB = DATA INPUT BUS bus used when transferring data from one section of a computer to another, such as between memory and CPU

dibit *noun* digit made up of two binary bits

dichotomizing search *noun* fast search method for use on ordered lists of data (the search key is compared with the data in the middle of the list and one half is discarded, this is repeated with the half remaining until only one data item remains)

dictionary *noun* (i) book which lists words and meanings; (ii) data management structure which allows files to be referenced and sorted; (iii) part of a spelling checker program: the list of correctly spelled words against the which the program checks a text

differ *verb* not to be the same as something else; *the two products differ considerably - one has an external hard disk, the other has internal hard disk and external magnetic tape drive*

◊ **difference** *noun* way in which two things are not the same; *what is the difference between these two products? differences in price or price differences;* **symmetric difference** = logical function whose output is true if either of the inputs is true, and false if both inputs are the same

◊ **different** *adjective* not the same; *our product range is quite different in design from the Japanese models; we offer ten models each in six different colours*

◊ **differential** *adjective* which shows a difference

diffuse *verb* to move *or* insert something over an area *or* through a substance; *the smoke from the faulty machine rapidly diffused through the building; the chemical was diffused into the substrate*

◊ **diffusion** *noun* means of transferring doping materials into an integrated circuit substrate

digit *noun* symbol *or* character which represents an integer that is smaller than the radix of the number base used; *a phone number with eight digits or an eight-digit phone number; the decimal digit 8; the* *decimal number system uses the digits 0123456789;* **check digit** = additional digit inserted into transmitted text to monitor and correct errors; **digit place** *or* **position** = position of a digit within a number; *see also* RADIX

◇ **digital** *adjective* which represents data *or* physical quantities in numerical form (especially using a binary system in computer related devices); **digital cassette** = high quality magnetic tape housed in a standard size cassette with write protect tabs, and a standard format leader; **digital circuit** = electronic circuit that operates on digital information providing logical functions *or* switching; **digital clock** = clock which shows the time as a series of digits (such as 12:22:04); **digital computer** = computer which processes data in digital form (that is data represented in discrete digital form); *compare* ANALOG; **digital data** = data represented in (usually binary) numerical form; **digital logic** = applying Boolean algebra to hardware circuits; **digital optical recording (DOR)** = recording signals in binary form as small holes in the surface of an optical *or* compact disk which can then be read by laser; **digital output** = computer output in digital form; *compare with* ANALOG OUTPUT; **digital plotter** = plotter whose pen position is controllable in discrete steps, so that drawings in the computer can be output graphically; **digital read-out** = data displayed in numerical form, such as numbers on an LCD in a calculator; **digital representation** = data *or* quantities represented using discrete quantities (digits); **digital resolution** = smallest number that can be represented with one digit, the value assigned to the least significant bit of a word *or* number; **digital signal** = electric signal that has only a number of possible states, as opposed to analog signals which are continuously variable; **digital signalling** = control and dialling codes sent down a (telephone line) in digital form; **digital signature** = unique identification code sent by a terminal *or* device in digital form; **digital speech** *see* SPEECH SYNTHESIS; **digital system** = system that deals with digital signals; **digital switching** = operating communications connections and switches only by use of digital signals; **digital to analog converter** *or* **D to A converter (DAC)** = circuit that converts a digital signal to an analog one (the analog signal is proportional to an input binary number); **digital transmission system** = communications achieved by converting analog signals to a digital form then modulating and transmitting this (the

signal is then converted back to analog form at the receiver)

◇ **digitally** *adverb* (quantity represented) in digital form; *the machine takes digitally recorded data and generates an image*

digitize *verb* to change analog movement *or* signals into a digital form which can be processed by computers, etc.; *we can digitize your signature to allow it to be printed with any laser printer;* **digitized photograph** = image *or* photograph that has been scanned to produce an analog signal which is then converted to digital form and stored *or* displayed on a computer; **digitizing pad** = sensitive surface that translates the position of a pen into numerical form, so that drawings can be entered into a computer

◇ **digitizer** *noun* analog to digital converter *or* device which converts an analog movement *or* signal to a digital one which can be understood by a computer

DIL = DUAL-IN-LINE PACKAGE standard layout for integrated circuit packages using two parallel rows of connecting pins along each side

dimension *noun* measurement of size; *the dimensions of the computer are small enough for it to fit into a case*

◇ **dimensioning** *noun* definition of the size of something (usually an array *or* matrix); *array dimensioning occurs at this line*

diminished radix complement *noun* number representation in which each digit of the number is subtracted from one less than the radix; *see also* ONE'S, NINE'S COMPLEMENT

DIN = DEUTSCHE INDUSTRIENORM German industry standards organization

diode *noun* electronic component that allows an electrical current to pass in one direction and not the other; **light-emitting diode (LED)** = semiconductor diode that emits light when a current is applied (used in clock and calculator displays, and as an indicator)

DIP = DUAL-IN-LINE PACKAGE standard layout for integrated circuit packages using two parallel rows of connecting pins along each side

direct 1 *verb* to manage *or* to organize; **directed scan** = file *or* array search method in which a starting point and a direction of scan is provided, either up *or* down from the starting point (an address *or* record number) **2** *adjective* straight *or* with no processing *or* going in a straight way; **direct access** = storage and retrieval of data without the need to read other data first; **direct (access) address** = ABSOLUTE ADDRESS; **direct access storage device (DASD)** = storage medium whose memory locations can be directly read *or* written to; **direct addressing** = method of addressing where the storage location address given in the instruction is the location to be used; **direct change-over** = switching from one computer to another in one go; **direct code** = binary code which directly operates the CPU, using only absolute addresses and values; **direct coding** = program instructions written in absolute code; **direct connect** = (modem) which plugs straight into the standard square telephone socket; **direct current (DC)** = constant value electric current that flows in one direction; **direct data entry (DDE)** = keying in data directly onto a magnetic disk *or* tape; **direct digital control (DDC)** = machine operated automatically by computer; **direct information access network for Europe (DIANE)** = services offered over the Euronet network; **direct-insert routine** *or* **subroutine** = routine which can be directly copied (inserted) into a larger routine *or* program without the need for a call instruction; **direct instruction** = program command that contains an operand and the code for the operation to be carried out; **direct memory access (DMA)** = direct, rapid link between a peripheral and a computer's main memory which avoids the use of accessing routines for each item of data required; *direct memory access transfer between the main memory and the second processor;* **direct memory access channel** = high speed data transfer link; **direct mode** = typing in a command which is executed once return is pressed; **direct page register** = register that provides memory page access data when a CPU is carrying out a direct memory access, to allow access to any part of memory; **direct reference address** = virtual address that can only be altered by indexing; **direct transfer** = bit for bit copy of the contents of one register into another register (including any status bits, etc.) **3** *adverb* straight *or* with no third party involved

◇ **direction** *noun* **(a)** organizing *or* managing; *he took over the direction of a software distribution group* **(b)** directions for use = instructions showing how to use something NOTE: no plural for (a)

◇ **directive** *noun* programming instruction used to control the language translator, compiler, etc.

◇ **directly** *adverb* **(a)** immediately **(b)** straight *or* with no third party involved; *we deal directly with the manufacturer, without using a wholesaler*

QUOTE directives are very useful for selecting parts of the code for particular purposes
Personal Computer World

directory *noun* **disk directory** = list of names and information about files in a backing storage device; *the disk directory shows file name, date and time of creation*

dirty bit *noun* flag bit set by memory-resident programs (a utility *or* the operating system) to indicate that they have already been loaded into main memory

disable *verb* to prevent a device *or* function from operating; *he disabled the keyboard to prevent anyone changing the data;* **disable interrupt** = command to the CPU to ignore any interrupt signals

disarm *verb* to prevent an interrupt having any effect; **disarmed state** = state of an interrupt that has been disabled, and cannot accept a signal

disassemble *verb* to translate machine code instructions back into assembly language mnemonics
◇ **disassembler** *noun* software that translates a machine code program back into an assembly language form

disaster dump *noun* program and data dump just before *or* caused by a fatal error *or* system crash

disc = DISK
NOTE: disc is the more usual spelling in the USA

discard *verb* to throw out something which is not needed

disclose *verb* to reveal details of something which were supposed to be secret
◇ **disclosure** *noun* act of telling details about something

disconnect *verb* to unplug *or* break a connection between two devices; *do not forget to disconnect the cable before moving the printer*

discrete *adjective* (values *or* events *or* energy *or* data) which occurs in small individual units; *the data word is made up of discrete bits*

discretionary *adjective* which can be used if wanted *or* not used if not wanted; **discretionary hyphen** *or* **soft hyphen** = hyphen which is inserted to show that a word is broken (as at the end of a line), but which is not present when the word is written normally

discrimination instruction *noun* conditional program instruction that directs control by providing the location of the next instruction to be executed (if a condition is met); *see also* BRANCH, JUMP, CALL

disjunction *noun* logical function that produces a true output if any input is true
◊ **disjunctive search** *noun* search for data items that match at least one of a number of keys

disk *noun* flat circular plate coated with a substance that is capable of being magnetized (data is stored on this by magnetizing selective sections to represent binary digits); **backup disk** = disk which contains a copy of the information from other disks, as a security precaution; **disk access** = operations required to read from or write to a magnetic disk, including device selection, sector and track address, movement of read/write head to the correct location, access location on disk; **disk-based (operating system)** = (operating system) held on floppy *or* hard disk; **disk cartridge** = protective case containing a removable hard disk; **disk controller** = IC *or* circuits used to translate a request for data by the CPU into control signals for the disk drive (including motor control and access arm movement); **disk-controller card** = add-on card that contains all the electronics and connectors to interface a disk drive to a CPU; **disk crash** = fault caused by the read/write head touching the surface of the disk; **disk drive** = device that spins a magnetic disk and controls the position of the read/write head; **disk file** = number of related records *or* data items stored under one name on disk; **disk formatting** = initial setting up of a blank disk with track and sector markers and other control information; **disk index holes** = holes around the hub of a disk that provide rotational information to a disk controller *or* number of holes providing sector location indicators on a hard-sectored disk; **disk map** = display of the organization of data on a disk; **disk operating system (DOS)** = section of the operating system software that controls disk and file management; **MS disk operating system** *or* **Microsoft DOS (MS-DOS)** = popular DOS for microcomputers; **disk pack** = number of disks on a single hub, each with its own read/write head; **disk sector** = smallest area on a magnetic disk that can be addressed by a computer; **disk storage** = using disks as a backing store; **disk track** = one of a series of (thin) concentric rings on a magnetic disk, which the read/write head accesses and along which data is stored in separate sectors; **disk unit** = disk drive; **fixed disk** = magnetic disk which cannot be removed from the disk drive; **floppy disk** = small disk for storing information which can be removed from a computer; **hard disk** = solid disk which will store a large amount of computer information in a sealed case, and cannot usually be removed from the computer; **optical disk** = disk which contains binary data in the form of small holes which are read by a laser beam (also called WORM (write one, read many) when used on computers; **Winchester disk** = hard disk with a large storage capacity sealed in a computer

COMMENT: the disk surface is divided into tracks and sectors which can be accessed individually; magnetic tapes cannot be accessed in this way

◊ **diskette** *noun* light, flexible disk that can store data in a magnetic form, used in most personal computers
◊ **diskless** *adjective* which does not use disks for data storage; *diskless system; they want to create a diskless workstation*

disorderly close-down *noun* system crash that did not provide enough warning to carry out an orderly close-down

dispatch *or* **despatch** *noun* action of sending material *or* information *or* messages to a location

dispersion *noun* logical function whose output is false if all inputs are true, and true if any input is false

displacement *noun* offset used in an indexed address

display 1 *noun* device on which information *or* images can be presented visually; **display adapter** = device which allows information in a computer to be displayed on a CRT (the adapter interfaces with both the computer and CRT); **display attribute** = variable which defines the shape *or* size *or* colour of text *or* graphics displayed; **display character** = graphical symbol which appears as a printed *or* displayed item, such as one of the letters of the alphabet *or* a number; **display character generator** = ROM that provides the display circuits with a pattern of dots which form the character; **display colour** = colour of characters in a (videotext) display system; **display controller** = device that accepts character *or* graphics codes and instructions, and converts them into dot-matrix patterns that are displayed on a screen; **display format** = number of characters that can be displayed on a screen, given as row and column lengths; **display highlights** = emphasis of certain words *or* paragraphs by changing character display colour; **display line** = horizontal printing positions for characters in a line of text; **display mode** = way of referring to the character set to be used, usually graphics *or* alphanumerics; **display processor** = processor that changes data to a format suitable for a display controller; **display register** = register that contains character *or* control *or* graphical data that is to be displayed; **display resolution** = number of pixels per unit area that a display can clearly show; **display screen** = the physical part of a Visual Display Unit *or* terminal *or* monitor, which allows the user to see characters *or* graphics (usually a Cathode Ray Tube, but sometimes LCD *or* LED displays are used); **display scrolling** = movement of a screenful of information up or down one line or pixel at a time; **display space** = memory *or* amount of screen available to show graphics *or* text; **display unit** = computer terminal *or* piece of equipment that is capable of showing data *or* information, usually by means of CRT; **gas discharge** *or* **plasma** *or* **electroluminescent display** = flat lightweight display screen that is made up of two flat pieces of glass covered with a grid of conductors, separated by a thin layer of gas which luminesces when a point of the grid is selected by two electrical signals; *see also* VISUAL DISPLAY UNIT **2** *verb* to show information; *the customer's details were displayed on the screen; by keying HELP, the screen will display the options available to the user*

QUOTE the review machine also came with a monochrome display card plugged into one of the expansion slots
Personal Computer World

distant *adjective* which is located some way away; *the distant printers are connected with cables*

distinguish *verb* to tell the difference between two things; *the OCR has difficulty in distinguishing certain characters*

distort *verb* to introduce unwanted differences between a signal input and output from a device
◊ **distortion** *noun* unwanted differences in a signal before and after it has passed through a piece of equipment

distribute *verb* (a) to send out data *or* information to users in a network *or* system; **distributed adaptive routing** = directing messages in a packet network switching system by an exchange of information between nodes; **distributed database system** = data system where the data is kept on different disks in different places; **distributed data processing (DDP)** = operations to derive information from data which is kept in different places; **distributed file system** = system that uses files stored in more than one location *or* backing store but are processed at a central point; **distributed intelligence** = decentralized system in which a number of small micros *or* mini-computers carry out a set of fixed (tasks rather than one large computer); **distributed (data) processing** = system of processing in a large organization with many small computers at different workstations instead of one central computer; **distributed system** = computer system which uses more than one processor in different locations, all connected to a central computer
◊ **distribution** *noun* act of sending information out, especially via a network; **distribution network** *see* LAN, WAN

divide *verb* (a) to divide a number by four = to find out how many fours can be contained in the other number; *twenty-one divided by three gives seven* (b) to cut *or* to split into parts; *in the hyphenation program, long words are automatically divided at the end of lines*
◊ **division** *noun* act of dividing

dividend *noun* operand that is divided by a divisor in a division operation

COMMENT: the dividend is divided by the divisor to form the quotient and a remainder

divisor *noun* operand used to divide a dividend in a division operation

DMA = DIRECT MEMORY ACCESS direct rapid link between a peripheral and a computer's main memory, which avoids the use of accessing routines for each item of data read; **DMA controller** = interface IC that controls high-speed data transfer between a high-speed peripheral and main memory, usually the controller will also halt *or* cycle steal from the CPU; **DMA cycle stealing** = CPU allowing the DMA controller to send data over the bus during clock cycles when it performs internal *or* NOP instructions

DML = DATA MANIPULATION LANGUAGE

do-nothing (instruction) *noun* programming instruction that does not carry out any action (except increasing the program counter to the next instruction address

document 1 *noun* piece of paper with writing on it *or* file containing text; **document assembly** *or* **document merge** = creating a new file by combining two or more sections *or* complete documents; **document processing** = processing of documents (such as invoices) by a computer; **document reader** = device which converts written *or* typed information to a form that a computer can understand and process; **document recovery** = program which allows a document which has been accidentally deleted to be recovered **2** *verb* to write a description of a process

◊ **documentation** *noun* **(a)** all documents referring to something; *please send all documentation concerning the product* **(b)** information, notes and diagrams that describe the function, use and operation of a piece of hardware *or* software
NOTE: no plural

dollar sign *noun* printed *or* written character ($) used in some languages to identify a variable as a string type

domain *noun* **public domain** = information *or* program which belongs to and is available to the public; **program which is in the public domain** = program which is not copyrighted

dongle *noun* coded circuit *or* chip that has to be present in a system before a piece of copyright software will run

dope *verb* to introduce a dopant into a substance

◊ **dopant** *noun* chemical substance that is diffused *or* implanted onto the substrate of a chip during manufacture, to provide it with n- or p-type properties

◊ **doped** *adjective* (chip) which has had a dopant added

◊ **doping** *noun* adding of dopant to a chip

DOR = DIGITAL OPTICAL READING recording signals in binary form as small holes in the surface of an optical *or* compact disk which can then be read by laser

DOS = DISK OPERATING SYSTEM section of the operating system software, that controls the disk and file access; *boot up the DOS after you switch on the PC*

dot *noun* small round spot; **dot command** = method of writing instructions with a full stop followed by the command, used mainly for embedded commands in word-processor systems; **dot matrix** = forming characters by use of dots inside a rectangular matrix; **dots per inch** *or* **d.p.i.** *or* **dpi** standard method used to describe the resolution capabilities of a page printer *or* scanner; *some laser printers offer high resolution printing: 400 dpi*

◊ **dot-matrix printer** *noun* printer in which the characters are made up by a series of closely spaced dots (it produces a page line by line; a dot-matrix printer can be used either for printing using a ribbon *or* for thermal *or* electrostatic printing)

> QUOTE the characters are formed from an array of dots like in a dot-matrix printer, except that much higher resolution is used
> *Practical Computing*

double *adjective* twice; twice as large; twice the size; **double buffering** = use of two buffers, allowing one to be read while the other is being written to; **double density** = system to double the storage capacity of a disk drive by doubling the number of bits which can be put on the disk surface; **double-density disk** = disk that can store two bits of data per unit area, compared to a standard disk; **double ended queue (deque)** = queue in which new items can be added to either end; **double-length** *or* **double precision arithmetic** = use of two data words to store a number, providing greater precision; **double-sided disk** = disk which can store information on both sides; **double-sided disk drive** = disk drive which can access data on double-sided disks; **double-sided printed circuit board** = circuit board with conducting tracks on both sides; **double word** = two bytes of data handled as one word, often used for address data

doublet *or* **diad** *noun* word made up of two bits

down *adverb (of computers or programs)* not working; *the computer system went down* *twice during the afternoon;* **down time** = period of time during which a computer system is not working *or* usable (NOTE: opposite is **up**)

download *verb* (i) to load a program *or* section of data from a remote computer via a telephone line; (ii) to load data from a CPU to a small computer; (iii) to send printer font data stored on a disk to a printer (where it will be stored in temporary memory *or* RAM); *there is no charge for downloading public domain software from the BBS*

◇ **downloadable** *adjective* which can be downloaded; **downloadable fonts** = fonts *or* typefaces stored on a disk, which can be downloaded *or* sent to a printer and stored in temporary memory *or* RAM

downward *adjective* towards a lower position; **downward compatibility** = ability of a complex computer system to work with a simple computer; *the mainframe is downward compatible with the micro*

dp *or* **DP** = DATA PROCESSING operating on data to produce useful information *or* to sort and organize data files

d.p.i. *or* **dpi** = DOTS PER INCH standard method used to describe the resolution capabilities of a dot-matrix *or* laser printer *or* scanner; *a 300 d.p.i. black and white A4 monitor; a 300 dpi image scanner*

COMMENT: 300 d.p.i. is the normal industry standard for a laser printer

DPM = DATA PROCESSING MANAGER

draft 1 *noun* rough copy of a document before errors have been corrected; **draft printing** = low quality, high speed printing **2** *verb* to make a rough copy *or* drawing; *he drafted out the details of the program on a piece of paper*

drag *verb* to move (a mouse) with a control key pressed, so moving an image on screen; *you can enlarge a frame by clicking inside its border and dragging to the position wanted*

QUOTE press the mouse button and drag the mouse: this produces a dotted rectangle on the screen
QUOTE you can easily enlarge the frame by dragging from any of the eight black rectangles round the border, showing that it is selected
Desktop Publishing

DRAM = DYNAMIC RANDOM ACCESS MEMORY

QUOTE cheap bulk memory systems are always built from DRAMs
Electronics & Power

drive 1 *noun* part of a computer which operates a tape *or* disk; **disk drive** = device which spins a magnetic disk and controls the position of the read/write head; **tape drive** = mechanism that carries magnetic tape over the drive heads **2** *verb* to make a tape *or* disk work; *the disk is driven by a motor*

◇ **driven** *adjective* operated by something; **control driven** = computer architecture where instructions are executed once a control sequence has been received; **event-driven** = computer program *or* process where each step of the execution relies on external actions

◇ **driver** *or* **handler** *noun* program *or* routine used to interface and manage an input/output device *or* other peripheral; **printer driver** = dedicated software that controls and formats users' commands ready for a printer

DRO = DESTRUCTIVE READOUT form of storage medium that loses its data after it has been read

drop *noun* **drop dead halt** *or* **dead halt** = program instruction from the user *or* an error that causes the program to stop without allowing recovery; **drop in** = small piece of dirt that is on a disk *or* tape surface, which does not allow data to be recorded on that section; **drop out** = failure of a small piece of tape *or* disk to be correctly magnetized for the accurate storage of data

drum *noun* early type of magnetic computer storage; **magnetic drum** = cylindrical magnetic storage device; **drum plotter** = computer output device that consists of a movable pen and a piece of paper around a drum that can be rotated, creating patterns and text when both are moved in various ways

dry cell *noun* battery that cannot be recharged; *compare with* RECHARGEABLE BATTERY

◇ **dry contact** *noun* faulty electrical connection, often causing an intermittent fault

◇ **dry run** *noun* running a program with test data to check everything works

DSR = DATA SET READY signal from a device that it is ready to accept data, this signal occurs after a DTR signal is received

DSW = DEVICE STATUS WORD data word transmitted from a device that contains information about its current status

DTE = DATA TERMINAL EQUIPMENT device at which a communications path starts *or* finishes

DTP = DESKTOP PUBLISHING the design, layout and printing of documents using special software, a desktop computer and a printer

DTR = DATA TERMINAL READY signal from a device that indicates that it is ready to send data

dual *adjective* using two *or* a pair; **dual channel** = two separate audio recording paths, as found in stereo equipment; **dual clocking** = multiplexed data, each set of data is available and valid on a different clock pulse *or* edge; **dual column** = two separate parallel lists of information; **dual-in-line package (DIL** *or* **DIP)** = standard layout for integrated circuit packages using two parallel rows of connecting pins along each edge; **dual port memory** = memory with two sets of data and memory lines to allow communications between CPUs; **dual processor** = computer system with two processors for faster program execution; **dual systems** = two computer systems, working in parallel on the same data, with the same instructions, to ensure high reliability

duct *noun* pipe containing cables, providing a tidy and protective surrounding for a group of cables

dumb terminal *noun* peripheral that can only transmit and receive data from a computer, but is not capable of processing data; *compare* INTELLIGENT TERMINAL

dummy *noun* imitation product to test the reaction of potential customers to its design; **dummy instruction** = instruction in a program that is only there to satisfy language syntax *or* to make up a block length; **dummy variable** = variable set up to satisfy the syntax of a language, but which is replaced when the program is executed

dump 1 *noun* (i) data which has been copied from one device to another for storage; (ii) transferring of data to a disk for storage; (iii) *US* printout of the contents of all *or* selected data in memory; **binary dump** = sections of memory dumped onto another medium *or* printed out in binary form; **change dump** = printout of all the locations whose contents have been changed during a program run; **dump and restart** = software that will stop a program execution, dump any relevant data or program status then restart the program; **dump point** = point in a program where the program and its data are saved onto backing store to minimize the effects of any future faults; **screen dump** = outputting the text *or* graphics displayed on a screen to a printer **2** *verb* to move data from one device *or* storage area to another; *the account results were dumped to the backup disk*

duodecimal number system *noun* number system with a radix of twelve

duplex *noun* simultaneous transmission of two signals on one line; **duplex circuit** = electronic circuit used to transmit data in two directions simultaneously; **duplex computer** = two identical computer systems used in an on-line application, with one used as a backup in case of failure of the other; **duplex operation** = transmission of data in two directions simultaneously; *see also* HALF-DUPLEX, FULL DUPLEX, SIMPLEX

durable *adjective* which will not be destroyed easily; *durable cartridge*

duration *noun* length of time for which something lasts

dustcover *noun* protective cover for a machine

duty-rated *adjective* maximum number of operations which a device can perform in a set time to a certain specification

QUOTE the laser printer can provide letter-quality print on ordinary cut-sheet paper and is duty-rated at up to 3,000 pages per month
Minicomputer News

dyadic operation *noun* binary operation using two binary operands

dynamic *adjective* referring to data which can change with time; **dynamic allocation** = system where resources allocated during a program run, rather than being determined in advance; **dynamic buffer** = buffer whose size varies with demand; **dynamic data structure** = structure of a data management system which can be changed *or* adapted; **dynamic dump** = dump that is carried out periodically during a program run; **dynamic memory** *or* **dynamic RAM** =

random access memory that requires its contents to be updated regularly; **dynamic relocation (program)** = program that is moved from one section of memory to another during its run-time without affecting it *or* its data; **dynamic stop** = stop in a process where the system tells the user that some action must be taken before the processing will continue; **dynamic storage allocation** = to allocate memory to a program when it needs it rather than reserving a block before it has run; **dynamically redefinable character set** = computer *or* videotext character set that can be changed when required; **dynamic subroutine** = subroutine whose function must be defined each time it is called; *compare* STATIC

Ee

E hexadecimal number equivalent to decimal number 14

EAPROM = ELECTRICALLY ALTERABLE PROGRAMMABLE READ-ONLY MEMORY version of EAROM which can be programmed

EAROM = ELECTRICALLY ALTERABLE READ-ONLY MEMORY

earth 1 *noun* connection in a circuit representing zero potential; *all loose wires should be tied to earth;* **earth wire** = connecting wire between an electrical device and the earth, representing zero potential **2** *verb* to connect an electrical device to the earth; *all appliances must be earthed*
NOTE: US English is **ground**

easy-to-use *adjective* that is simple to understand and operate

> QUOTE it is a really easy-to-use, menu-driven program that allows you to produce presentation quality graphics with little or no training
> *Soft*

EBCDIC = EXTENDED BINARY CODED DECIMAL INTERCHANGE CODE eight bit binary character coding system

EBNF = EXTENDED BACKUS-NAUR FORM more flexible way of defining the syntax of a language; *see also* BNF

EBR = ELECTRON BEAM RECORDING recording the output from a computer directly onto microfilm using an electron beam

echo 1 *noun* return of a signal back to the source from which it was transmitted; **echo check** = each character received at a terminal is returned to the transmitter and checked to ensure accurate data transmission **2** *verb* to return a received signal along the same transmission path

ECL = EMITTER COUPLED LOGIC high-speed logic circuit design using the emitters of the transistors as output connections to other stages

ECMA = EUROPEAN COMPUTER MANUFACTURERS ASSOCIATION; **ECMA symbols** = standard set of symbols used to draw flowcharts

EDAC = ERROR DETECTION AND CORRECTION forward error correction system for data communications

edge *noun* side of a flat object *or* signal *or* clock pulse; **edge board** *or* **card** = printed circuit board that has a series of contact strips along one edge allowing it to be inserted into an edge connector; **edge connector** = long connector with a slot containing metal contacts to allow it to make electrical contact with an edge card; **edge detection** = algorithm and routines used in image recognition to define the edges of an object; **edge notched card** = paper card which has punched holes along an edge to represent data; **edge-triggered** = process *or* circuit which is clocked *or* synchronized by the changing level (edge) of a clock signal rather than the level itself

edit *verb* to change, correct and modify text *or* programs; **edit commands** = sequence of characters or keys that must be pressed to accomplish a function in an editor; **edit key** = key that starts a function that makes an editor easier to use; *there are several special edit keys - this one will re-format the text;* **edit window** = area of the screen in which the user can display and edit text *or* graphics; **editing run** = processing carried out to check that new data meets certain requirements before actually analysing the data and its information content; **editing terms** = command words and instruction sequences used when editing; **linkage editing** = combining separate programs together, and standardizing the calls and references within them

◇ **editor** *noun* **editor program** = software that allows the user to select sections of a file and alter, delete or add to them; **line editor** = software in which only one line of a source program can be edited at a time; **text editor =** piece of software used to enter and correct text *or* modify programs under development

QUOTE an object orientated graphics editor enables you to add text to graphics
Byte
QUOTE while it has many formatting facilities, it does not include an editor with which to create the template for the report
Personal Computer World

EDP = ELECTRONIC DATA PROCESSING data processing using computers and electronic devices; **EDP capability =** word processor that is able to carry out certain data processing functions NOTE: **EDP** is more common in US English

EDS = EXCHANGEABLE DISK STORAGE disk drive using removable disk pack (as opposed to a fixed disk)

EEPROM = ELECTRICALLY ERASABLE PROGRAMMABLE READ-ONLY MEMORY

EEROM = ELECTRICALLY ERASABLE READ-ONLY MEMORY

QUOTE conventional EEPROM requires two transistors to store each bit of data
Electronics & Power

effective *adjective* which can be used to produce a certain result; **effective address =** address resulting from the modification of an address; **effective instruction =** the resulting instruction executed after the modification of an original instruction; **effective search speed =** rate of finding a particular section of information from a storage device; **effective throughput =** average throughput of a processor

efficient *adjective* which works well; *the program is highly efficient at sorting files*

◊ **efficiently** *adverb* in an efficient way; *the word-processing package has produced a series of labelled letters very efficiently*

◊ **efficiency** *noun* working well; *he is doubtful about the efficiency of the new networking system*

EFT = ELECTRONIC FUNDS TRANSFER (SYSTEM) system where computers are used to transmit money to and from banks

◊ **EFTPOS** = ELECTRONIC FUNDS TRANSFER POINT-OF-SALE terminal at a POS that is linked to a central computer which automatically transfers money from the customer's account to the shop's

EGA = ENHANCED GRAPHICS ADAPTER popular microcomputer high-resolution colour display standardized system

QUOTE although the video BIOS services are enhanced by adding an EGA card, the DOS functions are not
.EXE

EIA = ELECTRONIC INDUSTRY ASSOCIATION; **EIA interface =** standard defining interface signals, transmission rate and power, usually used to connect terminals to modems

eight-bit (system) *noun* referring to an (old) small, low cost, low power home computer in which the CPU can process eight-bit words; **eight-bit byte** *or* **octet =** byte made up of eight binary digits; *compare with* SIXTEEN, THIRTY-TWO BIT
◊ **eight-inch disk** *noun* high-capacity floppy disk which is eight inches in diameter; **eight-inch drive =** disk drive for a eight-inch disk
◊ **eighty-track disk** *noun* disk formatted to contain eighty tracks; **eighty-column screen =** screen that can display eighty characters horizontally

either-or operation *noun* logical function that produces a true output if any input is true
◊ **either-way operation** *noun* data transmission in one direction at a time over a bidirectional channel

elapsed time *noun* time taken by the user to carry out a task on a computer

elastic banding *noun* method of defining the limits of an image on a computer screen by stretching a boundary around it
◊ **elastic buffer** *noun* buffer size that changes according to demand

electric *adjective* worked by electricity; **electric current =** mass movement of electric charge in a conductor; **electric charge =** a number of atoms that are charged (due to excess *or* deficiency of electrons)
◊ **electrical** *adjective* referring to electricity; *the engineers are trying to repair an electrical fault*
◊ **electrically** *adverb* referring to electricity; *an electrically-powered motor;* **electrically alterable, programmable read-only memory (EAPROM) =** version of EAROM that can be programmed; **electrically alterable read-only memory (EAROM) =** read-only memory chip

whose contents can be programmed by applying a certain voltage to a write pin, and can be erased by light *or* a reverse voltage; **electrically erasable programmable read-only memory (EEPROM)** = ROM storage chip which can be programmed and erased using an electrical signal; **electrically erasable read-only memory (EEROM)** = EAROM memory chip whose contents can be programmed by applying a certain voltage to a write pin, and can be erased by light *or* a reverse voltage

electricity *noun* electric current used to provide light *or* heat *or* power; *the electricity was cut off, and the computers crashed; electricity prices are an important factor in the production costs*

electrographic printer *noun see* ELECTROSTATIC PRINTER

electroluminescence *noun* light emitted from a phosphor dot when it is struck by an electron *or* charged particle

◊ **electroluminescing** *adjective* (object) which is emitting light due to electroluminescence

◊ **electroluminescent** *adjective* capable of emitting light due to electroluminescence; *the screen coating is electroluminescent;* **electroluminescent display** = flat, lightweight display screen that is made up of two pieces of glass covered with a grid of conductors, separated by a thin layer of gas which luminesces when a point of the grid is selected by two electric signals

electromagnetic *adjective* generating a magnetic field *or* magnetic effect when supplied with electrical power; **electromagnetic interference** = corruption of data due to nearby electrically generated magnetic fields

electron beam recording (EBR) *noun* recording the output from a computer directly onto microfilm using an electron beam

electronic *adjective* referring to something which is controlled by *or* controls electron flow; **electronic blackboard** = means of transmitting handwritten text and diagrams over a telephone line; **electronic data processing (EDP)** = data processing using computers and electronic devices; **electronic data processing compatibility** = ability of a word processor to carry out certain data processing functions; **electronic digital computer** = digital computer constructed

with electronic components (the basic form uses a CPU, main memory, backing storage and input/output devices; these are all implemented with electronic components and integrated circuits); **electronic engineer** = person who specializes in work on electronic devices; **electronic industry association interface (EIA)** = standard defining interface signals, transmission rate and power usually used to connect terminals to modems; **electronic filing** = system of storage of documents which can be easily retrieved; **electronic funds transfer (EFT)** = using a computer to transfer money to and from banks; **electronic funds transfer point of sale (EFTPOS)** = terminal at a POS that is linked to a central computer which automatically transfers money from the customer's account to the shop's; **electronic keyboard** = keyboard that generates characters electronically in response to a switch making contact when pressed, rather than by mechanical means; **electronic mail** = sending and receiving messages over a telephone network, usually using a bulletin board; **electronic mailbox** = system for holding messages sent by electronic mail until the person to whom they were sent is ready to accept them; **electronic pen** *or* **stylus** *or* **wand** = light pen *or* wand; stylus used to draw on a graphics tablet; **electronic point-of-sale (EPOS)** = system that uses a computer terminal at a point-of-sale site for electronic funds transfer *or* stock control as well as product identification, etc.; **electronic publishing** = (i) use of desktop publishing packages and laser printers to produce printed matter; (ii) using computers to write and display information, such as viewdata; **electronic pulse** = short voltage pulse; **electronic shopping** = system of shopping from the home, using computerized catalogues and paying by credit card, all by means of a home computer terminal; **electronic smog** = excessive stray electromagnetic fields and static electricity generated by large numbers of electronic equipment (this can damage equipment *or* a person's health); **electronic traffic** = data transmitted in the form of electronic pulses

◊ **electronically** *adverb* referring to operations using electronic methods; *the text is electronically transmitted to an outside typesetter*

◊ **electronics** *noun* science of applying the study of electrons and their properties to manufactured products, such as components, computers, calculators or telephones; *the electronics industry; an electronics specialist* NOTE: takes a singular verb

electrosensitive *adjective* **electrosensitive paper** = metal-coated printing paper, which can display characters using localized heating with a special dot-matrix print head; **electrosensitive printing** = printing using electrosensitive paper

◇ **electrostatic** *adjective* referring to devices using the properties of static electrical charge; **electrostatic printer** = type of printer which forms an image on the paper by charging certain regions to provide character shapes, etc., and using ink with an opposite charge which sticks to the paper where required; **electrostatic screen** = metal cage surrounding sensitive equipment (and connected to ground) to protect it from interference; **electrostatic storage** = data stored in the form of small electric charged regions on a dielectric material

◇ **electrothermal printer** *noun* printer that uses a printing head with a dot-matrix of heating elements to form characters on electrosensitive paper

elegant *adjective* **elegant programming** = writing a well-structured program using the minimum number of instructions

element *noun* **(a)** small part of an object which is made up of many similar parts; **logic element** = gate *or* combination of gates; **picture element** *or* **pixel** = smallest single unit *or* point on a display whose colour *or* brightness can be controlled; **signal element** = smallest basic unit used when transmitting digital data **(b)** one number *or* cell of a matrix *or* array; **array element** = one individual piece of data within an array

◇ **elementary** *adjective* made of many similar small sections *or* objects

eliminate *verb* to remove something completely; *using a computer should eliminate all possibility of error in the address system; the spelling checker does not eliminate all spelling mistakes*

◇ **elimination** *noun* removing of something completely; **elimination factor** =

during a search, the section of data that is not used

else rule *noun* program logical rule used with an IF-THEN instruction to provide an alternative if the IF-THEN condition is not met; *IF X=20 THEN PRINT 'X is 20' ELSE PRINT 'X not 20'*

EM = END OF MEDIUM

E-mail *or* **email** = ELECTRONIC MAIL

embedded code *noun* sections *or* routines written in machine code, inserted into a high-level program to speed up *or* perform a special function; **embedded command** = printer command (such as indicating that text should be in italic) inserted into the text and used by a word-processing system when producing formatted printed text; **embedded computer** *or* **system** = dedicated computer controlling a machine; dedicated computer within a larger system that performs one fixed function

embrace *see* DEADLY

EMI = ELECTROMAGNETIC INTERFERENCE corruption of data due to nearby electrically generated magnetic fields

emitter-coupled logic (ECL) *noun* high-speed logic circuit design using the emitters of the transistors as output connections to other stages

empty *adjective* with nothing inside; **empty** *or* **null list** = list with no elements; **empty medium** = blank but formatted storage medium that is ready to receive data; **empty** *or* **null** *or* **void set** = reserved area for related data items, containing no data; **empty slot** = (i) packet of data in a packet-switching LAN that is carrying no information; (ii) unused expansion edge connector on a motherboard; **empty** *or* **null string** = variable containing no characters

emulate *verb* to copy *or* behave like something else; *some laser printers are able to emulate the more popular office printers*

◊ **emulation** *noun* behaviour by one computer *or* printer which is exactly the same as another, which allows the same programs to be run and the same data to be processed; **emulation facility** = feature of hardware *or* software which emulates another system

◊ **emulator** *noun* software *or* hardware that allows a machine to behave like another

QUOTE full communications error checking built into the software ensures reliable file transfers and a terminal emulation facility enables a user's terminal to be used as if it were a terminal to the remote computer

Byte

QUOTE some application programs do not have the right drivers for a laser printer, so look out for laser printers which are able to emulate the more popular office printers

Publish

emulsion laser storage *noun* digital storage technique using a laser to expose light sensitive material

enable *verb* (a) to allow something to happen; *a spooling program enables editing work to be carried out which printing is going on* (b) to use an electronic signal to start a process *or* access a function (on a chip *or* circuit); **enabling signal** = signal that starts a process *or* allows one to take place

encipher *verb* to convert plaintext into a secure coded form by means of a cipher system; *our competitors cannot understand our files - they have all been enciphered*

enclose *verb* to surround with something; to put something inside something else

◊ **enclosure** *noun* protective casing for equipment

encode *verb* to apply the rules of a code to a program *or* data

◊ **encoder** *noun* device that can translate data from one format to another

◊ **encoding** *noun* translation of a message *or* text according to a coding system; **binary encoding** = representing a character *or* element with a unique combination *or* pattern of bits in a word; **encoding format** = method of coding data stored on a magnetic disk (to avoid a series of similar bits); **magnetic encoding** = storage of binary data signals on a magnetic medium

encrypt *verb* to convert plaintext to a secure coded form, using a cipher system; *the encrypted text can be sent along ordinary telephone lines, and no one will be able to understand it*

◊ **encryption** *noun* conversion of plaintext to a secure coded form by means of a cipher system; **data encryption standard (DES)** = standard for a block data cipher system

end 1 *noun* (a) final point *or* last part; *at the end of the data transmission;* **in the end** = at last *or* after a lot of problems; *in the end the company had to pull out of the US market; in the end the company had to call in a consultant engineer* (b) statement *or* character to indicate the last word of a source file; **end about carry** = most significant digit is added into the least significant place (used in BCD arithmetic); **end about shift** = data movement to the left *or* right in a word, the bits falling outside the word boundary are discarded and replaced with zeros; **end of address (EOA)** = transmitted code which indicates that address data has been sent; **end of block (EOB)** = code which shows that the last byte of a block of data has been sent through a communications link; **end of data (EOD)** = code which shows that the end of a stored data file has been reached; **end of document** *or* **end of file (EOF)** = marker after the last record in a file; **end of job (EOJ)** = code used in batch processing to show that a job has been finished; **end of medium (EM)** = code that indicates the end of usable physical medium; **end of message (EOM)** = code used to separate the last character of one message from the first of another message; **end of page indicator** = indicator on a typewriter to show that a page is nearly finished; **end of record (EOR)** = code used to show the end of a record; **end of run routines** = routines carried out before a program run finishes to perform certain system housekeeping functions; **end of tape** = code used to indicate the end of a magnetic tape; **end of text (EOT** *or* **ETX)** = code sent after last character of text; **end of transmission (EOT)** = sequence of characters that indicate that all the data from a terminal *or* peripheral has been transmitted **2** *verb* to finish *or* to stop something

◊ **ending** *noun* (a) action of coming to an end *or* of stopping something (b) end part of something

◊ **endless** *adjective* with no end; **endless loop** = continuous piece of recording tape *or* number of computer instructions that are continuously repeated

◊ **end user** *noun* person who will use the device *or* program *or* product; *the company is creating a computer with a specific end user in mind*

enhance *verb* to make better *or* clearer; **enhanced dot matrix** = clearer character *or* graphics printout (using smaller dots and more dots per inch); **enhanced graphics adapter (EGA)** = popular standardized system of high-resolution colour display for microcomputers; **enhanced graphics adapter screen** = high-resolution colour monitor that can display EGA system signals and graphics; **enhanced small device interface (ESDI)** = interface standard between a CPU and peripherals such as disk drives

◇ **enhancement** *noun* add-on facility which improves the output *or* performance of equipment

◇ **enhancer** *noun* device *or* software which enhances a process *or* product

QUOTE the typefaces are fairly rudimentary, especially if you are not using an enhanced graphics adapter screen
Desktop Publishing

ENQ = ENQUIRY

enquiry *noun* request for data *or* information from a device *or* database; accessing data in a computer memory without changing the data; **enquiry character** = special control code that is a request for identification *or* status *or* data from a device

ensure *verb* to make sure; *pushing the write-protect tab will ensure that the data on the disk cannot be erased*

enter *verb* to type in information on a terminal *or* keyboard; *to enter a name on a list; the data has been entered on data capture forms;* **enter key** = key pressed to indicate the end of an input *or* line of text

◇ **entering** *noun* act of typing in data *or* writing items in a record
NOTE: no plural

entity *noun* subject to which the data stored in a file *or* database refers

entry *noun* (a) single record *or* data about one action *or* object in a database *or* library (b) place where you can enter; **entry condition** = condition that must be satisfied before a routine can be entered; **entry instruction** = first instruction executed in a called subroutine; **entry point** = address from which a program *or* subroutine is to be executed; **entry time** = point in time when a program *or* job *or* batch will be executed by the operating system scheduler

enumerated type *noun* data storage *or* classification using numbers to represent chosen convenient labels

COMMENT: if 'man', 'horse', 'dog', 'cat' are the items of data, stored by the machine simply as 0, 1, 2, 3, they can still be referred to in the program as man, horse, etc., to make it easier for the user to recognize them

envelope *noun* transmitted byte of data containing error and control bits

environment *noun* (a) condition in a computer system of all the registers and memory locations (b) surroundings *or* physical conditions

QUOTE one of the advantages of working in a PC-based environment is the enormous range of software which can run on the same computer
ESL Newsletter

EOA = END OF ADDRESS

EOB = END OF BLOCK

EOD = END OF DATA

EOF = END OF FILE

EOJ = END OF JOB

EOM = END OF MESSAGE

EOR = END OF RECORD

EOT = END OF TEXT *or* TRANSMISSION

EPOS = ELECTRONIC POINT-OF-SALE system that uses a computer terminal at a point-of-sale site for electronic funds transfer *or* stock control as well as product identification

EPROM *noun* (a) = ELECTRICALLY PROGRAMMABLE READ-ONLY MEMORY (b) = ERASABLE PROGRAMMABLE READ-ONLY MEMORY

QUOTE the densest EPROMs commercially available today are at the 1Mbit level
Electronics & Power

equal 1 *adjective* exactly the same **2** *verb* to be the same as; *production this month has equalled our best month ever* NOTE: **equalling - equalled** but US: **equaling - equaled**

◇ **equality** *noun* logical function whose output is true if either of two inputs is true, and false if both inputs are the same

◊ **equalize** *verb* to make equal (to preset values); *the received signal was equalized to an optimum shape*

◊ **equally** *adverb* in the same way; *they were both equally responsible for the successful launch of the new system*

equate *verb* to make the same as; *the variable was equated to the input data*

◊ **equation** *noun* formula; **machine equation** = formula which an analog computer has been programmed to solve

equip *verb* to provide with machinery *or* equipment

◊ **equipment** *noun* machinery and furniture required to make a factory *or* office work; *office equipment or business equipment; computer equipment supplier; office equipment catalogue;* **equipment failure** = hardware fault, rather than a software fault
NOTE: no plural

equivalent *adjective* **to be equivalent to** = to have the same value as *or* to be the same as; *the total characters keyboarded so far is equivalent to one day's printing time*

◊ **equivalence** *noun* **(a)** being equivalent **(b)** logical operation that is true if all the inputs are the same; **equivalence function** *or* **operation** = (i) AND function; (ii) logical function whose output is true if both inputs are the same; **equivalence gate** = gate which performs an equivalence function; **non-equivalence function (NEQ)** = logical function where the output is true if the inputs are not the same, otherwise the output is false

COMMENT: output is 1 if both inputs are 1 or if both are 0; if the two inputs are different, the output is 0

erase *verb* **(a)** to set all the digits in a storage area to zero **(b)** to remove any signal from a magnetic medium; **erase head** = small magnet that clears a magnetic tape *or* disk of recorded signals

◊ **erase character** *noun* character which means do nothing

◊ **erasable** *adjective* which can be erased; **erasable storage** *or* **erasable memory** = (i) storage medium that can be re-used; (ii) temporary storage; **erasable programmable read-only memory (EPROM)** = read-only memory chip that can be programmed by a voltage applied to a write pin and data applied to its output pins, usually erasable with ultraviolet light

◊ **eraser** *noun* device that erases the contents of an EPROM (usually using UV light)

EROM = ERASABLE READ-ONLY MEMORY *same as* EAROM

error *noun* mistake due to an operator; mistake caused by a hardware *or* software fault; mistake in a program that prevents a program *or* system running correctly; *he made an error in calculating the total; the secretary must have made a typing error;* **in error** *or* **by error** = by mistake; **margin of error** = number of mistakes which are acceptable in a document *or* in a calculation; **error ambiguity** = error due to an incorrect selection from ambiguous data; **error burst** = group of several consecutive errors (in a transmission); **error checking code** = general term used to describe all error correcting and error detecting codes; **error code** = code that indicates that a particular type of error has occurred; **error condition** = state that is entered if an attempt is made to operate on data containing errors; **error control** = routines that ensure that errors are minimised and any errors that occur are detected and dealt with rapidly; **error correcting code** = coding system that allows bit errors occurring during transmission to be rapidly corrected by logical deduction methods rather than re-transmission; *see also* GRAY CODE; **error correction** = hardware *or* software that can detect and correct an error in a transmission; **error detecting codes** = coding system that allows errors occurring during transmission to be detected but is not complex enough to correct the errors; **error detection** = using special hardware *or* software to detect errors in a data entry *or* transmission, then usually ask for re-transmission; **error detection and correction (EDAC)** = forward error correction system for data communications; **error diagnosis** = finding the cause of an error; **error diagnostics** = information and system messages displayed when an error is detected to help a user diagnose and correct an error; **error handling** *or* **management** = routines and procedures that diagnose and correct errors *or* minimise the effects of errors, so that a system will run when an error is detected; **error interrupts** = interrupt signals sent due to an error in hardware or software; **error logging** = recording errors that have occurred; *features of the program include error logging;* **error message** = report that an error has occurred; **error propagation** = one error causing another; **error rate** = (i) number of mistakes per thousand entries *or* per page; (ii) number of corrupt bits of data in relation to the total transmission length; *the error rate is less than 1%;* **error recovery** = software *or* hardware that can continue after an error has occurred; **error routine** = short routine within a main program that handles any errors when they occur; **error trapping** = detecting and correcting errors before they cause any problems; **compilation error** = error occurring during program compilation time; **diagnostic error message** = explanatory line of text displayed when an error has been found; **execution error** = error occurring during program execution, due to bad inputs *or* a faulty program; **logical error** = fault in a program design causing incorrect branching *or* operation; **permanent error** = error in a system which cannot be repaired; **quantization error** = error in converting an analog signal into a numerical form due to limited accuracy *or* a rapidly changing signal; **recoverable error** = error that does not cause complete system shut-down, and allows the user to restart the program; **syntax error** = error resulting from incorrect use of programming language syntax; **transient read error** = error which can be recovered from (caused by bad data recording); **undetected error** = error which is not detected by a coding system

> QUOTE syntax errors, like omitting a bracket, will produce an error message from the compiler
> *Personal Computer World*

ESC escape character code *or* key on a computer

escape character *noun* character used to represent an escape code; **escape codes** = transmitted code sequence which informs the receiver that all following characters represent control actions; **escape key** = key on a keyboard which allows the user to enter escape codes to control the computer's basic modes *or* actions

◊ **escapement** *noun* preset vertical movement of a sheet of paper in a printer

ESDI = ENHANCED SMALL DEVICE INTERFACE interface standard between a CPU and peripherals such as disk drives

establish *verb* (i) to discover and prove something; (ii) to define the use *or* value of something; *they established which component was faulty*

ETX = END OF TEXT

evaluate *verb* to calculate a value *or* a quantity

◊ **evaluation** *noun* action of calculating a value *or* a quantity

even *noun* quantity *or* number that is a multiple of two; *the first three even numbers are 2, 4, 6;* **even parity (check)** = error checking method that only transmits an even number of binary ones in each word; *compare* ODD PARITY

event *noun* an action *or* activity

◊ **event-driven** *noun* computer program *or* process where each step of the execution relies on external actions

except *preposition & conjunction* not including; *all the text has been keyboarded, except the last ten pages;* **except gate** = logical function whose output is true if either (of two) inputs is true, and false if both inputs are the same

◊ **exception** *noun* thing which is different from all others; **exception dictionary** = store of words and their special word-break requirements, for word-processing and photocomposition

◊ **exceptional** *adjective* not usual *or* different

excess *noun* too much of something; **excess-3 code** = code in which decimal digits are represented by the binary equivalent of three greater than the number; *the excess-3 code representation of 6 is 1001*

◊ **excessive** *adjective* too much *or* too large; *the program used an excessive amount of memory to accomplish the job*

exchange 1 *noun* giving of one thing for another; **part exchange** = giving an old product as part of the payment for a new one **2** *verb* **(a)** to exchange one article for another = to give one thing in place of something else; **exchange selection** = sorting method which repeatedly exchanges various pairs of data items until they are in order **(b)** to swap data between two locations

◊ **exchangeable** *adjective* which can be exchanged; **exchangeable disk storage (EDS)** = disk drive using a removable disk pack (as opposed to a fixed disk)

exclude *verb* to keep out *or* not to include

◊ **excluding** *preposition* not including

◊ **exclusion** *noun* **(a)** act of not including **(b)** restriction of access to a system

◇ **exclusive** *adjective* which excludes; **exclusive NOR (EXNOR)** = logical function whose output is true if all inputs are the same level, and false if any are different; **exclusive NOR gate** = electronic implementation of the EXNOR function; **exclusive OR (EXOR)** = logical function whose output is true if any input is true, and false if all the inputs are the same; **exclusive OR gate** = electronic implementation of the EXOR function

executable form *noun* program translated *or* compiled into a machine code form that a processor can execute

execute *verb* to run *or* carry out a computer program *or* process; **execute cycle** = events required to fetch, decode and carry out an instruction stored in memory; **execute mode** = state of a computer that is executing a program; *compare with* DIRECT MODE; **execute phase** = section of the execute cycle when the instruction is carried out; **execute signal** = signal that steps the CPU through the execute cycle; **execute statement** = basic operating system command to start a program run; **execute time** = EXECUTION TIME; **fetch-execute cycle** = EXECUTE CYCLE

◇ **execution** *noun* carrying out of a computer program *or* process; **execution address** = location in memory at which the first instruction in a program is stored; **execution cycle** = period of time during which the instruction is executed; **execution error** = error detected while a program is being run; **execution phase** = EXECUTE PHASE; **execution time** = (i) time taken to run *or* carry out a program *or* series of instructions; (ii) time taken for one execution cycle

QUOTE fast execution speed is the single most important feature of a C compiler

.EXE

executive *adjective* **executive program** *or* **supervisor program** = master program in a computer system that controls the execution of other programs; **executive control program** = OPERATING SYSTEM; **executive instruction** = instruction used to control and execute programs under the control of an operating system; *see also* SUPERVISOR INSTRUCTION

exerciser *noun* tester for a device

exhaustive search *noun* search through every record in a database

exit *verb* to stop program execution *or* to leave a program and return control to the operating system *or* interpreter; **exit point** = point in a subroutine where control is returned to the main program; *you have to exit to another editing system to add headlines*

exjunction *noun* logical function whose output is true if either (of two) inputs is true, and false if both inputs are the same

EXNOR = EXCLUSIVE NOR logical function whose output is true if all inputs are the same level, false if any are different; **EXNOR gate** = electronic implementation of the EXNOR function; *see also* NOR

EXOR = EXCLUSIVE OR logical function whose output is true if any input is true, and false if the all inputs are the same; **EXOR gate** = electronic implementation of the EXOR function; *see also* OR

expand *verb* to make larger; *if you want to hold so much data, you will have to expand the disk capacity*

◇ **expandable** *adjective* which can be expanded; **expandable system** = computer system that is designed to be able to grow (in power *or* memory) by hardware *or* software additions

◇ **expansion** *noun* increase in computing power *or* storage size; **expansion card** *or* **expansion board** = printed circuit board that is connected to a system to increase its functions *or* performance; **expansion slot** = connector inside a computer into which an expansion card can be plugged; *insert the board in the expansion slot;* **macro expansion** = process in which a macro call is replaced with the instuctions in the macro

QUOTE it can be attached to mast kinds of printer, and, if that is not enough, an expansion box can be fitted to the bus connector

Personal Computer World

expert *noun* person who knows a lot about something; *he is a computer expert; she is an expert in programming languages;* **expert system** = software that applies the knowledge, advice and rules defined by experts in a particular field to a user's data to help solve a problem

explicit address *noun* address provided in two parts, one is the reference point, the other a displacement *or* index value

exponent *noun* number indicating the power to which a base number is to be raised; **binary exponent** = one word that contains the sign and exponent of a binary number (expressed in exponent and mantissa form); *see also* MANTISSA

◇ **exponentiation** *noun* raising a base number to a certain power

express *verb* to state *or* to describe; *express the formula in its simplest form; the computer structure was expressed graphically*

◇ **expression** *noun* **(a)** mathematical formula *or* relationship **(b)** definition of a value *or* variable in a program

extend *verb* to make longer; **extended arithmetic element** = section of a CPU that provides hardware implementations of various mathematical functions; **extended binary coded decimal interchange code (EBCDIC)** = 8-bit character coding system; **extended BNF (EBNF)** = more flexible way of defining the syntax of a language; **extending serial file** = file that can be added to *or* that has no maximum size

◇ **extensible** *adjective* which can be extended; **extensible language** = computer programming language that allows the user to add his own data types and commands

◇ **extension** *noun* making longer; thing which makes something longer; **extension cable** = cable that allows a device located at some distance to be connected; **extension memory** = storage which is located outside the main computer system but which can be accessed by the CPU; **filename extension** = additional information after a filename, indicating the type *or* use of the file

external *adjective* outside a program *or* device; **external clock** = clock *or* synchronizing signal supplied from outside a device; **external data file** = file containing data for a program that is stored separately from it; **external device** = (i) item of hardware (such as terminals, printers, etc.) which is attached to a main computer; (ii) any device that allows communications between the computer and itself, but which is not directly operated by the main computer; **external disk drive** = device not built into the computer, but which is added to increase its storage capabilities; **external interrupts** = interrupt signal from a peripheral device indicating that attention is required; **external label** = identifying piece of paper stuck to the outside of a device *or* disk; **external memory** = memory which is located outside the main computer system confines but which can be accessed by the CPU; **external registers** = user's registers that are located in main memory rather than within the CPU; **external schema** = user's view of the structure of data *or* a program; **external sort** = method of sorting which uses a file stored in secondary memory, such as a disk, as its data source and uses the disk as temporary memory during sorting; **external storage** *or* **external store** = storage device which is located outside the main computer system but which can be accessed by the CPU

extra 1 *adjective* added *or* which is more than usual **2** *noun* item which is additional to the package; *the mouse and cabling are sold as extras*

◇ **extracode** *noun* short routines within the operating system that emulate a hardware function

extract *verb* to remove required data *or* information from a database; *we can extract the files required for typesetting;* **extract instruction** = instruction to select and read required data from a database *or* file

◇ **extractor** *noun see* MASK

eye-strain *noun* pain in the eyes, caused by looking at bright lights *or* at a VDU for too long

QUOTE to minimize eye-strain, it is vital to have good lighting conditions with this LCD system
Personal Computer World

Ff

f = FEMTO- *prefix* equal to one thousandth of a million millionth (10^{-15})

F hexadecimal number equivalent to decimal number 15

face *see* TYPEFACE

facet *noun* one surface *or* plane
◊ **faceted code** *noun* code which indicates various details of an item, by assigning each one a value

facility *noun* (a) being able to do something easily; *we offer facilities for processing a customer's own disks* (b) **facilities** = equipment *or* buildings which make it easy to do something; *storage facilities* (c) *US* single large building; *we have opened our new data processing facility*

facsimile *noun* exact copy of an original; **facsimile character generator** = means of displaying characters on a computer screen by copying preprogrammed images from memory; **facsimile copy** = exact copy of a document; **facsimile transmission (FAX)** = method of sending and receiving images in digital form over a telephone *or* radio link

factor *noun* (a) thing which is important *or* which has an influence on something else; **deciding factor** = most important factor which influences someone's decision; *the deciding factor was the superb graphics;* **elimination factor** = during a search, the section of data that is not used (b) any number in a multiplication that is the operand; **by a factor of ten** = ten times
◊ **factorial** *noun* the product of all the numbers below a number; *example: 4 factorial (written 4!) = 1x2x3x4 = 24*
◊ **factorize** *verb* to break down a number into two whole numbers which when multiplied will give the original number; *when factorized, 15 gives the factors 1, 15 or 3, 5*

factory *noun* building where products are manufactured; *computer factory; they have opened a new components factory;* **factory**

price *or* **price ex factory** = price not including transport from the maker's factory

fade *verb (of radio or electrical signal)* to become less strong

fail *verb* not to do something which should be done; not to work properly; *the company failed to carry out routine maintenance of its equipment; the prototype disk drive failed its first test; a computer has failed if you turn on the power supply and nothing happens;* **fail safe system** = system that has a predetermined state it will go to if a main program *or* device fails, so avoiding a total catastrophe that a complete system shutdown would produce; **fail soft system** = system that will still be partly operational even after a part of the system has failed; *see also* GRACEFUL DEGRADATION
◊ **failure** *noun* breaking down *or* stopping; not doing something which should be done; **failure logging** = section of the operating system that automatically saves the present system states and relevant data when an error *or* fault is detected; **failure rate** = number of a certain type of failure within a specified period of time; **failure recovery** = resuming a process *or* program after a failure has occurred and has been corrected; **induced failure** = failure of a device due to external effects; **mean time between failures (MTBF)** = average period of time that a piece of equipment will operate for between breakdowns; **power failure** = loss of the electric power supply; *see also* BLACKOUT, BROWN OUT

fall back *noun* special *or* temporary instructions *or* procedures *or* data used in the event of a fault *or* failure; **fall back recovery** = resuming a program after a fault has been fixed, from the point at which fall back routines were called; **fall back routines** = routines that are called *or* procedures which are executed by a user when a machine *or* system has failed

false *adjective* (i) wrong; not true *or* not correct; (ii) a logical term, equal to binary 0, opposite of true; **false code** = code that contains values not within specified limits; **false drop** *or* **retrieval** = unwanted files retrieved from a database through the use of incorrect search codes; **false error** = error warning given when no error has occurred

FAM = FAST ACCESS MEMORY

family *noun* **(a)** range of different designs of a particular typeface **(b)** range of machines from one manufacturer that are compatible with other products in the same line from the same manufacturer

fan 1 *noun* (i) mechanism that circulates air for cooling; (ii) a spread of data items *or* devices; *if the fan fails, the system will rapidly overheat* **2** *verb* (i) to cool a device by blowing air over it; (ii) to spread out a series of items *or* devices; **fan-in** = maximum number of inputs that a circuit *or* chip can deal with; **fan-out** = maximum number of outputs that a circuit *or* chip can drive without exceeding its power dissipation limit; **fanning strip** = cable supporting insulated strip

◊ **fanfold** *or* **accordion paper** *noun* method of folding continuous paper, one sheet in one direction, the next sheet in the opposite direction, allowing the paper to be stored conveniently and fed into a printer continuously

> QUOTE a filtered fan maintains positive air pressure within the cabinet, to keep dust and dirt from entering
> *Personal Computer World*

Faraday cage *noun* wire *or* metal screen, connected to ground, that completely encloses sensitive equipment to prevent any interference from stray electromagnetic radiation

fascia plate *noun* front panel on a device; *the fascia plate on the disk drive of this model is smaller than those on other models*

fast *adjective* which moves quickly; which works quickly; (storage *or* peripheral device) that performs its functions very rapidly; *fast program execution; this hard disk is fast, it has an access time of 28mS;* **fast access memory (FAM)** = storage locations that can be read from *or* written to

very rapidly; **fast core** = high speed, low access time working memory for a CPU; *the fast core is used as a scratchpad for all calculations in this system;* **fast line** = special telecommunications line which allows data to be transmitted at 48K *or* 96K baud rates; **fast peripheral** = peripheral that communicates with the computer at very high speeds, limited only by the speed of the electronic circuits, as opposed to a slow peripheral such as a card reader, where mechanical movement determines speed; **fast time-scale** = operation in which the time-scale factor is less than one

fatal error *noun* fault in a program *or* device that causes the system to crash

father file *noun* backup of the previous version of a file; *see also* GRANDFATHER, SON

fault *noun* situation where something has gone wrong with software *or* hardware, causing it to malfunction; *the technical staff are trying to correct a programming fault; we think there is a basic fault in the product design; see also* BUG, ERROR; **fault detection** = (automatic) process which logically *or* mathematically determines that a fault exists in a circuit; **fault diagnosis** = process by which the cause of a fault is located; **fault location program** = routine that is part of a diagnostic program that identifies the cause of faulty data *or* equipment; **fault time** = period of time during which a computer system is not working *or* usable; **fault trace** = program that checks and records the occurrences of faults in a system

◊ **fault tolerance** *noun* ability of a system to continue functioning even when a fault has occurred

◊ **fault-tolerant** *adjective* (system *or* device) that is able to continue functioning even when a fault occurs; *they market a highly successful range of fault-tolerant minis*

◊ **faulty** *adjective* which does not work properly; *there must be a faulty piece of equipment in the system; they traced the fault to a faulty cable;* **faulty sector** = sector of a magnetic disk that cannot be written to *or* read from correctly

> QUOTE before fault-tolerant systems, users had to rely on cold standby
> QUOTE fault tolerance is usually associated with a system's reliability
> *Computer News*

fax *or* **FAX** *noun* & *verb informal* = FACSIMILE COPY, FACSIMILE

TRANSMISSION *we will send a fax of the design plan; I've faxed the documents to our New York office; the fax machine is next to the telephone switchboard*

QUOTE investment in a good modem and communications system could reduce your costs considerably on both courier and fax services
Which PC?

fd *or* **FD** **(a)** = FULL DUPLEX data transmission down a channel in two directions simultaneously **(b)** = FLOPPY DISK

fdc = FLOPPY DISK CONTROLLER

fdx *or* **FDX** = FULL DUPLEX

feasibility *noun* ability to be done; *he has been asked to report on the feasibility of a project;* **feasibility study** = examination and report into the usefulness and cost of a new product that is being considered for purchase; **to carry out a feasibility study on a project** = to carry out an examination of costs and profits to see if the project should be started
NOTE: no plural

feature *noun* special function *or* ability *or* design of hardware *or* software; **key feature** = most important feature; *the key features of this system are: 20Mb of formatted storage with an access time of 60ms*

FEDS = FIXED AND EXCHANGEABLE DISK STORAGE magnetic disk storage system that contains some removable disks, such as floppy disks and some fixed *or* hard disk drives

feed **1** *noun* device which puts paper *or* tape into and through a machine, such as a printer *or* photocopier; **continuous feed** = device which feeds in continuous computer stationery into a printer; **front feed** *or* **sheet feed attachment** = device which can be attached to a line printer to allow individual sheets of paper to be fed in automatically; **feed holes** = punched sprocket holes along the edge of continuous paper; **feed reel** = reel of tape which is being fed into a machine; **paper feed** = mechanism which pulls paper through a printer; **sheet feed** = device which puts in one sheet at a time into a printer; **tractor feed** = method of feeding paper into a printer, sprocket wheels on the printer connect with sprocket holes on each edge of the paper **2** *verb* to put paper into a machine *or* information into a computer; *this paper should be manually fed into the printer; data is fed into the computer* NOTE: feeding - fed

◊ **feedback** *noun* information from one source which can be used to modify something *or* provide a constructive criticism of something; *we are getting customer feedback on the new system; they asked the sales teams for feedback on the reception of the new model; have you any feedback from the sales force about the customers' reaction to the new model?;* **feedback control** = information about the effects of a controlling signal on a machine *or* device, returned to the controlling computer NOTE: no plural

feeder *noun* **(a)** channel that carries signals from one point to another **(b)** mechanism that automatically inserts the paper into a printer

female *adjective* **female connector** = connector with connecting sockets into which the pins *or* plugs of a male connector can be inserted; **female socket** = hole into which a pin *or* plug can be inserted to make a connection

femto- **(f)** *prefix* equal to ten exponent minus fifteen (10^{-15}); **femto second** = thousandth of a picosecond

FEP = FRONT END PROCESSOR processor placed between an input source and the central computer, whose function is to preprocess received data to relieve the workload of the main computer

ferric oxide *or* **ferrite** *noun* substance (iron oxide) used as tape *or* disk coating that can be magnetized to store data *or* signals

◊ **ferrite core** *noun* small bead of magnetic material that can hold an electromagnetic charge, used in (old) core memory

◊ **ferromagnetic material** *noun* any ferrite material that can be magnetized

FET = FIELD EFFECT TRANSISTOR electronic device that can act as a variable current flow control, an external signal varies the resistance of the device and current flow by changing the width of a conducting channel

fetch *noun* command that retrieves the next instruction from memory; **demand fetching** = virtual page management system in which the pages are selected as required; **fetch cycle** = events that retrieve the next instruction to be executed from memory (by placing the program counter contents on the address bus); **fetch-execute cycle** = events required to retrieve, decode and carry out an instruction stored in memory; **fetch instruction** = computer instruction to select and read the next instruction *or* data to be processed; **fetch phase** = section of the fetch-execute cycle that retrieves and decodes the instructions from memory; **fetch protect** = to restrict access to a section of memory; **fetch signal** = signal that steps the CPU through the fetch cycle

FF (a) = FORM FEED **(b)** = FLIP-FLOP

fibre optics *noun* light transmission through thin strands of glass *or* plastic, which allows data to be transmitted; **fibre optic cable** *or* **connection** = fine strands of glass *or* plastic protected by a surrounding material, used for transmission of light signals; *fibre optic connections enabling nodes up to one kilometre apart to be used* ◊ **fibre ribbon** *noun* fabric-based ribbon used in printers

fiche *see* MICROFICHE

field *noun* **(a)** area of force and energy distribution, caused by magnetic *or* electric energy sources; **field effect transistor (FET)** = electronic device that can act as a variable current flow control, an external signal varies the resistance of the device and current flow by changing the width of a conducting channel; **field programmable device** *see* PLA; **field programming** = writing data into a PROM; *see also* BLOW **(b)** sections containing individual data items in a record; *the employee record has a field for age;* **address** *or* **operand field** = part of a computer instruction that contains the location of the operand; **card field** = part of a card column reserved for one type of data *or* record; **data field** = part of a computer instruction that contains the location of the data; **field label** = series of characters used to identify a field *or* its location; **field length** = number of characters that a field can contain; **field marker** *or* **separator** = code used to indicate the end of one field and the start of the next; **protected field** = storage *or* display area that cannot be altered by the user **(c) in the field** = outside an office *or* factory; **field engineer** = engineer who does not work at one single company, but travels between customers carrying out maintenance on their computers; **field tested** = product tested outside a company *or* research laboratory, in a real situation
◊ **fielding** *noun* arrangement of field allocations inside a record and file

FIFO = FIRST IN FIRST OUT storage read/write method in which the first item stored is the first read; **FIFO memory** = memory using a FIFO access scheme; *the two computers operate at different rates, but can transmit data using a FIFO memory;* **FIFO queue** = temporary (queue) storage, in which the first item written to the queue is the first to be read; *compare* LIFO

fifth generation computers *noun* next stage of computer system design using fast VLSI circuits and powerful programming languages to allow human interaction

figure *noun* printed number; **figures shift** = (i) transmitted code that indicates to the receiver that all following characters should be read as upper case; (ii) mechanical switch which allows a typewriter to print *or* keyboard to produce special characters and symbols located on the same keys as the numbers; **in round figures** = not totally accurate, but correct to the nearest 10 or 100; *they have a workforce of 2,500 in round figures*

file 1 *noun* **(a)** documents kept for reference; **to place something on file** = to keep a record of something **(b)** section of data on a computer (such as payroll, address list, customer accounts), in the form of individual records which may contain data, characters, digits *or* graphics; **data file** = file containing data (as opposed to a program file); **disk file** = number of related records *or* data items stored under one name on disk; **distributed file system** = system that uses files stored in more than one location *or* backing store, but which are processed at a central point; **file activity ratio** = ratio of the number of different records accessed within a file compared to the total number in store; **file cleanup** = tidying and removing out of date *or* unnecessary data from a file; **file collating** = putting the contents of a file into order; **file control block** = list (in main memory) of files in use within the system; **file conversion** = change of format *or* structure of a file system, usually when using a new program *or* file handling routine; **file creation** = writing file header information onto a disk and writing an entry into the directory; **file deletion** = erasing a file from storage; *see also* DELETE; **file descriptor** = code *or* series of characters used to identify a file; **file directory** = list of names and information about files in a backing storage device; **file extent** = actual area *or* number of tracks required to store a file; **file gap** = section of blank tape *or* disk that indicates the end of a file; **file handling routine** =

short computer program that manages the reading/writing and organization of stored files; **file identification** = unique label *or* name used to identify and locate a file stored on baking store; **file index** = sorted table of the main entries in a file, with their address, allowing the rapid location of entries; **file label** = character(s) used to identify a file; **file layout** = set of rules defining internal file structure; **file maintenance** = process of updating a file by changing, adding *or* deleting entries; **file management (system)** = section of a DOS that allocates disk space to files, keeping track of the sections and their sector addresses; **file manager** = routines used to create, locate and maintain files on backing store; **file merger** = (i) to combine two data files, but still retaining an overall structure; (ii) one file created from more than one file written one after the other (no order preserved); **file name** = word used to identify a particular stored file; **file organization** *see* FILE LAYOUT; **file processing** = applying a set of rules *or* search limits to a file, in order to update *or* find information; **file protection** = (i) software *or* physical device used to prevent any accidental deletion *or* modification of a file *or* its records; (ii) *see* FILE SECURITY; **file protect tab** = plastic tab on a disk which prevents accidental erasure of a file; **file purge** = erasing the contents of a file; **file-recovery utility** = software that allows files that have been accidentally deleted *or* damaged to be read again; *a lost file cannot be found without a file-recovery utility;* **file security** = hardware *or* software organization of a computer system to protect users' files from unauthorized access; **file server** = small microcomputer and large backing store device that is used for the management and storage of a users files in a network; **file set** = number of related files treated as one unit; **file sort** = to put the contents of a file into order; **file storage** = physical means of preserving data in a file, such as a disk drive *or* tape machine; **file store** = files that are available in main memory at any time; **file structure** = way in which a (data) file is organized; **file transfer** = moving a file from one area of memory to another *or* to another storage device; **file update** = (i) recent changes *or* transactions to a file; (ii) new version of software which is sent to users of an existing version; **file validation** = checking that a file is correct; **hidden file** = important system file which is not displayed in a directory and cannot normally be read by a user; **indexed file** = sequential file with an index of all the entries and their addresses; **inverted file** = file with an index entry for every data item;

output file = set of records that have been completely processed according to various parameters; **program file** = file containing a program rather than data; **text file** = file that contains text rather than digits *or* data; **threaded file** = file in which an entry will contain data and an address to the next entry that contains the same data (allowing rapid retrieval of all identical entries); **transaction** *or* **change** *or* **detail** *or* **movement file** = file containing recent changes to records *or* transactions used to update a master file **2** *verb* **to file documents** = to put documents in order so that they can be found easily; *the correspondence is filed under "complaints"; he filed the new papers in chronological order*

◇ **filename** *noun* unique identification code allocated to a program; **filename extension** = additional information after a filename, indicating the type *or* use of the file; *the filename extension SYS indicates that this is a system file*

QUOTE it allows users to back up or restore read-only security files and hidden system files independently
Minicomputer News
QUOTE the lost file, while inaccessible without a file-recovery utility, remains on disk until new information writes over it
Publish
QUOTE when the filename is entered at the prompt, the operating system looks in the file and executes any instructions stored there
PC User

filing *noun* documents which have to be put in order

◇ **filing system** *noun* **(a)** way of putting documents in order for reference **(b)** software which organizes files

fill 1 *verb* **(a)** to make something full; *the screen was filled with flickering images* **(b)** to put characters into gaps in a field so that there are no spaces left; **fill character** = character added to a string of characters to make up a required length **(c)** to draw an enclosed area in one colour *or* shading

◇ **fill up** *verb* to make something completely full; *the disk was quickly filled up*

filter 1 *noun* **(a)** electronic circuit that allows certain frequencies to pass while stopping others **(b)** (i) pattern of binary digits used to select various bits from a binary word (a one in the filter retains that bit in the source word); (ii) to select various records from a file **2** *verb* **(a)** to remove unwanted elements from a signal *or* file **(b)** to select various bits *or* records from a word *or* file

final *adjective* last *or* coming at the end of a period; *to keyboard the final data files; to make the final changes to a document*

find 1 *verb* to get something back which has been lost; *it took a lot of time to find the faulty chip; the debugger found the error very quickly* NOTE: **finding - found 2** *noun* command to locate a piece of information; **find and replace =** feature on a word-processor that allows certain words *or* sections of text to be located and replaced with others

fine *adjective* excellent *or* of very high quality
◊ **fine tune** *verb* to adjust by small amounts the features *or* parameters of hardware *or* software to improve performance; *fine-tuning improved the speed by ten per cent*

finish 1 *noun* **(a)** final appearance; *the product has an attractive finish* **(b)** end of a process *or* function **2** *verb* **(a)** to do something *or* to make something completely; *the order was finished in time; she finished all the keyboarding before lunch* **(b)** to come to an end; *the contract is due to finish next month*
◊ **finished** *adjective* which has been completed; **finished document =** document which is typed, and is ready to be printed; **finished goods =** manufactured goods which are ready to be sold

finite-precision numbers *noun* use of a fixed number of bits to represent numbers

firmware *noun* computer program *or* data that is permanently stored in a hardware memory chip, such as a ROM *or* EPROM; *compare with* HARDWARE, SOFTWARE

first-level address *noun* computer storage address that directly, without any modification, accesses a location *or* device
◊ **first fit** *noun* routine *or* algorithm that selects the first, largest section of free memory in which to store a (virtual) page
◊ **first generation computer** *noun* original computer made with valve based electronic technology, started around 1951; **first generation image =** master copy of an original image, text *or* document; **first in first out (FIFO) =** temporary queue where the first item stored is the first read

fix *verb* **(a)** to make something permanent *or* to attach something permanently; *the computer is fixed to the workstation;* **fixed and exchangeable disk storage (FEDS) =** magnetic disk storage system that contains some removable disks, such as floppy disks and some fixed *or* hard disk drives; **fixed cycle operation =** (i) process in which each operation is allocated a certain, fixed time limit; (ii) actions within a process that are synchronized to a clock; **fixed data =** data written to a file *or* screen for information *or* identification purposes and which cannot be altered by the user; **fixed disk storage =** hard disk *or* magnetic disk which cannot be removed from the disk drive; **fixed field =** area in a stored record that can only contain a certain amount of data; **fixed head disk (drive) =** use of a separate immovable read/write head over each disk track making access time very short; **fixed-length record =** record whose size cannot be changed; **fixed-length word =** preset number of bits that make up a computer word; **fixed program computer =** (hardwired) computer program that cannot be altered and is run automatically; **fixed routing =** communications direction routing that does not consider traffic *or* efficient paths; **fixed word length =** computer whose word size (in bits) cannot be changed **2** *verb* to mend; *the technicians are trying to fix the switchboard; can you fix the photocopier?*

◊ **fixed-point notation =** *noun* number representation that retains the position of the digits and decimal points in the computer, so limiting the maximum manageable numbers; *storage of fixed point numbers has two bytes allocated for the whole number and one byte for the fraction part;* **fixed-point arithmetic =** arithmetic rules and methods using fixed-point numbers; *compare with* FLOATING POINT

flag 1 *noun* (i) way of showing the end of field *or* of indicating something special in a database; (ii) method of reporting the status of a register after a mathematical *or* logical operation; *if the result is zero, the zero flag is set;* **carry flag =** indicator that a carry has occurred after a subtraction *or* addition; **device flag =** one bit in a device status word, used to show the state of a device; **overflow bit *or* flag =** single bit in a word that is set to one (1) if a mathematical overflow has occurred; **zero flag =** indicator that the contents of a register *or* result is zero; **flag bit =** single bit of a word used as a flag for certain operations; **flag code =** code sequence which informs the receiver that following characters represent control actions; **flag event =** process *or* state *or* condition that sets a flag; **flag register =** register that contains the status and flag bits of a CPU; **flag sequence =** sequence of codes sent on a packet switching network as identification of the start and finish of a frame of data **2** *verb* to attract the attention of a program while it is running to provide a result *or* to report an action *or* to indicate something special

◊ **flagging** *noun* putting an indicator against an item so that it can be found later

flash *verb* to switch a light on and off; to increase and lower the brightness of a cursor to provide an indicator; **flash A/D =** parallel high speed A/D converter; **flashing character =** character intensity that is switched on and off (as an indicator)

flat *adjective* **(a)** smooth (surface); **flat file =** two-dimensional file of data items; **flat pack =** integrated circuit package whose leads extend horizontally, allowing the device to be mounted directly onto a PCB without the need for holes **(b)** fixed *or* not changing; **flat rate =** set pricing rate that covers all the uses of a facility

◊ **flatbed** *noun* printing *or* scanning machine that holds the paper *or* image on a flat surface while processing; *scanners are either flatbed models or platen type, paper-fed models; paper cannot be rolled through flatbed scanners;* **flatbed plotter =** movable pen that draws diagrams under the control of a computer onto a flat piece of paper

flex *noun* wire *or* cable used to connect an appliance to the mains electricity supply
NOTE: no plural: **a piece of flex**

flexible *adjective* which can be altered *or* changed; **flexible array =** array whose size and limits can be altered; **flexible disk =** FLOPPY DISK; **flexible disk cartridge =** FLOPPY DISK; **flexible machining system (FMS) =** computer numeric control (CNC) *or* control of a machine by a computer; **flexible manufacturing system (FMS) =** use of CNC machines, robots and other automated devices in manufacturing

◊ **flexibility** *noun* ability of hardware *or* software to adapt to various conditions *or* tasks

flicker 1 *noun* computer graphic image whose brightness alternates due to a low image refresh rate *or* signal corruption **2** *verb* to move very slightly; *the image flickers when the printer is switched on*

◊ **flicker-free** *adjective* (display) that does not flicker

QUOTE the new 640 by 480 pixel standard, coupled with the flicker-free displays on the four new monitors and a maximum of 256 colours from a palette of more than quarter of a million
PC User

flip-flop (FF) *noun* electronic circuit *or* chip whose output can be one of two states, which is determined by one or two inputs, can be used to store one bit of digital data

flippy *noun* disk that is double-sided but used in a single-sided drive, so it has to be turned over to read the other side

float *noun* addition of the origin address to all indexed *or* relative addresses to check the amount of memory a program will require; **float factor =** location in memory at which the first instruction of a program is stored; **float relocate =** to convert floating addresses to absolute addresses

◊ **floating** *adjective* not fixed; character which is separate from the character it should be attached to; **floating address =** location specified in relation to a reference address; **floating head =** FLYING HEAD; **floating point arithmetic =** arithmetic operations on floating point numbers; **floating point (notation) =** numerical notation in which a fractional number is represented with a point after the first digit and a power, so that any number can be stored in a standard form; *the fixed number 56.47 in floating-point arithmetic would be 0.5647 and a power of 2;* **floating point number =** number represented using floating point notation; **floating point operation (FLOP) =** mathematical operation carried out on a floating point number; **floating point processor =** specialized CPU that can process floating point numbers very rapidly; *the floating point processor speeds up the processing of the graphics software; this model includes a built-in floating point processor;* **floating symbolic address =** symbol *or* label that identifies a particular instruction *or* word, regardless of its location

FLOP = FLOATING POINT OPERATION; **FLOPs per second =** measure of computing power as the number of floating point operations that a computer can execute every second

floppy disk *or* **floppy** *or* **FD** *noun* secondary storage device, in the form of a flat, circular flexible disk onto which data can be stored in a magnetic form (a floppy disk cannot store as much data as a hard disk, but is easily removed, and is protected by a flexible paper *or* plastic sleeve); **floppy disk controller (FDC) =** combination of hardware and software devices that control and manage the read/write operations of a disk drive from a computer; **floppy disk sector =** smallest area on a magnetic (floppy) disk that can be individually addressed by a computer; **floppy disk drive** or **unit** = disk drive for floppy disks and ancillary electronics as a separate assembly; **floppy tape** or **tape streamer** = continuous loop of tape, used for backing storage; *see also* MICROFLOPPY

COMMENT: floppies are available in various sizes: the commonest are 3.5 inch, 5.25 inch and 8 inch. The size refers to the diameter of the disk inside the sleeve

flow 1 *noun* regular movement; *automatic text flow across pages; the device controls the copy flow; current flow is regulated by a resistor;* **flow control** = management of the flow of data into queues and buffers, to prevent spillage or lost data **2** *verb* to move smoothly; *work is flowing normally again after the breakdown of the printer; data flow* = movement of data through a system

◊ **flowchart** or **flow diagram 1** *noun* chart which shows the arrangement of the steps in a process or program; **data flowchart** = diagram used to describe a computer or data processing system structure; **flowchart symbols** = special symbols used to represent devices, decisions and operations in a flowchart; **flowchart template** = plastic sheet with template symbols cut out, to allow symbols to be drawn quickly and clearly; **logical flowchart** = diagram showing where the logical decisions occur in a structure and their effects on program execution **2** *verb* to describe a process, its control and routes graphically; **flow diagram** = FLOWCHART; **flow direction** = order in which events occurring a flowchart; **flowline** = lines connecting flowchart symbols, showing the direction of flow within a flowchart

fluctuate *verb* to move up and down; *the electric current fluctuates between 1 Amp and 1.3 Amp*

◊ **fluctuating** *adjective* moving up and down; *fluctuating signal strength*

◊ **fluctuation** *noun* up and down movement; *voltage fluctuations can affect the functioning of the computer system*

flush 1 *verb* to clear or erase all the contents of a queue, buffer, file or section of memory; **flush buffers** = to erase any data remaining in a buffer, ready for a new job or after a job has been aborted **2** *adjective* level or in line with; **flush left** or **flush right** *see* JUSTIFY LEFT, JUSTIFY RIGHT

flutter *noun* fluctuations of tape speed due to mechanical or circuit problems, causing

signal distortion; *wow and flutter and common faults on cheap tape recorders*

flyback *noun* electron picture beam return from the end of a scan to the beginning of the next

flying head *noun* hard disk read/write head that is wing-shaped to fly just above the surface of the spinning disk

FMS = FLEXIBLE MACHINING SYSTEM, FLEXIBLE MANUFACTURING SYSTEM computer numeric control (CNC) or control of a machine by a computer

fold *verb* **accordion** or **fanfold** = method of folding continuous stationery, one sheet in one direction, the next sheet in the opposite direction

◊ **folding** *noun* hashing method (that generates an address by splitting the key into parts and adding them together)

◊ **-fold** *suffix* times; **four-fold** = four times

font or **fount** *noun* set of characters all of the same style, size and typeface; **font change** = function on a computer to change the style of characters used on a display screen; **font disk** = magnetic disk that contains the data to drive a character generator to make up the various fonts on a computer display; **downloadable fonts** or **resident fonts** = fonts or typefaces which are stored on a disk and can be downloaded to a printer and stored in temporary memory

QUOTE laser printers store fonts in several ways: as resident, cartridge and downloadable fonts
Desktop Publishing Today

foot *noun* bottom part; *he signed his name at the foot of the letter*

◊ **footer** or **footing** *noun* message at the bottom of all the pages in a printed document (such as the page number)

◊ **footnote** *noun* note at the bottom of a page, which refers to the text above it, usually using a superior number as a reference

◊ **footprint** *noun* **(a)** area covered by a transmitting device such as a satellite or antenna **(b)** area that a computer takes up on a desk

for-next loop *noun* loop or routine that is repeated until a condition no longer occurs; *for X=1 to 5: print X: next X - this will print out 1 2 3 4 5*

forbid *verb* to say that something must not be done; *the contract forbids sale of the goods to the USA;* **forbidden character** *or* **combination** = bit combination in a computer word that is not allowed according to the rules defined by the programmer *or* system designer
NOTE: **forbidding - forbade - forbidden**

force 1 *noun* strength; **to come into force** = to start to operate *or* work; *the new regulations will come into force on January 1st* **2** *verb* to make someone do something; *competition has forced the company to lower its prices;* **forced page break** = embedded code which indicates a new page start

foreground *noun* **(a)** front part of an illustration (as opposed to the background); **foreground colour** = colour of characters and text displayed on a screen **(b)** high priority task done by a computer; **foreground/background modes** = computer system in which two modes for program execution are possible: foreground mode for interactive user programs, background mode for housekeeping and other necessary system programs; **foreground processing** *or* **foregrounding** = region of a multitasking operating system in which high priority jobs *or* programs are executed; **foreground program** = high priority program in a multitasking system, whose results are usually visible to the user; *compare* BACKGROUND; **foregrounding** = execution of high priority jobs *or* programs in a multitasking operating system

forest *noun* number of interconnected data structure trees

form 1 *noun* **(a)** preprinted document with blank spaces where information can be entered **(b)** page of computer stationery; **form feed** = command to a printer to move to the next sheet of paper; **form flash** = text heading held in store and printed out at the same time as the text; **form handling equipment** = peripherals (such as decollator) which deal with output from a printer; **form letter** = standard letter into which personal details of each addressee are inserted, such as name, address and job; **form mode** = display method on a data entry terminal, the form is displayed on the screen and the operator enters relevant details; **form overlay** = heading *or* other matter held in store and printed out at the same time as the text; **form stop** = sensor on a printer which indicates when the paper has run out **2** *verb* to create a shape;

to construct; *the system is formed of five separate modules*

format 1 *noun* **(a)** specific method of arranging text *or* data; way of arranging data on disk; **address format** = way in which address data is stored including which bits select pages, memory protect, etc.; **card format** = way in which columns and rows are arranged to represent data *or* characters in a punched card; **data format** = rules defining the way in which data is stored *or* transmitted; **display format** = number of characters that can be displayed on a screen, given as row and column lengths; **format mode** = use of protected display fields on a screen to show a blank form *or* page which cannot be altered, but into which a user can enter information; **instruction format** = rules defining the way the operands, data and address are arranged in an instruction; **local format storage** = format of a empty form *or* repeated page stored in a terminal rather than being repeatedly transmitted; **variable format** = changing method of arranging data *or* text within an area **(b)** precise syntax of instructions and arguments; **symbolic-coding format** = assembly language instruction syntax, using a label, operation and operand fields **2** *verb* **(a)** to arrange text as it will appear in printed form on paper; *style sheets are used to format documents;* **formatted dump** = text *or* data printed in a certain format **(b)** **to format a disk** = (i) to set up a blank disk so that it is ready for data, by writing control and track location information on it; (ii) to define the areas of a disk reserved for data and control; **disk formatting** = setting up a blank disk by writing control and track location information on it; *disk formatting has to be done before you can use a new floppy disk*

◇ **formatter** *noun* hardware *or* software that arranges text *or* data according to certain rules; **print formatter** = software that converts embedded codes and print commands to printer control signals; **text formatter** = program that converts text to a new form *or* layout according to parameters *or* embedded codes (such as line width, page size, justification, etc.)

QUOTE there are three models, offering 53, 80 and 160 Mb of formatted capacity
Minicomputer News

formula *noun* set of mathematical rules applied to solve a problem; **formula portability** = feature in a spreadsheet program to find a value in a single cell from data in others, with the possibility of using

the same formula in other cells; **formula translator** = FORTRAN
NOTE: plural is **formulae**

FORTH computer programming language mainly used in control applications

> QUOTE the main attraction of FORTH over other computer languages is that it is not simply a language, rather it is a programming tool in which it is possible to write other application specific languages
>
> *Electronics & Power*

FORTRAN = FORMULA TRANSLATOR programming language developed in the first place for scientific use

forty-track disk *noun* floppy disk formatted to contain forty tracks of data

forward *adjective* moving in advance *or* in front; **forward error correction** = error detection and correction method that is applied to received data to correct errors rather than requesting another transmission
◊ **forward mode** *noun* to add a number *or* index *or* displacement to an origin

FOSDIC = FILM OPTICAL SCANNING DEVICE FOR INPUT INTO COMPUTERS storage device for computer data using microfilm

fount = FONT set of characters all of the same style, size and typeface

four-address instruction *noun* program instruction which contains four addresses within its address field, usually the location of the two operands, the result and the location of the next instruction; **four-plus-one address** = instruction that contains the locations of four registers and the location of the next instruction

fourth generation computers *noun* computer technology using LSI circuits, developed around 1970 and still in current use; **fourth generation languages** = languages that are user-friendly and have been designed with the non-expert in mind

fraction *noun* (i) part of a whole unit, expressed as one figure above another (such as ½, ⅓, ¼, etc.); (ii) mantissa of a floating point number
◊ **fractional** *adjective* made of fractions; referring to fractions; *the root is the fractional power of a number;* **fractional part** = mantissa of a floating point number

fragmentation *noun* main memory allocation to a number of files, which has resulted in many small, free sections *or* fragments that are too small to be of any use, but waste a lot of space

frame *noun* (i) space on magnetic tape for one character code; (ii) packet of transmitted data including control and route information; **frame error** = error due to a faulty bit within a frame on magnetic tape
◊ **framework** *noun* basic structure of a database *or* process *or* program; *the program framework was designed first*

fraud *noun* making money by tricking people *or* by making them believe something which is not true; **computer fraud** = theft of data *or* dishonest use *or* other crimes involving computers

> QUOTE the offences led to the arrest of nine teenagers who were all charged with computer fraud
>
> *Computer News*

free 1 *adjective* available for use *or* not currently being used; (spare bytes) available on disk *or* in memory; **free running mode** = interactive computer mode that allows more than one user to have simultaneous use of a program; **free wheeling** = transmission protocol where the computer transmitting receives no status signals from the receiver **2** *verb* to erase *or* remove *or* backup programs *or* files to provide space in memory
◊ **freedom** *noun* being free to do something without restriction; **freedom of information** = being able to examine computer records (referring both to government activities and to records kept about individuals)
◊ **freely** *adverb* with no restrictions

frequency *noun* number of cycles *or* periods of a regular waveform that are repeated per second; **clock frequency** = frequency of the main clock that synchronizes a computer system; *the main clock frequency is 10MHz*
◊ **frequent** *adjective* which comes *or* goes *or* takes place often
◊ **frequently** *adverb* often

friction feed *noun* printer mechanism where the paper is advanced by holding it between two rollers (as opposed to tractor feed)

FROM = FUSIBLE READ ONLY MEMORY

front *noun* part of something which faces away from the back; *the disks are inserted in slots in the front of the terminal;* **front panel** = main computer system control switches and status indicators

◇ **front-end** *adjective* located at the start *or* most important point of a circuit *or* network; **front-end processor (FEP)** = processor placed between an input source and the central computer whose function is to preprocess received data to relieve the workload of the main computer

full *adjective* **(a)** with as much inside as possible; *the disk is full, so the material will have to be stored on another disk* **(b)** complete *or* including everything; **full adder** = binary addition circuit that can produce the sum of two inputs and can also accept a carry input, producing a carry output if necessary; **full duplex** = data transmission down a channel in two directions simultaneously; *see also* DUPLEX, HALF-DUPLEX, SIMPLEX; **full-size display** = large screen VDU which can display a whole page of text; **full subtractor** = binary subtractor circuit that can produce the difference of two inputs and can also accept a carry input, producing a carry output if necessary

◇ **fully** *adverb* completely; **fully formed characters** = characters produced by a printer in a single action; *a daisy wheel printer produces fully formed characters*

QUOTE transmitter and receiver can be operated independently, making full duplex communication possible
Electronics & Power

function 1 *noun* **(a)** mathematical formula, where a result is dependent upon several other numbers **(b)** sequence of computer program instructions in a main program that perform a certain task; **function digit** = code used to instruct a computer as to which function *or* branch in a program to follow; **function table** = list that gives the relationship between two sets of instructions *or* data **(c)** special feature available on a computer *or* word-processor; *the word-processor had a spelling-checker function but no built-in text-editing function;* **function code** = printing codes that control an action rather than representing a character **2** *verb* to operate *or* perform correctly; *the new system has not functioned properly since it was installed*

◇ **functional** *adjective* which refers to the way something works; **functional diagram** = drawing of the internal workings and processes of a machine *or* piece of software; **functional specification** = specification which defines the results which a program is expected to produce; **functional unit** = hardware *or* software that works as it should

◇ **function key** *or* **programmable function key** *noun* key *or* switch that has been assigned a particular task *or* sequence of instructions; *tags can be allocated to function keys; hitting F5 will put you into insert mode*

COMMENT: function keys often form a separate group of keys on the keyboard, and have specific functions attached to them. They may be labelled F1, F2, etc.

QUOTE they made it clear that the PC was to take its place as part of a much larger computing function that comprised of local area networks, wide area networks, small systems, distributed systems and mainframes
Minicomputer News
QUOTE if your computer has a MOD function, you will not need the function defined in line 3010
Computing Today
QUOTE the final set of keys are to be found above the main keyboard and comprise 5 function keys, which together with shift, give 10 user-defined keys
Computing Today

fuse 1 *noun* electrical protection device consisting of a small piece of metal, which will melt when too much power passes through it; **to blow a fuse** = to melt a fuse by passing too much current through it **2** *verb* to draw too much current, causing a fuse to melt; *when the air-conditioning was switched on, it fused the whole system*

◇ **fusible link** *noun* small link in a PLA that can be blown to program the device permanently

◇ **fusible read only memory (FROM)** *noun* PROM that is made up of a matrix of fusible links which are selectively blown to program it

fuzzy logic *or* **fuzzy theory** *noun* type of logic applied to computer programming, which tries to replicate the reasoning methods of the human brain

Gg

G = GIGA *prefix* meaning one thousand million

> COMMENT: in computing G refers to 2^{30}, equal to 1,073,741,824

GaAs = GALLIUM ARSENIDE

gain 1 *noun* increase *or* becoming larger; amount by which a signal amplitude is changed as it passes through a circuit, usually given as a ratio of output to input amplitude **2** *verb* to obtain *or* to get; **to gain access to a file** = to be able to access a file; *the user cannot gain access to the confidential information in the file without a password*

gallium arsenide (GaAs) *noun* semiconductor compound, a new material for chip construction, that allows faster operation than silicon chips

game *noun* something which is played for enjoyment *or* relaxation; **computer game** = game played on a computer, using special software; **game paddle** = device held in the hand to move a cursor *or* graphics in a computer game

ganged *adjective* mechanically linked devices that are operated by a single action; **ganged switch** = series of switches that operate on different parts of a circuit, but which are all switched by a single action; *a ganged switch is used to select which data bus a printer will respond to*

gap *noun* **(a)** space between recorded data; **block** *or* **interblock gap (IBG)** = blank magnetic tape between the end of one block of data and the start of the next in backing store; **gap character** = an extra character added to a group of characters (for parity or another purpose, but not data *or* instructions); **gap digit** = an extra digit added to a group of data (for parity or another purpose, but not data *or* instructions); **record gap** = blank section of magnetic tape between two consecutive records **(b)** space between a read head and the magnetic medium; **gap loss** = signal attenuation due to incorrect alignment of the read/write head with the storage medium; **air** *or* **head gap** = narrow gap between a recording *or* playback head and the magnetic medium

garbage *noun* data *or* information that is no longer required because it is out of date *or* contains errors; **garbage collection** = reorganization and removal of unwanted *or* out of date files and records; clearing a section of memory of a program *or* its data that is not in use; **garbage in garbage out (GIGO)** = expression meaning that the accuracy and quality of information that is output depends on the quality of the input

> COMMENT: GIGO is sometimes taken to mean "garbage in gospel out": i.e. that whatever wrong information is put into a computer, people will always believe that the output results are true

gas discharge display *or* **gas plasma display** *noun* flat, lightweight display screen that is made of two flat pieces of glass covered with a grid of conductors, separated by a thin layer of a gas which luminesces when one point of the grid is selected by two electric signals

> COMMENT: mainly used in modern portable computer displays, but the definition is not as good as in cathode ray tube displays

gate *noun* **(a)** logical electronic switch whose output depends on the states of the inputs and the type of logical function implemented; **AND gate** = gate that performs a logical AND function; **coincidence gate** = gate that produces a logical output depending on various input coincidences (an AND gate requires the coincidence in time of all logically true inputs); **EXNOR gate** = electronic implementation of the EXNOR function; **EXOR** = electronic implementation of the EXOR function; **NAND gate** = electronic circuit that provides a NAND function; **negation** *or* **NOT gate** = single input gate whose output is equal to the logical inverse of the input; **NOR gate** = electronic circuit which performs a NOR function; **OR gate** = electronic circuit that provides the OR function; **gate array** = number of interconnected logic gates built into an integrated circuit to perform a complex function; **gate delay** or **propagation time** = time taken for a gate to produce an output after it has received inputs; **gate circuit** = electronic components that implement a logical function **(b)** connection pin of a FET device

◊ **gateway** noun hard or software protocol translation device that allows users working in one network to access another

gather verb to receive data from various sources (either directly from a data capture device or from a cartridge) and sort and insert in correct order into a database; **gather write** = to write a group of separate records as one block of data

gender changer noun informal device for changing a female connection to a male or vice versa

general adjective **(a)** ordinary or not special; **general office** = main administrative office **(b)** dealing with everything; **general purpose computer** = computer whose processing power may be applied to many different sorts of applications, depending on its hardware or software instructions; **general purpose interface bus (GPIB)** = standard for an interface bus between a computer and laboratory equipment; **general purpose program** = program or device able to perform many different jobs or applications; **general register** or **general purpose register (gpr)** = data register in a computer processing unit that can store items of data for many different mathematical or logical operations

generate verb to use software or a device to produce codes or a program automatically; *to generate an image from digitally recorded data; the graphics tablet generates a pair of co-ordinates each time the pen is moved;* **computer-generated** = produced using a computer; *they analyzed the computer-generated image;* **generated address** = location used by a program that has been produced by instructions within the program; **generated error** = error occurring due to inaccuracies in data used (such as a sum total error due to a series of numbers which are rounded up)

◊ **generation** noun **(a)** producing data or software or programs using a computer; *the computer is used in the generation of graphic images; code generation is automatic;* **program generation** see GENERATOR **(b)** state or age of the technology used in the design of a system; **first generation** = earliest type of technology; **first generation computers** = original computers made with valve-based electronic technology, started around 1951; **first generation image** = master copy of an original image, text or document; **second generation computers** = computers which used transistors instead of valves; **third generation computers** = computers which used integrated circuits instead of transistors; **fourth generation computers** = computer technology using LSI circuits, developed around 1970 and still in current use; **fourth generation languages** = languages that are user-friendly and have been designed with the non-expert in mind; **fifth generation computers** = next stage of computer system design using fast VLSI circuits and powerful programming languages to allow human interaction **(c)** distance between a file and the original version, used when making backups; *the father file is a first generation backup*

◊ **generator** noun **(a)** (program) that generates new programs according to rules or specifications set out by the user **(b)** device which generates electricity; *the computer centre has its own independent generator, in case of mains power failure*

QUOTE vector and character generation are executed in hardware by a graphics display processor

Computing Today

generic adjective (something) that is compatible with a whole family of hardware or software devices from one manufacturer

genuine adjective real or correct; *authentication allows the system to recognize that a sender's message is genuine*

get noun instruction to obtain a record from a file or database

ghost noun **ghost cursor** = second cursor which can be used in some programs

gibberish noun useless and meaningless information

giga- or **G** prefix meaning one thousand million; **gigabyte** = 10^9 bytes

COMMENT: in computing giga refers to 2^{30}, which is equal to 1,073,741,824

GIGO = GARBAGE IN GARBAGE OUT expression meaning that the accuracy and quality of information that is output depends on the quality of the input

> COMMENT: GIGO is sometimes taken to mean "garbage in gospel out": i.e. that whatever wrong information is put into a computer, people will always believe that the output results are true

GINO = GRAPHICAL INPUT OUTPUT graphical control routine written in FORTRAN

GKS = GRAPHICS KERNEL SYSTEM standard for software command and functions describing graphical input/output to provide the same functions etc. on any type of hardware

glare *noun* very bright light reflections, especially on a VDU screen; *the glare from the screen makes my eyes hurt*
NOTE: no plural

glitch *noun informal* anything which causes the sudden unexpected failure of a computer *or* equipment

global *adjective* covering everything; **global exchange** = replace function which replaces one piece of text (such as a word) with another throughout a whole text; **global knowledge** = all the knowledge about one problem *or* task; **global search and replace** = word-processor search and replace function covering a complete file *or* document; **global variable** = variable *or* number that can be accessed by any routine *or* structure in a program; *compare* LOCAL VARIABLE

GND = GROUND electrical circuit connection to earth *or* to a point with a zero voltage level

goal *noun* (i) aim *or* what you are trying to do; (ii) final state reached when a task has been finished *or* has produced satisfactory results

gold contacts *noun* electrical contacts, (usually for low-level signals) that are coated with gold to reduce the electrical resistance

golf-ball *noun* metal ball with characters on its surface, which produces printed characters by striking a ribbon onto paper; **golf-ball printer** = computer printer using a golf-ball as a printing head

gospel *see note at* GARBAGE

GOTO programming command which instructs a jump; *GOTO 105 instructs a jump to line 105*

> COMMENT: GOTO statements are frowned upon by software experts since their use discourages set, structured programming techniques

GPIB = GENERAL PURPOSE INTERFACE BUS standard for an interface bus between a computer and laboratory equipment

gpr = GENERAL PURPOSE REGISTER data register in a computer processing unit that can store items of data for many different mathematical *or* logical operations

grab *verb* to take something and hold it
◇ **grabber** *noun* **frame grabber** = high speed digital sampling circuit that stores a TV picture in memory so that it can then be processed by a computer

> QUOTE sometimes a program can grab all the available memory, even if it is not going to use it
> *Byte*
> QUOTE the frame grabber is distinguished by its ability to acquire a TV image in a single frame interval
> *Electronics & Wireless World*

graceful degradation *noun* allowing some parts of a system to continue to function after a part has broken down

grade *noun* level *or* rank; *a top-grade computer expert*

grammatical error *noun* incorrect use of a computer programming language syntax
◇ **grammar** *noun* rules for the correct use of language

grandfather file *noun* third most recent version of a backed up file, after father and son files; **grandfather cycle** = period in which the grandfather file is retrieved and updated to produce a new father file, the old father file becoming the new grandfather file

granularity *noun* size of memory segments in a virtual memory system

graph *noun* diagram showing the relationship between two *or* more variables as a line *or* series of points; **graph plotter** = printing device with a pen which takes data

graph 94 **group**

from a computer and plots it in graphic form

◊ **graphic** *adjective* (representation of information) in the form of pictures *or* plots instead of by text; **graphic data** = stored data that represents graphical information (when displayed on a screen); **graphic display** = computer screen able to present graphical information; **graphic display resolution** = number of pixels that a computer is able to display on the screen; **graphic language** = computer programming language with inbuilt commands that are useful when displaying graphics; *this graphic language can plot lines, circles and graphs with a single command*

◊ **graphical** *adjective* referring to something represented by graphics

◊ **graphically** *adverb* using pictures; *the sales figures are graphically represented as a pie chart*

◊ **graphics** *noun* pictures *or* lines which can be drawn on paper *or* on a screen to represent information; *graphics output such as bar charts, pie charts, line drawings, etc.;* **graphics character** = preprogrammed shape that can be displayed on a non-graphical screen instead of a character, used extensively in videotext systems to display simple pictures; **graphics kernel system (GKS)** = standard for software command and functions describing graphical input/output to provide the same functions etc. on any type of hardware; **graphics library** = number of routines stored in a library file that can be added to any user program to simplify the task of writing graphics programs; **graphics light pen** = high-accuracy light pen used for drawing onto a graphics display screen; **graphics mode** = videotext terminal whose displayed characters are taken from a range of graphics characters instead of text; **graphics pad** *or* **tablet** = flat device that allows a user to input graphical information into a computer by drawing on its surface; **graphics processor** = dedicated processor and memory used only to produce and control images on a display, to provide high speed graphics handling capabilities; **graphics software** = prewritten routines that perform standard graphics commands such as line drawing, plotting, etc., that can be called from within a program to simplify program writing; **graphics terminal** = special terminal with a high-resolution graphic display and graphics pad *or* other input device; **graphics VDU** = special VDU which can display high-resolution *or* colour graphics as well as text

Gray code *noun* coding system in which the binary representation of decimal numbers changes by only one bit at a time from one number to the next

COMMENT: used in communications systems to provide error detection facilities

green phosphor *noun* most commonly used phosphor for monochrome screen coating, which displays green characters on a black background

COMMENT: a new popular screen type is paper-white, using a white phosphor to display black characters on a white background

gremlin *noun informal* unexplained fault in a system; **line gremlin** = unexplained fault when data is lost during transmission

grey scale *noun* **(a)** shades of grey that are used to measure the correct exposure when filming **(b)** shades which are produced from displaying what should be colour information on a monochrome monitor

grid *noun* system of numbered squares used to help when drawing; matrix of lines at right angles allowing points to be easily plotted *or* located

grip *verb* to hold something tightly; *in friction feed, the paper is gripped by the rollers*

ground *noun* electrical circuit connection to earth *or* to a point with a zero voltage level NOTE: **ground** is more common in US English; the U.K. English is **earth**

group 1 *noun* **(a)** set of computer records that contain related information; **group mark** *or* **marker** = code used to identify the start and end of a group of related records *or* items of data; **group poll** = polling a number of devices at once **(b)** six-character word used in telegraphic communications **2** *verb* to bring several things together

guarantee *noun* legal document promising that a machine will work properly *or* that an item is of good quality; *the system is still under guarantee and will be repaired free of charge*

guard band *noun* section of magnetic tape between two channels recorded on the same tape

◊ **guard bit** *noun* one bit within a stored word that indicates to the computer whether it can be altered or if it is protected

guide bars *noun* special lines in a bar code that show the start and finish of the code; *the standard guide bars are two thin lines that are a little longer than the coding lines*

gulp *noun* a group of words, usually two bytes; *see also* BYTE, NIBBLE

gun *or* **electron gun** *noun* source of an electron beam located inside a cathode ray tube

COMMENT: black and white monitors have a single beam gun, while colour monitors contain three, one for each primary colour (Red, Green and Blue) used

Hh

H & J = HYPHENATION AND JUSTIFICATION

hack *verb* **(a)** to experiment and explore computer software and hardware **(b)** to break into a computer system for criminal purposes

◊ **hacker** *noun* person who hacks

> QUOTE software manufacturers try more and more sophisticated methods to protect their programs and the hackers use equally clever methods to break into them
> *Electronics & Wireless World*
> QUOTE the hackers used their own software to break into the credit card centre
> *Computer News*
> QUOTE any computer linked to the system will be alerted if a hacker uses its code number
> *Practical Computing*

half *noun* one of two equal parts; *half the data was lost in transmission; the second half of the program contains some errors;* **half adder** = binary adder that can produce the sum of two inputs, producing a carry output if necessary, but cannot accept a carry input; **half duplex** = data transmission in one direction at a time over a bidirectional channel; **half-duplex modem** = modem which works in one mode at a time (either transmitting *or* receiving); *some modems can operate in half-duplex mode if required; see also* DUPLEX; **half-height drive** = disk drive whose front is half the height of a standard drive (half height drives, usually 5.25 inches are now the norm on PCs); **half-intensity** = character *or* graphics display at half the usual display brightness; **half word** = sequence of bits occupying half a standard computer word, but which can be accessed as a single unit

hall effect *noun* description of the effect of a magnetic field on electron flow; **hall effect switch** = solid state electronic switch operated by a magnetic field

halt 1 *noun* computer instruction to stop a CPU carrying out any further instructions until restarted, or until the program is restarted, usually by external means (such as a reset button); **dead** *or* **drop-dead halt** = program instruction from the user *or* an error that causes the program to stop without allowing recovery; **halt instruction** = program instruction that causes a CPU to halt, suspending operations, usually until it is reset; **programmed halt** = instruction within a program which when executed, halts the processor (to restart the program, a reset is usually required); **halt condition** = operating state reached when a CPU reaches a fault or faulty instruction *or* halt instruction *or* halt instruction in the program that is being run **2** *verb* to stop; *hitting CTRL S will halt the program*

Hamming code *noun* coding system that uses check bits and checksums to detect and correct errors in transmitted data, mainly used in teletext systems; **Hamming distance** = the number of digits that are different in two equal length words

hand *noun* **hands off** = working system where: (i) the operator does not control the operation which is automatic; (ii) the operator does not need to touch the device in use; **hands on** = working system where the operator controls the operations by keying instructions on the keyboard; *the sales representatives have received hands-on experience of the new computer; the computer firm gives a two day hands-on training course*

◊ **hand-held** *adjective* which can be held in the hand; **hand-held computer** *or* **programmable** = very small computer which can be held in the hand, useful for basic information input, when a terminal is not available

◊ **handler** *or* **driver** *noun* section of the operating system *or* program which controls a peripheral

handshake *or* **handshaking** *noun* standardized signals between two devices to make sure that the system is working correctly, equipment is compatible and data transfer is correct (signals would include ready to receive, ready to transmit, data OK); **full handshaking** = signals transmitted between two communicating devices indicating ready-to-send, ready-to-receive, received, transmitted, etc.; **handshake I/O control** = use of handshake signals meaning ready-to-send and ready-to-receive, that allow a computer to communicate with a slower peripheral

hang *verb* to enter an endless loop and not respond to further instruction

◊ **hangover** *noun* sudden tone change on a document that is transmitted over a fax machine as a gradual change, caused by equipment faults

◊ **hangup** *noun* sudden stop of a working program (often due to the CPU executing an illegal instruction *or* entering an endless loop)

hard *adjective* solid, as opposed to soft; (parts of a computer system) that cannot be programmed *or* altered; **hard card** = board containing a hard disk drive and the required interfacing electronics, which can be slotted into a system's expansion connector; **hard copy** = printed document *or* copy of information contained in a computer *or* system, in a form that is readable (as opposed to soft copy); **hard copy interface** = serial *or* parallel interface used to transmit data between a computer and a printer; **hard disk** = rigid magnetic disk that is able to store many times more data than a floppy disk, and usually cannot be removed from the disk drive; **hard disk drive** = unit used to store and retrieve data from a spinning hard disk (on the commands of a computer); **hard disk model** = model of computer with a hard disk; **hard error** = error which is permanent in a system; **hard failure** = fault (in hardware) that must be mended before a device will function correctly; *the hard failure was due to a burnt-out chip*

◊ **hard-sectoring** *noun* method of permanently formatting a disk, where each track is split into sectors, sometimes preformatted by a series of punched holes around the central hub, where each hole marks the start of sector

hardware *noun* physical units, components, integrated circuits, disks and mechanisms that make up a computer *or* its peripherals; **hardware compatibility** = architecture of two different computers that allows one to run the programs of the other without changing any device drivers *or* memory locations, or the ability of one to use the add-on boards of the other; **hardware configuration** = way in which the hardware of a computer system is connected together; **hardware interrupt** = interrupt signal generated by a piece of hardware rather than by software;

hardware reliability = ability of a piece of hardware to function normally over a period of time; **hardware security** = making a system secure by means of hardware (such as keys, cards, etc.) NOTE: no plural *compare* SOFTWARE

> COMMENT: computer hardware can include the computer itself, the disks and disk drive, printer, VDU, etc.

hardwired connection *noun* permanent phone line connection, instead of a plug and socket

◊ **hardwired logic** *noun* logical function *or* program, which is built into the hardware, using electronic devices, such as gates, rather than in software

◊ **hardwired program** *noun* computer program built into the hardware, and which cannot be changed

hartley *noun* unit of information, equal to 3.32 bits, or the probability of one state out of ten equally probable states

hash 1 *verb* to produce a unique number derived from the entry itself, for each entry in a database; **hashing function** = algorithm used to produce a hash code for an entry and ensure that it is different from every other entry **2** *noun* **(a)** *see* HASHMARK **(b)** **hash code** = coding system derived from the ASCII codes, where the code numbers for the first three letters are added up, giving a new number used as hash code; **hash-code system** = coding system using hash codes; **hash index** = list of entries according to their hashed numbers; **hash table** = list of all entries in a file with their hashed key address; **hash total** = total of a number of hashed entries used for error detection; **hash value** = number arrived at after a key is hashed

◊ **hashmark** *or* **hash mark** *noun* printed sign (#) used as a hard copy marker *or* as an indicator
NOTE: in US usage (#) means number; #32 = number 32 (apartment number in an address, paragraph number in a text, etc.). In computer usage, the pound sign (£) is often used in the US instead of the hash to avoid confusion

hazard *noun* fault in hardware due to incorrect signal timing; **hazard-free implementation** = logical function design that has taken into account any hazards that could occur, and solved them

HD = HALF DUPLEX data transmission in one direction only, over a bidirectional channel

HDLC = HIGH LEVEL DATA LINK CONTROL

HDX = HALF DUPLEX

head 1 *noun* **(a) combined head** *or* **read/write head** = transducer that can read *or* write data from the surface of a magnetic storage medium, such as a floppy disk; **head alignment** = (i) correct position of a tape *or* disk head in relation to the magnetic surface, to give the best performance and correct track location; (ii) location of the read head in the same position as the write head was (in relation to the magnetic medium); **head cleaning disk** = special disk which is used to clean the disk read/write heads; **head crash** = component failure in a disk drive, where the head is allowed to hit the surface of the spinning disk, causing disk surface damage and data corruption; **head demagnetizer** = device used to remove any stray magnetic effects that might have built up on the tape head; **head park** = to move the read/write head in a (hard) disk drive to a safe position, not over the disk, so that if the unit is knocked *or* jarred the head will not damage the disk surface; **head wheel** = wheel that keeps video tape in contact with the head; **disk head** = head which reads *or* writes on a floppy disk; **flying head** = hard disk read/write head that uses a 'wing' to fly just over the surface of the spinning disk; **playback head** = transducer that reads signals recorded on a storage medium and usually converts them to an electrical signal; **read head** = transducer that can read data from a magnetic storage medium such as a floppy disk; **tape head** = head which reads *or* writes signals on a magnetic tape; **write head** = transducer that can write data onto a magnetic medium **(b)** data that indicates the start address of a list of items stored in memory **(c)** top edge of a book *or* of a page; **head of form** = first line on a form *or* sheet of paper that can be printed on **(d)** start of a reel of recording tape **(e)** top part of a device, network *or* body; **head end** = interconnection equipment between an antenna and a cable television network **2** *verb* to be the first item of data in a list; *the queue was headed by my file*

◇ **header** *noun* **(a)** in a local area network, a packet of data that is sent before a transmission to provide information on destination and routing **(b)** information at the beginning of a list of data relating to the rest of the data; **header block** = block of data at the beginning of a file containing data about file characteristics; **header card** = punched card containing information about the rest of the cards in the set; **header**

label = section of data at the beginning of a magnetic tape, that contains identification, format and control information; **tape header** = identification information at the beginning of a tape **(c)** words at the top of a page of a document (such as title, author's name, page number, etc.); *see also* FOOTER

◇ **heading** *noun* **(a)** title *or* name of a document or file **(b)** header *or* words at the top of each page of a document (such as the title, the page numbers, etc.)

◇ **headlife** *noun* length of time that a video *or* tape head can work before being serviced *or* replaced

◇ **headline** *noun* = HEADING

heap *noun* **(a)** temporary data storage area that allows random access; *compare with* STACK **(b)** binary tree

heat sensitive paper *noun see* ELECTROSTATIC PRINTING

heat-sink *noun* metal device used to conduct heat away from an electronic component to prevent damage

help *noun* **(a)** thing which makes it easy to do something; *he finds his word-processor a great help in the office; they need some help with their programming* **(b)** function in a program *or* system that provides useful information about the program in use; *hit the HELP key if you want information about what to do next*

Hertz *noun* SI unit of frequency, defined as the number of cycles per second of time

COMMENT: Hertz rate is the frequency at which mains electricity is supplied to the consumer. The Hertz rate in the USA and Canada is 60; in Europe it is 50

heterogeneous network *noun* computer network joining computers of many different types and makes; **heterogeneous multiplexing** = communications multiplexing system that can deal with channels with different transmission rates and protocols

heuristic *noun* which learns from past experiences; *a heuristic program learns from its previous actions and decisions*

hex *or* **hexadecimal notation** *noun* number system using base 16 and digits 0-9 and A-F; **hex dump** = display of a section of memory in hexadecimal form; **hex pad** =

keypad with keys for each hexadecimal digit

hidden *adjective* which cannot be seen; **hidden defect in a program** = defect which was not seen when the program was tested; **hidden files** = important system files which are not displayed in a directory listing and cannot normally be read by a user; *it allows users to backup or restore hidden system files independently;* **hidden lines** = lines which make up a three-dimensional object, but are obscured when displayed as a two-dimensional image; **hidden line algorithm** = mathematical formula that removes hidden lines from a two-dimensional computer image of a 3-D object; **hidden line removal** = erasure of lines which should not be visible when looking at a two-dimensional image of a three-dimensional object

hierarchy *noun* way in which objects *or* data *or* structures are organized, usually with the most important *or* highest priority *or* most general item at the top, then working down a tree structure; **data hierarchy** = data structure organized hierarchically

◇ **hierarchical communications system** *noun* network in which each branch has a number of separate minor branches dividing from it; **hierarchical computer network** = method of allocating control and processing functions in a network to the computers which are most suited to the task; **hierarchical database** = database in which records can be related to each other in a defined structure; **hierarchical directory** = directory listing of files on a disk, showing the main directory and its files, branches and any sub-directories

high *adjective* **(a)** large *or* very great; **high density storage** = very large number of bits stored per area of storage medium; *a hard disk is a high density storage medium compared to paper tape;* **high-level data link control (HLDLC)** = ISO defined communications interface protocol which allows several computers to be linked; **high-level data link control station** = equipment and programs which correctly receive and transmit standard HLDLC data frames; **high-level (programming) language (HLL)** = computer programming language that is easy to learn and allows the user to write programs using words and commands that are easy to understand and look like English words, the program is then translated into machine code, with one HLL command often representing a number of machine code instructions;

programmers should have a knowledge of high-level languages, particularly PASCAL; compare LOW-LEVEL LANGUAGE; **high order** = digit with the greatest weighting within a number; **high-order language** = HIGH-LEVEL LANGUAGE; **high performance equipment** = very good quality *or* high specification equipment; **high priority program** = program that is important *or* urgent and is processed before others; **high specification** *or* **high spec** = giving a high degree of accuracy *or* having a large number of features; *high spec cabling needs to be very carefully handled;* **high speed carry** = single operation in which a carry into an adder results in a carry out **(b) logical high** = equal to logic TRUE state or 1; *compare* LOGICAL LOW; FALSE

◇ **highlight 1** *noun* **highlights** = characters *or* symbols treated to make them stand out from the rest of the text, often by using bold type **2** *verb* to make part of the text stand out from the rest; *the headings are highlighted in bold*

◇ **high-resolution** *or* **hi-res** *noun* ability to display *or* detect a very large number of pixels per unit area; *high-resolution graphics; this high-resolution monitor can display 640 x 320 pixels; the new hi-res optical scanner can detect 300 dots per inch*

◇ **high-speed** *adjective* which operates faster than normal data transmission *or* processing; **high-speed skip** = rapid movement in a printer to miss the perforations in continuous stationery

◇ **highway** *or* **bus** *noun* communications link consisting of a set of leads *or* wires which connect different parts of a computer hardware system and over which data is transmitted and received by various circuits inside the system; **address highway** = physical connections that carry the address data in a parallel form between the central processing unit and memory *or* external devices; **data highway** = bus carrying the data signals in parallel form between the central processing unit and memory *or* external devices

QUOTE they have proposed a standardized high-level language for importing image data into desktop publishing and other applications programs
QUOTE the computer is uniquely suited to image processing because of its high-resolution graphics

Byte

hill climbing *noun* method of achieving a goal in an expert system

hi-res = HIGH RESOLUTION *hi-res graphics; this hi-res monitor can display 640* *x 320 pixels; the new hi-res optical scanner can detect 300 dots per inch*

histogram *noun* graph on which values are represented as vertical *or* horizontal bars

hit 1 *noun* successful match *or* search of a database; *there was a hit after just a few seconds; there are three hits for this search key;* **hit on the line** = short period of noise on a communications line, causing data corruption **2** *verb* to press a key; *to save the text, hit ESCAPE S*

> QUOTE the cause of the data disaster is usually due to your finger hitting the wrong key
> *PC Business World*

HLDLC – HIGH-LEVEL DATA LINK CONTROL

HLL = HIGH-LEVEL LANGUAGE

HMI = HUMAN-MACHINE INTERACTION facilities provided to improve the interaction betweeen a user and a computer system

HOF = HEAD OF FORM

hold 1 *noun* synchronization timing pulse for a television time base signal **2** *verb* to retain *or* keep a value *or* communications line *or* section of memory; **holding loop** = section of program that loops until it is broken by some action, most often used when waiting for a response from the keyboard *or* a device; **holding time** = time spent by a communications circuit on call ◊ **holdup** *noun* (i) time period over which power will be supplied by a UPS; (ii) pause in a program *or* device due to a malfunction

> COMMENT: the hold feature keeps the picture steady and central on the screen; some televisions have horizontal and vertical hold controls to allow the picture to be moved and set up according to various conditions

hole *noun* punched gap in a punched paper tape *or* card, representing data; **index hole** = hole in the edge of a hard-sectored disk

Hollerith code *noun* coding system that uses punched holes in a card to represent characters and symbols, the system uses two sets of twelve rows to provide possible positions for each code

hologram *noun* imagined three-dimensional image produced by the interference pattern when a part of a coherent light source, such as a laser, is reflected from an object and mixed with the main beam
◊ **holographic image** *noun* hologram of a three-dimensional object; **holographic storage** = storage of data as a holographic image which is then read by a bank of photocells and a laser (a new storage medium with massive storage potential)

home *noun* **(a)** place where a person lives; **home banking** = method of examining and carrying out bank transactions via a terminal and modem in the user's home; **home computer** = microcomputer designed for home use, whose applications might include teaching, games, personal finance and word-processing **(b)** starting point for printing on a screen, usually taken as the top left hand corner; **home record** = first *or* initial data record in a file

homogeneous computer network *noun* network made up of similar machines, that are compatible *or* from the same manufacturer; **homogeneous multiplexing** = switching multiplexer system where all the channels contain data using the same protocol and transmission rate

hood *noun* cover which protects something; **acoustic hood** = soundproof cover put over a line printer to cut down its noise

hopper *noun* device which holds punched cards and feeds them into the reader

horizontal *adjective* lying flat *or* going from side to side, not up and down; **horizontal check** = error detection method for transmitted data; *see also* CYCLIC CHECK; **horizontal wraparound** = movement of a cursor on a computer display from the end of one line to the beginning of the next

host *noun & adjective* **host adapter** = adapter which connects to a host computer; *the cable to connect the scanner to the host adapter is included*
◊ **host computer** *noun* **(a)** main controlling computer in a multi-user *or* distributed system **(b)** computer used to write and debug software for another computer, often using a cross compiler **(c)** computer in a network that provides

special services *or* programming languages to all users

> QUOTE you select fonts manually or through commands sent from the host computer along with the text
>
> *Byte*

hot chassis *noun* metal framework *or* case around a computer that is connected to a voltage supply rather than being earthed; **hot standby** = piece of hardware that is kept operational at all times and is used as backup in case of system failure; **hot zone** = text area to the left of the right margin in a word-processed document (if a word does not fit in completely, a hyphen is automatically inserted)

house 1 *noun* company (especially a publishing company); *one of the biggest software houses in the US;* **house style** = (i) style of spelling and layout, used by a publishing company in all its books; (ii) method *or* design of a company's products, used to identify them from the products of competitors **2** *verb* to put a device in a case; *the magnetic tape is housed in a solid plastic case*

◊ **housekeeping** *noun* tasks that have to be regularly carried out to maintain a computer system (checking backups, deleting unwanted files, etc.); **housekeeping routine** = set of instructions executed once, at the start of a new program to carry out system actions such as clear memory, configure function keys or change screen display mode; *see also* IN-HOUSE

◊ **housing** *noun* solid case; *the computer housing was damaged when it fell on the floor*

howler *noun* (a) buzzer that indicates to a telephone exchange operator that a user's telephone handset is not on the receiver (b) very bad and obvious mistake; *what a howler, no wonder your program won't work*

HRG = HIGH RESOLUTION GRAPHICS ability to display a large number of pixels per unit area; *the HRG board can control up to 300 pixels per inch*

hub *noun* central part of a disk, usually with a hole and ring which the disk drive grips to spin the disk

huffman code *noun* data compression code, where frequent characters occupy less bit space than less frequent ones

human-computer *or* **human-machine interface (HMI)** *noun* facilities provided to improve the interaction between a user and a computer system

hunting *noun* process of searching out a data record in a file

hybrid circuit *noun* connection of a number of different electronic components such as integrated circuits, transistors, resistors and capacitors in a small package, which since the components are not contained in their own protective packages, requires far less space than the individual discrete components; **hybrid computer** = combination of analog and digital circuits in a computer system to achieve a particular goal; **hybrid interface** = one-off interface between a computer and a piece of analog equipment; **hybrid system** = combination of analog and digital computers and equipment to provide an optimal system for a particular task

hyphen *noun* printing sign (-) to show that a word has been split; **soft** *or* **discretionary hyphen** = hyphen which is inserted when a word is split at the end of a line in word-processed text, but is not present when the word is written normally

◊ **hyphenated** *adjective* written with a hyphen; *the word 'high-level' is usually hyphenated*

◊ **hyphenation** *noun* splitting of a word (as at the end of a line, when the word is too long to fit); **hyphenation and justification** *or* **H & J** = justifying lines to a set width, splitting the long words correctly at the end of each line; *an American hyphenation and justification program will not work with British English spellings*

> QUOTE the hyphenation program is useful for giving a professional appearance to documents and for getting as many words onto the page as possible
>
> *Micro Decision*

Hz = HERTZ

Ii

IAM = INTERMEDIATE ACCESS MEMORY memory storage that has an access time between that of main memory and a disk based system

IAR = INSTRUCTION ADDRESS REGISTER register in a CPU that contains the location of the next instruction to be processed

IAS = IMMEDIATE ACCESS STORE high-speed main memory area in a computer system

IBG = INTERBLOCK GAP

IC = INTEGRATED CIRCUIT
NOTE: plural is **ICs**

icand *noun* = MULTIPLICAND

icon *or* **ikon** *noun* graphic symbol *or* small picture displayed on screen, used in an interactive computer system to provide an easy way of identifying a function; *the icon for the graphics program is a small picture of a palette; click twice over the wordprocessor icon - the picture of the typewriter*

> QUOTE the system has on-screen icons and pop-up menus and is easy to control using the mouse
> *Electronics & Power*
> QUOTE an icon-based system allows easy use of a computer without the need to memorize the complicated command structure of the native operating system
> *Micro Decision*

ID = IDENTIFICATION; **ID card** = card which identifies a person; **ID code** = password *or* word that identifies a user so that he can access a system; *after you wake up the system, you have to input your ID code then your password*

identical *adjective* exactly the same; *the two systems use identical software; the performance of the two clones is identical*

identify *verb* to establish who someone is *or* what something is; *the user has to identify himself to the system by using a password before access is allowed; the maintenance engineers have identified the cause of the system failure*

◇ **identification** *noun* procedure used by a host computer to establish the identity and nature of the calling computer *or* user (this could be for security and access restriction purposes *or* to provide transmission protocol information); **identification character** = single character sent to a host computer to establish the identity and location of a remote computer *or* terminal; **identification division** = section of a COBOL program source code, in which the identifiers and formats for data and variables to be used within the program are declared

◇ **identifier** *noun* set of characters used to distinguish between different blocks of data *or* files; **identifier word** = word that is used as a block *or* file identifier

◇ **identity** *noun* who someone *or* what something is; **identity burst** = pattern of bits before the first block of data on a magnetic tape that identifies the tape format used; **identity gate** *or* **element** = logical gate that provides a single output that is true if the inputs are both the same; **identity number** = unique number, used usually with a password to identify a user when logging into a system; *don't forget to log in your identity number;* **identity operation** = logical function whose output is true only if all the operands are of the same value

idle *adjective* (machine *or* telephone line *or* device) which is not being used, but is ready and waiting to be used; **idle character** = symbol *or* code that means 'do nothing' *or* a code that is transmitted when there is no data available for transmission at that time; **idle time** = period of time when a device is switched on but not doing anything

IDP = INTEGRATED DATA PROCESSING

IEE *U.K.* = INSTITUTION OF ELECTRICAL ENGINEERS

IEEE *USA* = INSTITUTE OF ELECTRICAL AND ELECTRONIC ENGINEERS; **IEEE bus**

= interface that conforms to IEEE standards; **IEEE-488** = interfacing standard as laid down by the IEEE, where only data and handshaking signals are used, mainly used in laboratories to connect computers to measuring equipment

ier *noun* = MULTIPLIER

IF statement *noun* computer programming statement, meaning do an action IF a condition is true (usually followed by THEN); **IF-THEN-ELSE** = high-level programming language statement, meaning IF something cannot be done, THEN do this, or ELSE do that

ignore *verb* not to recognize *or* not to do what someone says; *this command instructs the computer to ignore all punctuation;* **ignore character** = null *or* fill character

IH = INTERRUPT HANDLER

IKBS = INTELLIGENT KNOWLEDGE-BASED SYSTEM

ikon *or* **icon** *noun* graphic symbol *or* picture displayed on screen, used in an interactive computer system to provide an easy way of identifying a function; *see also* ICON

illegal *adjective* which is not legal *or* which is against the law *or* against rules of syntax; **illegal character** = invalid combination of bits in a computer word, according to preset rules; **illegal instruction** = instruction code not within the repertoire of a language; **illegal operation** = instruction *or* process that does not follow the computer system's protocol *or* language syntax

◇ **illegally** *adverb* against the law *or* against rules; *the company has been illegally copying copyright software*

illiterate *adjective* (person) who cannot read; **computer illiterate** = (person) who does not understand computer-related expressions *or* operations; *see also* LITERATE

image *noun* (a) exact duplicate of an area of memory (b) copy of an original picture *or* design; **image area** = region of microfilm *or* display screen on which characters *or* designs can be displayed; **image processing** = analysis of information contained in an image, usually by electronic means *or* using a computer which provide the analysis *or* recognition of objects in the image, etc.; **image processor** = electronic *or* computer system used for image processing, and to extract information from the image; **image scanner** = input device which converts documents *or* drawings *or* photographs into a digitized, machine-readable form; **image sensor** = photoelectric device that produces a signal related to the amount of light falling on it (this scans horizontally over an image, reading in one line at a time); **image stability** = ability of a display screen to provide a flicker-free picture; **image storage space** = region of memory in which a digitized image is stored; **image table** = two bit-mapped tables used to control input and output devices *or* processes

◇ **imaging** *noun* technique for creating pictures on a screen (in medicine used to provide pictures of sections of the body, using scanners attached to computers)

immediate *adjective* which happens at once; **immediate access store (IAS)** = high-speed main memory area in a computer system; **immediate addressing** = accessing data immediately because it is held in the address field of an instruction; **immediate instruction** = computer instruction in which the operand is included within the instruction, rather than an address of the operand location; **immediate mode** = mode in which a computer executes an instruction as soon as it is entered; **immediate operand** = operand which is fetched at the same time as the instruction (within an immediate addressing operation); **immediate processing** = processing data when it appears, rather than waiting for a synchronizing clock pulse *or* time; *compare with* BATCH

impact *noun* hitting *or* striking something; **impact printer** = printer that prints text and symbols by striking an ink ribbon onto paper with a metal character, such as a daisy-wheel printer (as opposed to a non-impact printer like a laser printer); *see also* DAISY-WHEEL PRINTER, DOT MATRIX PRINTER

impedance *noun* measurement of the effect an electrical circuit has on signal current magnitude and phase when a steady voltage is applied; *see also* OHM

implement *verb* to carry out *or* to put something into action

◊ **implementation** *noun* version of something that works; *the latest implementation of the software runs much faster*

implication *noun* logical operation that uses an IF-THEN structure, if A is true and if B is true this implies that the AND function of A and B will be true

implied addressing *noun* assembler instruction that operates on only one register (this is preset at manufacture and the user does not have to specify an address; *implied addressing for the accumulator is used in the instruction LDA,16*

import *verb* **(a)** to bring goods into a country for sale **(b)** to bring something in from outside a system; *you can import images from the CAD package into the DTP program*
◊ **importation** *noun* the act of importing something into a system from outside

QUOTE text and graphics importation from other systems is possible
Publish

impulse *noun* (voltage) pulse which lasts a very short time
◊ **impulsive** *adjective* lasting a very short time

inaccurate *adjective* not correct *or* wrong; *he entered an inaccurate password*
◊ **inaccuracy** *noun* mistake *or* error; *the bibliography is full of inaccuracies*

inactive *adjective* not working *or* running

inbuilt *adjective* (feature *or* device) included in a system; *this software has inbuilt error correction*

inches-per-second (ips) way of showing the speed of tape past the read/write heads

in-circuit emulator *noun* (circuit) that emulates a device *or* integrated circuit and is inserted into a new or faulty circuit to test it working correctly; *this in-circuit emulator is used to test the floppy disk controller by emulating a disk drive*

inclusion *noun* logical operation that uses an IF-THEN structure, if A is true and if B is true this implies that the AND function of A and B will be true

◊ **inclusive** *adjective* which counts something in with other things; *prices are inclusive of VAT;* inclusive **OR** *see* OR

incoming *adjective* which is coming in from outside; **incoming message** = message received in a computer; **incoming traffic** = amount of data *or* messages received

incompatible *adjective* not compatible *or* which cannot work together; *they tried to link the two systems, but found they were incompatible*

incorrect *adjective* not correct *or* with mistakes; *the input data was incorrect, so the output was also incorrect*
◊ **incorrectly** *adverb* not correctly *or* with mistakes; *the data was incorrectly keyboarded*

increment 1 *noun* **(a)** addition of a set number, usually one, to a register, often for counting purposes; *an increment is added to the counter each time a pulse is detected* **(b)** value of the number added to a register; *increase the increment to three* **2** *verb* **(a)** to add something *or* to increase a number; *the counter is incremented each time an instruction is executed* **(b)** to move forward to the next location **(c)** to move a document *or* card forward to its next preset location for printing *or* reading
◊ **incremental computer** *noun* computer that stores variables as the difference between their actual value and an absolute initial value; **incremental data** = data which represents the difference of a value from an original value; **incremental plotter** = graphical output device that can only move in small steps, with input data representing the difference between present position and the position required, so drawing lines and curves as a series of short straight lines

indent 1 *noun* space *or* series of spaces from the left margin, when starting a line of text **2** *verb* to start a line of text with a space in from the left margin; *the first line of the paragraph is indented two spaces*
◊ **indentation** *noun* leaving a space at the beginning of a line of text

independent *adjective* free *or* not controlled by anyone
◊ **independently** *adverb* freely *or* without being controlled *or* without being connected; *in spooling, the printer is acting independently of the keyboard; the item is indexed independently*

indeterminate system *noun* system whose logical (output) state cannot be predicted

index 1 *noun* **(a)** list of items in a computer memory, usually arranged alphabetically; **index build** = creation of an ordered list from the results of a database *or* file search; **index page** = videotext page that tells the user the locations of other pages *or* areas of interest **(b)** list of subjects and contents of a book in alphabetical order (usually at the back of a book) **(c)** list of terms classified into groups *or* put in alphabetical order; **index letter** *or* **index number** = letter *or* number which identifies an item in an index **(d)** address to be used that is the result of an offset value added to a start location; *see* INDEXED ADDRESSING; **index register (IR)** = computer address register that is added to a reference address to provide the location to be accessed; **index value word** = offset value added to an address to produce a usable address **(e)** guide marks along the edge of a piece of film *or* strip of microfilm; **index hole** = hole in the edge of a hand-sectored disk **2** *verb* to put marks against items, so that they will be selected and sorted to form an index; **indexed address** = address of the location to be accessed which is found in an index register; **indexed addressing** = method of addressing where the storage location is addressed with a start address and an offset word, which is added to give the destination address; **indexed file** = sequential file with an index of all entries and their addresses; **indexed instruction** = instruction that contains an origin and offset that are added to provide the location to be accessed; **indexed sequential access method (ISAM)** = data retrieval method using a list containing the address of each stored record, where the list is searched, then the record is retrieved from the address in the list; **indexed sequential storage** = method of storing records in a consecutive order, but in such a way that they can be accessed rapidly

◇ **indexing** *noun* **(a)** use of indexed addressing methods in a computer **(b)** process of building and sorting a list of records; **indexing language** = language used in building library *or* book indexes **(c)** writing an index for a book; **computer indexing** = using a computer to compile an index for a book by selecting relevant words *or* items from the text

indicate *verb* to show

◇ **indication** *noun* sign *or* thing which shows

◇ **indicator** *noun* something which shows the state of a process, usually a light *or* buzzer; **indicator chart** = graphical representation of the location and use of indicator flags within a program; **indicator flag** = register *or* single bit that indicates the state of the processor and its registers, such as a carry or overflow; **indicator light** = light used to warn *or* to indicate the condition of equipment

indirect *adjective* not direct; **indirect addressing** = way of addressing data, where the first instruction refers to an address which contains a second address

individual 1 *noun* single person; *each individual has his own password to access the system* **2** *adjective* single *or* belonging to a single person; *the individual workstations are all linked to the mainframe*

induce *verb* (i) to generate an electrical current in a coil of wire by electromagnetic effects; (ii) to prove (something) mathematically; **induced failure** = failure of a device due to external effects; **induced interference** = electrical noise on a signal due to induced signals from nearby electromagnetic sources

◇ **inductance** *noun* measurement of the amount of energy a device can store in its magnetic field

◇ **induction** *noun* (i) generation of an electrical current due to electromagnetic effects from a nearby source; (ii) mathematically proving a formula *or* fact

◇ **inductive coordination** *noun* agreement between electrical power suppliers and communication providers on methods of reducing induced interference

◇ **inductor** *noun* electrical component consisting of a coil of wire used to introduce inductance effects into a circuit (by storing energy in its magnetic field)

inert *adjective* (chemical substance *or* gas) that does not react with other chemicals

inequivalence *noun* logical function whose output is true if either of two inputs is true, and false if both inputs are the same

inference *noun* **(a)** deduction of results from data according to certain rules; **inference engine** *or* **machine** = set of rules used in an expert system to deduce goals *or* results from data **(b)** method of deducing a result about confidential information concerning an individual by using various data related to groups of people; **inference control** = determining which information may be released without disclosing personal information about a single individual

inferior figures *noun* smaller numbers *or* characters that are printed slightly below normal characters, used in mathematical and chemical formulae; *see also* SUBSCRIPT, SUPERSCRIPT, SUPERIOR
NOTE: used with figures: CO_2

infinite *adjective* with no end; **infinite loop** = loop which has no exit (except by ending the running of the program by switching off the machine *or* resetting)
◊ **infinity** *noun* **(a)** very large incomprehensible quantity even bigger than the biggest you can think of **(b)** distance of an object from a viewer where beams of light from the object would be seen to be parallel (i.e. very far away)

infix notation *noun* method of computer programming syntax where operators are embedded inside operands (such as C - D or X + Y); *compare with* PREFIX, POSTFIX NOTATION

informatics *noun* science and study of ways and means of information processing and transmission
NOTE: no plural

information *noun* **(a)** knowledge presented to a person in a form which can be understood **(b)** data that has been processed *or* arranged to provide facts which have a meaning; **information bearer channel** = communications channel that is able to carry control and message data, usually at a higher rate than a data only channel; **information content** = measurement of the amount of information conveyed by the transmission of a symbol *or* character, often measured in shannons; **information flow control** = regulation of access to certain information; **information input** = information received from an input device; **information line** = line running across the screen which gives

the user information about the program running *or* the file being edited, etc.; **information management system** = computer program that allows information to be easily stored, retrieved, searched and updated; **information networks** = number of databases linked together, usually by telephone lines and modems, allowing a large amount of data to be accessed by a wider group of users; **information output** = display of information on an output device; **information processing** = organizing, processing and extracting information from data; **information processor** = machine that processes a received signal, according to a program, using stored information and provides an output (this is an example of a computer that is not dealing with mathematical functions); **information provider (IP)** = company *or* user that provides an information source for use in a videotext system (such as the company providing weather information *or* stock market reports); **information rate** = amount of information content per character multiplied by the number of characters transmitted per second; **information retrieval (IR)** = locating quantities of data stored in a database and producing useful information from the data; **information storage** = storing data in a form which allows it to be processed at a later date; **information storage and retrieval (ISR)** = techniques involved in storing information and retrieving data from a store; **information structure** *see* DATA STRUCTURE; **information system** = computer system which provides information according to a user's requests; **information technology (IT)** = technology involved in acquiring, storing, processing and distributing information by electronic means (including radio, television, telephone, computers); **information theory** = formulae and mathematics concerned with data transmission equipment and signals; **information transfer channel** = connection between a data transmitter and a receiver; *see also* DATA TERMINAL EQUIPMENT

QUOTE Information Technology is still too young to be an established discipline. However, the national and international IT research programmes are reasonably agreed that it comprises electronics, computing and telecommunications
Electronics and Power

infrastructure *noun* basic structure *or* basic services

infringement *noun* breaking the law *or* a rule; **copyright infringement** = illegally making a copy of a program which is in copyright

inherent addressing *noun* instruction that contains all the data required for the address to be accessed with no further operation; *compare with* EXTENDED, INDEXED

inherited error *noun* error that is the result of a fault in a previous process *or* action

inhibit *verb* to stop a process taking place *or* to prevent an integrated circuit *or* gate from operating, (by means of a signal *or* command); **inhibiting input** = one input of a gate which blocks the output signal

in-house *adverb & adjective* working inside a company; *all the data processing is done in-house; the in-house maintenance staff deal with all our equipment*

initial 1 *adjective* first *or* at the beginning; **initial address** = address at which the first instruction of a program is stored; **initial condition** = condition that must be satisfied before a routine can be entered; **initial error** = error in data that is the difference between the value of the data at the start of processing and its present actual value; **initial instructions** = routine that acts as an initial program loader; **initial program header** = small machine-code program usually stored in a read-only memory device that directs the CPU to load a larger program *or* operating system from store into main memory (such as a boot up routine that loads the operating system when a computer is switched on); **initial program loader (IPL)** = short routine that loads a program (the operating system) from backing store into main memory; **initial value** = starting point (usually zero) set when initializing variables at the beginning of a program **2** *noun* first letter of a word, especially of a name; *what do the initials IBM stand for?*

◊ **initialization** *noun* process of initializing; *initialization is often carried out without the user knowing*

◊ **initialize** *verb* to set values *or* parameters *or* control lines to their initial values, to allow a program *or* process to be re-started

ink 1 *noun* dark liquid used to mark *or* write with; **ink-jet printer** = computer printer that produces characters by sending a stream of tiny drops of electrically charged ink onto the paper (the movement of the ink drops is controlled by an electric

field; this is a non-impact printer with few moving parts); *colour ink-jet technology and thermal transfer technology compete with each other* **2** *verb* to draw lines on paper using a plotter device

QUOTE ink-jet printers work by squirting a fine stream of ink onto the paper
Personal Computer World

inlay card *noun* identification card inside a tape *or* disk box

inline 1 *noun* connection pins on a chip arranged in one or two rows **2** *adverb* way in which unsorted *or* unedited data is processed; **in-line program** = program that contains no loops; **in-line processing** = processing data when it appears rather than waiting for a synchronizing *or* clock pulse

inner loop *noun* loop contained inside another loop; *see also* NESTED LOOP

input (i/p *or* **I/P) 1** *verb* to transfer data *or* information from outside a computer to its main memory; *the data was input via a modem* NOTE: **inputs - inputting - input 2** *noun* **(a)** action of inputting information **(b)** data *or* information that is transferred into a computer; **input area** = section of main memory that holds data transferred from backing store until it is processed *or* distributed to other sections; **input block** = block of data transferred to an input area; **input buffer register** = temporary store for data from an input device before it is transferred to main *or* backing store; **input device** = device such as a keyboard *or* bar code reader, which converts actions *or* information into a form which a computer can understand and transfers the data to the processor; **input lead** = lead which connects an input device to a computer; **input limited** = (program) which is not running as fast as it could due to limiting input rate from a slower peripheral; **input mode** = computer which is receiving data; **input port** = circuit *or* connector that allows a computer to receive data from other external devices; **input register** = temporary store for data received at slow speeds from an I/O device, the data is then transferred at high speed to main memory; **input routine** = set of instructions which control an I/O device and direct data received from it to the correct storage location; **input section** = (i) input routine; (ii) input area; **input statement** = computer programming command that waits for data entry from a port *or* keyboard; **input storage** *see* INPUT AREA; **input unit** = an input device; **input work queue** = list of commands to be carried out in the order they were entered (or in order by priority) **(c)** electrical signals which are applied to relevant circuits to perform the operation

◊ **input-bound** *or* **limited** *adjective* (program) which is not running as fast as it could due to limiting input rate from a slower peripheral

◊ **input/output (I/O)** *noun* receiving *or* transmitting data between a computer and its peripherals, and other points outside the system; **input/output buffer** = temporary storage area for data waiting to be output *or* data input; **input/output bus** = links allowing data and control signal transfer between a CPU and memory *or* peripheral devices; **input/output channel** = link between a processor and peripheral allowing data transfer; **input/output control program** = monitoring and control of I/O operations and data flow by a section of the operating system *or* supervisory program; **input/output controller** = intelligent device that monitors, directs and controls data flow between a CPU and I/O devices; **input/output device** *or* **unit** = peripheral (such as a terminal in a workstation) which can be used both for inputting and outputting data to a processor; **input/output executive** = master program that controls all the I/O activities of a computer; **input/output instruction** = computer programming instruction that allows data to be input *or* output from a processor; **input/output interface** = circuit allowing controlled data input and output from a CPU, consisting usually of: input/output channel, parallel input/output port and a DMA interface; **input/output interrupt** = interrupt signal from a peripheral device *or* to indicate that an input or output operation is required; **input/output library** = set of routines that can be used by the programmer to help simplify input/output tasks (such as printer drivers *or* port control routines); **input/output port** = circuit *or* connector that provides an input/output channel to another device; *the joystick can be connected to the input/output port;* **input/output processor (IOP)** = processor that carries out input/output transfers for a CPU, including DMA and error correction facilities; **input/output referencing** = use of labels to refer to specific input/output devices, the actual address of the device being inserted at run-time; **input/output register** = temporary store for data received from main memory before being transferred to an I/O device (or data from an I/O device to be stored in main memory *or* processed); **input/output request (IORQ)** = request signal from the CPU for data input or output; **input/output status word** = word whose bits describe the state of

peripheral devices (busy, free, etc.); **parallel input/output (PIO)** = data input *or* output from a computer

QUOTE inputs include raster scan files and ASCII files
Byte

inquiry *noun* (i) asking a question; (ii) accessing data held in a computer system; **inquiry character (ENQ)** = code transmitted by a computer to a remote terminal, asking for a response; **inquiry station** = terminal that is used to access and interrogate files stored on a remote computer; **inquiry/response** = interactive computer mode, in which a user's commands and enquiries are responded to very quickly

insert *verb* **(a)** to put something into something; *first insert the system disk in the left slot* **(b)** to add new text inside a word *or* sentence; **inserted subroutine** = series of instructions that are copied directly into the main program where a call instruction appears *or* where a user requires

◊ **insertion loss** *noun* attenuation to a signal caused by adding a device into an existing channel *or* circuit

◊ **insert mode** *noun* interactive computer mode used for editing and correcting documents

COMMENT: this is a standard feature on most word-processing packages where the cursor is placed at the required point in the document and any characters typed will be added, with the existing text moving on as necessary

install *verb* to put a machine into an office *or* factory; to set up a new computer system to the user's requirements *or* to configure a new program to the existing system capabilities; *the system is easy to install and simple to use*

◊ **installation** *noun* **(a)** computer and equipment used for one type of work and processing; *the engineers are still testing the new installation* **(b)** setting up a new computer system; *the installation of the equipment took only a few hours*

instantaneous access *noun* extremely short access time to a random access device

instruct *verb* to tell someone *or* a computer what to do

◊ **instruction** *noun* word used in a programming language that is understood by the computer to represent an action; *the instruction PRINT is used in this BASIC* *dialect as an operand to display the following data;* **absolute instruction** = instruction which completely describes the operation to be performed (i.e. no other data is required); **arithmetic instruction** = instruction to perform an arithmetic operation on data rather than a logical function; **blank** *or* **null** *or* **dummy instruction** = instruction in a program that is only there to satisfy language syntax *or* to make up a block length; **breakpoint instruction** = halt command inserted in a program to temporarily stop execution, allowing the programmer to examine data and registers whilst debugging a program; **decision** *or* **discrimination instruction** = conditional program instruction that directs control by providing the location of the next instruction to be executed (if a condition is met); **dummy instruction** = instruction in a program that is only there to satisfy language syntax *or* to make up a block length; **executive instruction** = instruction used to control and execute programs under the control of an operating system; **four-address instruction** = program instruction which contains four addresses within its address field, usually the location of the two operands, the result and the location of the next instruction; **indexed instruction** = instruction that contains an origin and location of an offset that are added together to provide the address to be accessed; **input/output instruction** = computer programming instruction that allows data to be input *or* output from a processor; **jump instruction** = program command to end one set of instructions and direct the processor to another section of the program; **macro instruction** = one programming instruction that refers to a number of instructions within a routine *or* macro; **no-op instruction** = instruction that does not carry out any functions, but increments the program counter; **n-plus-one instruction** = instruction made up of a number (n) of addresses and one other address that is the location of the next instruction to be executed; **supervisory instruction** = instruction used to control and execute programs under the control of an operating system; **three-address-instruction** = instruction format which contains the addresses of two operands and the location where the result is to be stored; **two-address-instruction** = instruction format containing the locations of two operands, the result being stored in one of the operand locations; **two-plus-one-address instruction** = instruction containing locations of two operands and an address for the storage of the result; **instruction address** = location of an instruction;

instruction address register (IAR) register in a CPU that contains the location of the next instruction to be processed; **instruction area** = section of memory that is used to store instructions; **instruction cache** = area of high-speed memory which stores the next few instructions to be executed by a processor; **instruction character** = special character that provides a control sequence rather than an alphanumeric character; **instruction codes** = set of symbols *or* codes that a CPU can directly understand and execute; **instruction counter** *or* **instruction address register (IAR)** *or* **program counter** = register in a CPU that contains the location of the next instruction to be processed; **instruction cycle** = sequence of events and their timing that is involved when fetching and executing an instruction stored in memory; **instruction cycle time** = amount of time taken for one instruction cycle; **instruction decoder** = program which decodes instructions in machine code; **instruction execution time** = time taken to carry out an instruction; **instruction format** = rules defining the way the operands, data and addresses are arranged in an instruction; **instruction modification** = altering a part of an instruction (data *or* operator) so that it carries out a different function when next executed; **instruction pipelining** = beginning processing a second instruction while still processing the present one (this increases program speed of execution); **instruction processor** = section of the central processing unit that decodes the instruction and performs the necessary arithmetic and logical functions; **instruction register (IR)** = register in a central processing unit that stores an instruction during decoding and execution operations; **instruction repertoire** *or* **set** = total number of instructions that a processor can recognize and execute; **instruction storage** *see* INSTRUCTION AREA; **instruction time** = amount of time taken for a central processing unit to carry out a complete instruction; **instruction word** = fixed set of characters used to initiate an instruction; *the manufacturers of this CPU have decided that JMP will be the instruction word to call the jump function*

COMMENT: in a high level language the instructions are translated by the compiler *or* interpreter to a form that is understood by the central processing unit

insulate *verb* to prevent energy from a conductor reaching another point by separating the two points with an insulation material

integer *noun* mathematical term to describe a whole number (it may be positive *or* negative *or* zero); **double-precision integer** = two computer words used to store an integer; **integer BASIC** = faster version of BASIC that uses only integer mathematics and cannot support fractions

◊ **integral** *noun* add-on device *or* special feature that is already built into a system; *the integral disk drives and modem reduced desk space*

QUOTE an integral 7 inch amber display screen, two half-height disk drives and terminal emulation for easy interfacing with mainframes
Computing Today

integrated *adjective* (system) that contains many peripherals grouped together in order to provide a neat, complete system; **integrated database** = database that is able to provide information for varied requirements without any redundant data; **integrated data processing (IDP)** = organizational method for the entry and retrieval of data to provide maximum efficiency; **integrated emulator** = emulator program run within a multitasking operating system; **integrated modem** = modem that is a internal part of the system; **integrated office** = office environment in which all operations are carried out using a central computer (to store information, print, etc.); **integrated services digital network (ISDN)** = international digital communications network which can transmit sound, fax and data over the same channel; **integrated software** = software such as an operating system *or* word-processor that is stored in the computer system and has been tailored to the requirements of the system

◊ **integrated circuit (IC)** *noun* circuit where all the active and passive components are formed on one small piece of semiconductor, by means of etching and chemical processes

◊ **integration** *noun* bringing several operations together; *small scale integration (SSI); medium scale integration (MSI); large scale integration (LSI); very large scale integration (VLSI)*

COMMENT: integrated circuits can be classified as follows: Small Scale Integration (SSI): 1 to 10 components per IC; Medium Scale Integration (MSI): 10 to 500 components per IC; Large Scale Integration (LSI): 500 to 10,000 components per IC; Very Large Scale Integration (VLSI): 10,000 to 100,000 components per IC

integrity *noun* reliability of data (when being processed *or* stored on disk); **integrity of a file** = the fact that a file that has been stored on disk is not corrupted *or* distorted in any way; **the data in this file has integrity** = the data has not been corrupted

QUOTE it is intended for use in applications demanding high data integrity, such as archival storage or permanent databases
Minicomputer News

intelligence *noun* (i) ability to reason; (ii) ability of a device to carry out processing *or* run a program; **artificial intelligence (AI)** = the design of computer programs and systems that attempt to imitate human intelligence and decision-making functions, providing basic reasoning and human characteristics

◊ **intelligent** *noun (of a machine)* (program *or* device) that is capable of limited reasoning facilities, giving it human-like responses; **intelligent device** = peripheral device that contains a central processing unit allowing it to process data; **intelligent knowledge-based system (IKBS)** *or* **expert system** = software that applies the knowledge, advice and rules defined by an expert in a particular field to a user's data to help solve a problem; **intelligent spacer** = facility on a word-processing system used to prevent words from being hyphenated *or* separated at the wrong point; **intelligent tutoring system** = computer-aided learning system that provides responsive and interactive teaching facilities for users; **intelligent terminal** = computer terminal which contains a CPU and memory, usually with a facility to allow the user to program it independently of the main CPU NOTE: the opposite is **dumb terminal**

intensity *noun* measure of the strength of a signal *or* the brightness of a light source

inter- *prefix* meaning between; **interblock** = between blocks

interact *verb (of two things)* to act on each other

◊ **interaction** *noun* action of two things on each other

◊ **interactive** *adjective* (system *or* piece of software) that allows communication between the user and the computer (in conversational mode); **interactive debugging system** = software development tool that allows the user to run a program under test, set breakpoints, examine source and object code, examine registers and memory contents and trace the instruction execution; **interactive graphics**

= display system that is able to react to different inputs from the user; *the space invaders machine has great interactive graphics, the player controls the position of his spaceship on the screen with the joystick*; **interactive media** = communication between a group of people using different transmission means; **interactive mode** *or* **processing** = computer mode that allows the user to enter commands *or* programs *or* data and receive immediate responses; *see also* INQUIRY/RESPONSE; **interactive routine** = computer program that can accept data from an operator, process it and provide a real-time reaction to it; **interactive system** = system which provides an immediate response to the user's commands *or* programs *or* data; **interactive terminal** = terminal in an interactive system which sends and receives information; **interactive videotext** = viewdata service that allows the operator to select pages, display them, ask questions use a service such as teleshopping

◊ **interactive video** *noun* system that uses a computer linked to a video disk player to provide processing power and real images *or* moving pictures

COMMENT: this system is often used in teaching to ask a student questions, which if answered correctly will provide him with a filmed sequence from the videodisk

QUOTE soon pupils will be able to go shopping in a French town from the comfort of their classroom - carried to their destination by interactive video, a medium which combines the power of the computer with the audiovisual impact of video
Electronics & Power
QUOTE interactivity is a buzzword you've been hearing a lot lately. Resign yourself to it because you're going to be hearing a lot more of it
Music Technology

interblock gap (IBG) *noun* blank magnetic tape between the end of one block of data and the start of the next in backing store

interchange 1 *noun* exchange of one thing for another; *the machine allows document interchange between it and other machines without reformatting* **2** *verb* to exchange one thing for another

◊ **interchangeable** *adjective* which can be exchanged

intercharacter spacing *noun* word-processor feature that provides variable spacing between words to create a justified line

interconnect *verb (of several things)* to connect together; *a series of interconnected terminals*

◊ **interconnection** *noun* section of connecting material between two devices

interface 1 *noun* (i) point at which one computer system ends and another begins; (ii) circuit *or* device *or* port that allows two or more incompatible units to be linked together in a standard communication system, allowing data to be transferred between them; (iii) section of a program which allows transmission of data to another program; **EIA interface** = standard defining interface signals, transmission rate and power usually used to connect terminals to modems; **general purpose interface adapter (GPIA)** = usually used to interface a processing unit to a IEEE-488 bus; **general purpose interface bus (GPIB)** = standard for an interface bus between a computer and laboratory equipment; **input/output interface** = circuit allowing controlled data input and output from a CPU, consisting usually of: input/output channel, parallel input/output port and a DMA interface; **interface card** = add-on board that allows a computer to interface to certain equipment *or* conform to a certain standard; **interface message processor** = computer in a packet switching network that deals with the flow of data, acting as an interface processor; **interface processor** = computer that controls data transfer between a processor and a terminal *or* network; **interface routines** = software that allows programs *or* data for one system to run on another; **parallel interface** = computer circuit *or* connector that allows parallel data to be transmitted *or* received NOTE: parallel interfaces are usually used to drive printers **serial interface** = circuit that converts parallel data in a computer to and from a serial form, allowing serial data to be transmitted to *or* received from other equipment NOTE: the most common serial interface is RS232C **2** *verb* (i) to modify a device by adding a circuit *or* connector to allow it to conform to a standard communications system; (ii) to connect two or more incompatible devices together with a circuit, to allow them to communicate

◊ **interfacing** *noun* hardware *or* software used to interface two computers *or* programs *or* devices

interfere *verb* to interfere with something = to stop something working properly *or* to get in the way

◊ **interference** *noun* noise on a signal; **electromagnetic interference** = corruption of data due to nearby electrically generated magnetic fields; **induced interference =** electrical noise on a signal due to induced signals from nearby electromagnetic sources

interior label *noun* identification label stored on a storage medium (magnetic tape *or* disk) rather than an exterior *or* physical label stuck to the case

interlace *verb* to build up an image on a television screen using two passes, each displaying alternate lines

COMMENT: this system uses two picture fields made up of alternate lines to reduce picture flicker effects

interleaved *adjective* sections of two programs executed alternately to give the impression that they are running simultaneously
◊ **interleaving** *noun* **(a)** processor dealing with slices *or* sections of processes alternately, so that they appear to be executed simultaneously **(b)** dividing data storage into sections so that each can be accessed separately

QUOTE there are two separate 40-bit arrays on each card to allow interleaved operation, achieving data access every 170ns machine cycle
Minicomputer News

interlock 1 *noun* security device which is part of the logon prompt and requires a password **2** *verb* to prevent a device from performing another task until the present one has been completed

interlude *noun* small initial routine at the start of a program that carries out housekeeping tasks

intermediate *adjective* which is at a stage between two others; **intermediate access memory (IAM) =** memory storage that has an access time between that of main memory and disk based systems; **intermediate code =** code used by a computer *or* assembler during the translation of a high-level code to machine code; **intermediate file =** series of records that contain partially processed data, that will be used at a later date to complete that task; **intermediate storage =** temporary area of memory for items that are currently being processed

intermittent error *noun* error which apparently occurs randomly in a computer

or communications system due to a program fault *or* noise

COMMENT: these errors are very difficult to trace and correct due to their apparent random appearance

internal *adjective* which is inside; **internal arithmetic =** arithmetic operations performed by the ALU; **internal character code =** representation of characters in a particular operating system; **internal format =** way in which data and instructions are represented within a CPU *or* backing store; **internal language =** language used in a computer system that is not under the direct control of the operator

COMMENT: many compiled languages are translated to an internal language

◊ **internal memory** *or* **store** *noun* section of RAM and ROM to which the central processing unit is directly connected without the use of an interface (as in external memory devices such as disk drives)
◊ **internal sort** *noun* sorting program using only the main memory of a system
◊ **internally stored program** *noun* computer program code that is stored in a ROM device in a computer system (and does not have to be loaded from backing store)

international *adjective* referring to different countries
◊ **International Standards Organization (ISO)** *noun* organization which regulates standards for many types of product; **International Standards Organization Open System Interconnection (ISO/OSI) =** standardized ISO network design which is constructed in layered form, with each layer having a specific task, allowing different systems to communicate if they conform to the standard

interpolation *noun* calculation of intermediate values between two points

interpret *verb* to translate what is said in one language into another; **interpreted language =** programming language that is executed by an interpreter
◊ **interpreter** *noun* software that is used to translate (at the time of execution) a user's high-level program into machine code; *compare with* COMPILER

COMMENT: a compiler translates the high-level language into machine code and then executes it, rather than the real-time translation by an interpreter

◊ **interpretative** *adjective* **interpretative code** = code used with an interpretative program; **interpretative program** = software that translates (at run-time) high level interpretative code into machine code instructions

interrecord gap = INTERBLOCK GAP

interrogation *noun* asking questions; **file interrogation** = questions asked to select various records *or* data items from a file

interrupt 1 *verb* to stop something happening while it is happening **2** *noun* **(a)** stopping of a transmission due to an action at the receiving end of a system **(b)** signal which diverts a central processing unit from one task to another which has higher priority, allowing the CPU to return to the first task later; *this printer port design uses an interrupt line to let the CPU know it is ready to receive data;* **armed interrupt** = interrupt line which has been made active (using an interrupt mask); **interrupt enable** = to arm an interrupt (by setting a bit in the interrupt mask); **interrupt disable** = to disable an interrupt (by resetting a bit in the interrupt mask to zero); **interrupt handler (IH)** = software that accepts interrupt signals and acts on them (such as running a special routine *or* sending data to a peripheral); **interrupt level** = priority assigned to the interrupt from a peripheral; **interrupt line** = connection to a central processing unit from outside the system that allows external devices to use the CPU's interrupt facility; **interrupt mask** = term in computer programming that selects which interrupt lines are to be activated; **interrupt priorities** = deciding which interrupt is given highest priority; *see also* NON-MASKABLE INTERRUPT; **interrupt request** = signal from a device that indicates to the CPU that it requires attention; **interrupt servicing** = carrying out some action when an interrupt is detected, such as running a routine; **interrupt signal** *see* INTERRUPT; **interrupt stacking** = storing interrupts in a queue and processing according to priority; **maskable interrupt** = interrupt line that can be disabled and ignored using an interrupt mask; **non-maskable interrupt (NMI)** = high priority interrupt signal that cannot be blocked and overrides all other commands; **polled interrupt** = interrupt signal determined by polling; **transparent interrupt** = mode in which if an interrupt occurs, all machine and program states are saved, the interrupt is serviced then the system restores all previous states and continues normally; **vectored interrupt** = interrupt which directs the CPU to transfer to a particular location

intersection *noun* logical function whose output is only true if both its inputs are true

interval *noun* short pause between two actions; *there was an interval between pressing the key and the starting of the printout*

intervention *noun* acting to make a change in a system

interword spacing *noun* variable spacing between words in a text, used to justify lines

intimate *noun* software that operates and interacts closely with hardware in a system

introduce *verb* to put something into something; *errors were introduced into the text at keyboarding*

invalid *adjective* not valid; *he tried to use an invalid password; the message was that the instruction was invalid*

inverse *noun* changing the logical state of a signal *or* device to its logical opposite; *the inverse of true is false; the inverse of 1 is 0;* **inverse video** = television effect created by swapping the background and foreground text display colours

◊ **inversion** *noun* changing over the numbers in a binary word (one to zero, zero to one); *the inversion of a binary digit takes place in one's complement*

◊ **invert** *verb* to change all binary ones to zeros and zeros to ones; **inverted commas** = printing sign (") which is usually used to indicate a quotation; **inverted file** = file with an index entry for all the data items

◊ **inverter** *noun* **(a)** logical gate that provides inversion facilities **(b)** circuit used to provide alternating current supply from a DC battery source; **inverter (AC/DC)** = device which changes alternating current to direct current, or direct current to alternating current

invitation *noun* action by a processor to contact another device to allow it to send a message; **invitation to send (ITS)** = special character transmitted to indicate to a device that the host computer is willing to receive messages

◊ **invite** *verb* to ask someone to do something

invoke *verb* to start *or* run a program (often a memory resident utility)

QUOTE when an error is detected, the editor may be invoked and positioned at the statement in error
Personal Computer World

involve *verb* to have to do with; to include (something) in a process; *backing up involves copying current working files onto a separate storage disk*

I/O = INPUT/OUTPUT referring to the receiving *or* transmitting of data; **I/O bound** = processor that is doing very little processing since its time is taken up reading *or* writing data from a I/O port; **I/O buffer** = temporary storage area for data waiting to be input *or* output; **I/O bus** = links allowing data and control signal transfer between a CPU and memory *or* peripheral devices; **I/O channel** = link between a processor and peripheral, allowing data transfer; **I/O device** = peripheral (such as a terminal in a workstation) which can be used for both inputting and outputting data to a processor; **I/O file** = file whose contents have been *or* will be transferred from storage to a peripheral; **I/O instruction** = computer programming instruction that allows data to be input *or* output from a processor; **I/O mapping** = method of assigning a special address to each I/O port that does not use any memory locations; *compare with* MEMORY MAPPING; **I/O port** = circuit *or* connector that provides an input/output channel to another device; *see also* SERIAL PORT, PARALLEL PORT

IOP = INPUT/OUTPUT PROCESSOR

IORQ = INPUT/OUTPUT REQUEST

i/p *or* **I/P** = INPUT

ip = INFORMATION PROVIDER company *or* user that provides an information source for use in a videotext system; **ip terminal** = special visual display unit that allows users to create and edit videotext pages before sending to the main videotext page database

IPL = INITIAL PROGRAM LOADER

ips = INCHES PER SECOND

IPSE = INTEGRATED PROJECT SUPPORT ENVIRONMENT

QUOTE one of the first aims of an IPSE is to provide a centralized information base into which all project data can be deposited in a form which enables all tools to exchange data
Electronics & Power

IR (a) = INFORMATION RETRIEVAL **(b)** = INDEX REGISTER **(c)** = INSTRUCTION REGISTER

irretrievable *adjective* which cannot be retrieved; *the files are irretrievable since the computer crashed*

irreversible process *noun* process which, once carried out, cannot be reversed

ISAM = INDEXED SEQUENTIAL ACCESS METHOD

ISDN = INTEGRATED SERVICES DIGITAL NETWORK

ISO = INTERNATIONAL STANDARDS ORGANIZATION; **ISO/OSI** = INTERNATIONAL STANDARDS ORGANIZATION OPEN SYSTEM INTERCONNECTION

isolate *verb* (i) to separate something from a system; (ii) to insulate (something) electrically; **isolated location** = (hardware) storage location which cannot be directly accessed by a user's program, protecting it against accidental erasure
◊ **isolation** *noun* being isolated; **isolation transformer** = transformer used to isolate equipment from direct connection with the mains electricity supply, in case of voltage spikes etc.
◊ **isolator** *noun* device *or* material which isolates

ISR = INFORMATION STORAGE AND RETRIEVAL

IT = INFORMATION TECHNOLOGY

italic *adjective & noun* type of character font in which the characters slope to the right; *the headline is printed in italic and underlined;* **italics** = italic characters; *all the footnotes are printed in italics; hit CTRL I to print the text in italics*

item *noun* single thing among many; *a data item can be a word or a series of figures or a record in a file;* **item size** = number of characters *or* digits in an item of data

iterate *or* **iterative routine** *noun* loop *or* series of instructions in a program which repeat over and over again until the program is completed

◇ **iteration** *noun* repeated application of a program to solve a problem

◇ **iterative process** *noun* process that is continuously repeated until a condition is met

ITS = INVITATION TO SEND

Jj

jack *noun* plug which consists of a single pin; **data jack** = plug that allows a modem to be connected directly to the telephone system

jam 1 *noun* process *or* mechanism which has stopped working due to a fault; *a jam in the paper feed* **2** *verb (of a device)* to stop working because something is blocking the functioning; *the recorder's not working because the tape is jammed in the motor; lightweight copier paper will feed without jamming*

jar *verb* to give a sharp shock to a device; *you can cause trouble by turning off or jarring the PC while the disk read heads are moving; hard disks are very sensitive to jarring*

JCL = JOB CONTROL LANGUAGE commands that describe the identification of and resources required by a job that a computer has to process

jet *see* INK-JET

jitter *noun* fault where there is rapid small up-and-down movement of characters *or* pixels on a screen of image bits in a facsimile transmission; *looking at this screen jitter is giving me a headache*

JK-flip-flop *noun* flip-flop device with two inputs (J and K) and two complementary outputs that are dependent on the inputs

job *noun* task *or* number of tasks *or* work to be processed as a single unit; *the next job to be processed is to sort all the records;* **job control file** = file which contains instructions in a JCL; **job control language (JCL)** = commands that describe the identification of and resources required by a job that a computer has to process; **job control program** = short program of job control instructions loaded before a particular application is run, that sets up the system as required by the application; **job file** = file containing jobs *or* job names waiting to be processed; **job mix** = the jobs being executed at any one time in a system; **job number** = number which is given to a job in a queue, waiting to be processed; **job orientated language** = computer programming language that provides specialized instructions relating to job control tasks and processing; **job orientated terminal** = computer terminal designed for and used for a particular task; **job priority** = importance of a job compared to others; **job processing** = to read in job control instructions from an input source and execute them; **job queue** *or* **job stream** = number of tasks arranged in an order waiting to be processed in a multitasking *or* batch system; **job scheduling** = arranging the order in which jobs are processed; **job statement control** = use of instructions and statements to control the actions of the operating system of a computer; **job step** *or* **stream** = one unit of processing involved in a task; **remote job entry (RJE)** = use of an interactive user terminal to enter job control instructions; **stacked job control** = queue of job control instructions that are processed in the order in which they were received

join *verb* **(a)** to put several things together **(b)** to combine two or more pieces of information to produce a single unit of information; **join files** = instruction to produce a new file consisting of one file added to the end of another **(c)** logical function that produces a true output if any input is true

joint denial *noun* logical function whose output is false if any input is true

journal *noun* **(a)** record of all communications to and from a terminal; **journal file** = stored record of every communication between a user and the central computer, used to help retrieve files after a system crash *or* fault **(b)** list of any changes *or* updates to a file; *the modified records were added to the master file and noted in the journal*

joystick *noun* device that allows a user to move a cursor around the screen by moving an upright rod connected to an I/O port on the computer; **joystick port =** circuit and connector used to interface a joystick with a computer; *a joystick port is provided with the home computer*

COMMENT: mostly used for computer games or CAD or desktop publishing packages

jumbo chip *noun* integrated circuit made using the whole of a semiconductor wafer; *see also* WAFER SCALE INTEGRATION

COMMENT: these devices are very new and proving rather difficult to manufacture without faults to any of the thousands of gates on the surface; when working, these devices will be extremely powerful

jump (instruction) 1 *noun* programming command to end one set of instructions and direct the processor to another section of the program; **conditional jump =** situation where the processor is directed to another section of the program only if a condition is met; **jump operation =** situation where the CPU is sent from the instruction it is currently executing to another point in the program; **unconditional jump =** instruction which transfers control from one point in the program to another, without requiring any condition to be met **2** *verb* to direct a CPU to another section of a program; **jump on zero =** conditional jump executed if a flag *or* register is zero

◊ **jumper** *noun* temporary wire connection on a circuit board; **jumper-selectable =** circuit *or* device whose options can be selected by positioning various wire connections; *the printer's typeface was jumper-selectable*

junction *noun* connection between wires *or* cables; **junction box =** small box where a number of wires can be interconnected

junk 1 *noun* information *or* hardware which is useless *or* out-of-date *or* non-functional **2** *verb* to get rid of a file; to make a file *or* piece of hardware redundant; **to junk a file =** to erase *or* delete from storage a file that is no longer used

justify *verb* **(a)** to change the spacing between words *or* characters in a document so that the left and right margins will be straight; **justify inhibit =** to prevent a word processor justifying a document; **justify margin** *see* LEFT *or* RIGHT JUSTIFY; **hyphenate and justify =** to break long words correctly where they split at the ends of lines, so as to give a straight right margin; **left justify =** to print with a straight left-hand margin; **right justify =** to print with a straight right-hand margin **(b)** to shift the contents of a computer register by a set amount

◊ **justification** *noun* moving data bits *or* characters to the left *or* right so that the lines have straight margins; **hyphenation and justification** *or* **H & J =** justifying lines to a set width, splitting the long words correctly at the end of each line; *an American hyphenation and justification program will not work with British English spellings*

juxtaposition *noun* arranging *or* placing items next to or adjacent to each other

Kk

K *prefix* **(a)** = KILO symbol used to represent one thousand **(b)** symbol used to represent 1,024, equal to 2^{10}

◇ **Kb** = KILOBIT measure of 1,024 bits

◇ **KB** *or* **K byte** = KILOBYTE unit of measure for high capacity storage devices meaning 1,024 bytes; *the new disk drive has a 100KB capacity; the original PC cannot access more than 640K bytes of RAM*

COMMENT: 1,024 is the strict definition in computer or electronics applications, being equal to a convenient power of two; these abbreviations can also be taken to equal approximately one thousand, even in computing applications. 1KB is roughly equal to one thousand output characters

Karnaugh map *noun* graphical representation of states and conditions in a logic circuit; *the prototype was checked for hazards with a Karnaugh map*

kernel *noun* basic essential instruction routines required as a basis for any operations in a computer system; **graphics kernel system (gks)** = number of basic commands required to illuminate in various shades and colours the pixels on a screen (these are then used to provide more complex functions such as line *or* shape plotting)

COMMENT: kernel routines are usually hidden from the user; they are used by the operating system for tasks such as loading a program or displaying text on a screen

key 1 *noun* **(a)** button on a keyboard that operates a switch; *there are 64 keys on the keyboard;* **key click** = sound produced by a computer to allow the operator to know that the key he pressed has been registered; **key number** = numeric code used to identify which key has been pressed; **key overlay** = paper placed over the keys on a keyboard describing their functions for a particular application; *without the key overlay, I would never remember which function key does what;* **key punch** = machine used for punching data into punched cards by means of a keyboard; **key rollover** = use of a buffer between the keyboard and computer to provide rapid key stroke storage for fast typists who hit several keys in rapid succession; **key strip** = piece of paper above certain keys used to remind the operator of their special functions **(b)** *(names of keys)* **alphanumeric key** *or* **character key** = key which produces a character (letter *or* symbol *or* figure); **carriage return key** = key which moves a cursor *or* printhead to the beginning of the next line on screen *or* on a typewriter *or* in printing; **function key** = key which has a specific task *or* sequence of instructions; *tags can be allocated to function keys;* **shift key** = key which provides a second function for a key (usually by moving the output into upper case) **(c)** important object *or* group of characters in a computer system, used to represent an instruction *or* set of data; **key terminal** = most important terminal in a computer system *or* one with the highest priority **(d)** special combination of numbers *or* characters that are used with a cipher to encrypt *or* decrypt a message; *type this key into the machine, that will decode the last message* **(e)** identification code *or* word used for a stored record *or* data item; *we selected all the records with the word disk in their keys;* **index key** = one field which is used to index a record; **key field** = field which identifies entries in a record; **keyed sequential access method (KSAM)** = file structure that allows data to be accessed using key fields *or* key field content **2** *verb* **to key in** = to enter text *or* commands via a keyboard; *they keyed in the latest data*

◇ **keyboard 1** *noun* number of keys fixed together in some order, used to enter information into a computer *or* to produce characters on a typewriter; **keyboard to disk entry** = system where information entered on a keyboard is stored directly on to disk with no processing; **ANSI keyboard** = standard for a keyboard that provides either upper case or upper and lower case characters on a typewriter style keyboard; **ASCII keyboard** = keyboard that provides a key for every ASCII code; **ASR keyboard** = communications console keyboard that has all the characters and punctuation keys and special control, send and receive keys; **AZERTY keyboard** = non-English language key layout (the first six letters on the top left row of the keyboard being AZERTY); **interactive keyboard** = keyboard that helps to direct the user or prompts for an input by lighting up certain keys on the keyboard (under program control); **keyboard contact bounce** = multiple signals from a key pressed just once, due to a faulty switch and key bounce; **keyboard encoder** = way in which each key generates a unique word when pressed; **keyboard layout** = way in which various function and character keys are arranged; **keyboard overlay** = paper placed over the keys on a keyboard describing their special functions for a particular application; **keyboard send/receive (KSR)** = terminal which has a keyboard and monitor, and is linked to a CPU; **keyboard to disk entry** = system where information entered on a keyboard is stored directly onto disk with no processing; **QWERTY keyboard** = standard English language key layout (the first six letters on the top left row of keys are QWERTY); **touch sensitive keyboard** = thin, flat membrane type keyboard whose keys are activated by touching the particular key, with no movement involved (often used for heavy duty or dirty environments where normal keys would not function correctly) **2** verb to enter information by using a keyboard; *it was cheaper to have the manuscript keyboarded by another company*

◇ **keyboarder** noun person who enters data via a keyboard

◇ **keyboarding** noun action of entering data using a keyboard; *the cost of keyboarding is calculated in keystrokes per hour*

◇ **keypad** noun group of special keys used for certain applications; *you can use the numeric keypad to enter the figures;* **hex keypad** = keypad with 16 keys (0-9 and A-F) for all the hexadecimal digits; **numeric keypad** = set of ten keys with figures (0-9), included in most computer keyboards as a separate group, used for entering large amounts of data in numeric form

◇ **keystroke** noun action of pressing a key; *he keyboards at a rate of 3500 keystrokes per hour;* **keystroke count** = counting of each keystroke made, often used to calculate keyboarding costs; **keystroke verification** = check made on each key pressed to make sure it is valid for a particular application

◇ **key-to-disk** noun system where data is keyed in and stored directly on disk without any processing

◇ **keyword** noun (i) command word used in a programming language to provide a function; (ii) important or informative word in a title or document that describes

its contents; (iii) word which is relevant or important to a text; *the BASIC keyword PRINT will display text on the screen; computer is a keyword in IT*

> QUOTE where large orders are being placed over the telephone it is easy to key them into the micro
>> *Micro Decision*
> QUOTE the new keyboard is almost unchanged, and features sixteen programmable function keys
>> *Micro Decision*
> QUOTE it uses a six button keypad to select the devices and functions
>> *Byte*
> QUOTE the main QWERTY typing area is in the centre of the keyboard with the 10 function keys on the left
>> *Personal Computer World*

kill verb to erase a file or stop a program during execution; **kill file** = command to erase a stored file completely; **kill job** = command to halt a computer job while it is running

kilo prefix **(a)** meaning one thousand; **kilobaud** = = 1,000 bits per second; **kilo instructions per second (KIPS)** = one thousand computer instructions processed every second, used as a measure of computer power **(b)** meaning 1,024 units, equal to 2^{10} (used only in computer and electronics applications); **kilobit** or **Kb** = 1,024 bits of data; **kilobyte** or **KB** or **Kbyte** = unit of measurement for high capacity storage devices meaning 1,024 bytes of data; **kiloword** or **KW** = unit of measurement of 1,024 computer words

KIPS = KILO INSTRUCTIONS PER SECOND one thousand computer instructions processed every second, used as a measure of computer power

kludge or **kluge** noun informal (i) temporary correction made to a badly written or constructed piece of software or to a keyboarding error; (ii) hardware which should be used for demonstration purposes only

◇ **kluged** adjective temporarily repaired

knob noun round button (such as on a monitor), which can be turned to control some process; *turn the on/off knob; the brightness can be regulated by turning a knob at the back of the monitor*

knowledge noun what is known; **intelligent-knowledge based system (IKBS)** = software that applies the knowledge, advice and rules defined by experts in a particular subject, to a user's data to help solve a problem; **knowledge-based system =** computer system that applies the stored reactions, instructions and knowledge of experts in a particular field to a problem; *see also* EXPERT SYSTEM; **knowledge engineering =** designing and writing expert computer systems

KSR = KEYBOARD SEND/RECEIVE terminal which has a keyboard and monitor, and is linked to a CPU; *compare with* ASR

KW = KILOWORD

LI

label 1 (a) *noun* (i) word *or* other symbol used in a computer program to identify a routine *or* statement; (ii) character(s) used to identify a variable *or* piece of data *or* a file; *BASIC uses many program labels such as line numbers;* **label field** = an item of data in a record that contains a label; **label record** = record containing identification for a stored file **(b)** piece of paper *or* card attached to something to show instructions for use *or* an address; **external label** = identifying piece of paper stuck to the outside of a device *or* disk **2** *verb* to print an address on a label
NOTE: **labelling - labelled** but US **labeling - labeled**

◇ **labelling** *noun* printing labels; *the word-processor has a special utility allowing simple and rapid labelling*
NOTE: no plural

lag *noun* time taken for an image to be no longer visible after it has been displayed on a CRT screen (this is caused by long persistence phosphor)

LAN *or* **lan** = LOCAL AREA NETWORK network where various terminals and equipment are all within a short distance of one another (at a maximum distance of about 500m, for example in the same building), and can be interconnected by cables; **LAN server** = dedicated computer and backing storage facility used by terminals and operators of a LAN; *compare* WAN

> QUOTE since most of the LAN hardware is already present, the installation costs are only $50 per connection
> *Practical Computing*

language *noun* system of words *or* symbols which allows communication with computers (such as one that allows computer instructions to be entered as words which are easy to understand, and then translates them into machine code); **assembly language** *or* **assembler language** = programming language using mnemonics to code instructions which will then be converted to machine code; **command language** = programming language made up of procedures for various tasks, that can be called up by a series of commands; **control language** = commands that identify and describe the resources required by a job that a computer has to perform; **graphic language** = computer programming language with inbuilt commands that are useful when displaying graphics; **high-level language (HLL)** = computer programming language that is easy to learn and allows the user to write programs using words and commands that are easy to understand and look like English words, the program is then translated into machine code, with one HLL instruction often representing more than one machine code instruction; **low-level language (LLL)** = language which is fast, but long and complex to program in, where each instruction represents a single machine code instruction; **machine language** = programming language that consists of commands in binary code form that can be directly understood by the CPU; **programming language** = software that allows a user to enter a program in a certain language and then to execute it; **query language** = language in a database management system that allows a database to be easily searched and queried; **source language** = original language in which a program is written prior to processing by a computer; **language assembler** = program used to translate and assemble a source code program into a machine executable binary form; **language compiler** = software that converts an encoded source program into another (machine code) form, and then executes it; **language interpreter** = any program that takes each consecutive line of source program and translates it into another (machine code) form at runtime; **language processor** = language translator from one language to machine code (there are three types of language processor: assembler, compiler and interpreter); **language rules** = syntax and format for instructions and data items used in a particular language; **language support environment** = hardware and software tools supplied to help the programmer write programs in a particular language; **language translation** = using a computer to translate text from one language to another; **language translator** = program that converts code written in one language into equivalent instructions in another language

COMMENT: There are three main types of computer languages: machine code, assembler and high-level language. The higher the level the language is, the easier it is to program and understand, but the slower it is to execute. The following are the commonest high-level languages: ADA, ALGOL, APL, BASIC, C, COBOL, COMAL, CORAL, FORTH, FORTRAN, LISP, LOGO, PASCAL, PL/1, POP-2, PROLOG. Assembly language uses mnemonics to represent machine code instructions; machine code is the basic binary patterns that instruct the processor to perform various tasks

lap *noun* **(a)** a person's knees, when he is sitting down; *he placed the computer on his lap and keyboarded some orders while sitting in his car* **(b)** overlap of printed colours which prevents any gaps showing

◊ **lapheld computer** *or* **laptop computer** *noun* computer that is light enough to carry but not so small as to fit in a pocket, usually containing a screen, keyboard and disk drive

QUOTE in our summary of seven laphelds we found features to admire in every machine
QUOTE the idea of a hard disk in a lapheld machine which runs on batteries is not brand new
PC Business World

large-scale computer *noun* high-powered (large word size) computer system that can access high capacity memory and backing storage devices as well as multiple users

◊ **large-scale integration (LSI)** *noun* integrated circuit with 500 to 10,000 components

laser *noun* = LIGHT AMPLIFICATION BY STIMULATED EMISSION OF RADIATION device that produces coherent light of a single wavelength in a narrow beam, by exciting a material so that it emits photons of light; **laser emulsion storage** = digital storage technique using a laser to expose light-sensitive material; **laser printer** = high-resolution computer printer that uses a laser source to print high-quality dot matrix character patterns on paper (these have a much higher resolution than normal printers, usually 300 dpi)

last in first out (LIFO) *noun* queue system that reads the last item stored, first;

this computer stack uses a last in first out data retrieval method; compare with FIRST IN FIRST OUT

latch *verb* to set an output state; *the output latched high until we reset the computer*

latency *noun* time delay between the moment when an instruction is given to a computer and the execution of the instruction *or* return of a result (such as the delay between a request for data and the data being transferred from memory)

launch 1 *noun* putting a new product on the market; *the launch of the new PC has been put back six months; the launch date for the network will be September* **2** *verb* to put a new product on the market; *the new PC was launched at the Computer Show; launching costs for the computer range were calculated at $250,000*

layer *noun* **(a)** ISO/OSI standards defining the stages a message has to pass through when being transmitted from one computer to another over a local area network; **application layer** = the program that requests a transmission; **data link layer** = layer that sends packets of data to the next link, and deals with error correction; **network layer** = layer that decides on the routes to be used, the costs, etc.; **physical layer** = layer that defines the rules for bit rate, power, medium for transmission, etc.; **presentation layer** = section that agrees on format, codes and request for start/end of a connection; **session layer** = layer that makes the connection/disconnection between a transmitter and receiver; **transport layer** = layer that checks and controls the quality of the connection

◊ **layered** *adjective* consisting of layers; *the kernel has a layered structure according to user priority*

◊ **layout** *noun* rules governing the data input and output from a computer

LCD = LIQUID CRYSTAL DISPLAY liquid crystal that turns black when a voltage is applied, used in many watches, calculators and other small digital displays

QUOTE LCD screens can run for long periods on ordinary or rechargeable batteries
Micro Decision

LCP = LINK CONTROL PROCEDURE rules defining the transmission of data over a channel

lead *noun* **(a)** electrical conducting wire

◊ **lead in page** *noun* videotext page that directs the user to other pages of interest

◊ **leader** *noun* section of magnetic tape that contains no signal, used at the beginning of the reel for identification and to aid the tape machine to pick up the tape; **leader record** = initial record containing information (such as titles, format, etc.) about following records in a file

◊ **leading edge** *noun* first edge of a punched card that enters the card reader

◊ **leading zero** *noun* zero digit used to pad out the beginning of a stored number

leaf *noun* final node in a tree structure

leap-frog test *noun* memory location test, in which a program skips from one location to another random location, writing data then reading and comparing for faults, until all locations have been tested; **crippled leap-frog test** = standard leap-frog test that uses a single memory location rather than a changing location

lease 1 *noun* written contract for letting *or* renting a piece of equipment for a period against payment of a fee **2** *verb* **(a)** to let *or* rent equipment for a period; *the company has a policy of only using leased equipment;* **leased line** = communications channel, such as a telephone line, which is rented for the exclusive use of the subscriber **(b)** to use equipment for a time and pay a fee; *the company leases all its computers*

least cost design *noun* best money-saving use of space *or* components; *the budget is only £1000, we need the least cost design for the new circuit*

◊ **least recently used algorithm** *noun* algorithm which finds the page of memory that was last accessed before any other, and erases it to make room for another page

◊ **least significant digit (LSD)** *noun* digit which occupies the right hand position in a number and so carries the least power (equal to the number radix raised to zero = 1); **least significant bit (LSB)** = binary digit occupying the right hand position of a word and carrying the least power of two in the word (usually equal to two raised to zero = 1)

leaving files open *phrase* meaning that a file has not been closed *or* does not contain an end of text marker (this will result in the loss of data since the text will not have been saved)

LED = LIGHT EMITTING DIODE semiconductor diode that emits light when a current is applied

COMMENT: LED displays are used to display small amounts of information, as in pocket calculators, watches, indicators, etc.

left justification *noun* **(a)** shifting a binary number to the left hand end of the word containing it **(b)** making the left hand margin of the text even

◊ **left justify** *verb* printing command that makes the left hand margin of the text even

◊ **left shift** *noun* left arithmetic shift by one bit of data in a word, a binary number is doubled for each left shift

leg *noun* one possible path through a routine

legal *adjective* statement or instruction that is acceptable within language syntax rules

length *noun* how long something is; the number of data items in a variable *or* list; **block length** = number of records *or* fields *or* characters in a block of data; **buffer length** = number of data item that can be stored in a buffer while waiting for the processor to attend to them; **field length** = number of characters stored in a field; **file length** = number of characters *or* bytes in a stored file; **length of filename** = number of characters allowed for identification of a file; **line length** = number of characters which can be displayed horizontally on one line of a display (CRT displays often use an 80 character line length); **record length** = total number of characters contained in the various fields within a stored record; **register length** = number of bits that make up a register

letter *noun* piece of writing sent from one person to another *or* from a company to another, to give information, to send an instructions, etc.; **form letter** *or* **standard letter** = letter sent to several addressees by name without any change to the text

◊ **letter-quality (LQ) printing** *noun* feature of some dot-matrix printers to provide characters of the same quality as a typewriter by using dots which are very close together; **near-letter-quality (NLQ) printing** = printing by a dot-matrix printer that provides higher quality type, which is almost as good as a typewriter, by decreasing the space between the dots

level *noun* quantity of bits that make up a digital transmitted signal; **quaternary level quantization** = use of four bits of data in an A/D conversion process

lexical analysis *noun* stage in program translation when the compiling *or* translating software replaces program keywords with machine code instructions

LF = LINE FEED

library *noun* (a) collection of files *or* documents *or* books *or* records, etc., which can be consulted *or* borrowed by the public, usually kept in a public place (b) collection of programs *or* books belonging to a person; *he has a large library of computer games;* **library function** = software routine that a user can insert into his program to provide the function with no effort; **library program** = (i) number of specially written *or* relevant software routines, which a user can insert into his own program, saving time and effort; (ii) group of functions which a computer needs to refer to often, but which are not stored in main memory; *the square root function is already in the library program;* **macro library** = number of useful, independent routines that can be incorporated into any program to ease program writing; **library routine** = prewritten routine that can be inserted into a main program and called up when required; **library subroutine** = tried and tested subroutine stored in a library, and which can be inserted into a user's program when required; **library track** = one track on a magnetic disk *or* tape used to store information about the contents (such as titles, format and index data)

licence *noun* permission given by one manufacturer to another manufacturer to make copies of his products against payment of a fee; *the software is manufactured in this country under licence*

LIFO = LAST IN FIRST OUT queue system that reads the last item stored, first; *this computer stack uses a LIFO data retrieval method; see also* FIFO

lifter *noun* mechanical device that lifts magnetic tape away from the heads when rewinding the tape

light *noun* perception of brightness due to electromagnetic effects in the frequency range 400 - 750 nm, which allows a person to see; *the VDU should not be placed under a bright light;* **light emitting diode (LED)** = semiconductor diode that emits light when a current is applied (used in calculators and clock displays and as indicators); **light pen** = computer accessory in the shape of a pen that contains a light-sensitive device that can detect pixels on a video screen (often used with suitable software to draw graphics on a screen *or* position a cursor)
◊ **lightweight** *adjective* which is not heavy; *a lightweight computer which can easily fit into a suitcase*

limits *noun* predefined maximum ranges for numbers in a computer
◊ **limited distance modem** *noun* data transmission device with a very short range that sends pure digital data rather than on a modulated carrier

line *noun* (a) physical connection for data transmission (such as a cable between parts of a system *or* a telephone wire); **access line** = permanently connected communications line between a terminal and a DSE; **fast line** = special communications link that allows data to be transmitted at 48K *or* 96K baud; **line communications** = signal transmission using a cable link *or* telegraph wire; **line control** = special codes used to control a communications channel; **line driver** = high power circuit and amplifier used to send signals over a long distance line without too much loss of signal; **line level** = amplitude of a signal transmitted over a cable; **line speed** = rate at which data is sent along a line; **line switching** = communications line and circuit established on demand and held until no longer required (b) single long thin mark drawn by a pen *or* printed on a surface; *the printer has difficulty in reproducing very fine lines* (c) one trace by the electron picture beam on a screen *or* monitor; **line flyback** = electron beam returning from the end of one line to the beginning of the next; **line frequency** = number of picture lines that are scanned per second (d) row of characters (printed on a page *or* displayed on a computer screen *or* printer); *each page has 52 lines of text; several lines of manuscript seem to have been missed by the keyboarder; can we insert an extra line of spacing between the paragraphs?;* **command**

line = program line that contains a command; **information line** = line running across the screen which gives the user information about the program being executed *or* the file being edited; **line editor** = piece of software that allows the operator to modify one line of text from a file at a time; **line ending** = character which shows that a line has ended (instructed by pressing the carriage return key); **line feed (LF)** = control on a printer *or* computer terminal that moves the cursor down by one line; **line length** = number of characters contained in a displayed line (on a computer screen this is normally 80 characters, on a printer often 132 characters); **line spacing** = distance between two rows of characters; **lines per minute (LPM)** = number of lines printed by a line printer per minute **(e)** series of characters received as a single input by a computer; **line input** = command to receive all characters including punctuation entered up to a carriage return code **(f)** one row of commands *or* arguments in a computer program; **line number** = number that refers to a line of program code in a computer program

COMMENT: the programming language will sort out the program into order according to line number

QUOTE straight lines are drawn by clicking the points on the screen where you would like the line to start and finish
Personal Computer World
QUOTE while pixel editing is handy for line art, most desktop scanners have trouble producing the shades of grey or half-tones found in black and white photography
Publish

◇ **line printer** *noun* device for printing draft quality information at high speeds, typical output is 200 to 3000 lines per minute

COMMENT: line printers print a whole line at a time, running from right to left and left to right, and are usually dot matrix printers with not very high quality print. Compare page printers, which print a whole page at a time

linear *adjective* **linear list** = list that has no free space for new records within its structure; **linear program** = computer program that contains no loops *or* branches; **linear programming** = method of mathematically breaking down a problem so that it can be solved by computer; **linear search** = search method which compares each item in a list with the search key until the correct entry is found (starting with the first item and working sequentially towards the end)

link 1 *noun* **(a)** communications path *or* channel between two components *or* devices; *to transmit faster, you can use the direct link with the mainframe;* **data link layer** = ISO/OSI layer that sends packets of data to the next link, and deals with error correction; **link control procedure (LCP)** = rules defining the transmission of data over a channel **(b)** software routine that allows data transfer between incompatible programs; **link trials** = testing computer programs so as to see if each module works in conjunction with the others **2** *verb* to join *or* interface two pieces of software *or* hardware; *the two computers are linked;* **link files** = command to merge together a list of separate files; **linked list** = list of data where each entry carries the address of the next consecutive entry; **linked subroutine** = number of computer instructions in a program that can be called at any time, with control being returned on completion to the next instruction in the main program

◇ **linkage** *noun* act of linking two things; **linkage editing** = combining separate programs together, and standardizing the calls *or* references within them; **linkage software** = special software which links sections of program code with any library routines *or* other code; *graphics and text are joined without linkage software*

◇ **linking** *noun* merging of a number of small programs together to enable them to run as one unit; **linking loader** = short software routine that merges sections of programs to allow them to be run as one

LIPS = LOGICAL INFERENCES PER SECOND standard for the measurement of processing power of an inference engine

COMMENT: one inference often requires thousands of computer instructions

liquid crystal display (LCD) *noun* liquid crystals that turn black when a voltage is applied, used in many watch, calculator and digital displays

COMMENT: LCDs do not generate light and so cannot be seen in the dark without an external light source (as opposed to LEDs)

LISP = LIST PROCESSING high-level language used mainly in processing lists of instructions *or* data and in artificial intelligence work

list 1 *noun* series of ordered items of data; **chained list** = list in which each element contains data and an address to the next element in the list; **linear list** = list that has no free space for new records within its structure; **linked list** = list of data where each entry carries the address of the next consecutive entry; **pushdown list** = temporary storage, in a LIFO format, for a list of items of data; **reference list** = list of routines *or* instructions and their location within a program; **stop list** = list of words that are not to be used *or* are not significant for a file search; **list processing** = (i) computation of a series of items of data such as adding *or* deleting *or* sorting *or* updating entries; (ii) LISP *or* a high-level language used mainly in processing lists of instructions *or* data, and in artificial intelligence work **2** *verb* to print *or* display certain items of information; **to list a program** = to display a program line by line in correct order

◊ **listing** *noun* program lines printed *or* displayed in an ordered way; **computer listing** = printout of a list of items, taken from data stored in a computer; **a program listing** = a printed copy of the lines of a program; **listing paper** = continuous stationery

literal *noun* **(a)** (operand) computer instruction that contains the actual number *or* address to be used, rather than a label *or* its location **(b)** printing error when one character is replaced by another *or* when two characters are transposed

literate *adjective* (person) who can read; **computer-literate** = able to understand expressions relating to computers and how to use a computer

◊ **literacy** *noun* being able to read; **computer literacy** = understanding the basic principles of computers, related expressions and being able to use computers for programming *or* applications

liveware *noun* the operators and users of a computer system (as opposed to the hardware and software)

LLL = LOW-LEVEL LANGUAGE

load 1 *noun* job *or* piece of work to be done; **load sharing** = use of more than one computer in a network to even out the work load on each processor; **work load** = number of tasks that a machine has to complete **2** *verb* **(a)** to transfer a file *or* program from disk *or* tape to main memory; **scatter load** = loading sequential data into various non-continuous locations in memory; **load and run** *or* **load and go** = computer program that is loaded into main memory and then starts to execute itself automatically **(b)** to put a disk *or* tape into a computer, so that it can be run

◊ **loading** *noun* action of transferring a file *or* program from disk to memory; *loading can be a long process*

◊ **load point** *noun* start of a recording section in a reel of magnetic tape

◊ **loader** *noun* program which loads another file *or* program into computer memory; **absolute loader** = program that loads a section of code into main memory; *compare* BOOTSTRAP; **binary loader** = short section of program code that allows programs in binary form (such as object code from a linker *or* assembler) to be loaded into memory; **card loader** = short program that transfers data from a punched card into main memory; **initial program loader (IPL)** = short routine that loads the first section of a program, after which it continues the loading process itself

QUOTE this windowing system is particularly handy when you want to load or save a file or change directories

Byte

local *adjective & noun* **(a)** (variable *or* argument) that is only used in a certain section of a computer program *or* structure; **local declaration** = assignment of a variable that is only valid in a section of a computer program *or* structure; **local memory** = high speed RAM that is used instead of a hardware device to store bit streams *or* patterns; **local variable** = variable which can only be accessed by certain routines in a certain section of a computer program; *compare* GLOBAL VARIABLE **(b)** referring to a system with limited access; *(of a terminal)* **on local** = not working with a CPU, but being used as a stand-alone terminal; **local mode** = operating state of a computer terminal that does not receive messages

◊ **local area network (LAN** *or* **lan)** *noun* network where various terminals and equipment are all a short distance from one another (at a maximum distance of about 500m, for example in the same building) and can be interconnected by cables; *compare with* WAN; **local area network server** = dedicated computer and backing storage facility used by terminals and operators of a LAN

COMMENT: LANs use cables *or* optical fibre links; WANs use modems, radio and other long distance transmission methods

locate *verb* (i) to place *or* to set; (ii) to find; *the computer is located in the main office building; have you managed to locate the programming fault?*

◊ **location** *noun* number *or* absolute address which specifies the point in memory where a data word can be found and accessed

lock *verb* to prevent access to a system *or* file; **locking a file** = the action of preventing any further writing to a file; **to lock onto** = to synchronize an internal clock with a received signal

◊ **lockout** *noun* preventing a user sending messages over a network by continuously transmitting data

◊ **lock up** *noun* faulty operating state of computer that cannot be recovered from without switching off the power

COMMENT: this can be caused by an infinite program loop *or* a deadly embrace

log 1 *noun* record of computer processing operations **2** *verb* to record a series of actions; **to log in** *or* **log on** = to enter various identification data, such as a password, usually by means of a terminal, to the central computer before accessing a program *or* data (used as a means of making sure that only authorized users can access the computer system); **automatic log on** = telephone number, password and user number transmitted when requested by a remote system to automate logon; **to log off** *or* **log out** = to enter a symbol *or* instruction at the end of a computing session to close all files and break the channel between the user's terminal and the main computer NOTE: the verbs can be spelled **log on, log-on,** or **logon; log off, log-off** or **logoff**

◊ **logging** *noun* input of data into a system; **logging on** *or* **logging off** = process of opening *or* ending operations with a system; **error logging** = recording errors met; *features of the program include error logging*

logic *noun* (a) science which deals with thought and reasoning; **formal logic** = treatment of form and structure, ignoring content (b) mathematical treatment of formal logic operations such as AND, OR, etc., and their transformation into various circuits; *see also* BOOLEAN ALGEBRA; **logic map** graphical representation of states and conditions in a logic circuit; **logic state** = one out of two possible levels in a digital circuit, the levels being 1 and 0 or TRUE and FALSE; **logic state analyzer** = test equipment that displays the logic states of a number of components *or* circuits; **logic symbol** = graphical symbol used to represent a type of logic function (c) system for deducing results from binary data; **logic bomb** = section of code that performs various unpleasant functions such as system crash when a number of conditions are true (the logic bomb is installed by unpleasant hackers *or* very annoyed programmers); **logic level** = voltage used to represent a particular logic state (this is often five volts for a one and zero volts for a zero); **logic operation** = computer operation *or* procedure in which a decision is made (d) components of a computer *or* digital system; **sequential logic** = logic circuit whose output depends on the logic state of the previous inputs; **logic card** *or* **logic board** = printed circuit board containing binary logic gates rather than analog components; **logic circuit** = electronic circuit made up of various logical gates such as AND, OR and EXOR; **logic element** = gate *or* combination of logic gates; **logic flowchart** = graphical representation of logic elements, steps and decisions and the interconnections; **logic gate** = electronic circuit that applies a logical operator to an input signal and produces an output; *see also* GATE

◊ **logical** *adjective* that uses logic in its operation; *logical reasoning can be simulated by an artificial intelligence machine;* **logical channel** = electronic circuit between a terminal and a network node in a packet switching system; **logical chart** = graphical representation of logic elements, steps and decisions and their interconnections; **logical comparison** = function to see if two logic signals are the same; **logical decision** = one of two paths chosen as a result of one of two possible answers to a question; **logical error** = fault in a program design causing incorrect branching *or* operations; **logical expression** = function made up from a series of logical operators such as AND and OR; **logical high** = equal to logic true state *or* 1; **logical low** = equal to logic false state *or* 0; **logical operator** = character *or* word that describes the logical action it will perform (the most common logical operators are AND, NOT, and OR); **logical record** = unit of information ready for processing that is not necessarily the same as the original data item in storage, which might contain control data, etc.; **logical shift** = data movement to the left or right in a word, the bits falling outside the word boundary are discarded, the free positions are filled with zeros; *compare with* ARITHMETIC SHIFT

◊ **logic-seeking** *adjective* printer that can print the required information with the minimum head movement, detecting ends of lines, justification commands, etc.

> QUOTE a reduction in the number of logic gates leads to faster operation and lower silicon costs
> QUOTE the removal of complex but infrequently used logic makes the core of the processor simpler and faster, so simple operations execute faster
>
> *Electronics & Power*

login = LOGGING IN

LOGO *noun* high-level programming language used mainly for educational purposes, with graphical commands that are easy to use

◊ **logo** *noun* special printed set of characters or symbols used to identify a company or product

logoff = LOG OFF, LOGGING OFF
◊ **logon** = LOG ON, LOGGING ON
◊ **logout** = LOGGING OUT

long haul network *noun* communications network between distant computers that usually uses the public telephone system

look ahead *noun* action by some CPUs to fetch instructions and examine them before they are executed (to speed up operations); **carry look ahead** = high speed adder that can predict if a carry will be generated by a sum and add it in, removing the delay found in a ripple through carry adder

◊ **binary look-up** *noun* fast search method for use on ordered lists of data; the search key is compared with the data in the middle of the list and one half is discarded, this is repeated with remaining half until only one data item remains

◊ **look-up table** or **LUT** *noun* collection of stored results that can be accessed very rapidly by a program without the need to calculate each result whenever needed; *lookup tables are preprogrammed then used in processing so saving calculations for each result required*

> QUOTE a lookup table changes a pixel's value based on the values in a table
>
> *Byte*

loop 1 *noun* procedure or series of instructions in a computer program that are performed again and again until a test shows that a specific condition has been met or until the program is completed; **closed loop** = computer control operation in which data is fed back from the output of the controlled device to the controlling loop; **endless loop** or **infinite loop** = loop which has no end, except when the program is stopped; **holding loop** = section of program that loops until it is broken by some action, most often used when waiting for a response from the keyboard or a device; **modification loop** = instructions within a loop that change other instructions or data within a program; **nested loop** = loop contained inside another; **loop body** = main section of instructions within a loop that carry out the primary function rather than being used to enter or leave or setup the loop; **loop check** = check that data has been correctly transmitted down a line by returning the data to the transmitter; **loop counter** = register that contains the number of times a loop has been repeated; **loop program** = sequence of instructions that are repeated until a condition is met **2** *verb* to make a piece of wire or tape into a circle; **looping program** = computer program that runs continuously

lose *verb* not to have something any more; *all the current files were lost when the system crashed and we had no backup copies*

low-priority work *noun* task which is not particularly important; **low-resolution graphics** or **low-res graphics** = ability to display character-sized graphic blocks or preset shapes on a screen rather than using individual pixels; *compare* HIGH-RESOLUTION; **low speed communications** = data transmission at less than 2400 bits per second

◊ **lower case** *noun* small characters (such as a, b, c, as opposed to upper case A, B, C)

◊ **low-level language (LLL)** *noun* programming language similar to assembler and in which each instruction has a single equivalent machine code instruction (the language is particular to one system or computer); *see also* HIGH-LEVEL LANGUAGE

◊ **low-order digit** *noun* digit in the position within a number that represents the lowest weighting of the number base;

the number 234156 has a low-order digit of 6

◇ **low-res** *see* LOW-RESOLUTION

LPM = LINES PER MINUTE

LQ = LETTER QUALITY

LSB = LEAST SIGNIFICANT BIT binary digit occupying the right hand position of a word and carrying the least power of two in the word, usually equal to two raised to zero = 1

LSD = LEAST SIGNIFICANT DIGIT digit which occupies the right hand position in a number and so carries least power (equal to the number radix raised to zero = 1)

LSI = LARGE SCALE INTEGRATION system with between 500 and 10,000 circuits on a single IC

luggable *noun* personal computer that is just about portable and usually will not run off batteries (it is much heavier and less compact than a lap-top or true transportable machine)

LUT LOOK-UP TABLE

QUOTE an image processing system can have three LUTs that map the image memory to the display device

Byte

Mm

m *prefix* = MILLI one thousandth

M *prefix* = MEGA **(a)** one million; **Mbps** = MEGA BITS PER SECOND number of million bits transmitted every second; **MFLOPS** = MEGA FLOATING POINT OPERATIONS PER SECOND measure of computing power and speed, equal to one million floating point operations per second **(b)** symbol for 1,048,576, used only in computer and electronic related applications, equal to 2^{20}; **Mbyte (MB)** = measurement of mass storage equal to 1,048,576 bytes; *the latest model has a 30Mbyte hard disk*

MAC = MESSAGE AUTHENTICATION CODE special code transmitted at the same time as a message as proof of its authenticity

machine *noun* **(a)** number of separate moving parts *or* components, acting together to carry out a process **(b)** computer *or* system *or* processor made of various components connected together to provide a function *or* perform a task; **clean machine** = computer that contains only the minimum of ROM based code to boot its system from disk, any languages required must be loaded separately; **source machine** = computer which can compile source code; **virtual machine** = simulated machine and its operations; **machine address** = number *or* absolute address which specifies the point in memory where a data word can be found and accessed; **machine check** = fault caused by equipment failure; **machine code** *or* **machine language** = programming language that consists of commands in binary code that can be directly understood by the central processing unit without the need for translation; **machine code format** = a machine code instruction is usually made up of 1,2 or 3 bytes for operand, data and address; **machine code instruction** = instruction that directly controls the CPU and is recognized without the need for translation; **machine cycle** = minimum period of time taken by the CPU for the execution of an instruction; **machine dependent** = not standardized *or* which cannot be used on hardware *or* software from a different manufacturer without modifications; **machine equation** = formula which an analog computer has been programmed to solve; **machine independent** = (computer software) that can be run on any computer system; **machine independent language** = programming language that can be translated and executed on any computer that has a suitable compiler; **machine instruction** = an instruction which can be recognized by a machine and is part of its limited set of commands; **machine intelligence** = the design of computer programs and devices that attempt to imitate human intelligence and decision-making functions, providing basic reasoning and other human characteristics; **machine intimate** = software that operates and interacts closely with the hardware in a system; **machine language** = (i) the way in which machine code is written; (ii) MACHINE CODE; **machine language compile** = to generate a machine code program from a HLL program by translating and assembling each HLL instruction; **machine language programming** = slowest and most complex method of programming a CPU, but the fastest in execution, achieved by entering directly into RAM or ROM the binary representation for the machine code instructions to be carried out (rather than using an assembler with assembly language programs *or* a compiler with HLL programs); **machine-readable** = (commands *or* data) stored on a medium that can be directly input to the computer; *the disk stores data in machine-readable form;* **machine run** = action of processing instructions in a program by a computer; **machine translation** = computer system that is used to translate text and commands from one language and syntax to another; **machine word** = number of bits of data operated on simultaneously by a CPU in one machine cycle, often 8, 16 or 32 bits

macro- *prefix* very large *or* applying to the whole system

◊ **macro** *noun* program routine *or* block of instructions identified by a single word *or* label; **macro assembler** *or* **assembly program** = assembler program that is able to decode macro instructions; **macro call** = use of a label in an assembly language program to indicate to an assembler that the macro routine is to be inserted at that point; **macro code** *or* **macro command** *or* **macro instruction** = one word that is used to represent a number of instructions, simplifying program writing; **macro definition** = description (in a program *or* to the operating system) of the structure, function and instructions that make up a macro operation; **macro expansion** = process in which a macro call is replaced with the instructions in the macro; **macro flowchart** = graphical representation of the logical steps, stages and actions within a routine; **macro language** = programming language that allows the programmer to define and use macro instructions; **macro programming** = writing a program using macro instructions *or* defining macro instructions

◊ **macroelement** *noun* number of data items treated as one element

◊ **macroinstruction** *noun* one programming instruction that refers to a number of instructions within a routine *or* macro

magazine *noun* number of pages in a videotext system

magnet *noun* something that produces a magnetic field

◊ **magnetic** *adjective* which has a magnetic field associated with it; **magnetic bubble memory** = method of storing large amounts of binary data as small magnetized areas in the medium (made of certain pure materials); **magnetic card** = plastic card with a strip of magnetic recording material on its surface, allowing data to be stored (used in automatic cash dispensers); **magnetic card reader** *or* **magnetic strip reader** = machine that can read data stored on a magnetic card; **magnetic cartridge** *or* **cassette** = small box containing a reel of magnetic tape and a pick up reel; **magnetic cell** = small piece of material whose magnetic field can be altered to represent the two states of binary data; **magnetic core** = early main memory system for storing data in the first types of computer, each bit of data was stored in a magnetic cell; **magnetic disk** = flat circular piece of material coated with a substance, allowing signals and data to be stored magnetically; *see also* FLOPPY DISK, HARD DISK; **magnetic disk unit** = computer peripheral made up of a disk drive and necessary control electronics; **magnetic drum** = computer data storage peripheral that uses a coated cylinder to store data magnetically(not often used now); **magnetic encoding** = storage of (binary) data signals on a magnetic medium; **magnetic field** = description of the polarity and strength of magnetic effects at a point; **magnetic flux** = measure of magnetic field strength per unit area; **magnetic head** = electromagnetic component that converts electrical signals into a magnetic field, allowing them to be stored on a magnetic medium; **magnetic ink** = printing ink that contains a magnetic material, used in some character recognition systems; **magnetic ink character recognition (MICR)** = system that identifies characters by sensing the magnetic ink patterns (as used on bank cheques); **magnetic master** = original version of a recorded tape *or* disk; **magnetic material** *or* **medium** = substance that will retain a magnetic flux pattern after a magnetic field is removed; **magnetic media** = magnetic materials used to store signals, such as disk, tape, etc.; **magnetic memory** *or* **store** = storage that uses a medium that can store data bits as magnetic field changes; **magnetic recording** = transferring an electrical signal onto a moving magnetic tape *or* disk by means of an magnetic field generated by a magnetic head; **magnetic strip** = layer of magnetic material on the surface of a plastic card, used for recording data; **magnetic transfer** = copy signals stored on one type of magnetic medium to another

◊ **magnetic tape** *noun* narrow length of thin plastic coated with a magnetic material used to store signals magnetically; **magnetic tape cartridge** *or* **cassette** = small box containing a reel of magnetic tape and a pick up reel, used in a cassette player *or* tape drive; **magnetic tape encoder** = device that directly writes data entered at a keyboard onto magnetic tape; **magnetic tape reader** = machine that can read signals stored on magnetic tape and convert them to an electrical form that can be understood by a computer; **magnetic tape recorder** = device with a magnetic head, motor and circuitry to allow electrical signals to be recorded onto *or* played back from a magnetic tape; **magnetic tape transport** = computer-controlled magnetic tape drive mechanism

◊ **magnetize** *verb* to convert a material *or* object into a magnet

COMMENT: magnetic tape is available on spools of between 200 and 800 metres. The tape is magnetized by the read/write head. Tape is a storage medium which only allows serial access, that is, all the tape has to be read until the required location is found (as opposed to disk storage, which can be accessed randomly)

mag tape *noun informal* = MAGNETIC TAPE

magnitude *noun* level *or* strength of a signal *or* variable

mail 1 *noun* (a) system of sending letters and parcels from one place to another (b) letters sent *or* received (c) electronic messages to and from users of a bulletin board *or* network; **electronic mail** *or* **email** *or* **e-mail** = messages sent between users of a bulletin board *or* interconnecting network **2** *verb* to send something by post; *to mail a letter; we mailed our order last Wednesday*

◇ **mailbox** *or* **mail box** *noun* electronic storage space with an address in which a user's incoming messages are stored

◇ **mailing** *noun* sending something using the post

◇ **mail-merge** *noun* word-processing program which allows a standard form letter to be printed out to a series of different names and addresses

main *adjective* most important; **main clock** = clock signal that synchronizes all the components in a system; **main entry** = entry in a catalogue under which is contained the most important information about the document; **main index** = more general index that directs the user gradually to more specific index areas; **main memory** *or* **main storage** = fast access RAM whose locations can be directly and immediately addressed by the CPU; *the 16-bit system includes up to 3Mb of main memory*; **main routine** = section of instructions that make up the main part of a program (a program often consists of a main routine and several subroutines, which are called from the main routine)

◇ **mainframe (computer)** *noun* large-scale high power computer system that can handle high capacity memory and backing storage devices as well as a number of operators simultaneously; **mainframe access** = using microcomputers to access a mainframe computer

mains electricity *noun* normal domestic electricity supply to consumers

COMMENT: in UK this is 240 volts at 50Hz; in the USA, it is 120 volts at 60Hz

maintain *verb* to ensure a system is in good condition and functioning correctly; **well maintained** = well looked after

◇ **maintainability** *noun* the ability to have repairs carried out quickly and efficiently if a failure occurs

◇ **maintenance** *noun* (i) keeping a machine in good working condition; (ii) tasks carried out in order to keep a system running, such as repairing faults, replacing components, etc.; **file maintenance** = process of updating a file by changing *or* adding *or* deleting entries; **preventive maintenance** = regular inspection and cleaning of a system to prevent faults occurring; **maintenance contract** = arrangement with a repair company that provides regular checks and special repair prices in the event of a fault; **maintenance routine** = software diagnostic tool used by an engineer during preventative maintenance operations

major cycle *noun* minimum access time of a mechanical storage device

male connector *noun* plug with conducting pins that can be inserted into a female connector to provide an electrical connection

malfunction 1 *noun* (*of hardware or software*) not working correctly; *the data was lost due to a software malfunction*; **malfunction routine** = software routine used to find and help diagnose the cause of an error *or* fault **2** *verb* not to work properly; *some of the keys on the keyboard have started to malfunction*

◇ **malfunctioning** *noun* not working properly

man machine interface (MMI) *noun* hardware and software designed to make it easier for users to communicate effectively with a machine

manage *verb* to direct *or* to be in charge of

◇ **manageable** *adjective* which can be dealt with easily; *processing problems which are still manageable; the problems are too large to be manageable; data should be split into manageable files*

◇ **management** *noun* directing *or* organizing (work *or* a business); **network management** = organization, planning, running and upkeep of a network

◇ **manager** *noun* (a) user-friendly front end software that allows easy access to operating system commands; **file manager** = section of a disk operating system that allocates disk space to files, keeping track of the file sections (if it has to be split) and their sector addresses; **queue manager** = software which orders tasks waiting to be processed; **records manager** = program which maintains records and can access and process them; **text manager** = facilities that allow text to be written, stored, retrieved, edited and printed (b) head of a department in a company; *a department manager; data processing manager; production manager*

manipulate *verb* to move, edit and change text *or* data; *an image processor that captures, displays and manipulates video images*
◇ **manipulation** *noun* moving *or* editing *or* changing text *or* data; *the high-speed database management program allows the manipulation of very large amounts of data*

mantissa *noun* fractional part of a number; *the mantissa of the number 45.897 is 0.897*

manual 1 *noun* document containing instructions about the operation of a system *or* piece of software; *the manual is included with the system;* **installation manual** = booklet showing how a system should be installed; **instruction manual** = document describing how to use a system *or* software; **user's manual** = booklet showing how a device *or* system should be used 2 *adjective* (work) done by hand; (process) carried out by the operator without the help of a machine; **manual data processing** = sorting and processing information without the help of a computer; **manual entry** *or* **manual input** = act of entering data into a computer, by an operator via a keyboard
◇ **manually** *adverb* done by hand, not automatically; *the paper has to be fed into the printer manually*

map 1 *noun* diagram representing the internal layout of a computer's memory *or* communications regions; **memory map** = diagram indicating the allocation of address ranges to various memory devices, such as RAM, ROM and memory-mapped input/output devices 2 *verb* to retrieve data and display it as a map; **database mapping** = description of the way in which the records and fields in a database are related; **I/O mapping** = method of assigning a special address to each (I/O) port in a microcomputer rather than a memory location; **to map out** = to draw *or* set down the basic way in which something should be done; **memory-mapped (input/output)** = allocation of addresses to a computer's input/output devices to allow them to be accessed as if they are a memory location; *a memory-mapped screen has an address allocated to each pixel allowing direct access to the screen by the CPU; see also* BIT-MAP, BIT-MAPPED

MAR = MEMORY ADDRESS REGISTER register within the CPU that contains the next location to be accessed

marching display *noun* display device that contains a buffer to show the last few characters entered

margin *noun* (a) blank space around a section of printed text; *when typing the contract leave wide margins; the left margin and right margin are the two sections of blank paper on either side of the page;* **to set the margin** = to define the size of a margin (b) extra time *or* space; **safety margin** = time *or* space allowed for something to be safe; **margin of error** = number of mistakes which are accepted in a document *or* in a calculation

mark 1 *noun* (a) sign put on a page to show something (b) transmitted signal that represents a logical one *or* true condition; **mark space** = two-state transmission code using a mark and a space (without a mark) as signals 2 *verb* to put a mark on something; **mark block** = to put a block marker at the beginning and end of a block of text; **mark sense** = to write characters with conductive *or* magnetic ink so that they are then machine readable; **mark sense device** *or* **reader** = device that reads data from special cards containing conductive *or* magnetic marks; **mark sensing card** = preprinted card with spaces for mark sense characters
◇ **marker** *noun* code inserted in a file *or* text to indicate a special section; **block markers** = two markers inserted at the start and finish of a section of data *or* text to indicate a special block which can then be moved *or* deleted *or* copied as a single unit; **field marker** = code used to indicate the end of one field and the start of the next; **word marker** = symbol indicating the start of a word in a variable word length machine

mask 1 *noun* (a) integrated circuit layout that is used to define the pattern to be etched *or* doped onto a slice of semiconductor; *a mask or stencil is used to transfer the transistor design onto silicon* (b) pattern of binary digits used to select various bits from a binary word (a one in the mask retains that bit in the word); **mask bit** = one bit used to select the required bit from a word *or* string; **mask register** = storage location in a computer that contains the pattern of bits used as a mask; **interrupt mask** = data word in a computer that selects which interrupt lines are to be activated **2** *verb* to cover an area of (something) with (something); **masked ROM** = read-only memory device that is programmed during manufacture, by depositing metal onto selected regions dictated by the shape of a mask

◊ **maskable** *adjective* which can be masked; **maskable interrupt** = interrupt which can be activated by using an interrupt mask; **non-maskable interrupt (NMI)** = high priority interrupt signal that cannot be deactivated

◊ **masking** *noun* operation used to select various bits in a word

QUOTE the device features a maskable interrupt feature which reduces CPU overheads
Electronics & Power

mass storage *noun* storage and retrieval of large amounts of data; **mass storage device** = computer backing store device that is able to store large amounts of data; *the hard disk is definitely a mass storage device;* **mass storage system** = data storage system that can hold more than one million million bits of data

master 1 *noun* main *or* most important device *or* person in a system; most up-to-date and correct file; *the master computer controls everything else;* **master card** = first punched card in a pack that provides information about the rest of the pack; **master clock** = timing signal to which all components in a system are synchronized; **master computer** = computer in a multiprocessor system that controls the other processors and allocates jobs, etc.; **master control program (MCP)** = software that controls the operations in a system; **master data** = reference data which is stored in a master file; **master disk** = (i) disk containing all the files for a task; (ii) disk containing the code for a computer's operating system that must be loaded before the system will operate; **master file** = set of all the reference data required for an application, which is updated periodically; **master/master computer system** = system in which each processor is a master, dedicated to one task; **master program file** = magnetic medium which

contains all the programs required for an application; **master/slave computer system** = system with a master controlling computer and a slave that takes commands from the master; **master tape** = magnetic tape which contains all the vital operating system routines, loaded once when the computer is switched on (by the initial program loader); **master terminal** = one terminal in a network that has priority over any other, used by the system manager to set up the system *or* carry out privileged commands **2** *verb* to learn and understand a language *or* process; *we mastered the new word-processor quite quickly; the user-friendly package is easier to master*

match *verb* (a) to search through a database for a similar piece of information (b) to set a register equal to another

material *noun* substance which can be used to make a finished product; *gold is the ideal material for electrical connections*

mathematics *noun* study of the relationship between numbers, their manipulation and organization to (logically) prove facts and theories; *see also* ALGEBRA

◊ **mathematical** *adjective* referring to mathematics; **mathematical model** = representation of a system using mathematical ideas and formulae; **mathematical subroutines** = library routines that carry out standard mathematical functions, such as square root, logarithm, cosine, sine, etc.

◊ **maths** *or US* **math** *informal* = MATHEMATICS; **maths chip** *or* **coprocessor** = dedicated IC that can be added to a system to carry out mathematical functions far more rapidly than a standard CPU, speeding up the execution of a program

matrix *noun* (a) array of numbers *or* data items arranged in rows and columns; **matrix rotation** = swapping the rows with the columns in an array (equal to rotating by 90 degrees) (b) array of connections between logic gates providing a number of possible logical functions; **key matrix** = way in which the keys of a keyboard are arranged as an array of connections (c) pattern of the dots that make up a character on a computer screen *or* dot-matrix *or* laser printer; **matrix printer** *or* **dot-matrix printer** = printer in which the characters are made up by a series of dots printed close together, producing a page line by line; a dot-matrix printer can be used either for printing using a ribbon or for thermal *or* electrostatic printing; **character matrix =** pattern of dots that makes up a displayed character

matter *noun* **(a)** question *or* problem to be discussed **(b)** main section of text on a page as opposed to titles *or* headlines
NOTE: no plural for (b)

maximum *adjective & noun* highest value used *or* which is allowed; **maximum capacity =** greatest amount of data that can be stored; **maximum transmission rate =** greatest amount of data that can be transmitted every second; **maximum users =** greatest number of users that a system can support at any one time

MB *or* **Mb** *or* **Mbyte** = MEGABYTE equal to 1,048,576 bytes of storage, equal to 2^{20} bytes

◇ **Mbps** = MEGA BITS PER SECOND

QUOTE the maximum storage capacity is restricted to 8 Mbytes
Micro Decision

MBR = MEMORY BUFFER REGISTER register in a CPU that temporarily buffers all inputs and outputs

MCP = MASTER CONTROL PROGRAM

MDR = MEMORY DATA REGISTER register in a CPU that holds data before it is processed *or* moved to a memory location

mean 1 *noun & adjective* average value of a set of numbers *or* values; **mean time between failures (MTBF) =** average period of time that a piece of equipment will operate between failures; **mean time to failure (MTF) =** average period of time for which a device will operate (usually continuously) before failing; **mean time to repair =** average period of time required to repair a faulty piece of equipment **2** *verb* to signify something; *the message DISK FULL means that there is no more room on the disk for further data*

measure 1 *noun* **(a)** way of calculating size *or* quantity; **square measure =** area in square feet *or* metres, calculated by multiplying width and length **(b)** total width of a printed line of text **(c)** type of action; **to take measures to prevent something happening =** to act to stop something happening; **safety measures =** actions to make sure that something is safe **2** *verb* to find out the size *or* quantity of something; to be of a certain size *or* quantity

◇ **measurement** *noun* **(a)** measurements = size; *to write down the measurements of a package* **(b)** way of judging something; *performance measurement or measurement of performance is carried out by running a benchmark program*

mechanical *adjective* referring to machines

◇ **mechanism** *noun* piece of machinery; *the printer mechanism is very simple; the drive mechanism appears to be faulty*

media *see* MEDIUM; **magnetic media =** magnetic materials used to store signals, such as disk, tape, etc.

medium 1 *adjective* middle *or* average; *a medium-sized computer system* **2** *noun* storage medium = any physical material that can be used to store data for a computer application; *data storage mediums such as paper tape, magnetic disk, magnetic tape, paper, card and microfiche are available;* data medium = medium which allows data to be stored *or* displayed such as magnetic disk *or* a VDU; **empty medium =** blank but formatted storage medium that is ready to accept data; **magnetic medium** *or* **material =** substance that will retain a magnetic flux pattern after a magnetic field is removed NOTE: plural is **mediums** or **media**

◇ **medium scale integration (MSI)** *noun* integrated circuit with 10 to 500 components

◇ **medium speed** *noun* data communication speed between 2400 and 9600 bits per second

COMMENT: medium speed transmission describes the maximum rate of transfer for a normal voice grade channel

meet *noun* logical function whose output is true if both inputs are true

mega- *prefix* **(a)** meaning one million; **megabits per second (Mbps) =** number of million bits transmitted every second; **megaflops (MFLOPS)** measure of computing power and speed equal to one million floating point instructions per second **(b)** meaning 1,048,576 (equal to 2^{20}) and used only in computing and electronic related applications; **megabit (Mb) =** equal to 1,048,576 bits; **megabyte (MB)** equal to 1,048,576 bytes of storage

QUOTE adding multiple megabytes of memory is a simple matter of plugging memory cards into the internal bus
Byte

member *noun* individual record *or* item in a field

memory *noun* storage space in a computer system *or* medium that is capable of retaining data *or* instructions; **associative memory** = method of data retrieval that uses part of the data rather than an address to locate data; **backing memory** = any data storage medium, such as a magnetic tape *or* floppy disk, that is not the main high speed memory; **bootstrap memory** = permanent memory within a terminal *or* microcomputer, that allows a user to customize the attributes, booting the system and loading programs; **bubble memory** = method of storing large amounts of binary data, as small magnetized areas in the medium (certain pure materials); **cache memory** = section of high-speed memory which stores data that the CPU needs to access quickly; **charge coupled device (CCD) memory** = volatile, low-cost, high-storage capability memory device; **content-addressable memory** = memory that is addressed and accessed by its contents rather than a location; **control memory** = memory which decodes control instructions into microinstructions which operate the computer *or* microcontroller; **core memory** *or* **primary memory** = central fast-access memory which stores the programs and data currently in use; **disk memory** = data stored on magnetic disk, not on tape; **dynamic memory** = random access memory that requires its contents to be updated regularly; **external memory** = memory which is located outside the main computer system confines, but which can be accessed by the CPU; **fast access memory (FAM)** = storage locations that can be read from *or* written to very rapidly; **FIFO memory** *or* **first in first out memory** = memory using a FIFO access scheme; **internal memory** = storage available within and under the direct control of the main computer, such as main memory; **magnetic memory** = storage that uses a medium that can store data bits as magnetic field changes; **main memory** = fast access RAM whose locations can be directly and immediately addressed by a CPU; **nonvolatile memory** = storage medium that retains data even when power has been switched off; **random access memory (RAM)** = memory that allows access to any location in any order without having to access the rest of memory; **read only memory (ROM)** = memory device that has had data written into it at manufacture, which can only be read; **scratchpad memory** = workspace *or* area of high-speed memory that is used for the temporary storage of data currently in use; **serial memory** = storage whose locations can only be accessed in a serial way, locating one item requires a search through every location; *magnetic tape is a high capacity serial memory;* **static memory** = non-volatile memory that does not require refreshing; **virtual memory** = system where the workspace is held in both backing store and memory at the same time; **volatile memory** = memory *or* storage medium which loses data stored in it when its power supply is switched off; **memory access time** = time delay between requesting access to a location and being able to do so; **memory address register (MAR)** = register within the CPU that contains the address of the next location to be accessed; **memory bank** = number of smaller storage devices connected together to form one large area of memory; **memory board** = printed circuit board containing memory chips; **memory buffer register (MBR)** = register in a CPU that temporarily buffers all inputs and outputs; **memory capacity** = number of bits *or* bytes that can be stored within a memory device; **memory cell** = smallest location that can be individually accessed; **memory chip** = electronic component that is able to store binary data; **memory cycle** = period of time from when the CPU reads *or* writes to a location and the action being performed; **memory data register (MDR)** = register in a CPU which holds data before it is processed *or* moved to a memory location; **memory diagnostic** = software routine that checks each memory location in main memory for faults; **memory dump** = printout of all the contents of an area of memory; **memory edit** = to change (selectively) the contents of various memory locations; **memory hierarchy** = the different types (capacity and access time) of memory available in a system; **memory intensive** = software that uses large amounts of RAM or disk storage during run-time, such as programs whose entire code has to be in main memory during execution; **memory management** = software that controls and regulates the flow and position in memory of files and data; **memory map** = diagram indicating the allocation of address ranges to various devices such as RAM, ROM and memory-mapped input/output devices; **memory-mapped** = with addresses allocated to a computer's input *or* output devices to allow them to be accessed as if they were a memory location; *a memory-mapped screen has an address allocated to each pixel, allowing direct access to the screen by the CPU;* **memory-mapped I/O** = an I/O port which can be accessed as if it were a memory location within the CPU's normal address range; **memory page** = one section of main store which is divided into pages, which contains data *or* programs; **memory protect** = feature on most storage systems to prevent the accidental overwriting of data; **memory-resident** = (program) that is held permanently in memory; *the system can bomb if you set up too many memory-resident programs at the same time;* **memory switching system** = system which communicates information, stores it in memory and then transmits it according to instructions; **memory workspace** = amount of extra memory required by a program to store data used during execution

◊ **memorize** *verb* to remember *or* to retain in the memory

QUOTE when a program is loaded into memory, some is used for the code, some for the permanent data, and some is reserved for the stack which grows and shrinks for function calls and local data
Personal Computer World

menu *noun* list of options *or* programs available to the user; **menu-driven software** = program where commands *or* options are selected from a menu by the operator; **menu selection** = choosing commands from a list of options presented to the operator; **main menu** = list of primary options available; **pop-up menu** *or* **pull-down menu** = menu of options that can be displayed at any time, usually overwriting any other text; *the pull-down menu is viewed by clicking over the icon at the top of the screen*

QUOTE when the operator is required to make a choice a menu is displayed
Micro Decision

mercury delay line *noun* (old) method of storing serial data as pulses in a length of mercury, the data was constantly read, regenerated and fed back into the input

merge *verb* to combine two data files, but still retaining an overall order; *the system automatically merges text and illustrations into the document;* **merge sort** = software application in which the sorted files are merged into a new file; *see also* MAIL-MERGE

mesh *noun* any system with two *or* more possible paths at each interconnection; **mesh network** = method of connecting several machines together, where each pair of devices has two *or* more connections

message *noun* (a) information sent from one person to another (b) certain defined amount of information; **message format** =

predetermined rules defining the coding, size and speed of transmitted messages; **message heading** = section of a message that contains routing and destination information; **message routing** = selection of a suitable path between the source and destination of a message in a network; **message slot** = number of bits that can hold a message which circulates around a ring network; **message text** = information that concerns the user at the destination without routing *or* network control data

metabit *noun* extra identifying bit for each data word

◊ **metacompilation** *noun* compiling a program that will compile other programs when executed

◊ **metalanguage** *noun* language which describes a programming language

metal oxide semiconductor (MOS) *noun* production and design method for a certain family of integrated circuits using patterns of metal conductors and oxide deposited onto a semiconductor; **complementary metal oxide semiconductor (CMOS)** = integrated circuit design and construction method, using a pair of complementary p- and n-type transistors

MFLOPS = MEGA FLOATING POINT INSTRUCTIONS PER SECOND

MHz = MEGAHERTZ one million cycles per second

MICR = MAGNETIC INK CHARACTER RECOGNITION system that identifies characters by sensing magnetic ink patterns (as used on bank cheques)

micro *noun* = MICROCOMPUTER

micro- *prefix* (a) meaning one millionth of a unit; **micrometre** = one millionth of a metre; **microsecond** = one millionth of a second (b) meaning very small; **microcassette** = small format audio cassette used mainly in pocket dictating equipment; **microchip** = circuit in which all the active and passive components are formed on one small piece of semiconductor, by means of etching and chemical processes; **microcircuit** = complex integrated circuit; **microcode** = ALU control instructions implemented as hardwired software

microcomputer *or* **micro** *noun* complete small-scale, cheap, low-power computer system based around a microprocessor chip and having limited memory capacity; **microcomputer architecture** = layout and interconnection of a microcomputer's internal hardware; **microcomputer backplane** = main printed circuit board of a system, containing most of the components and connections for expansion boards, etc.; **microcomputer bus** = main data, address and control buses in a microcomputer; **microcomputer development kit** = basic computer based around a new CPU chip that allows hardware and software designers to experiment with the new device; **single-board microcomputer** = microcomputer whose components are all contained on a single printed circuit board

◊ **microcomputing** *noun* referring to microcomputers and their use; *the microcomputing industry*

COMMENT: micros are particularly used as home computers *or* as small office computers

microcontroller *noun* small self-contained microcomputer for use in dedicated control applications; **single-chip microcontroller** = one integrated circuit that contains a CPU, I/O ports, RAM and often a basic programming language

◊ **microcycle** *noun* unit of time (usually a multiple of the system clock period) used to give the execution time of instructions

◊ **microdevice** *noun* very small device, such as a microprocessor

◊ **microelectronics** *noun* design and manufacture of electronic circuits with integrated circuits and chips

◊ **microfloppy** *noun* small size magnetic floppy disk (usually refers to 3.5 inch disks)

◊ **microinstruction** *noun* one hardwired instruction (part of a microcode) that controls the actions of the ALU

◊ **micron** *noun* one millionth of a metre

◊ **microprocessor** *noun* central processing unit elements, often contained on a single integrated circuit chip, which when combined with other memory and I/O chips will make up a microcomputer; **bit-slice microprocessor** = large word size CPU constructed by joining a number of smaller word size blocks; *the bit-slice microprocessor uses four 4-bit processors to make a 16-bit word processor;* **microprocessor addressing capabilities** = highest address that a CPU can directly address, without special features (this depends on the address word size - the bigger the word the greater the addressing capacity); **microprocessor architecture** = layout of the basic parts within a CPU (I/O, ALU, etc.); **microprocessor chip** =

integrated circuit that contains all the elements of a central processing unit, connected with other memory and I/O chips to make a microcomputer; **microprocessor unit (MPU)** = unit containing the main elements of a microprocessor

◊ **microprogram** *noun* series of microinstructions; **microprogram assembly language** = each assembly language instruction of a computer is carried out by a microprogram; **microprogram counter** = register that stores the address of the next microinstruction to be carried out (the microprogram counter is the same as the memory address register); **microprogram instruction set** = complete set of basic microinstructions available in a CPU; **microprogram store** = storage device used to hold a microprogram

◊ **microprogramming** *noun* writing microcode using microinstructions

◊ **microsecond** *noun* one millionth of a second

◊ **microsequence** *noun* series of microinstructions

◊ **microwriter** *noun* portable keyboard and display, used for keyboarding when travelling

mid-user *noun* operator who retrieves relevant information from a database for a customer *or* end user

middleware *noun* system software that has been customized by a dealer for a particular user

migration *noun* **data migration** = moving data between a high priority or on-line device to a low-priority or off-line device

milk disk *noun* disk used to transfer data from a small machine onto a larger computer, which provides greater processing power

◊ **milking machine** *noun* portable machine which can accept data from different machines, then transfer it to another larger computer

milli- *prefix* meaning one thousandth; **milliampere** *or* **mA** = electrical current measure equal to one thousandth of an ampere; **millisecond** *or* **mS** = one thousandth of a second

MIMD = MULTIPLE INSTRUCTION STREAM - MULTIPLE DATA STREAM architecture of a parallel processor that uses a number of ALUs and memory devices in parallel to provide high speed processing

mini- *prefix* meaning small; **miniaturization** = making something very small; **minidisk** = magnetic disk smaller than the 5.25 inch standard, usually 3.5 inch; **minifloppy** = magnetic disk (usually refers to the 5.25 inch standard); *(slang)* **miniwinny** = small Winchester hard disk

minicomputer *or* **mini** *noun* small computer, with a greater range of instructions and processing power than a microcomputer, but not able to compete with the speed *or* data handling capacity of a mainframe computer

minimal latency coding *see* MINIMUM ACCESS CODE

◊ **minimal tree** *noun* tree whose nodes are organized in the optimum way, providing maximum efficiency

minimum *noun* the smallest amount of something; **minimum access code** *or* **minimum delay code** = coding system that provides the fastest access and retrieval time for stored data items

◊ **minimize** *verb* to make as small as possible; *we minimized costs by cutting down the number of components*

minmax *noun* method used in artificial intelligence to solve problems

minuend *noun* number from which another is subtracted

minus *or* **minus sign** *noun* printed *or* written sign (like a small dash) to indicate subtraction *or* to show a negative value

MIPS = MILLION INSTRUCTIONS PER SECOND measure of computing power of a computer

mirror *verb* to create an identical copy

QUOTE disks are also mirrored so that the system can continue to run in the event of a disk crash
QUOTE mirroring of the database is handled automatically by systems software
Computer News

MIS = MANAGEMENT INFORMATION SYSTEM

MISD = MULTIPLE INSTRUCTION STREAM - SINGLE DATA STREAM architecture of a parallel computer that has a single ALU and data bus with a number of control units

MMI = MAN MACHINE INTERFACE hardware and software designed to make it easier for users to communicate effectively with a machine

mnemonic *noun* shortened form of a word *or* function that is helpful as a reminder (such as INCA for increment register A); **assembler mnemonics** *or* **mnemonic operation codes** = standard word abbreviations used when writing a program for a particular CPU in assembly language (such as LDA for load register A)

mock-up *noun* model of a new product for testing *or* to show to possible customers

mode *noun* way of doing something; method of operating a computer; *when you want to type in text, press this function key which will put the terminal in its alphanumeric mode;* **burst mode** = data transmission using intermittent bursts of data; **byte mode** = data transmitted one byte at a time; **control mode** = state of a device in which control signals can be received to select options *or* functions; **deferred mode** = entering a command as a program line, then executing the program; **direct mode** = typing in a command which is executed once carriage return has been pressed; **execute mode** = command entered in direct mode to start a program run; **form mode** = display method on a data entry terminal, the form is displayed on the screen and the operator enters relevant details; **input mode** = computer which is receiving data; **insert mode** = interactive computer mode in which new text is entered within the previous text, which adjusts to make room for it; **interactive mode** = computer that allows the user to enter commands *or* programs *or* data and receive an immediate response; **noisy mode** = floating point arithmetic in which a digit other than a zero is deliberately added in the least significant position during the normalization of a floating point number; **replace mode** = interactive computer mode in which new text entered replaces any previous text; **sequential mode** = each instruction in a program is stored in consecutive locations

◊ **modal** *adjective* referring to modes

QUOTE the printer gives print quality in three modes: high speed, data processing and letter-quality
Minicomputer News

model 1 *noun* **(a)** small copy of something to show what it will look like when finished; *he showed us a model of the new computer centre building* **(b)** style *or* type of product; version of a product; *the new model B has taken the place of model A; this is the latest model; the model on display is last year's; they are selling off the old models at half price;* **demonstration model** = piece of equipment used in demonstrations (and then sold cheaply) **2** *adjective* which is a perfect example to be copied; *a model agreement* **3** *verb* to make a computerized model of a new product *or* of the economic system, etc. NOTE: **modelling - modelled** but US **modeling - modeled**

◊ **modelling** *noun* creating computer models

modem *or* **MODEM** *noun* = MODULATOR/DEMODULATOR device that allows data to be sent over telephone lines by converting binary signals from a computer into analog sound signals which can be transmitted over a telephone line; **dial-in modem** = auto-answer modem that can be called at any time to access a system; *see also* STANDARD *compare with* ACOUSTIC COUPLER

COMMENT: the process of converting binary signals to analog is called "modulation". When the signal is received, another modem reverses the process (called "demodulation"). Both modems must be working according to the same standards

modify *verb* to change something *or* to make something fit a different use; *the keyboard was modified for European users; we are running a modified version of the mail-merge system; the software will have to be modified to run on a small PC*

◊ **modification** *noun* change made to something; *the modifications to the system allow it to be run as part of a LAN;* **modification loop** = instructions within a loop that changes other instructions *or* data within a program

◊ **modifier** *noun* programming instruction that alters the normal action of a command

modular *adjective* (method of constructing hardware *or* software products) by connecting several smaller blocks together to produce a customized product; **modular programming** = programming small individually written sections of computer code that can be made to fit into a structured program and can be called up from a main program

◊ **modularity** *noun* being made up from modules; *the modularity of the software or hardware allows the system to be changed*

◊ **modularization** *noun* designing programs from a set of standard modules

modulate *verb* to change a carrier wave so that it can carry data; **modulated signal** = constant frequency and amplitude carrier signal that is used in a modulated form to transmit data; **modulating signal** = signal to be transmitted that is used to modulate a carrier

◊ **modulator** *noun* electronic circuit that varies a carrier signal according to an applied signal; **modulator/demodulator** = MODEM

module *noun* **(a)** small section of a large program that can if required function independently as a program in its own right **(b)** self-contained piece of hardware that can be connected with other modules to form a new system; *a multifunction analog interface module includes analog to digital and digital to analog converters*

modulo arithmetic *noun* branch of arithmetic that uses the remainder of one number when divided by another; **modulo-N** = modulo arithmetic using base N; **modulo-N check** = error detection test using the remainder from a modulo arithmetic operation on data

modulus *or* **MOD** *noun* the remainder after the division of one number by another; *7 mod 3 = 1*

momentary switch *noun* switch that only conducts while it is being pressed

monadic (Boolean) operator *noun* logical operator with only one operand; *the monadic operator NOT can be used here;* **monadic operation** = operation that uses one operand to produce one result

monitor 1 *noun* **(a)** visual display unit used to display high quality text *or* graphics, generated by a computer; **multi-scan** *or* **multi-sync monitor** = monitor which has circuitry to lock onto the required scanning frequency for any type of graphics card; **monitor unit** *see* VDU **(b)** **monitor program** = computer program that allows basic commands to be entered to operate a system (such as load a program, examine the state of devices, etc.); *see also* OPERATING SYSTEM; **firmware monitor** = monitor program that is resident in a ROM device, used to load in the operating system when a machine is switched on **(c)** system that watches for faults *or* failures in a circuit; **power monitor** = circuit that shuts off the electricity supply if it is faulty *or* likely to damage equipment **2** *verb* (i) to check *or* to examine how something is working; (ii) to look after and supervise a process *or* experiment to make sure it is operating correctly; *he is monitoring the progress of the trainee programmers; the machine monitors each signal as it is sent out*

mono- *prefix* meaning single *or* one

◊ **monochrome** *adjective & noun* (image) in one colour, usually shades of grey and black and white; **monochrome monitor** = computer monitor that displays text and graphics in black, white and shades of grey instead of colours

◊ **monoprogramming system** *noun* computer batch processing system that executes one program at a time; *compare with* MULTIPROGRAMMING SYSTEM

Monte Carlo method *noun* statistical analysis technique

MOS = METAL OXIDE SEMICONDUCTOR production and design method for a certain family of integrated circuits using patterns of metal conductors and oxide deposited onto a semiconductor; *see also* MOSFET; **MOS memory** = solid-state memory using MOSFETs to store binary data; **CMOS** = = COMPLEMENTARY METAL OXIDE SEMICONDUCTOR integrated circuit design and construction (using a pair of complementary p and n type transistors)

QUOTE integrated circuits fall into one of two distinct classes, based either on bipolar or metal oxide semiconductor (MOS) transistors
Electronics & Power

mosaic *noun* display character used in videotext systems that is made up of small dots

MOSFET = METAL OXIDE SEMICONDUCTOR FIELD EFFECT TRANSISTOR high power and high speed field effect transistor manufactured using MOS techniques

most significant bit *or* **msb** *or* **MSB** *noun* bit in a word that represents the greatest value *or* weighting (usually the bit which is furthest to the left); *the most significant bit in an eight bit binary word represents 128 in decimal notation*

◊ **most significant character** *or* **most significant digit (MSD)** *noun* digit at the far

left of a number, that represents the greatest power of the base NOTE: the opposite is **LSB, LSD**

motherboard *noun* main printed circuit board of a system, containing most of the components and connections for expansion boards, etc.

mount *verb* to fix a device *or* a circuit onto a base; *the chips are mounted in sockets on the PCB*

mouse *noun* small hand-held input device moved on a flat surface to control the position of a cursor on the screen; **mouse-driven** = (software) which uses a mouse rather than a keyboard for input; **mouse driver** = program which converts data from a mouse to a standard form that can be used by any software NOTE: the plural is **mice** or sometimes **mouses**

QUOTE a powerful new mouse-based editor:- you can cut, paste and copy with the mouse
Personal Computer World
QUOTE you can use a mouse to access pop-up menus and a keyboard for a word-processor
Byte

M out of N code *noun* coding system providing error detection, each valid character which is N bits long must contain M binary "one" bits

move *verb* to change the place of something; **move block** = command which changes the place of a block of text identified by block markers

◊ **movable** *adjective* which can be moved; **movable head disk** = magnetic disk head assembly that moves across the disk until the required track is reached

◊ **movement** *noun* changing the place of something; **movement file** = file continuing recent changes *or* transactions to records, which is then used to update a master file

MPS = MICROPROCESSOR SYSTEM

MPU = MICROPROCESSOR UNIT

ms = MILLISECOND one thousandth of a second

msb *or* **MSB** = MOST SIGNIFICANT BIT bit in a word that represents the greatest value *or* weight (usually the bit furthest to the left)

MSD = MOST SIGNIFICANT DIGIT

MSI = MEDIUM SCALE INTEGRATION

MSX *noun* hardware and software standard for home computers that can use interchangeable software

MTBF = MEAN TIME BETWEEN FAILURES average period of time that a piece of equipment will operate between failures

MTF = MEAN TIME TO FAILURE average period of time for which a device will operate (usually continuously) before failing

multi- *prefix* meaning many *or* more than one; *multimegabyte memory card; a multistandard unit;* **multi-access system** = computer system that allows several users to access one file *or* program at the same time; *see also* MULTI-USER; **multi-address** *or* **multi-address instruction** = instruction that contains more than one address (of data *or* locations *or* input/output)

◇ **multi-board computer** *noun* computer which has several integrated circuit boards connected with a mother board

◇ **multi-bus system** *noun* computer architecture that uses a high speed bus between CPU and main memory and a slower bus between CPU and other peripherals

◇ **multichannel** *adjective* with more than one channel

◇ **multicolour** *adjective* with several colours

◇ **multidimensional** *adjective* with features in more than one dimension; **multidimensional array** = number of arrays arranged in parallel, providing depth; **multidimensional language** = programming language that can be represented in a number of ways

◇ **multi-disk** *adjective* referring to several types of disk; **multi-disk option** = system that can have disk drives installed in a number of sizes; **multi-disk reader** = device which can read from various sizes and formats of disk

◇ **multidrop circuit** *noun* network allowing communications between a number of terminals and a central computer, but not directly between terminals

◇ **multifunction** *adjective* which has several functions; *a multifunction analog interface module includes analog to digital and digital to analog converters;* **multifunction card** = add-on circuit board that provides many features to upgrade a computer; **multifunction workstation** = workstation where several tasks can be carried out

◇ **multifunctional** *adjective* which has several functions; *a multifunctional scanner*

◇ **multilayer** *noun* printed circuit board that has several layers *or* interconnecting conduction tracks

◇ **multilevel** *noun* signal with a number of possible values (quaternary signals have four levels)

◇ **multilink system** *noun* system where there is more than one connection between two points

◇ **multimedia** *adjective* referring to several forms of media

◇ **multi-part stationery** *noun* continuous stationery with two or more sheets together, either with carbons between *or* carbonless

◇ **multipass overlap** *noun* system of producing higher quality print from a dot matrix printer by repeating the line of characters but shifted slightly, so making the dots less noticeable

◇ **multiphase program** *noun* program that requires more than one fetch operation before execution is complete

multiple *adjective* having many parts *or* acting in many ways; **multiple access** *see* MULTI-ACCESS; **multiple address code** = instruction with more than one address for the operands, result and the location of the next instruction to be executed; *see also* THREE-PLUS-ONE; FOUR-PLUS-ONE ADDRESS; **multiple bus architecture** = computer architecture that uses a high speed bus between CPU and main memory and a slower bus between CPU and other peripherals; **multiple instruction stream - multiple data stream (MIMD)** = architecture of a parallel processor that uses a number of ALUs and memories in parallel to provide high speed processing; **multiple instruction stream - single data stream (MISD)** = architecture of a parallel computer that has a single ALU and data bus with a number of control units; **multiple precision** = use of more than one byte of data for number storage to increase possible precision

multiplex *verb* to combine several messages in the same transmission medium; **multiplexed bus** = one bus used to carry address, data and control signals at different times; **dynamic multiplexing** = multiplexing method which allocates time segments to signals according to demand; **homogeneous multiplexing** = switching multiplexor system where all the channels contain data using the same protocol and transmission rate

◇ **multiplexor (MUX)** *noun* circuit that combines a number of inputs into a smaller number of outputs; *compare with* DEMULTIPLEXOR *a 4 to 1 multiplexor combines four inputs into a single output*

QUOTE the displays use BCD input signals and can be multiplexed to provide up to six digits
Electronics & Power

multiply *verb* to perform a multiplication of a number (the multiplier)

◇ **multiplicand** *noun* number which is multiplied by another number

◇ **multiplication** *noun* mathematical operation that adds one number to itself a number of times; *the multiplication of 5 and 3 = 15;* **multiplication sign** = printed *or* written sign (x) used to show that numbers are multiplied

◇ **multiplier** *noun* number which multiplies a multiplicand

multipoint *adjective* (connection) with several lines, attaching several terminals to a single line to a single computer

◇ **multiprecision** *noun* use of more than one data word to represent numbers (increasing the range *or* precision possible)

◇ **multiprocessing system** *noun* system where several processing units work together sharing the same memory

◇ **multiprocessor** *noun* number of processing units acting together *or* separately but sharing the same area of memory; **multiprocessor interleaving** = each processor in a multiprocessor system dealing with a section of one or more processes

◇ **multi-programming** *noun* operating system used to execute more than one program apparently simultaneously (each program being executed a little at a time)

◇ **multi-scan** *or* **multi-sync monitor** *noun* monitor which contains circuitry to lock onto the required scanning frequency of any type of graphics card

◇ **multi statement line** *noun* line from a computer program that contains more than one instruction *or* statement

◇ **multi-strike printer ribbon** *noun* inked ribbon in a printer that can be used more than once

multitasking *or* **multi-tasking** *noun* ability of a computer system to run two or more programs at the same time; *the system is multi-user and multi-tasking;* **real-time multitasking** = executing several (real-time) tasks simultaneously without slowing the execution of any of the processors

COMMENT: few small systems are capable of simultaneous multitasking, since each program would require its own processor; this is overcome by allocating to each program an amount of processing time, executing each a little at a time so that they will appear to run simultaneously due to the speed of the processor and the relatively short gaps between programs

QUOTE this is a true multi-tasking system, meaning that several computer applications can be running at the same time
Which PC?
QUOTE page management programs are so greedy for memory that it is not a good idea to ask them to share RAM space with anything else, so the question of multi-tasking does not arise here
Desktop Publishing

multi-terminal system *noun* system where several terminals are linked to a single CPU

◇ **multithread** *noun* program design using more than one logical path through it, each path being concurrently executed

◇ **multi-user system** *noun* computer system that can support more than one user at a time; *the program runs on a standalone machine or a multi-user system*

◇ **multi-window editor** *noun* program used for creating and editing a number of applications programs independently, each in a separate window on screen at the same time

Murray code *noun* code used for teleprinters that uses only 5 bits

music chip *noun* integrated circuit capable of generating musical sounds and tunes

MUX = MULTIPLEXOR circuit that combines a number of inputs into a smaller number of outputs; *compare* DEMULTIPLEXOR

Nn

n *prefix* meaning nano-

N-key rollover *noun* facility on a keyboard where each keystroke (up to a maximum of N) is registered in sequence even if they are struck very fast

NAK = NEGATIVE ACKNOWLEDGEMENT

name *noun* **(a)** word used to call a thing *or* a person; **brand name** = name of a particular make of product; **corporate name** = name of a large corporation; *the company buys computer parts from several suppliers, and packages them together to make their own name product* **(b)** ordinary word used to identify an address in machine language; **file name** = word used to identify a particular stored file; **program name** = identification name for a stored program file; **name table** *or* **symbol table** = list of reserved words *or* commands in a language and the addresses in the computer that refer to them; **variable name** = word used to identify a variable in a program

NAND function *noun* logical function whose output is false if all inputs are true, and true if any input is false; **NAND gate** = electronic circuit that provides a NAND function NOTE: the NAND function is equivalent to an AND function with a NOT function at the output

COMMENT: the output is 0 only if both inputs are 1; if one input is 1 and the other 0, or if both inputs are 0, then the output is 1

nano- *or* **n** *prefix* meaning one thousand millionth *or*, *US* one billionth; **nanocircuit** *or* **nanosecond circuit** = electronic and logic circuits that can respond to impulses within nanoseconds; **nanosecond** *or* **ns** = one thousand millionth of a second NOTE: US billion is the same as UK one thousand million (10 to the power of nine); UK billion is one million million (10 to the power of 10)

QUOTE the cache's internal RAM is accessed in under 70ns from address strobe to ready signal
Electronics & Power

narrative *noun* explanatory notes or comments to help a user operate a program
◇ **narrative statement** *noun* statement which sets variables and allocates storage at the start of a program

native *adjective* **native format** = first *or* basic format

natural *adjective* occurring in nature *or* not created artificially; **natural binary coded decimal (NBCD)** = representation of single decimal digits as a pattern of 4 bits; **natural language** = language that is used *or* understood by humans; *the expert system can be programmed in a natural language*

QUOTE there are two main types of natural-language interface: those based on menus, and those where the user has to discover what questions the computer will respond to by trial and error
Electronics & Power

NBCD = NATURAL BINARY CODED DECIMAL

NC = NUMERICAL CONTROL machine operated automatically by computer *or* circuits controlled by a stored program *or* data

NDR = NON DESTRUCTIVE READOUT display system that continues to display previous characters when new ones are displayed

near letter-quality (NLQ) *noun* printing by a dot-matrix printer that provides higher quality type, which is almost as good as a typewriter, by decreasing the spaces between the dots; *switch the printer to NLQ for these form letters*

needle *noun* tiny metal pin on a dot matrix printer which prints one of the dots

negate *verb* to reverse the sign of a number; *if you negate 23.4 the result is -23.4*
◇ **negation** *noun* reversing the sign of a number (such as from 5 to -5)

◇ **negative** *adjective* meaning "no"; **negative acknowledgement (NAK) =** signal sent by a receiver to indicate that data has been incorrectly *or* incompletely received; **negative number =** number which represents the number subtracted from zero, indicated by a minus sign in front of the number; **negative-true logic =** use of a lower voltage level to represent binary 1 than for binary 0

neither-nor function *noun* logical function whose output is false if any input is true

NEQ = NON-EQUIVALENCE; **NEQ function =** logical function where the output is true if the inputs are not the same, otherwise the output is false; **NEQ gate =** electronic implementation of an NEQ function

nest *verb* (i) to insert a subroutine within a program *or* another routine; (ii) to use a routine that calls itself recursively; **nested loop =** loop inside another loop in the same program; **nested macrocall =** a macro called from within another macro; **nesting level =** number of subroutines within a subroutine; **nesting store =** hardware stack (normally stacks are implemented with software)

network 1 *noun* any system made of a number of points *or* circuits that are interconnected; **communications network =** group of devices such as terminals and printers that are interconnected with a central computer allowing the rapid and simple transfer of data; **computer network =** shared use of a series of interconnected computers, peripherals and terminals; **information network =** number of databases linked together, usually using telephone lines and modems, allowing a large amount of data to be accessed by a wider number of users; **local area network (LAN) =** network where the various terminals and equipment are all within a short distance of one another (at a maximum distance of 500m, for example in the same building) and can be interconnected by cables; **long haul network =** communications network between distant computers that usually uses the public telephone system; **wide area network (WAN) =** network where the various terminals are far apart and linked by radio *or* satellite; **network analysis =** study of messages, destinations and routes in a network to provide a better operation;

network architecture = method in which a network is constructed, such as layers in an OSI system; **network control program =** software that regulates the flow of and channels for data transmitted in a network; **network controller =** network user responsible for allocating disk space, answering queries and solving problems from other users of the same network; **network database =** database structure in which data items can be linked together; **network diagram =** graphical representation describing the interconnections between points; **network hardware =** physical links, computers and control equipment that make up a network; **network layer =** ISO/OSI standard layer that decides on the routes to be used, the costs, etc.; *see also* LAYER; **network management =** organization, planning, running and upkeep of a network; **network processor =** signal multiplexer controlled by a microprocessor in a network; **network redundancy =** extra links between points allowing continued operation in the event of one failing; **network software =** software which is used to establish the link between a user's program and the network; **network structure =** data structure that allows each node to be connected to any of the others; **network timing =** signals that correctly synchronize the transmission of data; *see also* BUS, MESH, PROTOCOL, RING, STAR, TOPOLOGY **2** *verb* to link points together in a network; *they run a system of networked micros; the workstations have been networked together rather than used as standalone systems*

◇ **networking** *noun* (i) working *or* organization of a network; (ii) interconnecting two *or* more computers either in the same room *or* different buildings, in the same town *or* different towns, allowing them to exchange information; **networking hardware** *or* **network hardware =** physical links, computers and control equipment that make up a network; **networking software** *or* **network software =** software which is used to establish the link between a user's program and the network; **networking specialist =** company *or* person who specializes in designing and setting up networks; *this computer firm is a UK networking specialist*

COMMENT: networking allows a machine with a floppy disk drive to use another PC's hard disk when both machines are linked by a cable and are using networking software

neutral *adjective* with no state *or* bias *or* voltage; **neutral transmission** = (transmission) system in which a voltage pulse and zero volts represent the binary digits 1 and 0

new *adjective* recent *or* not old; *they have installed a new computer system; the new programmer does not seem as efficient as the old one;* **new (command)** = program command that clears main memory of the present program ready to accept a new program to be entered; **new line character** = character that moves a cursor *or* printhead to the beginning of the next line; *see also* CARRIAGE RETURN (CR); LINEFEED (LF); **new technology** = electronic instruments which have recently been invented

next instruction register *noun* register in a CPU that contains the location where the next instruction to be executed is stored; *see also* REGISTER

nexus *noun* connection point between units in a network

nibble *or* **nybble** *noun* half the length of a standard byte
NOTE: a nibble is normally 4 bits, but can vary according to different micros or people

nil pointer *noun* pointer used to indicate the end of a chained list of items

nine's complement decimal complement (equivalent to the binary one's complement) formed by subtracting each digit in the number from nine; *see also* TEN'S COMPLEMENT

n-level logic *noun* logic gate design in which no more than n gates occur in a series

NLQ = NEAR LETTER-QUALITY

NMI NON-MASKABLE INTERRUPT

no-address operation *noun* instruction which does not require an address within it

◊ **no op** *or* **no operation instruction** = NO OPERATION programming instruction which does nothing

node *noun* interconnection point in a structure *or* network; *a tree is made of branches that connect together at nodes; this network has fibre optic connection with nodes up to one kilometre apart*

noise *noun* random signal present in addition to any wanted signal, caused by static, temperature, power supply, magnetic or electric fields and also from stars and the sun; **noise immunity** = ability of a circuit to ignore *or* filter out *or* be protected from noise; **impulsive noise** = interference on a signal caused by short periods of noise

◊ **noisy mode** *noun* floating point arithmetic system, in which a digit other than a zero is deliberately added in the least significant position during the normalization of a floating point number; **noisy digit** = digit, usually not zero, added during the normalization of a floating point number when in noisy mode

nomenclature *noun* predefined system for assigning words and symbols to represent numbers or terms

nomogram *or* **nomograph** *noun* graphical system for solving one value given two others

non- *prefix* meaning not
◊ **nonaligned** *adjective* two devices that are not correctly positioned in relation to each other, for optimum performance; **nonaligned read head** = read head that is not in the same position on a magnetic medium as the write head was, producing a loss of signal quality
◊ **non-arithmetic shift** *see* LOGICAL SHIFT
◊ **noncompatibility** *noun* two or more pieces of hardware *or* software that cannot exchange data *or* use the same peripherals
◊ **non-destructive cursor** *noun* cursor on a display that does not erase characters already displayed as it passes over them; *the screen quickly became unreadable when using a non-destructive cursor;* **non-destructive readout (NDR)** = display device that retains previous characters when displaying new characters; **non-destructive test** = series of tests carried out on a piece of equipment without destroying it; *I will carry out a number of non-destructive tests on your computer, if it passes, you can start using it again;* **non-scrollable** = part of the screen display which is always displayed

(in a WP, the text can scroll whilst instructions, etc., are non-scrollable); *see also* STATUS LINE

◊ **non-equivalence function (NEQ)** *noun* logical function where the output is true if the inputs are not the same, otherwise the output is false; **non-equivalence gate** = electronic implementation of an NEQ function

◊ **nonerasable storage** *noun* storage medium that cannot be erased and re-used; *paper tape is a nonerasable storage*

◊ **non-impact printer** *noun* printer (like an ink-jet printer) where the character form does not hit a ribbon onto the paper

◊ **nonlinear** *adjective* electronic circuit whose output does not change linearly in proportion to its input

◊ **non-maskable interrupt (NMI)** *noun* high priority interrupt signal that cannot be blocked by software and overrides other commands

◊ **non-operable instruction** *noun* instruction that does not carry out any function, but increments the program counter

◊ **non-printing codes** *noun* codes that represent an action of the printer rather than a printed character; *the line width can be set using one of the non-printing codes, .LW, then a number*

◊ **non return to zero (NRZ)** *noun* signalling system in which a positive voltage represents one binary digit and a negative voltage the other; representation of binary data in which the signal changes when the data changes state, and does not return to zero volts after each bit of data

◊ **non-volatile** *adjective* **non-volatile memory** *or* **non-volatile store** *or* **storage** = storage medium *or* memory that retains data even when the power has been switched off; *bubble memory is a non-volatile storage; using magnetic tape provides non-volatile memory*
NOTE: opposite is **volatile**

COMMENT: disks (both hard and floppy) and tapes are non-volatile memory stores; solid-state memory, such as RAM chips are volatile unless battery backed

NOR function = *noun* logical function whose output is false if either input is true; **NOR gate** = electric circuit *or* chip which performs a NOR function

COMMENT: the output is 1 only if both inputs are 0; if the two inputs are different or if both are 1, the output is 0

normal *adjective* usual *or* which happens regularly; *the normal procedure is for*

backup copies to be made at the end of each day's work; **normal format** = standardized format for data storage; **normal range** = expected range for a result *or* number, any outside this range are errors

◊ **normalize** *verb* **(a)** to convert data into a form which can be read by a particular computer system **(b)** to convert characters into just capitals or into just a lower case form **(c)** to store and represent numbers in a pre-agreed form, usually to provide maximum precision; *all the new data has been normalized to 10 decimal places;* **normalized form** = floating point number that has been normalized so that its mantissa is within a certain range

◊ **normalization** *noun* process of normalizing data; **normalization routine** = routine that normalizes a floating point number and adds extra (noisy) digits in the least significant position

NOT function *noun* logical inverse function where the output is true if the input is false; **NOT-AND** = equivalent to the NAND function; **NOT gate** = electronic circuit *or* chip which performs a NOT function

COMMENT: if the input is 1, the output is 0; if the input is 0, the output is 1

notation *noun* method of writing *or* representing numbers; **binary notation** = base two numerical system using only the digits 0 and 1; **decimal notation** = number representation in base 10, using the digits · 0-9; **hexadecimal notation** = number system using base 16 and the digits 0-9 and A-F; **infix notation** = mathematical syntax where operators are embedded inside operands (such as C - D or X + Y); **octal notation** = number system using base 8 and the digits 0-7; **postfix notation** = mathematical operations written in a logical way, so that the operator appears after the operands, this removes the need for brackets; *normal notation: (x-y) + z, but using postfix notation: xy - z +;* **prefix notation** = mathematical operations written in a logical way, so that the operator appears before the operands, this removes the need for brackets

notched *see* EDGE NOTCHED CARD

notepad *noun* **screen notepad** = part of the screen used to store information even when the terminal is switched off

notice board *noun* (i) board fixed to a wall where notices can be pinned up; (ii) type of bulletin board on which messages to all users can be left

n-plus-one address instruction *noun* instruction made up of a number (n) of addresses and one other address that is the location of the next instruction

npn transistor *noun* bipolar transistor design using p-type semiconductor for the base and n-type for the collector and emitter; *see also* TRANSISTOR, BIPOLAR

NRZ = NON RETURN TO ZERO

ns *abbreviation* nanosecond

n-type material *or* **N-type material** *or* **n-type semiconductor** *noun* semiconductor that has been doped with a substance that provides extra electrons in the material, giving it an overall negative charge compared to the intrinsic semiconductor; *see also* NPN TRANSISTOR

null *noun* nothing; **null character** = character which means nothing (usually code 0); **null instruction** = program instruction that does nothing; **null list** = list which contains nothing; **null modem** = emulator circuit that allows two pieces of equipment, that normally require modems to communicate, to be connected together over a short distance; *this cable is configured as a null modem, which will allow me to connect these 2 computers together easily;* **null set** = set that only contains zeros; **null string** = string that contains no characters

> QUOTE you have to connect the two RS232 ports together using a crossed cable, or null modem
> *PC Business World*

number 1 *noun* **(a)** representation of a quantity; **number cruncher** = dedicated

processor used for high-speed calculations; **number crunching** = performing high-speed calculations; *a very powerful processor is needed for graphics applications which require extensive number crunching capabilities;* **number range** = set of allowable values **(b)** written figure; *each piece of hardware has a production number; please note the reference number of your order;* **check number** = number produced from data for parity *or* error detection **2** *verb* **(a)** to put a figure on a document; *the pages of the manual are numbered 1 to 395* **(b)** to assign digits to a list of items in an ordered manner

◊ **numeral** *noun* character *or* symbol which represents a number; **Arabic numerals** = figures written 1, 2, 3, 4, etc.; **Roman numerals** = figures written I, II, III, IV, etc.

◊ **numeric** *adjective* (i) referring to numbers; (ii) (field, etc.) which contains only numbers; **numeric array** = array containing numbers; **numeric character** = letter used in some notations to represent numbers (for example in hex the letters A-F are numeric characters); **numeric keypad** = set of ten keys with figures, included in most computer keyboards as a separate group, used for entering large amounts of data in numeric form; **numeric operand** = operand that only uses numerals; **numeric pad** = numeric keypad; **numeric punch** = punched hole in rows 0-9 of a punched card

◊ **numerical** *adjective* referring to numbers; **numerical analysis** = study of ways of solving mathematical problems; **numerical control (NC)** *or* **computer numerical control (CNC)** = machine operated automatically by computer *or* circuits controlled by stored data

nybble *or* **nibble** *noun informal* half the length of a standard byte
NOTE: a nybble is normally 4 bits, but can vary according to different micros

Oo

OA = OFFICE AUTOMATION

object *noun* **(a)** variable used in an expert system within a reasoning operation **(b)** data in a statement which is to be operated on by the operator; *see also* ARGUMENT, OPERAND; **object** *or* **object-orientated architecture** = structure where all files, outputs, etc., in a system are represented as objects; **object code** = binary code which directly operates a central processing unit (a program code after it has been translated, compiled or assembled into machine code); **object computer** = computer system for which a program has been written and compiled; **object deck** = punched cards that contain a program; **object language** = the language of a program after it has been translated; *compare with* SOURCE LANGUAGE; **object program** = computer program in object code form, produced by a compiler *or* assembler

◊ **objective** *noun* something which someone tries to do

obtain *verb* to get *or* to receive; *to obtain data from a storage device*

OCCAM computer programming language, used in large multiprocessor *or* multi-user systems

COMMENT: this is the development language for transputer systems

occur *verb* to happen *or* to take place; *data loss can occur because of power supply variations*

OCP = ORDER CODE PROCESSOR *(in a multiprocessor system)* a processor which decides and performs the arithmetic and logical operations according to the program code

OCR (a) = OPTICAL CHARACTER READER device which scans printed *or* written characters, recognizes them, and converts them into machine-readable form for processing in a computer **(b)** = OPTICAL CHARACTER RECOGNITION process that allows printed *or* written characters to be recognized optically and converted into machine-readable code that can be input into a computer, using an optical character reader; **OCR font** = character design that can be easily read using an OCR reader

COMMENT: there are two OCR fonts in common use: OCR-A, which is easy for scanners to read, and OCR-B, which is easier for people to read than the OCR-A font

octal (notation) *noun* number notation using base 8, with digits 0 to 7; **octal digit** = digit (0 to 7) used in the octal system; **octal scale** = power of eight associated with each digit position in a number

COMMENT: in octal, the digits used are 0 to 7; so decimal 9 is octal 11

octet *noun* a group of eight bits treated as one unit; word made up of eight bits; *see also* BYTE

odd *adjective* (number, such as 5 or 7) which cannot be divided by two; **odd-even check** = method of checking that transmitted binary data has not been corrupted; **odd parity (check)** = error checking system in which any series of bits transmitted must have an odd number of binary ones (NOTE: opposite is **even)**

OEM = ORIGINAL EQUIPMENT MANUFACTURER company which produces equipment using basic parts made by other manufacturers, and customizes the product for a particular application

office *noun* room *or* building where a company works *or* where business is done; **office automation (OA)** = use of machines and computers to carry out normal office tasks; **office computer** = small computer (sometimes with a hard disk and several terminals) suitable for office use

off-line *adverb & adjective* (i) (processor *or* printer *or* terminal) that is not connected to

a network *or* central computer (usually temporarily); (ii) (peripheral) connected to a network, but not available for use; *before changing the paper in the printer, switch it off-line;* **off-line printing** = printout operation that is not supervised by a computer; **off-line processing** processing by devices not under the control of a central computer
NOTE: opposite is **on-line**

offset *noun* quantity added to a number *or* address to give a final number; **offset value** *or* **offset word** = value to be added to a base address to provide a final indexed address

O.K. used as a prompt in place of 'ready' in some systems

omission factor *noun* number of relevant documents that were missed in a search

OMR (a) = OPTICAL MARK READER device that can recognize marks *or* lines on a special forms (such as on an order form *or* a reply to a questionnaire) and that inputs them into a computer **(b)** = OPTICAL MARK RECOGNITION process that allows certain marks *or* lines on special forms (such as on an order form *or* a reply to a questionnaire) to be recognized by an optical mark reader, and input into a computer

on-board *adjective* (feature *or* circuit) which is contained on a motherboard *or* main PCB

QUOTE the electronic page is converted to a printer-readable video image by the on-board raster image processor
QUOTE the key intelligence features of these laser printers are emulation modes and on-board memory
Byte

on chip *noun* circuit constructed on a chip

◇ **on-chip** *adjective* (circuit) constructed on a chip; *the processor uses on-chip bootstrap software to allow programs to be loaded rapidly*

one address computer *noun* computer structure whose machine code only uses one address at a time; **one address instruction** = instruction made up of an operator and one address

◇ **one element** *noun* logical function that produces a true output if any input is true

◇ **one for one** *noun* programming language, usually assembler, that produces one machine code instruction for each

instruction *or* command word in the language

COMMENT: compilers and interpreters are usually used for translating high-level languages which use more than one machine code instruction for each high-level instruction

◇ **one-level address** *noun* storage address that directly, without any modification, accesses a location *or* device; **one-level code** = binary code which directly operates the CPU, using only absolute addresses and values (this is the final form of a program after a compiler *or* assembler pass); **one-level store** = organization of storage in which each different type of storage device is treated as if it were the same; **one-level subroutine** = subroutine which does not call another subroutine during its execution

◇ **one's complement** *noun* inverse of a binary number; *the one's complement of 10011 is 01100; see also* COMPLEMENT; TWO'S COMPLEMENT

◇ **one-pass assembler** *noun* assembler program that translates the source code in one action; *this new one-pass assembler is very quick in operation*

◇ **one-plus-one address** *noun* address format that provides the location of one register and the location of the next instruction

◇ **one-time pad** *noun* coding system that uses a unique cipher key each time it is used

COMMENT: two identical pieces of paper with an encrypted alphabet printed on each one are used, one by the sender, one by the receiver; this is one of the most secure cipher systems

◇ **one to zero ratio** *noun* ratio between the amplitude of a binary one and zero output

onion skin architecture *noun* design of a computer system in layers, according to function *or* priority; *the onion skin architecture of this computer is made up of a kernel at the centre, an operating system, a low-level language and then the user's program*

◇ **onion skin language** *noun* database manipulation language that can process hierarchical data structures

on-line *adverb & adjective* (terminal *or* device) connected to and under the control of a central processor; *the terminal is on-line to the mainframe;* **on-line database** = interactive search, retrieve and update of database records, with a terminal that is on-line; **on-line information retrieval** =

system that allows an operator of an on-line terminal to access, search and display data held in a main computer; **on-line processing** = processing by devices connected to and under the control of the central computer (the user remains in contact with the central computer while processing); **on-line storage** = data storage equipment that is directly controlled by a computer; **on-line system** = computer system that allows users who are on-line to transmit and receive information; **on-line transaction processing** = interactive processing in which a user enters commands and data on a terminal which is linked to a central computer, with results being displayed on the screen

on-screen *adjective* (information) that is displayed on a computer screen rather than printed out

◊ **on-site** *adjective* at the place where something is; *the new model has an on-site upgrade facility*

on the fly *adverb* (to examine and modify data) during a program run without stopping the run

O/P *or* **o/p** = OUTPUT

op code = OPERATION CODE part of the machine code instruction that defines the action to be performed

QUOTE the subroutine at 3300 is used to find the op code corresponding to the byte whose hex value is in B
Computing Today

open 1 *adjective* (a) command to prepare a file before reading *or* writing actions can occur; *you cannot access the data unless the file is open* (b) not closed; **open access** = system where many workstations are available for anyone to use; **open code** = extra instructions required in a program that mainly uses macroinstructions; **open-ended program** = program designed to allow future expansion and easy modification; **open reel** = magnetic tape on a reel that is not enclosed in a cartridge *or* cassette; **open routine** = routine which can be inserted into a larger routine *or* program without using a call instruction; **open subroutine** = code for a subroutine which is copied into memory whenever a call instruction is found, rather than executing a jump to the subroutine's address; **open system** = system which is constructed in such a way that different operating systems can work together; **Open System Interconnection (OSI)** = standardized ISO network which is constructed in layered

form, with each layer having a specific task, allowing different systems to communicate if they conform to the standard; *see also* ISO/OSI LAYERS, INTERNATIONAL **2** *verb* (a) to take the cover off *or* to make a door open; *open the disk drive door; open the top of the computer by lifting here* (b) to prepare a file before accessing *or* editing *or* carrying out other transactions on stored records; *you cannot access the data unless the file has been opened*

operand *noun* data (in a computer instruction) which is to be operated on by the operator; *in the instruction ADD 74, the operator ADD will add the operand 74 to the accumulator;* **immediate operand** = within an immediate addressing operation, the operand is fetched at the same time as the instruction; **literal operand** = actual number *or* address to be used rather than a label *or* its location; **numeric operand** = operand that only contains numerals; **operand field** = space allocated for an operand in a program instruction; *see also* ARGUMENT, MACHINE-CODE INSTRUCTION

operate *verb* to work *or* to make a machine work; *do you know how to operate the telephone switchboard ?;* **disk operating system (DOS)** = section of the operating system software that controls disk and file management; **operating code (op code)** = part of the machine code instruction that defines the action to be performed; **operating console** = terminal in an interactive system which sends and receives information; **operating instructions** = commands and instructions used to operate a computer; **operating system (OS)** = software that controls the basic, low-level hardware operations, and file management, without the user having to operate it (the operating system is usually supplied with the computer as part of the bundled software in ROM); **operating time** = total time required to carry out a task

◊ **operation** *noun* working (of a machine); **arithmetic operation** = mathematical function carried out on data; **binary operation** = (i) operation on two operands; (ii) operation on an operand in binary form; **block operation** = process carried out on a block of data; **Boolean operation** = logical operation on a number of operands, conforming to Boolean algebra rules; **complete operation** = operation that retrieves the necessary operands from memory, performs the operation and returns the results and operands to memory, then reads the next instruction to be processed; **dyadic Boolean operation** = logical operation that produces an output from two inputs; **no-address operation** = instruction which does not require an address within it; **no-operation instruction (no-op)** = programming instruction which does nothing; **operation code (op code)** = part of a machine-code instruction that defines the action to be performed; **operation cycle** = section of the machine cycle during which the instruction is executed; *see also* FETCH-EXECUTE CYCLE, MACHINE CYCLE; **operation decoder** = hardware that converts a machine-code instruction (in binary form) into actions; **operation field** = part of an assembly language statement that contains the mnemonic or symbol for the op code; **operation priority** = the sequence order in which the operations within a statement are carried out; **operation register** = register that contains the op code during its execution; **operation time** = period of time that an operation requires for its operation cycle; **operation trial** = series of tests to check programs and data preparation; **operations manual** *see* INSTRUCTION MANUAL

◊ **operational** *adjective* which is working or which refers to the way a machine works; **operational information** = information about the normal operations of a system

operator *noun* (a) person who makes a machine or process work; *the operator was sitting at his console;* **computer operator** = person who operates a computer; **operator's console** = input and output devices used by an operator to control a computer (usually consisting of a keyboard and VDU; **operator precedence** = order in which a number of mathematical operations will be carried out; **operator procedure** = set of actions that an operator has to carry out to work a machine or process (b) character or symbol or word that defines a function or operation; *x is the multiplication operator;* **arithmetic operator** = symbol which indicates an arithmetic function (such as + for addition, x for multiplication)

op register *noun* register that contains the operating code for the instruction that is being executed

optic fibres = OPTICAL FIBRES; **fibre optics** = using optical fibres (fine strands of glass or plastic protected by a surrounding material) for the transmission of light signals which can carry data

optical *adjective* referring to or making use of light; *an optical reader uses a light beam to scan characters or patterns or lines;* **optical bar reader** *or* **bar code reader** *or* **optical wand** = optical device that reads data from a bar code; **optical character reader (OCR)** = device which scans printed or written characters, recognizes them, and converts them into machine-readable code for processing in a computer; **optical character recognition (OCR)** = process that allows printed or written characters to be recognized optically and converted into machine-readable code that can be input into a computer, using an optical character reader; **optical communication system** = communication system using fibre optics; **optical data link** = connection between two devices to allow the transmission of data using light signals (either line-of-sight or optic fibre); **optical disk** = disk that contains binary data in the form of small holes in the surface which are read with a laser beam NOTE: also called WORM (write once, read many times) which can be programmed once or compact disk (CD) which is programmed at manufacture **optical fibre** = fine strand of glass or plastic protected by a surrounding material, that is used for the convenient transmission of light signals; **optical font** *or* **OCR font** = character design that can be easily read using an OCR reader; **optical mark reader (OMR)** = device that can recognize marks or lines on a special forms (such as on an order form or a reply to a questionnaire) and convert them into a form a computer can process; **optical mark recognition (OMR)** = process that allows certain marks or lines on special forms (such as on an order form or a reply to a questionnaire) to be recognized by an optical mark reader, and input into a computer; **optical memory** = optical disks; **optical scanner** = equipment that converts an image into electrical signals which can be stored in and displayed on a computer; **optical storage** = data storage using mediums such as optical disk, etc.; **optical transmission** = use of fibre optic cables, laser beams and other light sources to carry data, in the form of pulses of light; **optical wand** = OPTICAL BAR READER

optimization *noun* making something work as efficiently as possible

◊ **optimize** *verb* to make something work as efficiently as possible; **optimized code** = program that has been passed through an optimizer to remove any inefficient code or statements

◊ **optimizer** *noun* program which adapts another program to run more efficiently

optimum *noun & adjective* best possible; **optimum code** *or* **minimum access code** *or* **minimum delay code** = coding system that provides the fastest access and retrieval time for stored data items

option *noun* action which can be chosen; *there are usually four options along the top of the screen; the options available are described in the main menu*

◇ **optional** *adjective* which can be chosen; *the system comes with optional 3.5 or 5.25 disk drives*

> QUOTE with the colour palette option, remarkable colour effects can be achieved on an RGB colour monitor
> *Electronics & Wireless World*

OR function *noun* logical function that produces a true output if any input is true; **OR gate** = electronic implementation of the OR function

> COMMENT: the result of the OR function will be 1 if either or both inputs is 1; if both inputs are 0, then the result is 0

order *noun* **(a)** instruction; **order code** = operation code; **order code processor (OCP)** = *(in a multiprocessor system)* a processor which decodes and performs the arithmetic and logical operations according to the program code **(b)** sorted according to a key; *in alphabetical order;* **ordered list** = list of data items which has been sorted into an order **2** *verb* to direct *or* instruct

organize *verb* to arrange something so that it works efficiently

◇ **organization** *noun* way of arranging something so that it works efficiently

◇ **organizational** *adjective* referring to the way in which something is organized

orientated *adjective* aimed towards; **problem-orientated language (POL)** = high-level programming language that allows caertain problems to be expressed easily

◇ **orientation** *noun* direction *or* position of an object

origin *noun* **(a)** position on a display screen to which all coordinates are referenced, usually the top left hand corner of the screen **(b)** location in memory at which the first instruction of a program is stored; *see also* INDEXED

original 1 *adjective* used *or* made first **2** *noun* (first) master data disk used, from which a copy can be made

◇ **original equipment manufacturer (OEM)** *noun* company which produces equipment using basic parts made by other manufacturers, and customizes the product for a particular application; *one OEM supplies the disk drive, another the monitor; he started in business as a manufacturer of PCs for the OEM market*

◇ **originate** *verb* to start *or* come from; *the data originated from the new computer*

◇ **origination** *noun* work involved in creating something

orthogonal *adjective* (instruction) made up of independent parameters *or* parts

OS = OPERATING SYSTEM software that controls the basic, low-level hardware operations, and file management, without the user having to operate it (the operating system is usually supplied with the computer as part of the bundled software in ROM)

OSI = OPEN SYSTEM INTERCONNECTION *see also* ISO/OSI

out of range *adjective* (number *or* quantity) that is outside the limits of a system

outage *noun* time during which a system is not operational

outlet *noun* connection *or* point in a circuit *or* network where a signal *or* data can be accessed

outline *noun* the main features of something; **outline flowchart** = flowchart of the main features, steps and decisions in a program *or* system

output (o/p *or* **O/P) 1** *noun* **(a)** information *or* data that is transferred from a CPU *or* the main memory to another device such as a monitor *or* printer *or* secondary storage device; **computer output** = data *or* information produced after processing by a computer NOTE opposite is **input (b)** action of transferring the information *or* data from store to a user; **output area** *or* **block** = section of memory that contains data to be transferred to an output device; **output bound** *or* **limited** = processor that cannot function at normal speed because of a slower peripheral; **output buffer register** = temporary store for data that is waiting to be output; **output device** = device (such as a monitor *or* printer) which allows information to be displayed; **output file** = set of records that

have been completely processed according to various parameters; **output formatter =** (i) software used to format data or programs (and output them) so that they are compatible with another sort of storage medium; (ii) part of a word processor program that formats text according to embedded commands; **output mode =** computer mode in which data is moved from internal storage or the CPU to external devices; **output register =** register that stores data to be output until the receiver is ready or the channel is free; **output stream =** communications channel carrying data output to a peripheral; **output port =** circuit and connector that allow a computer to output or transmit data to other devices or machines; *connect the printer to the printer output port;* **input/output (I/O) =** (i) receiving or transmitting of data between a computer and its peripherals and other points outside the system; (ii) all data received or transmitted by a computer; *see also* INPUT **2** *verb* to transfer data from a computer to a monitor or printer; *finished documents can be output to the laser printer*
NOTE: **outputting - output**

QUOTE most CAD users output to a colour plotter
PC Business World

OV = OVERFLOW

overflow *or* **OV** *noun* **(a)** mathematical result that is greater than the limits of the computer's number storage system; **overflow bit** *or* **flag** *or* **indicator =** single bit in a word that is set to one (1) if a mathematical overflow has occurred; **overflow check =** examining an overflow flag to see if an overflow has occurred **(b)** situation in a network when the number of transmissions is greater than the line capacity and are transferred by another route

overhead *noun* extra code that has to be stored to organize the program; *the line numbers in a BASIC program are an overhead;* **overhead bit =** single bit used for error detection in a transmission; **polling overhead =** amount of time spent by a computer calling and checking each terminal in a network

overheat *verb* to become too hot; *the system may overheat if the room is not air-conditioned*

overlap 1 *noun* two things where one covers part of the other *or* two sections of data that are placed on top of each other;

multipass overlap = system of producing higher quality print from a dot matrix printer by repeating the line of characters but shifted slightly, so making the dots less noticeable (used to produce NLQ print) **2** *verb* to cover part of an item with another

overlay *noun* **(a) keyboard overlay =** strip of paper that is placed above keys on a keyboard to indicate their function **(b)** small section of a program that is larger than the main memory capacity of a computer, and is loaded into memory when required, so that main memory only contains the sections it requires to run a program; **form overlay =** heading or other matter held in store and printed out at the same time as the text; **overlay manager =** system software that manages (during run-time) the loading and execution of sections of a program when they are required; **overlay region =** area of main memory that can be used by the overlay manager to store the current section of the program being run; **overlay segments =** short sections of a long program that can be loaded into memory when required and executed

COMMENT: contrast with virtual memory management

overload *verb* to demand more than the device is capable of; *the computer is overloaded with that amount of processing;* **channel overload =** transmission of data at a rate greater than the channel capacity

overpunching *noun* altering data on a paper tape by punching additional holes

overrun *verb* data that was missed by a receiver because it was not synchronized with the transmitter or because it operates at a slower speed than the transmitter and has no buffer

overwrite *verb* to write data to a location (memory or tape or disk) and, in doing so, to destroy any data already contained in that location; *the latest data input has overwritten the old information*

over-voltage protection *noun* safety device that prevents a power supply voltage exceeding certain specified limits

oxide *noun* chemical compound of oxygen; **ferric oxide =** iron oxide used as a coating for magnetic disks and tapes; **metal oxide semiconductors (MOS) =** production and design method for a certain family of integrated circuits using patterns of metal conductors and oxide deposited onto a semiconductor; *see also* MOSFET, CMOS

Pp

p = PICO-

P-code *noun* intermediate code produced by a compiler that is ready for an interpreter to process, usually from PASCAL programs

pack 1 *noun* number of punched cards or magnetic disks; **disk pack** = number of magnetic disks on a single spindle, either fixed or removable (from the drive) **2** *verb* **(a)** to put things into a container for selling *or* sending; *to pack goods into cartons; the diskettes are packed in plastic wrappers; the computer is packed in expanded polystyrene before being shipped* **(b)** to store a quantity of data in a reduced form, often by representing several characters of data with one stored character; **packed decimal** = way of storing decimal digits in a small space, by using only four bits for each digit; **packed format** = two binary coded decimal digits stored within one computer word *or* byte (usually achieved by removing the check *or* parity bit)
NOTE: opposite is **padding**

package *noun* **(a)** group of different items joined together in one deal; **package deal** = agreement where several different items are agreed at the same time; *we are offering a package deal which includes the whole office computer system, staff training and hardware maintenance* **(b)** **applications package** = set of computer programs and manuals that cover all aspects of a particular task (such as payroll, stock control, invoicing, etc.); **packaged** *or* **canned software** *or* **software package** = computer programs and manuals designed for a special purpose; *the computer is sold with accounting and word-processing packages*

◊ **packaging** *noun* material used to protect goods which are being packed; attractive material used to wrap goods for display; *airtight packaging; packaging material* NOTE: no plural

packet *noun* group of bits of uniform size which can be transmitted as a group, using a packet switched network; **packet assembler/disassembler (PAD)** =

dedicated computer that converts serial data from asynchronous terminals to a form that can be transmitted along a packet switched (synchronous) network; *the remote terminal is connected to a PAD device through which it accesses the host computer;* **packet switched data service** *or* **packet switched network (PSN)** = service which transmits data in packets of a set length; **packet switching** = method of sending messages *or* data in uniform-sized packets, and processing and routing packets rather than bit streams

packing *noun* **(a)** action of putting goods into boxes and wrapping them for shipping; *what is the cost of the packing? packing is included in the price* **(b)** putting large amounts of data into a small area of storage; **packing density** = amount of bits of data which can be stored in a unit area of a disk *or* tape; **packing routine** = program which packs data into a small storage area **(c)** material used to protect goods; *packed in airtight packing*
NOTE: no plural

PAD = PACKET ASSEMBLER/DISASSEMBLER

pad 1 *noun* number of keys arranged together; **cursor pad** = group of cursor control keys; **keypad** = group of special keys used for certain applications; **hex keypad** = set of sixteen keys, with all the figures (0-9, A-F) needed to enter hexadecimal numbers; **numerical keypad** = set of ten keys with figures (0-9), included on most computer keyboards as a separate group, used for entering large amounts of data in numeric form **2** *verb* to; **pad character** = extra character added to a string *or* packet *or* file until it is a required size

◊ **padding** *noun* material (characters or digits) added to fill out a string *or* packet until it is the right length
NOTE: opposite is **packing**

paddle *noun* computer peripheral consisting of a knob *or* device which is turned to move a cursor *or* pointer on the screen; **games paddle** = device held in the hand to move a cursor *or* graphics in a computer game

page *noun* **(a)** sheet of paper **(b)** amount of text, displayed on a computer monitor *or* screen (which if printed out will fill a page of paper *or* which fills the screen); **page break** = (i) point at which a page ends and a new page starts (in continuous text); (ii) marker used when word-processing to show where a new page should start; **page description language (PDL)** = software that controls a printer's actions to print a page of text to a particular format according to a user's instructions; **page display** = showing on the screen a page of text as it will appear when printed out; **page length** = length of a page (in word-processing); **pages per minute (ppm)** = measurement of the speed of a printer as the number of pages of text printed every minute; **page printer** = printer which composes one page of text and then prints it rapidly **(c)** section of main store, which contains data *or* programs; **multiple base page** = multi-user system in which each user and the operating system have one page of main memory, which can then call up other pages within main memory; **page addressing** = main memory which has been split into blocks, with a unique address allocated to each block of memory which can then be called up and accessed individually, when required; **page boundary** = point where one page ends and the next starts; **page protection** = software controls to ensure that pages are not overwritten by accident *or* copied into a reserved section of memory; **page table** = list of all the pages and their locations within main memory, used by the operating system when accessing a page **(d)** one section of a main program which can be loaded into main memory when required **2** *verb* **(a)** to make up a text into pages **(b)** to divide computer backing store into sections to allow long programs to be executed in a small main memory

◇ **pagination** *noun* putting a text into pages; arrangement of pages in a book

◇ **paging** *noun* virtual memory technique that splits main memory into small blocks (pages) which are allocated an address and which can be called up when required; **paging algorithm** = formula by which the memory management allocates memory to pages, also covering the transfer from backing storage to main memory in the most efficient way

COMMENT: a virtual memory management system stores data as pages in memory to provide an apparently larger capacity main memory by storing unused pages in backing store, copying them into main memory only when required

paired registers *noun* two basic word size registers used together as one large word size register (often used for storing address words); *the 8-bit CPU uses a paired register to provide a 16-bit address register*

palette *noun* range of colours which can be used (on a printer *or* computer display)

QUOTE the colour palette option offer sixteen colours from a range of over four thousand
Electronics & Wireless World

panel *noun* flat section of a casing with control knobs *or* sockets; *the socket is on the back panel;* **control panel** = panel with indicators and switches which allows an operator to monitor and control the actions of a computer *or* peripheral; **front panel** = main computer system control switches and status indicators

paper *noun* thin material used for making books *or* newspapers *or* stationery items; **paper feed** = slot into which paper is introduced (in a printer); *US* **paper slew** = PAPER THROW; **paper tape** = long strip of paper on which data can be recorded, usually in the form of punched holes; **paper tape punch** = device which punches holes in paper tape to carry data; **paper tape reader** = device which accepts punched paper tape and converts the punched information stored on it into signals which a computer can process; **paper tape feed** = method by which paper tape is passed into a machine; **paper throw** = rapid vertical movement of paper in a printer; **paper tray** = container used to hold paper to be fed into a printer

◇ **paper-fed** *adjective* (device) which is activated when paper is introduced into it; *a paper-fed scanner*

◇ **paperless** *adjective* without using paper; **paperless office** = electronic office *or* office which uses computers and other electronic devices for office tasks and avoids the use of paper

parallel *adjective* (i) (computer system) in which two or more processors operate simultaneously on one or more items of data; (ii) two or more bits of a word transmitted over separate lines at the same time; **parallel access** = data transfer between two devices with a number of bits

(usually one byte wide) being sent simultaneously; **parallel adder** = number of adders joined together in parallel, allowing several digits to be added at once; **parallel computer** = computer with one or more logic or arithmetic units, allowing parallel processing; **parallel connection** = transmission link that handles parallel data; *their average transmission rate is 60,000 bps through parallel connection;* **parallel data transmission** = transmission of bits of data simultaneously along a number of data lines; **parallel input/output (PIO)** = data input or output from a computer in a parallel form; **parallel input/output chip** = dedicated integrated circuit that performs all handshaking, buffering, etc., needed when transferring parallel data to and from a CPU; **parallel input/parallel output (PIPO)** = device that can accept and transmit parallel data; **parallel input/serial output (PISO)** = device that can accept parallel data and transmit serial data; **parallel interface** or **port** = circuit and connector that allows parallel data to be received or transmitted; **parallel operation** = number of processes carried out simultaneously on a number of inputs; **parallel port** *see* PARALLEL INTERFACE; **parallel priority system** = number of peripherals connected in parallel to one bus, if they require attention, they send their address and an interrupt signal, which is then processed by the computer according to device priority; **parallel printer** = printer that accepts character data in parallel form; **parallel processing** = computer operating on several tasks simultaneously; **parallel running** = running an old and a new computer system together to allow the new system to be checked before it becomes the only system used; **parallel search storage** = data retrieval from storage that uses part of the data other than an address to locate the data; **parallel transfer** = data transfer between two devices with a number of bits (usually one byte wide) being sent simultaneously; **parallel transmission** = number of data lines carrying all the bits of a data word simultaneously
NOTE: opposite is **serial transmission**

parameter *noun* information which defines the limits or actions of something, such as a variable or routine or program; *the X parameter defines the number of characters displayed across a screen; the size of the array is set with this parameter;* **parameter-driven software** = software whose main functions can be modified and tailored to a user's needs by a number of variables; **parameter testing** = program to examine the parameters and set up the

system or program accordingly; **parameter word** = data word that contains information defining the limits or actions of a routine or program; **physical parameter** = description of the size, weight, voltage or power of a system

◊ **parametric (subroutine)** *noun* subroutine that uses parameters to define its limits or actions

◊ **paramterization** *noun* action of setting parameters for software

parity *noun* being equal; **block parity** = parity check on a block of data; **column parity** = parity check on every punched card or tape column; **even parity (check)** = error checking system in which any series of bits transmitted must have an even number of binary ones; **odd parity (check)** = error checking system in which any series of bits transmitted must have an odd number of binary ones; **parity bit** = extra bit added to a data word as a parity checking device; **parity check** = method of checking (odd or even parity check) for errors and that transmitted binary data has not been corrupted; **parity flag** = indicator that shows if data has passed a parity check or if data has odd or even parity; **parity interrupt** = interrupt signal from an error checking routine that indicates that received data has failed a parity check and is corrupt; **parity track** = one track on magnetic or paper tape that carries the parity bit

parsing *noun* operation to break down high-level language code into its element parts when translating into machine code

part *noun* **(a)** section of something; **part page display** = display of only a section of a page, and not the whole page **(b) spare part** = small piece of a machine which is needed to replace a piece which is broken or missing; *the printer won't work - we need to get a spare part*

partial carry *noun* temporary storage of all carries generated by parallel adders rather than a direct transfer

◊ **partial RAM** *noun* RAM chip in which only a certain area of the chip functions correctly, usually in newly released chips (partial RAM's can be used by employing more than one to make up the capacity of one fully functional chip)

partition 1 *noun* section of computer memory set aside as foreground or background memory; **partitioned file** = one file made up of several smaller sequential files, each part can be accessed individually by the control program **2** *verb* to divide a large file *or* block into several smaller units which can be accessed and handled more easily

PASCAL high-level structured programming language used both on micros and for teaching programming

pass 1 *noun* (i) the execution of a loop, once; (ii) single operation; **single-pass assembler** = assembler program that translates the source code in one action; **sorting pass** = single run through a list of items to put them into order **2** *verb* action of moving the whole length of a magnetic tape over the read/write heads

password *noun* word *or* series of characters which identifies a user so that he can access a system; *the user has to key in the password before he can access the database*

> QUOTE the system's security features let you divide the disk into up to 256 password-protected sections
>
> *Byte*

patch *noun* (temporary) correction made to a program; small correction made to software by the user, on the instructions of the software publisher

path *noun* possible route or sequence of events *or* instructions within the execution of a program

pattern *noun* series of regular lines *or* shapes which are repeated again and again; **pattern recognition** = algorithms *or* program functions that can identify a shape from a video camera, etc.

◇ **patterned** *adjective* with patterns

PC (a) = PERSONAL COMPUTER low cost microcomputer intended mainly for home and light business use; **PC compatible** = computer that is compatible with another common make (usually the IBM PC) **(b)** = PRINTED CIRCUIT (BOARD) **(c)** = PROGRAM COUNTER

> QUOTE in the UK, the company is known not for PCs but for PC printers
>
> *Which PC?*

PCB = PRINTED CIRCUIT BOARD

PCM = PLUG-COMPATIBLE MANUFACTURER company that produces add-on boards which are compatible with another manufacturer's computer

PCU = PERIPHERAL CONTROL UNIT device that converts input and output signals and instructions to a form that a peripheral device will understand

PDL = PAGE DESCRIPTION LANGUAGE, PROGRAM DESIGN LANGUAGE

PDN = PUBLIC DATA NETWORK

peak 1 *noun* highest point; maximum value of a variable *or* signal; **peak period** = time of the day when most power is being used; **time of peak demand** = time when something is being used most; **peak output** = highest output **2** *verb* to reach the highest point

peek *noun* BASIC computer instruction that allows the user to read the contents of a memory location; *you need the instruction PEEK 1452 here to examine the contents of memory location 1452;* compare POKE

pel *see* PIXEL

pen *see* LIGHT PEN; **pen recorder** = peripheral which moves a pen over paper according to an input (a value or coordinate)

per *preposition* **(a)** as per = according to; **as per sample** = as shown in the sample; **as per specification** = according to the details given in the specification **(b)** at a rate of; **per hour** *or* **per day** *or* **per week** *or* **per year** = for each hour *or* day *or* week *or* year **(c)** out of; *the rate of imperfect items is about twenty-five per thousand; the error rate has fallen to twelve per hundred*

◇ **percentile** *noun* one of a series of ninety-nine figures below which a certain percentage of the total falls

perfect 1 *adjective* completely correct *or* with no mistakes; *we check each batch to make sure it is perfect; she did a perfect typing test* **2** *verb* to make something which is completely correct; *he perfected the process for making high grade steel*

◇ **perfectly** *adverb* with no mistakes *or* correctly; *she typed the letter perfectly*

perforations *noun* line of very small holes in a sheet of paper *or* continuous stationery, to help when tearing

◊ **perforated tape** *noun* paper tape *or* long strip of tape on which data can be recorded in the form of punched holes

◊ **perforator** *noun* machine that punches holes in a paper tape

perform *verb* to do well *or* badly

◊ **performance** *noun* way in which someone *or* something acts; **as a measure of the system's performance** = as a way of judging if the system is working well; *in benchmarking, the performances of several systems or devices are tested against a standard benchmark;* **high performance** = high quality *or* high specification equipment

period *noun* **(a)** length of time; *for a period of time or for a period of months or for a six-year period; sales over a period of three months* **(b)** *US* full stop *or* printing sign used at the end of a piece of text

◊ **periodic** *or* **periodical** *adjective* **(a)** from time to time; *a periodic review of the company's performance* **(b)** periodic = (signal *or* event) that occurs regularly; *the clock signal is periodic*

◊ **periodically** *adverb* from time to time

peripheral 1 *adjective* which is not essential *or* which is attached to something else **2** *noun* (i) item of hardware (such as terminals, printers, monitors, etc.) which is attached to a main computer system; (ii) any device that allows communication between a system and itself, but is not directly operated by the system; *peripherals such as disk drives or printers allow data transfer and are controlled by a system, but contain independent circuits for their operation;* **fast peripheral** = peripheral that communicates with the computer at very high speeds, limited only by the speed of the electronic circuits; **slow peripheral** = peripheral such as a card reader, where mechanical movement determines speed; **peripheral control unit (PCU)** = device that converts the input/output signals and instructions from a computer to a form and protocol which the peripheral will understand; **peripheral driver** = program *or* routine used to interface, manage and control an input/output device *or* peripheral; **peripheral equipment** = (i) external devices that are used with a computer, such as a printer *or* scanner; (ii) (communications) equipment external to a central processor that provides extra features; **peripheral interface adapter (PIA)** = circuit that allows a computer to communicate with a peripheral by providing serial and parallel ports and other handshaking signals required to

interface the peripheral; **peripheral limited** = CPU that cannot execute instructions at normal speed because of a slow peripheral; **peripheral memory** = storage capacity available in a peripheral; **peripheral processing units (PPU)** = device used for input, output or storage which is controlled by the CPU; **peripheral software driver** = short section of computer program that allows a user to access and control a peripheral easily; *same as* DEVICE DRIVER; **peripheral transfer** = movement of data between a CPU and peripheral; **peripheral unit** = (i) item of hardware (such as terminal, printer, monitor, etc.) which is attached to a main computer system; (ii) any device that allows communication between a system and itself, but is not operated only by the system

permanent *adjective* which will last for a very long time *or* for ever; **permanent dynamic memory** = storage medium which retains data even when power is removed; **permanent error** = error in a system which cannot be mended; **permanent file** = data file that is stored in a backing storage device such as a disk drive; **permanent memory** = computer memory that retains data even when power is removed; *see also* NON-VOLATILE MEMORY

◊ **permanently** *adverb* done in a way which will last for a long time; *the production number is permanently engraved on the back of the computer casing*

permutation *noun* number of different ways in which something can be arranged; *the cipher system is very secure since there are so many possible permutations for the key*

persistence *noun* length of time that a CRT will continue to display an image after the picture beam has stopped tracing it on the screen; *slow scan rate monitors need long persistence phosphor to prevent the image flickering*

person *noun* human being

◊ **personal** *adjective* referring to one person; **personal computer (PC)** = low-cost microcomputer intended mainly for home and light business use; **personal identification device (PID)** = device (such as a card) connected *or* inserted into a system to identify *or* provide authorization for a user; **personal identification number (PIN)** = unique sequence of digits that identifies a user to provide authorization to access a system (often used on automatic cash dispensers *or* with a PID or password to enter a system)

◊ **personalize** *verb* to customize *or* to adapt a product specially for a certain user

PERT = PROGRAM EVALUATION AND REVIEW TECHNIQUE definition of tasks *or* jobs and the time each requires, arranged in order to achieve a goal

petal printer = DAISY WHEEL PRINTER

phantom ROM *noun* duplicate area of read-only memory that is accessed by a special code

phase 1 *noun* one part of a larger process; **run phase** = period of time when a program is run; **compile phase** = period of time during which a program is compiled **2** *verb* **to phase in** *or* **to phase out** = to introduce something gradually *or* to reduce something gradually; **phased change-over** = new device that is gradually introduced as the old one is used less and less

phone 1 *noun* telephone *or* machine used for speaking to someone over a long distance; *we had a new phone system installed last week;* **phone call** = speaking to someone on the phone; **to make a phone call** = to speak to someone on the telephone; **to answer the phone** *or* **to take a phone call** = to reply to a call on the phone; **phone number** = set of figures for a particular telephone; *he keeps a list of phone numbers in a little black book; the phone number is on the company notepaper; can you give me your phone number?*

phosphor *noun* substance that produces light when excited by some form of energy, usually an electron beam, used for the coating inside a cathode ray tube; *see* TELEVISION; **phosphor coating** = thin layer of phosphor on the inside of a CRT screen; **phosphor dots** = individual dots of red, green and blue phosphor on a colour CRT screen; **phosphor efficiency** = measure of the amount of light produced in ratio to the energy received from an electron beam; **long persistence phosphor** = television screen coating that retains the displayed image for a period of time longer than the refresh rate, so reducing flicker effects

COMMENT: a thin layer of phosphor is arranged in a pattern of small dots on the inside of a television screen which produces an image when scanned by the picture beam

photo 1 *prefix* referring to light
◊ **photodigital memory** *noun* computer memory system that uses a LASER to write

data onto a piece of film which can then be read many times but not written to again NOTE: also called WORM (Write Once Read Many times memory)
◊ **photoresist** *noun* chemical *or* material that hardens into an etch resistant material when light is shone on it; *to make the PCB, coat the board with photoresist, place the opaque pattern above, expose, then develop and etch, leaving the conducting tracks;* **positive photoresist** = method of forming photographic images where exposed areas of photoresist are removed, used in making PCBs

physical *adjective* solid *or* which can be touched; **physical database** = organization and structure of a stored database; **physical layer** = the ISO/OSI defined network layer that defines rules for bit rate, power and medium for signal transmission; *see also* LAYER
◊ **physical record** *noun* **(a)** maximum unit of data that can be transmitted in a single operation **(b)** all the information, including control data for one record stored in a computer system

PIA = PERIPHERAL INTERFACE ADAPTER circuit that allows a computer to communicate with a peripheral by providing serial and parallel ports and other handshaking signals required to interface the peripheral

pica *noun* typeface used on a printer, giving ten characters to the inch

pickup reel *noun* empty reel used to take the tape as it is played from a full reel

pico- (p) *prefix* representing one million millionth of a unit; **picosecond (pS)** = one million millionth of a second

picture 1 *noun* printed *or* drawn image of an object or scene; *this picture shows the new design;* **picture beam** = moving electron beam in a TV, that produces an image on the screen by illuminating the phosphor coating and by varying its intensity according to the received signal; **picture element** *or* **pixel** = smallest single unit *or* point on a display whose colour *or* brightness can be controlled; *see also* PIXEL; **picture processing** = analysis of information contained in an image, usually by computer *or* electronic methods, providing analysis *or* recognition of objects in the image; **picture transmission** = transmission of images over a telephone line; *see also* FACSIMILE TRANSMISSION **2** *verb* to visualize an object *or* scene; *try to* *picture the layout before starting to draw it in*

PID = PERSONAL IDENTIFICATION DEVICE device (such as a card) connected *or* inserted into a system to identify or provide authorization for a user

piggyback *verb* to connect two integrated circuits in parallel, one top of the other to save space; *piggyback those two memory chips to boost the memory capacity;* **piggyback entry** = to gain unauthorized access to a computer system by using an authorized user's password *or* terminal

◊ **piggybacking** *noun* using transmitted messages to carry acknowledgements from a message which has been received earlier

PILOT computer programming language that uses a text-based format and is mainly used in computer-aided learning

pilot 1 *noun* used as a test, which if successful will then be expanded into a full operation; *the company set up a pilot project to see if the proposed manufacturing system was efficient; the pilot factory has been built to test the new production process;* **pilot system** = system constructed to see if it can be manufactured, if it works and if the end-user likes it **2** *verb* to test; *they are piloting the new system*

PIN = PERSONAL IDENTIFICATION NUMBER unique sequence of digits that identifies the user

COMMENT: the PIN is commonly used in automatic cash machines in banks, along with a card (PID) which allows the user to be identified

pin *noun* **(a)** one of several short pieces of wire attached to an integrated circuit package that allows the IC to be connected to a circuit board **(b)** short piece of metal, part of a plug which fits into a hole in a socket; *use a three-pin plug to connect the printer to the mains;* **three-pin mains plug** = plug with three pins (one neutral, one live and one earthed); **two-pin mains plug** = plug with two pins (one neutral, one live)

◊ **pinfeed** *noun see* TRACTOR FEED

pinchwheel *noun* small rubber wheel in a tape machine that holds the tape in place and prevents flutter

PIO = PARALLEL INPUT/OUTPUT *see also* PIPO, PISO

pipeline (computer) 1 *noun* CPU or ALU that is constructed in blocks and executes instructions in steps, each block dealing with one part of the instruction, so speeding up program execution **2** *verb* **(a)** to schedule inputs to arrive at the microprocessor when nothing else is happening, so increasing apparent speed **(b)** to begin processing of a second instruction while still processing the present one to increase speed of execution of a program

PIPO = PARALLEL INPUT/PARALLEL OUTPUT

pirate 1 *noun* person who copies a patented invention *or* a copyright work and sells it; *the company is trying to take the software pirates to court; a pirate copy of a computer program* **2** *verb* to manufacture copies of an original copyrighted work illegally; *a pirated tape or a pirated design; the designs for the new system were pirated in the Far East; he used a cheap pirated disk and found the program had bugs in it*

◊ **piracy** *noun* copying of patented inventions *or* copyright works NOTE: no plural

COMMENT: the items most frequently pirated are programs on magnetic disks and tapes which are relatively simple to copy

PISO = PARALLEL INPUT/SERIAL OUTPUT

pitch *noun* measurement of the horizontal spacing of typed characters

pix *noun* picture *or* pictures

◊ **pixel** *or* **picture element** *noun* smallest single unit *or* point of a display whose colour *or* brightness can be controlled

COMMENT: in high resolution display systems the colour or brightness of a single pixel can be controlled; in low resolution systems a group of pixels are controlled at the same time

QUOTE an EGA display and driver give a resolution of 640 x 350 pixels and support sixteen colours
PC Business World
QUOTE adding 40 to each pixel brightens the image and can improve the display's appearance
Byte

PL/1 = PROGRAMMING LANGUAGE/1 high level programming language mainly used in commercial and scientific work on large computers, containing features of ALGOL, COBOL and FORTRAN

PLA = PROGRAMMABLE LOGIC ARRAY IC that can be permanently programmed to perform logic operations on data

COMMENT: a PLA consists of a large matrix of paths between input and output pins, with logic gates and a fusible link at each connection point which can be broken or left to conduct when programming to define a function from input to output

place *noun* position of a digit within a number

plaintext *noun* text *or* information that has not been encrypted *or* coded; *the messages were sent as plaintext by telephone; enter the plaintext message into the cipher machine*

PLAN low-level programming language

plan 1 *noun* **(a)** organized way of doing something **(b)** drawing which shows how something is arranged *or* how something will be built **2** *verb* to organize carefully how something should be done NOTE: **planning - planned**
◇ **planner** *noun* software program that allows appointments and important meetings to be recorded and arranged in the most efficient way
◇ **planning** *noun* organizing how something should be done; *long-term planning or short-term planning*
NOTE: no plural

plant *verb* to store a result in memory for later use

plasma display *or* **gas plasma display** *noun* display screen using the electroluminescing properties of certain gases to display text

COMMENT: this is a modern thin display usually used in small portable computers

QUOTE the disadvantage of using plasma technology is that it really needs mains power to work for any length of time
QUOTE the plasma panel came out of the extended use test well
Micro Decision

plastic bubble keyboard *noun* keyboard whose keys are small bubbles in a plastic sheet over a contact which when pressed completes a circuit

COMMENT: these are very solid and cheap keyboards but are not ideal for rapid typing

play back *verb* to read data *or* a signal from a recording medium; *after you have recorded the music, press this button to play back the tape and hear what it sounds like*
◇ **playback head** *noun* transducer that reads signals recorded on a storage medium and usually converts them to an electrical signal; *disk playback head; tape playback head*

player missile graphics *see* SPRITES

PLD = PROGRAMMABLE LOGIC DEVICE

plex database *noun* database structure in which data items can be linked together
◇ **plex structure** *noun* network structure *or* data structure in which each node is connected to all the others

PL/M = PROGRAMMING LANGUAGE FOR MICROPROCESSORS high level programming language derived from PL/1 for use on microprocessors

plot 1 *noun* graph *or* map **2** *verb* to draw an image (especially a graph) based on information supplied as a series of coordinates; **plotting mode** = ability of some word-processors to produce graphs by printing a number of closely spaced characters rather than individual pixels (this results in a broad low-resolution line)
◇ **plotter** *noun* computer peripheral that draws straight lines between two coordinates; **plotter driver** = dedicated software that converts simple instructions issued by a user into complex control instructions to direct the plotter; **plotter pen** = instrument used in a plotter to mark the paper with ink as it moves over the paper; **digital plotter** = plotter which receives the coordinates to plot to in a digital form; **drum plotter** = computer output device that consists of a movable pen and a piece of paper wrapped around a drum that rotates, creating patterns and text; **incremental plotter** = plotter which receives positional data as increments to its current position rather than separate coordinates; **printer-plotter** = high-resolution printer that is able to mimic a plotter and produce low-resolution plots; **x-y plotter** *or* **graph plotter** = plotter which plots to coordinates supplied, by moving the pen in two planes while the paper remains stationary

COMMENT: plotters are used for graph and diagram plotting and can plot curved lines as a number of short straight lines

plug 1 *noun* connector with protruding pins that is inserted into a socket to provide an electrical connection; *the printer is supplied with a plug;* **adapter plug** = plug which allows devices with different plugs (two-pin, three-pin, etc.) to be fitted into the same socket; **plug-compatible** = equipment manufactured to operate with another system when connected to it by a connector *or* cable; *this new plug-compatible board works much faster than any of its rivals, we can install it by simply plugging it into the expansion port* **2** *verb* **to plug in** = to make an electrical connection by pushing a plug into a socket; *no wonder the computer does nothing, you have not plugged it in at the mains;* **plug-in unit** = small electronic circuit that can be simply plugged into a system to increase its power NOTE: opposite is **unplug**

QUOTE it allows room for up to 40K of RAM via plug-in memory cartridges
Which PC?
QUOTE adding memory is simply a matter of plugging a card into an expansion bus connector
Byte

plus *or* **plus sign** *noun* printed *or* written sign (+) showing that figures are added *or* showing a positive value

PMOS = P-channel METAL OXIDE SEMICONDUCTOR metal oxide semiconductor transistor that conducts via a small region of p-type semiconductor

pnp transistor *noun* layout of a bipolar transistor whose collector and emitter are of p-type semiconductor and whose base is n-type semiconductor

point 1 *noun* **(a)** place *or* position; **access point** = point on a circuit board *or* in software, allowing an engineer to check signals *or* data; **breakpoint** = symbol inserted into a program which stops its execution at that point to allow registers, variables and memory locations to be examined (used when debugging a program); **re-entry point** = point in a program *or* routine where it is re-entered; **starting point** = place where something starts **(b)** **binary point** = dot which indicates the division between the bits for the numbers' whole units and the fractional part of the binary number; **decimal point** = dot (in a decimal number) which indicates the division between a whole unit and its fractional parts (such as 4.25); **percentage point** = 1 per cent **2** *verb* **to point out** = to show

◊ **point-of-sale (POS)** place in a shop where goods are paid for; **electronic point-of-sale (EPOS)** = system that uses a computer terminal at a point-of-sale site for electronic fund transfer *or* stock control as well as product pricing, etc.

◊ **pointer** *noun* **(a)** variable in a computer program that contains the address to a data item *or* instruction; *increment the contents of the pointer to the address of the next instruction;* **pointer file** = file of pointers referring to large amounts of stored data **(b)** graphical symbol used to indicate the position of a cursor on a computer display; *desktop publishing on a PC is greatly helped by the use of a pointer and mouse*

◊ **point to point** *noun* communications network where every point is connected to every other

COMMENT: this provides rapid reliable transmissions but is very expensive and wasteful in cabling

QUOTE the arrow keys, the spacebar or the mouse are used for pointing, and the enter key or the left mouse button are to pick
PC User
QUOTE pointing with the cursor and pressing the joystick button eliminates use of the keyboard entirely
Soft

poke *noun* computer instruction that modifies an entry in a memory by writing a number to an address in memory; *poke 1423,74 will write the data 74 into location 1423; compare with* PEEK

POL = PROBLEM-ORIENTATED LANGUAGE

polar *adjective* referring to poles; **polar coordinates** = system of defining positions as an angle and distance from the origin; *compare with* CARTESIAN COORDINATES

◊ **polarized** *adjective* **polarized plug** = plug which has a feature (usually a peg *or* a special shape) so that it can only be inserted into a socket in one way; **polarized edge connector** = edge connector that has a hole or key to prevent it being plugged in the wrong way round

◊ **polarity** *noun* definition of direction of flow of flux *or* current in an object; **electrical polarity** = definition of whether an electrical signal is positive *or* negative, indicating if a point is a source *or* collector of electrical current (positive polarity terminals are usually marked red, negative are black); **magnetic polarity** = method of indicating if a point is a source *or* collector of magnetic flux patterns; **polarity test** = check to see which electrical terminal is positive and which negative; **reverse polarity** = situation where positive and negative terminals have been confused, resulting in the equipment not functioning

Polish notation *see* REVERSE

poll *verb (of computer)* to determine the state of a peripheral in a network; **polled interrupt** = interrupt signal determined by polling a device

◊ **polling** *noun* system of communication between a controlling computer and a number of networked terminals (the computer checks each terminal in turn to see if it is ready to receive *or* transmit data, and takes the required action); **polling characters** = special sequence of characters for each terminal to be polled (when a terminal recognises its sequence, it responds); **polling interval** = period of time between two polling operations; **polling list** = order in which terminals are to be polled by a computer; **polling overhead** = amount of time spent by a computer in calling and checking each terminal in a network

COMMENT: the polling system differs from other communications systems in that the computer asks the terminals to transmit *or* receive, not the other way round

polynomial code *noun* error detection system that uses a set of mathematical rules applied to the message before it is transmitted and again when it is received to reproduce the original message

POP 2 high level programming language used for list processing applications

pop *verb* (instruction to a computer) to read and remove the last piece of data from a stack; **pop-down menu** *or* **pop-up menu** = menu that can be displayed on the screen at any time by pressing the appropriate key, usually displayed over material already on the screen

QUOTE you can use a mouse to access pop-up menus and a keyboard for word processing
Byte

port *noun* socket *or* physical connection allowing data transfer between a computer's internal communications channel and another external device; **asynchronous port** = connection to a computer allowing asynchronous data communications; **input port** = circuit *or* connector that allows a computer to receive data from other external devices; **joystick port** = socket and interfacing circuit into which a joystick can be

plugged; **output port** = circuit *or* connector that allows a computer to output *or* transmit data to another machine *or* device; **parallel port** = circuit and connector that allows parallel data to be received *or* transmitted; **printer port** = output port of a computer with a standard connector to which a printer is connected to receive character data (either serial *or* parallel); **serial port** = circuit that converts parallel data in a computer to and from a serial form, allowing serial data access; **port selector** = switch that allows the user to choose which peripheral a computer (via its o/p port) is connected to; **port sharing** = device that is placed between one I/O port and a number of peripherals, allowing the computer access to all of them

QUOTE the 40 Mbyte hard disk model is provided with eight terminal ports
Micro Decision

portable 1 *noun* compact self-contained computer that can be carried around and used either with a battery pack *or* mains power supply **2** *adjective* (any hardware *or* software *or* data files) that can used on a range of different computers; **portable software** *or* **portable programs** = programs that can be run on several different computer systems

◊ **portability** *noun* extent to which software *or* hardware can be used on several systems

QUOTE although portability between machines is there in theory, in practice it just isn't that simple
Personal Computer World

POS = POINT-OF-SALE place in a shop where goods are paid for; **EPOS** = ELECTRONIC POINT-OF-SALE system that uses a computer terminal at a point-of-sale site for electronic fund transfer *or* stock control as well as product pricing, etc.

position 1 *noun* place where something is; *this is the position of that chip on the PCB* **2** *verb* to place something in a special place; *the VDU should not be positioned in front of a window; position this photograph at the top right-hand corner of the page;* **positioning time** = amount of time required to access data stored in a disk drive *or* tape machine, including all mechanical movements of the read head and arm

◊ **positional** *adjective* referring to position; in a certain position

positive *adjective* **(a)** meaning "yes"; **positive response** = communication signal that indicates correct reception of a message; **positive terminal** = connection to a power supply source that is at a higher electrical potential than ground and supplies current to a component **(b)** (image) which shows objects as they are seen; **positive display** = (screen) where the text and graphics are shown as black on a white background to imitate a printed page; **positive presentation** = screen image which is coloured on a white background; *compare* NEGATIVE **(c)** electrical voltage greater than zero; **positive logic** = logic system in which a logical one is represented by a positive voltage level, and a logical zero represented by a zero or negative voltage level

post *verb* **(a)** to enter data into a record in a file **2** *prefix* action that occurs after another; **post-editing** = editing and modifying text after it has been compiled *or* translated by a machine; **post-formatted** = (text) arranged at printing time rather than on screen; **post mortem** = examination of a computer program *or* piece of hardware after it has failed to try to find out why the failure took place

◊ **postbyte** *noun* in a program instruction, the data byte following the op code that defines the register to be used

◊ **postfix** *noun* word *or* letter written after another; **postfix notation** = mathematical operations written in a logical way, so that the operator appears after the operands, this removes the need for brackets; *normal notation: (x-y) + z, but using postfix notation: xy - z +* (NOTE: often referred to as **reverse Polish notation**)

◊ **postprocessor** *noun* **(a)** microprocessor that handles semi-processed data from another device **(b)** program that processes data from another program, which has already been processed

potential *noun* ability of energy to carry out work (by transformation); **potential difference** = voltage difference between two points in a circuit

power *noun* **(a)** unit of energy in electronics equal to the product of voltage and current, measured in Watts; **automatic power off** = equipment that will switch itself off if it has not been used for a certain time; **power dump** = to remove all power from a computer; **power failure** = stoppage of the electrical power supply (for a long *or* very short period of time) which will cause electrical equipment to stop working or malfunction, unless they are battery backed; **power loss** = amount of power lost (in transmission *or* due to connection equipment); **"power off"** = switching off *or* disconnecting an electrical device from its power supply; **"power on"** = indication that a voltage is being supplied to a piece of electrical equipment; **power-on reset** = automatic reset of a CPU to a known initial state immediately after power is applied (some CPUs will not automatically start with clear registers, etc., but might contain garbage); **power pack** = self-contained box that will provide a voltage and current supply for a circuit; **power supply** *or* **power supply unit (PSU)** = electrical circuit that provides certain direct current voltage and current levels from an alternating current source for use in other electrical circuits (a PSU will regulate, smooth and reduce the mains voltage level for use in low power electronic circuits); **power up** = to switch on *or* apply a voltage to a electrical device; **uninterruptable power supply (UPS)** = power supply that can continue to provide a regulated supply to equipment even after mains power failure **(b)** mathematical term describing the number of times a number is to be multiplied by itself; *5 to the power 2 is equal to 25* NOTE: written as small figures in superscript: 10^5 : say: "ten to the power five"

◊ **powered** *adjective* driven by a type of energy

ppm = PAGES PER MINUTE

pre- *prefix* meaning before; **pre-agreed** = which has been agreed in advance; **pre-allocation** = execution of a process which does not begin until all memory and peripheral requirements are free for use; **pre-fetch** = instructions read and stored in a short temporary queue with a CPU that contains the next few instructions to be processed, increasing the speed of execution

precede *verb* to come before; *instruction which cancels the instruction which precedes it*

◊ **precedence** *noun* computational rules defining the order in which mathematical operations are calculated (usually multiplications are done first, then divisions, additions, and subtractions last); **operator precedence** = order in which a number of mathematical operations will be carried out

precise *adjective* very exact; *the atomic clock will give the precise time of starting the process*

◊ **precision** *noun* being very accurate; **double precision** = using two data words to store a number, providing greater precision; **multiple precision** = using more than one byte of data for number storage to increase possible precision; **precision of a number** = number of digits in a number; **single precision** = number stored in one word; *compare with* MULTIPLE, DOUBLE

precompiled code *noun* code that is output from a compiler, ready to be executed

precondition *verb* to condition data before it is processed

predefined *adjective* which has been defined in advance

predicate *noun* function *or* statement used in rule-based programs such as expert systems

QUOTE we should stick to systems which we know are formally sound, such as predicate logic
Personal Computer World

pre-edit *verb* to change text before it is run through a machine to make sure it is compatible

prefix *noun* (a) code *or* instruction *or* character at the beginning of a message *or* instruction (b) word attached to the beginning of another word to give it a special meaning
◊ **prefix notation** *noun* mathematical operations written in a logical way, so that the operator appears before the operands, this removes the need for brackets

preformatted *adjective* which has been formatted already; *a preformatted disk*

preparation *noun* getting something ready; **data preparation** = conversion of data into a machine-readable form (usually by keyboarding) before data entry

preprocessor *noun* (a) software that partly processes *or* prepares data before it is compiled *or* translated (b) small computer that carries out some initial processing of raw data before passing it to the main computer
◊ **preprocess** *verb* to carry out initial organization and simple processing of data

QUOTE the C preprocessor is in the first stage of converting a written program into machine instructions
QUOTE the preprocessor can be directed to read in another file before completion, perhaps because the same information is needed in each module of the program
Personal Computer World

preprogrammed *adjective* (chip) which has been programmed in the factory to perform one function

presentation layer *noun* ISO/OSI standard network layer that agrees on formats, codes and requests for start and end of a connection; *see also* ISO/OSI, LAYER

preset *verb* to set something in advance; *the printer was preset with new page parameters*
NOTE: **presetting - preset**

press *verb* to push with the fingers; *to end the program press ESCAPE*

prestore *verb* to store data in memory before it is processed

presumptive address *noun* initial address in a program, used as a reference for others
◊ **presumptive instruction** *noun* unmodified program instruction which is processed to obtain the instruction to be executed

prevent *verb* to stop something happening; *the police prevented anyone from leaving the building; we have changed the passwords to prevent hackers getting into the database*
◊ **preventive** *or* **preventative** *adjective* which tries to stop something happening; **preventive maintenance** = regular checks on equipment to correct and repair any small faults before they cause a major problem; *we have a preventive maintenance contract for the system*
◊ **prevention** *noun* preventing something happening

preview *verb* to display text *or* graphics on a screen as it will appear when it is printed out
◊ **previewer** *noun* feature that allows a user to see on screen what a page will look like when printed; *the built-in previewer allows the user to check for mistakes*

previous *adjective* which happens earlier; *copy data into the present workspace from the previous file*
◊ **previously** *adverb* happening earlier; *the data is copied onto previously formatted disks*

primary *adjective* first *or* basic *or* most important; **primary key** = unique identifying word that selects one entry from a database; **primary memory** or **store** or **main memory** = (i) small fast-access internal memory of a computer system (whose main memory is slower secondary storage) which stores the program currently being used; (ii) main internal memory of a computer system; **primary station** = the single station in a data network that can select a path and transmit the primary station status is temporary and is transferred from one station to another

◊ **primarily** adverb mainly

prime 1 adjective very important; **prime attribute** = most important feature or design of a system 2 noun number that can only be divided by itself and by one; *the number seven is a prime*

primer noun manual or simple instruction book with instructions and examples to show how a new program or system operates

primitive noun basic unit

print 1 noun (a) characters made in ink on paper; *he was very pleased to see his book in print; the print from the daisy-wheel printer is clearer than that from the line printer;* **print control character** = special character sent to a printer that directs it to perform an action or function (such as change font), rather than print a character; **print format** = way in which text is arranged when printed out, according to embedded codes, etc., used to set the margins, headers, etc.; **print hammer** = moving arm in a daisy-wheel printer that presses the metal character form onto the printer ribbon leaving a mark on the paper; **print life** = number of characters a component can print before needing to be replaced; *the printhead has a print life of over 400 million characters;* **print modifiers** = codes in a document that cause a printer to change mode, i.e. from bold to italic; **print pause** = temporarily stopping a printer while printing (to change paper, etc.); **print spooling** = automatic printing of a number of different documents in a queue at the normal speed of the printer, while the computer is doing some other task; **print style** = typeface used on a certain printer or for a certain document 2 verb to put letters or figures in ink on paper; *printed agreement; printed regulations; the printer prints at 60 characters per second*

◊ **printed circuit** or **printed circuit board (PCB)** noun flat insulating material that has conducting tracks of metal printed or etched onto its surface which complete a circuit when components are mounted on it

◊ **printer** noun (a) device that converts input data in an electrical form into a printed readable form; **computer printer** or **line printer** = machine which prints information from a computer, printing one line at a time; **barrel printer** = type of printer where characters are located around a rotating barrel; **bi-directional printer** = printer which is able to print characters from left to right or from right to left as the head moves backwards and forwards across the paper; **chain printer** = printer whose characters are located on a continuous belt; **daisy-wheel printer** = printer with characters arranged on interchangeable daisy-wheels; **dot-matrix printer** = printer which forms characters from a series of tiny dots printed close together; **impact printer** = printer that prints text and symbols by striking an inked ribbon onto paper with a metal character; **ink-jet printer** = printer that produces characters by sending a stream of tiny drops of electrically charged ink onto the paper (the movement of the ink drops is controlled by an electric field); **laser printer** = high-resolution printer that uses a laser source to print high quality dot-matrix characters; **line printer** = printer which prints draft-quality information at high speed (typical output is 200 - 3000 lines per minute); **page printer** = printer which composes one page of text, then prints it rapidly; **thermal printer** = printer where the character is formed on thermal paper with a printhead containing a matrix of small heating elements; **printer buffer** = temporary store for character data waiting to be printed (used to free the computer before the printing is completed making the operation faster); **printer control characters** = command characters in a text which transmit printing commands to a printer; **printer driver** = dedicated software that converts and formats users' commands ready for a printer; **printer-plotter** = high resolution printer that is able to operate as a low resolution plotter; **printer port** = output port of a computer to which a printer is connected to receive character data (either parallel or serial); **printer quality** = standard of printed text from a particular printer (high resolution dot-matrix printers produce near letter-quality, daisy-wheel printers produce letter-quality text); **printer ribbon** = roll of inked material which passes between a printhead and the paper

◊ **printhead** noun (i) row of needles in a dot-matrix printer that produce characters as a series of dots; (ii) metal form of a character that is pressed onto an inked ribbon to print the character on paper

◊ **printing** *noun* action of printing

◊ **print out** *verb* to print information stored in a computer with a printer

◊ **printout** *noun* **computer printout** = printed copy of information from a computer; *the sales director asked for a printout of the agents' commissions*

◊ **printwheel** *noun* daisy-wheel *or* the wheel made up of a number of arms, with a character shape at the end of each arm, used in a daisy-wheel printer

prior *adjective* happening before; **prior to** = before; *the password has to be keyed in prior to accessing the system*

◊ **priority** *noun* importance of a device *or* software routine in a computer system; *the operating system has priority over the application when disk space is allocated; the disk drive is more important than the printer, so it has a higher priority;* **job priority** = importance of a job compared to others; **priority interrupt** = signal to a computer that takes precedence over any other task; *see also* INTERRUPT, NON-MASKABLE INTERRUPT; **priority interrupt table** = list of peripherals and their priority when they send an interrupt signal (used instead of a hardware priority scheduler); **priority sequence** = the order in which various devices that have sent an interrupt signal are processed, according to their importance or urgency (a disk drive will usually come before a printer in a priority sequence); **priority scheduler** = system that organizes tasks into correct processing priority (to improve performance)

privacy *noun* the right of an individual to limit the extent of and control the access to the data that is stored about him; **privacy of data** = rule that data is secret and must not be accessed by users who have not been authorized; **privacy of information** = rule that unauthorized users cannot obtain data about private individuals from databases *or* that each individual has the right to know what information is being held about him *or* her on a database

private *adjective* belonging to an individual *or* to a company, not to the public; **private address space** = memory address range that is reserved for a single user, not for public access

privilege *noun* status of a user referring to the type of program he can run and the resources he can use; *the systems manager has a privileged status so he can access any file on the system;* **privileged account** = computer account that allows special programs *or* access to sensitive system data; *the system manager can access anyone else's account from his privileged account;* **privileged instructions** = computer commands which can only be executed via a privileged account, such as delete another account *or* set up a new user *or* examine passwords

problem *noun* **(a)** question to which it is difficult to find an answer; **to solve a problem** = to find an answer to a problem; **problem definition** = the clear explanation, in logical steps, of a problem that is to be solved; **problem-orientated language (POL)** = high-level programming language that allows certain problems to be expressed easily **(b)** malfunction *or* fault with hardware or software; **problem diagnosis** = finding the cause and method of repairing a fault *or* error

procedure *noun* **(a)** small section of computer instruction code that provides a frequently used function and can be called upon from a main program; *this procedure sorts all the files into alphabetic order, you can call it from the main program by the instruction SORT; see also* SUBROUTINE **(b)** method *or* route used when solving a problem; *you should use this procedure to retrieve lost files; the procedure is given in the manual;* **procedure-orientated language** = high-level programming language that allows procedures to be programmed easily

◊ **procedural** *adjective* using a procedure (to solve a problem); **procedural language** = high-level programming language in which the programmer enters the actions required to achieve the result wanted

proceed *verb* to move forward; *after spellchecking the text, you can proceed to the printing stage*

process 1 *noun* a number of tasks that must be carried out to achieve a goal; *the process of setting up the computer takes a long time; there are five stages in the process;* **process bound** = program that spends more time executing instructions and using the CPU than in I/O operations; **process chart** = diagram that shows each step of the computer procedures needed in a system; **process control** = automatic control of a process by a computer; **process control computer** = dedicated computer that controls and manages a process; **process control system** = complete input, output modules, a CPU with memory and a program (usually stored in ROM) and control and feedback devices such as A/D and D/A converters that completely monitors, manages and regulates a process **2** *verb* to carry out a number of tasks to produce a result (such as sorting data *or* finding the solution to a problem); *we processed the new data; processing all the information will take a long time*

◊ **processing** *noun* sorting of information; using a computer to solve a problem *or* organize data; *page processing time depends on the complexity of a given page; see also* CPU; **batch processing** = computer system, where information is collected into batches before being loaded into the computer; **data processing** *or* **information processing** = selecting and examining data in a computer to produce information in a special form; **image processing** = analysis of information contained in an image (usually by electronic means or by using a computer to provide the analysis or for recognition of objects in the image); **immediate processing** = processing data when it appears, rather than waiting for a certain clock pulse or time; **off-line processing** = processing by devices not under the control of a central computer; **on-line processing** = processing by devices connected to and under the control of the central computer (the user remains in contact with the central computer while processing); **query processing** = processing of queries, either by extracting information from a database *or* translating query commands from a query language; **real-time processing** = processing operations that take a time of the same order of magnitude as the problem to be solved; **serial processing** = executing one instruction at a time; *compare with* PARALLEL PROCESSING; **word-processing** *or* **text processing** = working with words, using a computer to produce, check and change texts, reports, letters, etc. NOTE: no plural

COMMENT: the central processing unit is a hardware device that allows a computer to manipulate and modify data; a compiler is a software language processor that translates data and instructions in one language into another form

processor *noun* hardware *or* software device that is able to manipulate *or* modify data according to instructions; **array processor** = computer that can act upon several arrays of data simultaneously for very fast mathematical applications; **associative processor** = processor that uses associative storage; **attached processor** = separate microprocessor in a system that

performs certain functions under the control of a central processor; **auxiliary processor** = extra, specialized processor, such as an array or numerical processor, that can work with a main processor to improve performance; **back-end processor** = special purpose auxiliary processor; **bit-slice processor** = construction of a large word size CPU by joining a number of smaller word size blocks; **distributed processor** = using many small computers at different workstations instead of one central computer; **front-end processor (FEP)** = processor placed between an input source and the central computer, whose function is to preprocess received data to reduce the main computer's workload; **input/output processor** = processor that handles data communications, including DMA and error correcting functions; **language processor** = program that translates from one language to machine code (there are three type of translator: (i) assembler; (ii) compiler; (iii) interpreter); **network processor** = signal multiplexer controlled by a microprocessor in a network; *(in a multiprocessor system)* **order code processor** = a processor which decodes and performs the arithmetic and logical operations according to the program code; **processor controlled keying** = data entry by an operator which is prompted and controlled by a computer; **processor interrupt** = to send an interrupt signal to a processor requesting attention, that will usually cause it to stop what it is doing and attend to the calling device; **processor status word (PSW)** = word which contains a number of status bits, such as carry flag, zero flag and overflow flag; **processor-limited** = (operation *or* execution time) that is set by the speed of the processor rather than a peripheral; **dual processor** = computer system with two processors for faster program execution; **image processor** = electronic *or* computer system used for image processing; **word-processor** = small computer which is used for working with words, to produce texts, reports, letters, etc.

QUOTE each chip will contain 128 processors and one million transistors
Computer News

produce *verb* to make *or* manufacture

◊ **producer** *noun* person *or* company *or* country which manufactures; *country which is a producer of high quality computer equipment; the company is a major magnetic tape producer*

◊ **producing** *adjective* which produces; **producing capacity** = capacity to produce

product *noun* **(a)** item which is made *or* manufactured; **basic product** = main product made from a raw material; **end product** *or* **final product** *or* **finished product** = product made at the end of a production process **(b)** manufactured item for sale; **product engineer** = engineer in charge of the equipment for making a product; **product line** *or* **product range** = series of different products made by the same company which form a group (such as printers in different models *or* different colours, etc.) **(c)** result after multiplication

◊ **production** *noun* making *or* manufacturing of goods for sale; *production will probably be held up by industrial action; we are hoping to speed up production by installing new machinery;* **batch production** = production in batches; **mass production** = manufacturing of large quantities of goods; *mass production of monitors or of calculators;* **rate of production** *or* **production rate** = speed at which items are made; **production control** = control of the manufacturing of a product (using computers)
NOTE: no plural

◊ **productive** *adjective* during *or* in which something useful is produced; **productive time** = period of time during which a computer can run error-free tasks

program 1 *noun* complete set of instructions which direct a computer to carry out a particular task; **assembly program** = number of assembly code instructions which perform a task; **background program** = computer program with a very low priority; **blue-ribbon program** = perfect program that runs first time with no errors; **control program/monitor** *or* **control program for microcomputers (CP/M)** = popular operating system for microcomputers; **diagnostic program** = software that helps find faults in a computer system; **executive program** = master program in a computer system that controls the execution of other programs; **foreground program** = high priority program in a multitasking system; **hardwired program** = computer program built into the hardware (and which cannot be changed); **job control program** = short program of job control instructions loaded before a particular application is run, that sets up the system as required by the application; **library program** = (i) number of specially written *or* relevant software routines, which a user can insert into his own program, saving time and effort; (ii) group of functions which a computer needs to refer to often, but which are not stored in main memory; **linear program** =

computer program that contains no loops *or* branches; **user program** = program written by a user (often in a high-level language); **program address counter** = register in a CPU that contains the location of the next instruction to be processed; **program branch** = one or more paths that can be followed after a conditional statement; **program cards** = punched cards that contain the instructions that make up a program; **program coding sheet** = specially preprinted form on which computer instructions can be written, simplifying program writing; **program compatibility** = ability of two pieces of software to function correctly together; **program compilation** = translation of an encoded source program into machine code; **program counter (PC)** *or* **instruction address register (IAR)** = register in a CPU that contains the location of the next instruction to be processed; *see also* INSTRUCTION ADDRESS REGISTER; SEQUENCE CONTROL REGISTER; **program crash** = unexpected failure of a program due to a programming error *or* a hardware fault; *I forgot to insert an important instruction which caused a program to crash, erasing all the files on the disk!;* **program design language (PDL)** = programming language used to design the structure of a program; **program development** = all the operations involved in creating a computer program from first ideas to initial writing, debugging and the final product; **program development system** = all the hardware and software needed for program development on a system; **program documentation** = set of instruction notes, examples and tips on how to use a program; *see also* MANUAL; **program editor** = software that allows the user to alter, delete and add instructions to a program file; **program execution** = instructing a processor to execute in sequence the instructions in a program; **program file** = file containing a program rather than data; **program flowchart** = diagram that graphically describes the various steps in a program; **program generator** = software that allows users to write complex programs using a few simple instructions; **program instruction** = single word *or* expression that represents one operation (in a high level program each program instruction can consist of a number of low level machine code instructions); **program library** = collection of useful procedures and programs which can be used for various purposes and included into new software; **program line** = one row of commands *or* arguments in a computer program; **program line number** = number that refers to a line of program code in a computer program; **program listing** = list of the set of instructions that make up a program (program listings are displayed in an ordered manner, BASIC listings by line number, assembly listings by memory location; they do not necessarily represent the order in which the program will be executed, since there could be jumps *or* subroutines); **program maintenance** = keeping a program free of errors and up to date; **program name** = identification name for a stored program file; **program origin** = address at which the first instruction of a program is stored; **program relocation** = moving a stored program from one area of memory to another; **program register** = register in a CPU that contains an instruction during decoding and execution operations; **program report generator** = software that allows users to create reports from files, databases and other stored data; **program run** = executing (in correct order) the instructions in a program; **program segment** = section of a main program that can be executed in its own right, without the rest of the main program being required; *see also* OVERLAY; **program specification** = document that contains details on all the functions and abilities of a computer program; **program stack** = section of memory reserved for storing temporary system *or* program data; **program statement** = high level program instruction that is made up of a number of machine code instructions; **program step** = one operation within a program, usually a single instruction; **program storage** = section of main memory in which programs (rather than operating system or data) can be stored; **program structure** = the way in which sections of program code are interlinked and operate; **program testing** = testing a new program with test data to ensure that it functions correctly; **program verification** = number of tests and checks performed to ensure that a program functions correctly **2** *verb* to write *or* prepare a set of instructions which direct a computer to perform a certain task; **programmed halt** = instruction within a program that when executed, halts the processor (to restart the CPU a reset action is required); **programmed learning** = using educational software which allows a learner to follow a course of instruction NOTE: **programs - programming - programmed**

◊ **programmable** *adjective* & *noun* (device) that can accept and store instructions then execute them; **programmable calculator** = small calculator

which can hold certain basic mathematical calculating programs; **programmable logic array (PLA)** *or* **programmable logic device (PLD)** = integrated circuit that can be permanently programmed to perform logic operations on data using a matrix of links between input and output pins; **programmable interrupt controller** = circuit *or* chip which can be programmed to ignore certain interrupts, accept only high priority interrupts and select the priority of interrupts; **programmable key** = special key on a computer terminal keyboard that can be programmed with various functions *or* characters; **programmable memory (PROM)** = electronic device in which data can be stored; *see also* EAROM; EEPROM; EPROM; ROM; **programmable read only memory (PROM)** = memory integrated circuit that can be programmed with data by a user (some PROMs provide permanent storage, others such as EPROMs are erasable); **hand-held programmable** = very small computer, which can be held in the hand, used for inputting information when a larger terminal is not available (as by a salesman on a call)

◊ **programmer** *noun* **(a)** person who is capable of designing and writing a working program; *the programmer is still working on the new software;* **applications programmer** = programmer who writes applications software; **systems programmer** = programmer specializes in writing systems software **(b)** device that allows data to be written into a programmable read only memory

◊ **programming** *noun* **(a)** writing programs for computers; **programming in logic** = PROLOG; **programming language** = software that allows a user to write a series of instructions to define a particular task, which will then be translated to a form that is understood by the computer; **programming standards** = rules to which programs must conform to produce compatible code **(b)** writing data into a PROM device

COMMENT: programming languages are grouped into different levels: the high-level languages such as BASIC and PASCAL are easy to understand and use, but offer slow execution time since each instruction is made up of a number of machine code instructions; low-level languages such as assembler are more complex to read and program in but offer faster execution time

project 1 *noun* planned task; *his latest project is computerizing the sales team; the design project was entirely worked out on computer; CAD is essential for accurate project design* **2** *verb* to forecast future figures from a set of data; *the projected sales of the new PC*

◇ **projection** *noun* forecast of a situation from a set of data; *the projection indicates that sales will increase*

PROLOG = PROGRAMMING IN LOGIC high-level programming language using logical operations for artificial intelligence and data retrieval applications

PROM (a) = PROGRAMMABLE READ-ONLY MEMORY read-only memory which can be programmed by the user (as opposed to ROM, which is programmed by the manufacturer); **PROM burner** *or* **programmer** = electronic device used to program a PROM; *see also* EPROM **(b)** = PROGRAMMABLE MEMORY electronic memory in which data can be stored

prompt *noun* message *or* character displayed to remind the user that an input is expected; *the prompt READY indicates that the system is available to receive instructions;* **command prompt** = symbol displayed to indicate a command is expected

propagate *verb* to travel *or* spread; **propagated error** = one error in a process that has affected later operations; **propagating error** = an error that occurs in one place *or* operation and affects another operation *or* process

◇ **propagation delay** *noun* time taken for an output to appear in a logic gate after the input is applied

proportion *noun* size of something as compared to others

◇ **proportional spacing** *noun* printing system where each letter takes a space proportional to the character width ('i' taking less space than 'm'); *compare* MONOSPACING

protect *verb* to stop something being damaged; **protected location** = memory location that cannot be altered *or* cannot be accessed without authorization; **protected storage** = section of memory that cannot be altered; **copy protect** = switch used to prevent copies of a disk being made; *all the disks are copy protected;* **crash protected** = (disk) which uses a head protection *or* data corruption protection system; *if the disk is crash protected, you will never lose your work*

◇ **protection** *noun* action of protecting; **protection key** = signal checked to see if a program can access a section of memory; **protection master** = spare copy of a master film *or* tape; **copy protection** = preventing copies being made; *a hard disk may crash because of faulty copy protection; the new product will come without copy protection;* **data protection** = making sure that data is not copied by an unauthorized user; **Data Protection Act** = act which prevents confidential data about people being copied without authority (also every organization that keeps information subject to the act on a computer, must protect it adequately)

◇ **protective** *adjective* which protects; *the disks are housed in hard protective cases*

protocol *noun* pre-agreed signals, codes and rules to be used for data exchange between systems; **protocol standards** = standards laid down to allow data exchange between any computer system conforming to the standard

prototype *noun* first working model of a device *or* program, which is then tested and adapted to improve it

◇ **prototyping** *noun* making a prototype

provider *noun* **information provider (ip)** = company *or* user that provides an information source for use in a videotext system (such as the company providing weather information *or* stock exchange reports)

pS = PICOSECOND

pseudo- *prefix* meaning similar to something, but not genuine

◇ **pseudo-code** *noun* English sentence structures, used to describe program instructions which are translated at a later date into machine code

◇ **pseudo-digital** *adjective* (modulated analog signals) produced by a modem and transmitted over telephone lines

◇ **pseudo-instruction** *noun* label (in an assembly language program) that represents a number of instructions

◇ **pseudo-operation** *noun* command in an assembler program that controls the assembler rather than producing machine code

◇ **pseudo-random** *noun* generated sequence that appears random but is repeated over a long period; **pseudo-random number generator** = hardware *or* software that produces pseudo-random numbers

PSN = PACKET SWITCHED NETWORK

PSU = POWER SUPPLY UNIT electrical circuit that provides certain direct current voltage and current levels from an alternating current source to other electrical circuits

COMMENT: a PSU will regulate, smooth and step down a higher voltage supply for use in small electronic equipment

PSW = PROCESSOR STATUS WORD

PTR = PAPER TAPE READER

public *adjective* open to anyone to use; made for the use of everyone; **public data network (PDN)** = data transmission service for the public; **public domain (PD)** = documents *or* text *or* program that has no copyright and can be copied by anyone; **public key cipher system** = cipher that uses a public key to encrypt messages and a secret key to decrypt them (conventional cipher systems use one secret key to encrypt and decrypt messages); *see also* CIPHER, KEY

publish *verb* to produce and sell software; **desktop publishing (DTP)** = design, layout and printing of documents using special software, a small computer and a printer; **electronic publishing** = (i) use of desktop publishing packages and laser printers to produce printed matter; (ii) using computers to write and display information (such as viewdata)

pull *verb* to remove data from a stack; *compare with* PUSH

pull-down *or* **pull-up menu** *noun* menu that can be displayed on screen at any time by pressing an appropriate key, usually displayed over the material already on screen

◇ **pull up** *verb* **to pull up a line** = to connect *or* set a line to a voltage level; *pull up the input line to a logic one by connecting it to 5 volts*

QUOTE the gated inputs lower the standby current and also eliminate the need for input pull-up or pull-down resistors
Electronics & Power

pulse 1 *noun* short period of a voltage level; **pulse stream** *or* **train** = continuous series of similar pulses **2** *verb* to apply a short-duration voltage level to a circuit; *we pulsed the input but it still would not work*

COMMENT: electric pulse can be used to transmit information, as the binary digits 0 and 1 correspond to 'no pulse' and 'pulse' (the voltage level used to distinguish the binary digits 0 and 1, is often zero and 5 or 12 volts, with the pulse width depending on transmission rate)

punch 1 *noun* device for making holes in punched cards **2** *verb* to make a hole; **punch** *or* **punched card** = small piece of card which contains holes which represent various instructions *or* data; **punched card reader** = device that transforms data on a punched card to a form that can be recognized by a computer; **punched tag** = card attached to a product in a shop, with punched holes containing data about the product; **punched (paper) tape** = strip of paper tape that contains holes to represent data

punctuation mark *noun* printing symbol, which cannot be spoken, but which helps to understand the text

COMMENT: the main punctuation marks are the question mark and exclamation mark; inverted commas (which show the type of text being written); the comma, full stop, colon and semicolon (which show how the words are broken up into sequences); the apostrophe (which shows that a letter or word is missing); the dash and hyphen and brackets (which separate or link words)

pure *adjective* clean *or* not mixed with other things; **pure code** = code that does not modify itself during execution

purge *verb* to remove unnecessary *or* out of date data from a file

push *verb* to press something *or* to move something by pressing on it; **push-down list** *or* **stack** = temporary storage queue system where the last item added is at the top of the list; *see also* LIFO; **push instruction** *or* **operation** = computer instruction that stores data on a LIFO list *or* stack; **push-up list** *or* **stack** = temporary storage queue system where the last item added is at the bottom of the list; *see also* FIFO

◇ **pushbutton** *adjective* which works by pressing on a button

put *verb* to push *or* place data onto a stack

Qq

QBE = QUERY BY EXAMPLE

QISAM = QUEUED INDEXED SEQUENTIAL ACCESS METHOD indexed sequential file that is read item by item into a buffer

QSAM = QUEUED SEQUENTIAL ACCESS METHOD queue of blocks that are waiting to be processed, retrieved using a sequential access method

QL = QUERY LANGUAGE

quad *noun* meaning four times; **quad density** = four bits of data stored in the usual place of one

◇ **quadding** *noun* insertion of spaces into text to fill out a line

QUOTE in this case, interfacing is done by a single quad-wide adapter
Minicomputer News

quadr- *prefix* meaning four

◇ **quadruplex** *noun* four signals combined into a single one
NOTE: no plural

quality *noun* what something is like *or* how good or bad something is; *there is a market for good quality secondhand computers;* **high quality** *or* **top quality** = very best quality; *the store specializes in high quality imported items;* **printer quality** = standard of printed text from a particular printer (high-resolution dot-matrix printers produce near-letter quality, daisy-wheel printers produce letter-quality text); *see also* LETTER, NEAR-LETTER, DRAFT; **quality control** = checking that the quality of a product is good NOTE: no plural

QUOTE the computer operates at 120cps in draft quality mode and 30cps in near letter-quality mode
Minicomputer News

quantify *verb* to quantify the effect of something = to show the effect of something in figures; *it is impossible to quantify the effect of the new computer system on our production*

◇ **quantifiable** *adjective* which can be quantified; *the effect of the change in the pricing structure is not quantifiable*

◇ **quantifier** *noun* sign *or* symbol which indicates the quantity *or* range of a predicate

quantity *noun* (a) amount *or* number of items; *a small quantity of illegal copies of the program have been imported; he bought a large quantity of spare parts* (b) large amount; *the company offers a discount for quantity purchases*

quantize *verb* to convert an analog signal into a numerical representation; *the input signal is quantized by an analog to digital converter;* **quantizing noise** = noise on a signal due to inaccuracies in the quantizing process

◇ **quantizer** *noun* device used to convert an analog input signal to a numerical form, that can be processed by a computer

◇ **quantization** *noun* conversion of an analog signal to a numerical representation; **quantization error** = error in converting an analog signal into a numerical form due to limited accuracy *or* rapidly changing signal; *see also* A/D

quartz (crystal) clock *noun* small slice of quartz crystal which vibrates at a certain frequency when an electrical voltage is supplied, used as a very accurate clock signal for computers and other high precision timing applications

quasi- *prefix* almost *or* which seems like; **quasi-instruction** = label (in an assembly program) that represents a number of instructions

quaternary *adjective* referring to four bits *or* levels *or* objects

query 1 *noun* question; **query by example (QBE)** = way of finding information in a database by stating the items that are to be found; **query facility** = program (usually a database *or* retrieval system) that allows the user to ask questions and receive answers *or* access certain information according to the query; **query language (QL)** = language in a database management system, that allows a database to be searched and queried easily; **query processing** = processing of queries, either by extracting information from a database *or* by translating query commands from a query language **2** *verb* to ask a question about something *or* to suggest that something may be wrong

queue 1 *noun* **(a)** line of people waiting one behind the other; *to form a queue or to join a queue* **(b)** list of data *or* tasks that are waiting to be processed; series of documents (such as orders, application forms) which are dealt with in order; **channel queue** = (i) queue of requests to use a channel; (ii) queue of data that has yet to be sent over a channel; **file queue** = number of files temporarily stored in order before being processed; *output devices such as laser printers are connected on-line with an automatic file queue;* **job queue** = number of tasks arranged in order waiting to be processed in a batch system; **his order went to the end of the queue** = his order was dealt with last; **queue discipline** = method used as the queue structure, either LIFO or FIFO; **queue management** *or* **queue manager** = software which orders tasks to be processed; *this is a new software spooler with a built-in queue management* **2** *verb* to add more data *or* tasks to the end of a queue; **queued indexed sequential access method (QISAM)** = indexed sequential file that is read item by item into a buffer; **queued sequential access method (QSAM)** = queue of blocks that are waiting to be processed, retrieved using a sequential access method; **queuing time** = period of time messages have to wait before they can be processed *or* transmitted

quick *adjective* fast *or* not taking any time; *the company made a quick recovery; he is looking for a quick return on his investment; we are hoping for a quick sale*

◊ **quickly** *adverb* without taking much time

◊ **quicksort** *noun* very rapid file sorting and ordering method

quiescent *adjective* state of a process *or* circuit *or* device when no input signal is applied ·

quiet *adjective* not making very much noise; *laser printers are much quieter than dot-matrix*

quintet *noun* byte made up of five bits

quit *verb* to leave a system *or* a program; *do not forget to save your text before you quit the system*
NOTE: **quitting - quit**

quote 1 *verb* to repeat words used by someone else; to repeat a reference number **2** *noun* **quotes** = quotation marks *or* inverted commas; **single quotes** = single inverted commas; **double quotes** = double inverted commas; *the name of the company should be put in double quotes*

◊ **quotation marks** *noun* inverted commas *or* signs printed at the beginning and end of text to show that it has been quoted from another source

quotient *noun* result of one number divided by another

COMMENT: when two numbers are divided, the answer is made up of a quotient and a remainder (the fractional part), 16 divided by 4 is equal to a quotient of 4 and zero remainder, 16 divided by 5 is equal to a quotient of 3 and a remainder of 1

QWERTY *noun* **QWERTY keyboard** = English language keyboard for a typewriter *or* computer, where the top line of letters are Q-W-E-R-T-Y; *the computer has a normal QWERTY keyboard; see also* AZERTY

QUOTE the keyboard does not have a QWERTY layout but is easy to use
Micro Decision

Rr

R & D = RESEARCH AND DEVELOPMENT; **R & D department** = department in a company that investigates new products, discoveries and techniques

race *verb* error condition in a digital circuit, in which the state *or* output of the circuit is very dependent on the exact timing between the input signals (faulty output is due to unequal propagation delays on the separate input signals at a gate)

rack *noun* metal supporting frame for electronic circuit boards and peripheral devices such as disk drives; **rack mounted** = system consisting of removable circuit boards in a supporting frame

radial transfer *noun* data transfer between two peripherals *or* programs that are on different layers of a structured system (such as an ISO/OSI system)

radix *noun* the value of the base of the number system being used; *the hexadecimal number has a radix of 16;* **radix complement** *see* TEN'S, TWO'S COMPLEMENT; **radix notation** = numbers represented to a certain radix; *see also* BASE NOTATION; **radix point** = dot which indicates the division between a whole unit and its fractional parts

ragged *adjective* not straight *or* with an uneven edge; **ragged left** = printed text with a flush right-hand margin and uneven left-hand margin; **ragged right** = printed text with a flush left-hand margin and uneven right-hand margin; **ragged text** = unjustified text, text with a ragged right margin

RAM = RANDOM ACCESS MEMORY memory that allows access to any location in any order, without having to access the rest first; *compare* SEQUENTIAL ACCESS MEMORY; **partial RAM** = RAM chip in which only a certain area of the chip functions correctly, usually in newly released chips (partial RAM's can be used by employing more than one to make up

the capacity of one fully functional chip); **RAM chip** = chip which stores data, allowing random access; **RAM disk** = section of RAM that is made to look like and behave as a high-speed disk drive (using special software); **RAM loader** = routine that will transfer a program from external backing store into RAM; **RAM refresh** = signals used to update the contents of dynamic RAM chips every few thousandths of a second, involving reading and rewriting the contents, needed to retain data; **RAM refresh rate** = number of times every second that the data in a dynamic RAM chip has to be read and rewritten; **self-refreshing RAM** = dynamic RAM chip that has built-in circuitry to generate refresh signals, allowing data to be retained when the power is off by using a battery; **dynamic RAM** = most common RAM ICs, which use capacititive charge to retain data but which must be refreshed (read from and rewritten to) every few thousandths of a second; **static RAM** = RAM ICs that do not have to be refreshed but cannot store as much data per chip as dynamic RAM; *see also* CHIP, ROM NOTE: there is no plural for RAM, and it often has no article: **512K of RAM; the file is stored in RAM**

COMMENT: dynamic RAM which uses a capacitor to store a bit of data (as a charge) needs to have each location refreshed from time to time to retain the data, but is very fast and can contain more data per unit area than static RAM which uses a latch to store the state of a bit, and has the advantage of not requiring to be refreshed to retain its data, and will keep data for as long as power is supplied

random *adjective* (event) that cannot be anticipated; **pseudo-random** = generated sequence that appears random but is repeated over a long period; **random number** = number that cannot be predicted; **random number generator** =

program which generates random numbers (used in lotteries, games, etc.); **random process** or **direct access** = system whose output cannot be related to its input or internal structure

◊ **random access** noun ability to access immediately memory locations in any order; *disk drives are random access, magnetic tape is sequential access memory;* **random access device** = device whose access time to retrieve data is not dependent on the location or type of data; **random access files** = file in which each item or record can be immediately accessed by its address, without searching through the rest of the file, and is not dependent on the previous location; **random access storage** = storage medium that allows access to any location in any order; **random access memory (RAM)** = memory that allows access to any location in any order, usually in the form of ICs

◊ **random processing** noun processing of data in the order required rather than the order in which it is stored

range 1 noun **(a)** series of items from which the customer can choose; *a wide range of products; the catalogue lists a wide range of computer stationery* **(b)** set of allowed values between a maximum and minimum; **number range** = set of allowable values **2** verb **(a)** to vary or to be different; *the company's products range from a cheap lapheld micro to a multistation mainframe* **(b)** to put text in order to one side; **range left** = move text to align it to the left margin; to move the contents of a word to the left edge

rank verb to sort data into an order, usually according to size or importance

rapid adjective fast; **rapid access** = device or memory whose access time is very short; **rapid access memory** or **fast access memory (FAM)** = storage locations that can be read from or written to very quickly

raster noun system of scanning the whole of a CRT screen with a picture beam by sweeping across it horizontally, moving down one pixel or line at a time; **raster graphics** = graphics where the picture is built up in lines across the screen or page; **raster image processor** = raster which translates software instructions into an image or complete page which is then printed by the printer; *an electronic page can be converted to a printer-readable video image by an on-board raster image processor;* **raster scan** = one sweep of the picture beam horizontally across the front of a CRT screen

rate 1 noun quantity of data or tasks that can be processed in a set time; *the processor's instruction execution rate is better than the older version;* **error rate** = number of errors that occur within a certain time; **information rate** = amount of information content per character multiplied by the number of characters transmitted per second **2** verb to evaluate how good something is or how large something is; **rated throughput** = maximum throughput of a device that will still meet original specifications

ratio noun proportion of one number to another; *the ratio of 10 to 5 is 2:1; the ratio of corrupt bits per transmitted message is falling with new technology*

◊ **rational number** noun number that can be written as the ratio of two whole numbers; *24 over 7 is a rational number; 0.333 can be written as the rational number 1/3*

raw adjective in the original state or not processed; **raw data** = (i) pieces of information that have not yet been input into a computer system; (ii) data in a database which has to be processed to provide information to the user; *this small computer collects raw data from the sensors, converts it and transmits it to the mainframe*

react verb **to react to something** = to act in response to something; **to react with something** = to change because a substance is present

◊ **reactive mode** noun computer operating mode in which each entry by the user causes something to happen but does not provide an immediate response; *compare with* INTERACTIVE; BATCH

read verb **(a)** to look at printed words and understand them; *conditions of sale are printed in such small characters that they are difficult to read; can the OCR read typeset characters?* **(b)** to retrieve data from a storage medium; *this instruction reads the first record of a file; access time can be the time taken to read from a record;* **destructive read** = read operation in which the stored data is erased as it is retrieved; **read back check** = system to ensure that data was correctly received, in which the transmitted data is sent back and checked against the original for any errors; **read cycle** = period of time between address data being sent to a storage device and the data being returned; **read head** =

transducer that reads signals stored on a magnetic medium and converts them back to their original electrical form; **read only =** device *or* circuit whose stored data cannot be changed; **read only memory (ROM) =** memory device that has had data written into it at the time of manufacture, and now its contents can only be read; *the manufacturer provided the monitor program in two ROM chips;* **read rate =** number of bytes *or* bits that a reader can read in a certain time; **read/write channel =** channel that can carry signals travelling in two directions; **read/write cycle =** sequence of events used to retrieve and store data; **read/write head =** transducer that can read *or* write data from the surface of a magnetic storage medium, such as a floppy disk; **read/write memory =** storage medium that can be written to and read from; *compare with* READ ONLY

◊ **readable** *adjective* that can be read *or* understood by someone *or* an electronic device; *the electronic page is converted to a printer-readable video image;* **machine readable =** (commands *or* data) stored on a medium that can be directly input to the computer

◊ **reader** *noun* device that reads data stored on one medium and converts it into another form; **card reader =** device that transforms data on a punched card to a form that can be recognized by the computer; **tape reader =** machine that reads punched holes in paper tape *or* signals on magnetic tape; *see also* OPTICAL

◊ **read-in** *or* **read in** *verb* to transfer data from an external source to main memory; *the computer automatically read-in thirty values from the A/D converter*

◊ **reading** *noun* note taken of figures *or* degrees, especially of degrees on a scale

◊ **readout** *noun* display of data; *the readout displayed the time; the clock had a digital readout;* **destructive readout =** display device that erases previous characters when displaying new ones; **readout device =** device that allows information (numbers *or* characters) to be displayed

> QUOTE some OCR programs can be taught to read typefaces that are not in their library
> *Publish*

> QUOTE the machine easily reads in text from typewriters and daisy-wheel printers
> *PC Business World*

ready *adjective* fit to be used *or* sold; (equipment) that is waiting and able to be used; *the green light indicates the system is ready for another program; the programming will not be ready until next week; the maintenance people hope that the system will be ready for use in 24 hours;* **ready state =** communications line *or* device that is waiting to accept data

real memory *noun* actual physical memory that can be addressed by a CPU; *compare with* VIRTUAL MEMORY

◊ **real number** *noun* (*in computing*) number that is represented with a fractional part (sometimes refers to numbers represented in a floating-point form)

◊ **real time** *noun* actions *or* processing time that is of the same order of magnitude as the problem to be solved (i.e. the processing time is within the same time as the problem to be solved, so that the result can influence the source of the data); *a navigation system needs to be able to process the position of a ship in real time and take suitable action before it hits a rock;* US **real-time clock =** clock in a computer that provides the correct time of day; *compare* RELATIVE-TIME CLOCK; **real-time input =** data input to a system as it happens *or* is required; **real-time multi-tasking =** executing several real-time tasks simultaneously without slowing the execution of any of the processes; **real-time processing =** processing operation that takes a time of the same order of magnitude as the problem to be solved; **real-time simulation =** computer model of a process where each process is executed in a similar time to the real process

◊ **real-time system** *noun* system whose processing time is within that of the problem, so that it can influence the source of the data; *in a real-time system, as you move the joystick left, the image on the screen moves left. If there is a pause for processing it is not a true real-time system*

> QUOTE a real-time process is one which interacts with a real external activity and respects deadlines imposed by that activity
> *.EXE*
> QUOTE define a real-time system as any system which is expected to interact with its environment within certain timing constraints
> *British Telecom Technology Journal*

reboot *verb* to reload an operating system during a computing session; *we rebooted and the files reappeared; see also* BOOT

recall 1 *noun* bringing back text *or* files from store **2** *verb* to bring back text *or* files from store for editing

> QUOTE automatic recall provides the facility to recall the last twenty commands and to edit and re-use them
> *Practical Computing*

receive *verb* to accept data from a communications link; *the computer received data via the telephone line;* **receive only** = computer terminal that can only accept and display data (but not transmit)

◇ **receiver** *noun* electronic device that can detect transmitted signals and present them in a suitable form; **receiver register** = temporary storage register for data inputs, before processing

recode *verb* to code a program which has been coded for one system, so that it will work on another

recognition *noun* (i) being able to recognize something; (ii) process that allows something to be recognized, such as letters on a printed text *or* bars on bar codes, etc.; **recognition logic** = logical software used in OCR, AI, etc.; **optical character recognition** = process that allows printed *or* written characters to be recognized optically (using an optical character reader), and converted into a form that can be input into a computer; **optical mark recognition** = process that allows certain marks *or* lines *or* patterns to be recognized optically (using an optical character reader), and converted into a form that can be input into a computer

◇ **recognize** *verb* to see something and remember that it has been seen before; *the scanner will recognize most character fonts*

◇ **recognizable** *adjective* which can be recognized

recompile *verb* to compile a source program again, usually after changes *or* debugging

reconfigure *verb* to alter the structure of data in a system

◇ **reconfiguration** *noun* altering the structure of data in a system; *I reconfigured the field structure in the file; this program allows us to reconfigure the system to our own requirements; see also* CONFIGURE, SET UP

reconstitute *verb* to return a file to a previous state, usually to restore a file after a crash *or* corruption

record 1 *noun* set of items of related data; *your record contains several fields that have been grouped together under the one heading; this record contains all their personal details;* **chained record** = data record in a chained file; **change** *or* **transaction record** = record containing new data which is to be used to update a master

record; **logical record** = number of items of related data that are held in temporary memory ready to be processed; **physical record** = record and control data combination stored on a backing device; **record count** = number of records within a stored file; **record format** *or* **layout** = organization and length of separate fields in a record; **record length** = quantity of data in a record; **records manager** = program which maintains records and can access and process them to provide information **2** *verb* to store data *or* signals on tape *or* on disk *or* in a computer; *record the results in this column; this device records signals onto magnetic tape; digitally recorded data are used to generate images;* **record button** = key pressed on a recorder when ready to record signals onto a medium; **record gap** *see* BLOCK GAP; **record head** *or* **write head** = transducer that converts an electrical signal into a magnetic field to write the data onto a magnetic medium

> QUOTE you can echo the previous record if a lot of replication is involved
> QUOTE records may be sorted before the report is created, using up to nine sort fields
> *Byte*
> QUOTE file and record-locking procedures have to be implemented to make sure that files cannot be corrupted when two users try to read or write to the same record simultaneously
> *Micro Decision*

recorder *noun* equipment able to transfer input signals onto a storage medium; **magnetic tape recorder** = device with a motor, read/write head and circuitry to allow electrical signals to be recorded onto *or* played back from magnetic tape

> COMMENT: the signal recorded is not always in the same form as the input signal: many recorders record a modulated carrier signal for better quality. A recorder is usually combined with a suitable playback circuit since the read and write heads are often the same physical device

recording *noun* action of storing signals *or* data on tape *or* in a computer; **recording density** = number of bits of data that can be stored in a unit area on a magnetic disk *or* tape

recover *verb* to get back something which has been lost; *it is possible to recover the data but it can take a long time*

◇ **recoverable error** *noun* error type that allows program execution to be continued after it has occurred

◇ **recovery** *noun* **(a)** returning to normal operating after a fault; **automatic recovery**

program = software that is automatically run when a piece of equipment fails, to ensure that the system continues to operate; **failure recovery** = resuming a process *or* program after a failure has occurred and has been corrected; **fall back recovery** = resuming a program after a fault has been fixed, from a point at which the fall back routines were called; **sense recovery time** = time that a RAM device takes to switch from read to write mode; **recovery procedure** = processes required to return a system to normal operation after an error **(b)** getting back something which has been lost; *the recovery of lost files can be carried out using the recovery procedure*

rectify *verb* to correct something *or* to make something right; *they had to rectify the error at the printout stage*

recursion *or* **recursive routine** *noun* subroutine in a program that calls itself during execution; **recursive call** = subroutine that calls itself when it is run

redefine *verb* to change the function *or* value assigned to a variable *or* object; *we redefined the initial parameters;* **to redefine a key** = to change the function of a programmable key; *I have redefined this key to display the figure five when pressed*

◊ **redefinable** *adjective* which can be redefined

QUOTE the idea of the packages is that they enable you to redefine the keyboard
Practical Computing
QUOTE one especially useful command lets you redefine the printer's character-translation table
Byte

red, green, blue (RGB) *noun* **(a)** high-definition monitor system that uses three separate input signals controlling red, green and blue colour picture beams **(b)** the three colour picture beams used in a colour TV

COMMENT: there are three colour guns producing red, green and blue beams acting on groups of three phosphor dots at each pixel location

redirect *verb* to send a message to its destination by another route

◊ **redirection** *noun* sending a message to its destination by another route; *call forwarding is automatic redirection of calls*

redo *verb* to do something again; **redo from start** = start again from the beginning

redraw *verb* to draw again; *can the computer redraw the graphics showing the product from the top view ?*

reduce *verb* **(a)** to make smaller **(b)** to convert raw data into a more compact form which can then be easily processed

◊ **reduced instruction set computer (RISC)** *noun* CPU design whose instruction set contains a small number of simple fast-executing instructions, that makes program writing more complex, but increases speed; *compare with* WISC

redundant *adjective* **(a)** (data) that can be removed without losing any information; *the parity bits on the received data are redundant and can be removed;* **redundant character** = character added to a block of characters for error detection *or* protocol purposes, and carries no information; **redundant code** = check bit *or* data added to a block of data for error detection purposes, and carries no information **(b)** extra piece of equipment kept ready for a task in case of faults

◊ **redundancy** *noun* providing extra components in a system in case there is a breakdown; **longitudinal redundancy check** = check on received blocks of data to detect any errors; **network redundancy** = extra links between points allowing continued operation in the event of one failing; **vertical redundancy check** = (odd) parity check on each character of a block received, to detect any errors; **redundancy checking** = checking of received data for correct redundant codes to detect any errors

reel *noun* holder round which a tape is rolled; *he dropped the reel on the floor and the tape unwound itself;* **pick-up reel** = empty reel used to store tape as it is played from a full reel

◊ **reel to reel** *noun* copying one tape of data onto another magnetic tape; **reel to reel recorder** = magnetic tape recording machine that uses tape held on one reel and feeds it to a pick-up reel

re-entrant program *or* **code** *or* **routine** *noun* one program *or* code shared by many users in a multi-user system (it can be interrupted *or* called again by another user before it has finished its previous run, and returns to the point at which it was interrupted when it has finished that run)

◊ **re-entry** *noun* calling a routine from within that routine; running a program from within that program; **re-entry point** =

point in a program *or* routine where it is re-entered

refer *verb* to mention *or* to deal with *or* to write about something; *the manual refers to the serial port, but I cannot find it*

◊ **reference 1** *noun* **(a)** value used as a starting point for other values, often zero; **reference address** = initial address in a program used as an origin *or* base for others **(b)** mentioning *or* dealing with something; **reference file** = file of data which is kept so that it can be referred to; **reference instruction** = command that provides access to sorted *or* stored data; **reference list** = list of routines *or* instructions and their location within a program; **reference mark** = printed symbol to indicate the presence of a note *or* reference not in the text; **reference retrieval system** = index which provides a reference to a document; **reference table** = list of ordered items; **reference time** = point in time that is used as an origin for further timings *or* measurements **2** *verb* to access a location in memory; *the access time taken to reference an item in memory is short*

> QUOTE a referencing function dynamically links all references throughout a document
>
> *Byte*

reflected code *noun* coding system in which the binary representation of decimal numbers changes by only one bit at a time from one number to the next

reformat *verb* to format a disk that already contains data, and erasing the data by doing so; *do not reformat your hard disk unless you can't do anything else*

◊ **reformatting** *noun* act of formatting a disk which already contains data; *reformatting destroys all the data on a disk;* *see also* FORMAT

refresh *verb* **(a)** to update regularly the contents of dynamic RAM by reading and rewriting stored data to ensure data is retained; *memory refresh signal;* **RAM refresh rate** = number of times every second that the data in a dynamic RAM chip has to be read and rewritten; **self-refreshing RAM** = dynamic RAM chip that has built-in circuitry to generate refresh signals, allowing data to be retained when the power is off, using a battery backup **(b)** **screen refresh** = to update regularly the images on a CRT screen by scanning each pixel with a picture beam to make sure the image is still visible; **refresh rate** = number of times

every second that the image on a CRT is redrawn

regenerate *verb* (i) to redraw an image on a screen many times a second so that it remains visible; (ii) to receive distorted signals, process and error check them, then retransmit the same data

◊ **regenerative memory** *noun* storage medium whose contents need to be regularly refreshed to retain its contents; *dynamic RAM is regenerative memory - it needs to be refreshed every 250ns; the CRT display can be thought of as regenerative memory, it requires regular refresh picture scans to prevent flicker;* **regenerative reading** = reading operation that automatically regenerates and rewrites the data back into memory

region *noun* special *or* reserved area of memory or program

◊ **regional breakpoint** *noun* breakpoint that can be inserted anywhere within a program that is being debugged; *see also* BREAKPOINT, DEBUGGING

register 1 *noun* (i) special location within a CPU (usually one or two words wide) that is used to hold data and addresses to be processed in a machine code operation; (ii) reserved memory location used for special storage purposes; **accumulator register** = most important internal storage register in a CPU, containing the data to be processed; **address register** = register in a computer that is able to store all the bits of an address which can then be processed as a single unit; **base register** = register in a CPU (not usually in small computers) that contains the address of the start of a program; **buffer register** = temporary storage for data being written to *or* read from memory; **circulating register** = shift register whose output is fed back into its input (to form a closed loop); **control register** = storage location for control data; **data register** = area within a CPU used to store data temporarily before it is processed; **external register** = registers which are located outside the main CPU, in locations within main memory, allowing the user to access them easily; **index register** = computer address register that is added to a reference address to provide the location to be accessed; **input/output register** = temporary storage for data received from memory before being transferred to an I/O device or data from an I/O device waiting to be stored in main memory or to be processed; **instruction register** = temporary storage for the instruction that is being executed;

instruction address register (IAR) = register in a CPU that stores the location where instructions are found; **memory address register (MAR)** = register within the CPU that contains the address of the next location to be accessed; **next instruction register** = register in the CPU that contains the address of the next instruction to be processed; **program status word register (PSW register)** = register which contains a number of status bits, such as carry flag, zero flag, overflow flag; **sequence control register (SCR)** = CPU register that contains the address of the next instruction to be processed; *see also* NEXT INSTRUCTION ADDRESS REGISTER; **shift register** = temporary storage into which data can be shifted; **register addressing** = instruction whose address field contains the register in which the operand is stored; **register file** = number of registers used for temporary storage; **register length** = size (in bits) of a register; *in this small micro, the data register is eight bits wide, an address register is sixteen bits wide;* **register map** = display of the contents of all the registers **2** *verb* to react to a stimulus

regulate *verb* to control a process (usually using sensors and a feedback mechanism); **regulated power supply** = constant, controlled voltage *or* current source whose output will not vary with input supply variation

COMMENT: a regulated power supply is required for all computers where components cannot withstand voltage variations

rehyphenation *noun* changing the hyphenation of words in a text after it has been put into a new page format *or* line width

reject *verb* to refuse to accept something; *the computer rejects all incoming data from incompatible sources*

◊ **rejection** *noun* refusing to accept something; **rejection error** = error by a scanner which cannot read a character and so leaves a blank

relational database *noun* set of data where all the items are related; **relational operator** *or* **logical operator** symbol that compares two items; **relational query** = database query that contains relational operators; *the relational query 'find all men under 35 years old' will not work on this system*

◊ **relationship** *noun* way in which two similar things are connected

relative *adjective* which is compared to something; **relative address** = location specified in relation to a reference address; **relative coding** = writing a program using relative address instructions; **relative coordinates** = positional information given in relation to a reference point; **relative data** = data that gives new coordinate information relative to previous coordinates; **relative error** = difference between a number and its correct value (caused by rounding off); **relative-time clock** = regular pulses that allow software in a computer to calculate the real time

relay 1 *noun* electromagnetically controlled switch; *there is a relay in the circuit; it is relay-rated at 5 Amps* **2** *verb* to receive data from one source and then retransmit it to another point; *all messages are relayed through this small micro*

release 1 *noun* **(a)** version of a product; *the latest software is release 5; see also* VERSION **(b)** putting a new product on the market

relevant *adjective* which has an important connection

◊ **relevance** *noun* (i) way in which something has a connection with something else; (ii) importance of something in a situation *or* process

reliability *noun* the ability of a device to function as intended, efficiently and without failure; *it has an excellent reliability record; the product has passed its reliability tests*

◊ **reliable** *adjective* which can be trusted to work properly; *the early version of the software were not completely reliable*

reload *verb* to load again; *we reloaded the program after the crash; see also* LOAD

relocate *verb* to move data from one area of storage to another; *the data is relocated during execution;* **self-relocating program** = program that can be loaded into any part of memory (that will modify its addresses depending on the program origin address)

◊ **relocatable** *adjective* which can be moved to another area of memory without affecting its operation; **relocatable program** = computer program that can be loaded into and executed from any area of memory; *the operating system can load and* *run a relocatable program from any area of memory*

◊ **relocation** *noun* moving to another area in memory; **dynamic relocation** = moving data *or* coding *or* assigning absolute locations during a program execution; **relocation constant** = quantity added to all addresses to move them to another section of memory, (equal to the new base address); **static relocation** = moving data *or* coding *or* assigning absolute locations before a program is run

REM = REMARK statement in a BASIC program that is ignored by the interpreter, allowing the programmer to write explanatory notes

remainder *noun* number equal to the dividend minus the product of the quotient and divider; *7 divided by 3 is equal to 2 remainder 1; compare with* QUOTIENT

remedial maintenance *noun* maintenance to repair faults which have developed in a system

remote *adjective* (communications) with a computer at a distance from the systems centre; *users can print reports on remote printers;* **remote console** *or* **device** = input/output device located away from the computer (and send data to it by line *or* modem); **remote job entry (RJE)** = batch processing system where instructions are transmitted to the computer from a remote terminal; **remote station** = communications station that can be controlled by a central computer; **remote terminal** = computer terminal connected to a distant computer system

remove *verb* to take away *or* to move to another place; *the file entry was removed from the floppy disk directory*

◊ **removable** *adjective* which can be removed; *a removable hard disk*

◊ **removal** *noun* taking away; *the removal of this instruction could solve the problem*

rename *verb* to give a new name to a file; *save the file and rename it CUSTOM*

renumber *noun* feature of some computer languages that allows the programmer to allocate new values to all *or* some of a program's line numbers; *see also* LINE NUMBER

reorganize *verb* to organize again; *wait while the spelling checker database is being reorganized*

repaginate *verb* to change the lengths of pages of text before they are printed; *the dtp package allows simple repagination; the text was repaginated with a new line width*

repeat *verb* to do an action again; **repeat counter** = register that holds the number of times a routine *or* task has been repeated; **repeat key** = key on a keyboard which repeats the character pressed

◊ **repeating group** *noun* pattern of data that is duplicated in a bit stream

reperforator *noun* machine that punches paper tape according to received signals; **reperforator transmitter** = reperforator and a punched tape transmitter connected together

repertoire *noun* the range of functions of a device *or* software; *the manual describes the full repertoire;* **character repertoire** = list of all the characters that can be displayed *or* printed; **instruction repertoire** = all the commands that a system can recognise and execute; *see also* RESERVED WORD

QUOTE the only omissions in the editing repertoire are dump, to list variables currently in use, and find
Computing Today

repetitive letter *noun* form letter *or* standard letter into which the details of each addressee (such as name and address) are inserted

replace *verb* (a) to put something back where it was before; to put something in the place of something else; *the printer ribbons need replacing after several thousand characters* (b) instruction to a computer to find a certain item of data and put another in its place; *see also* SEARCH AND REPLACE

replay 1 *noun* playback *or* reading back data *or* a signal from a recording **2** *verb* to play back (something which has been recorded)

replenish *verb* to charge a battery with electricity again

replicate *verb* to copy; *the routine will replicate your results with very little effort*

◊ **replication** *noun* (i) extra components in a system in case there is a breakdown *or* fault in one; (ii) copying a record *or* data to another location

report generator *noun* software that allows data from database files to be merged with a document (in the form of graphs or tables) to provide a complete report

◊ **report program generator (RPG)** *noun* programming language used mainly on personal computers for the preparation of business reports, allowing data in files, databases, etc., to be included

represent *verb* **(a)** to act as a symbol for something; *the hash sign is used to represent a number in a series* **(b)** to act as a salesman for a product

◊ **representation** *noun* action of representing something; **character representation** = combination of bits used for each character code

reproduce *verb* to copy data *or* text from one material *or* medium to another similar one

reprogram *verb* to alter a program so that it can be run on another type of computer

request 1 *noun* thing which someone asks for; **request to send signal (RTS)** = signal sent by a transmitter to a receiver asking if the receiver is ready to accept data (used in the RS232C serial connection) **2** *verb* to ask for something

require *verb* to need something *or* to demand something; *delicate computer systems require careful handling*

◊ **requirements** *noun* things which are needed; *memory requirements depend on the application software in use*

re-route *verb* to send by a different route

rerun *verb* to run a program *or* a printing job again; **rerun point** = place in the program from where to start a running again after a crash *or* halt

res *see* RESOLUTION; **hi-res** = HIGH RESOLUTION; **lo-res** = LOW RESOLUTION

resave *verb* to save again; *it automatically resaves the text*

rescue dump *noun* data saved on disk automatically when a computer fault occurs (it describes the state of the system at that time, used to help in debugging)

research *noun* scientific investigation to learn new facts about a field of study;

research and development (R & D) = investigation of new products, discoveries and techniques; *the company has spent millions of dollars on R & D*

reserved sector *noun* area of disk space that is used only for control data storage; **reserved word** = word *or* phrase used as an identifier in a programming language (it performs a particular operation *or* instruction and so cannot be used for other uses by the programmer *or* user)

> QUOTE sometimes a process will demand cache space when the only free cache space is reserved for higher priority processes
>
> .*EXE*

reset *verb* **(a)** to return a system to its initial state, to allow a program *or* process to be started again; **reset button** *or* **key** = switch that allows a program to be terminated and reset manually; **hard reset** = electrical signal that usually returns the system to its initial state when it was switched on, requiring a reboot; **soft reset** = instruction that terminates any program execution and returns the user to the monitor *or* BIOS **(b)** to set a register *or* counter to its initial state; *when it reaches 999 this counter resets to zero* **(c)** to set data equal to zero

> COMMENT: hard reset is similar to soft reset but with a few important differences: it is a switch that directly signals the CPU, while soft reset signals the operating system; hard reset clears all memory contents, a soft reset does not affect memory contents; hard reset should always reset the system, a soft reset does not always work (if for example, you have really upset the operating system, a soft reset will not work)

resident *adjective* (data *or* program) that is always in a computer; **resident engineer** = engineer who works permanently for one company; **resident software** *or* **memory-resident software** = program that is held permanently in memory (whilst the machine is on)

residual *adjective* which remains behind; **residual error rate** = ratio between incorrect and undetected received data and total data transmitted

◊ **residue check** *noun* error detection check in which the received data is divided by a set number and the remainder is checked against the required remainder

resist 1 *verb* to fight against something *or* to refuse to do something **2** *noun* substance used to protect a pattern of tracks on a PCB, that is not affected by etching chemicals; see also PHOTORESIST

resolution *noun* number of pixels that a screen *or* printer can display per unit area; *the resolution of most personal computer screens is not much more than 70 dpi (dots per inch)*; **graphic display resolution** = number of pixels that a computer is able to display on the screen; **high resolution (hi-res)** = ability to display *or* detect a very large number of pixels per unit area; *the high resolution screen can display 640 by 450 pixels;* **limiting resolution** = maximum number of lines that make up an image on a CRT screen; **low resolution (low-res)** = ability of a display system to control a number of pixels at a time rather than individual pixels

QUOTE the resolution is 300 dots per inch and the throughput is up to eight pages per minute
Practical Computing

resolving power *noun* measurement of the ability of an optical system to detect fine black lines on a white background (given as the number of lines per millimetre)

resonance *noun* situation where a frequency applied to a body being the same as its natural frequency, causes it to oscillate with a very large amplitude

resource *noun* products *or* programs which are useful; **resource allocation** = dividing available resources in a system between jobs; **resource sharing** = the use of one resource in a network *or* system by several users

respond *verb* to reply *or* to react because of something

◇ **response** *noun* reaction caused by something; **response frame** = page in a videotext system that allows a user to enter data; **response position** = area of a form that is to be used for optical mark reading data; **response time** = (i) time which passes between the user starting an action (by pressing a key) and the result appearing on the screen; (ii) speed with which a system responds to a stimulus; *the response time of this flight simulator is very good*

restart *verb* to start again; *first try to restart your system*

restore *verb* to put back into an earlier state

QUOTE first you have to restore the directory that contains the list of deleted files
Personal Computer World

restrict *verb* to keep something within a certain limit; to allow only certain people to access information; *the document is restricted, and cannot be placed on open access*

◇ **restriction** *noun* something which restricts (data flow *or* access)

result *noun* answer *or* outcome of an arithmetic *or* logical operation

resume *verb* to restart the program from the point where it was left, without changing any data

retain *verb* to keep

◇ **retention** *noun* keeping; **image retention** = time taken for a TV image to disappear after it has been displayed, caused by long persistence phosphor

retrieval *noun* the process of searching, locating and recovering information from a file *or* storage device; **information retrieval** = locating quantities of data stored in a database and producing information from the data; **information retrieval centre** = research system, providing specific information from a database for a user; **text retrieval** = information retrieval system that allows the user to examine complete documents rather than just a reference to a document

◇ **retrieve** *verb* to extract information from a file *or* storage device; *these are the records retrieved in that search; this command will retrieve all names beginning with S*

retro- *prefix* meaning going back; progress backwards; **retrofit** = device *or* accessory added to a system to upgrade it

retrospective parallel running *noun* running a new computer system with old data to check if it is accurate

◇ **retrospective search** *noun* search of documents on a certain subject since a certain date

return *noun* (a) instruction that causes program execution to return to the main program from a subroutine; *the program is not working because you missed out the return instruction at the end of the subroutine;* **return address** = address to be returned to after a called routine finishes (b) key on a keyboard used to indicate that all the required data has been entered; *you type in your name and code number then press return* (c) indication of an end of line (in printing); **carriage return (CR)** = code *or* key to indicate the end of an input line and to move the cursor to the start of the next line

◇ **return to zero signal** recording reference mark taken as the level of unmagnetized tape NOTE: opposite is **non return to zero**

COMMENT: the return address is put on the stack by the call instruction and provides the address of the instruction after the call, which is to be returned to after the called routine has finished

reveal *verb* to display previously hidden information once a condition has been met

reverse 1 *adjective* going in the opposite direction; **reverse channel** = low speed control data channel between a receiver and transmitter; **reverse characters** = characters which are displayed in the opposite way to other characters for emphasis (as black on white *or* white on black, when other characters are the opposite); **reverse index** = movement of a printer head up half a line to print superscripts; **reverse interrupt** = signal sent by a receiver to request the termination of transmissions; **reverse polarity** = situation where the positive and negative terminals have been confused, resulting in the equipment not functioning; **reverse Polish notation (RPN)** = mathematical operations written in a logical way, so that the operator appears after the numbers to be acted upon, this removes the need for brackets; *three plus four, minus two is written in RPN as 3 4 + 2 - = 5; normal notation: (x-y) + z, but using RPN: xy - z +; same as* POSTFIX NOTATION; **reverse video** = screen display mode where white and black are reversed (colours are complemented) **2** *verb* to go *or* travel in the opposite direction; to send (control) data from a receiver to a transmitter

QUOTE the options are listed on the left side of the screen, with active options shown at the top left in reverse video
PC User

revert *verb* to return to a normal state; *after the rush order, we reverted back to our normal speed;* **revert command** = command (in text) that returns a formatted page to its original state

review *verb* to see again *or* replay and check; *the program allows the user to review all wrongly spelled words*

revise *verb* to update *or* correct a version of a document *or* file; *the revised version has no mistakes*

rewind *verb* to return a tape *or* film *or* counter to its starting point; *the tape rewinds onto the spool automatically*

rewrite 1 *verb* to write something again; *see also* REGENERATE **2** *noun* act of writing something again; *the program is in its second rewrite*

RGB = RED, GREEN, BLUE high-definition monitor system that uses three separate input signals controlling red, green and blue colour picture beams

COMMENT: there are three colour guns producing red, green and blue beams acting on groups of three phosphor dots at each pixel location

ribbon *noun* long thin flat piece of material; **printer ribbon** = roll of inked material which passes between a printhead and the paper; **ribbon cable** = number of insulated conductors arranged next to each other forming a flat cable

right *adjective* not left; **right justify** = to align the right margin so that the text is straight; **right justification** = aligning the text and spacing characters so that the right margin is straight; **right shift** = to move a section of data one bit to the right; *see also* LOGICAL SHIFT, ARITHMETIC SHIFT

rigid *adjective* hard *or* which cannot bend

ring 1 *noun* data list whose last entry points back to the first entry; **ring (data) network** = type of network where each terminal is connected one after the other in a circle; *see also* CHAINED LIST **2** *verb* to telephone; **ring back system** = remote computer system in which a user attempting to access it phones once, allows it to ring a number of times, disconnects, waits a moment, then redials (usually in a bulletin board system)

◇ **ring shift** *noun* data movement to the left *or* right in a word, the bits falling outside the word boundary are discarded, the free positions are filled with zeros

ripple-through carry *noun* one operation producing a carry out from a sum and a carry in

RISC = REDUCED INSTRUCTION SET COMPUTER CPU design whose instruction set contains a small number of simple fast-executing instructions, that makes program writing more complex, but increases speed; *see also* WISC

RJE = REMOTE JOB ENTRY batch processing system where instructions are transmitted to the computer from a remote terminal

RO = RECEIVE ONLY computer terminal that can only accept and display data, not transmit

robot *noun* device which can be programmed to carry out certain manufacturing tasks which are similar to tasks carried out by people
◇ **robotics** *noun* study of artificial intelligence, programming and building involved with robot construction

QUOTE so far no robot sensor has been devised which can operate quickly enough to halt the robot if a human being is in its path of work
IEE News

robust *adjective* solid *or* (system) which can resume working after a fault
◇ **robustness** *noun* **(a)** strength of a system's casing and its ability to be knocked *or* dropped; *this hard disk is not very robust* **(b)** system's ability to continue functioning even with errors *or* faults during a program execution

rogue indicator *noun* special code used only for control applications such as end of file marker
◇ **rogue value** *or* **terminator** *noun* item in a list of data, which shows that the list is terminated

role indicator *noun* symbol used to show the role of a index entry in its particular context

rollback *noun* reloading software after the master software has been corrupted
◇ **roll-in** *verb* to transfer data from backing store into main memory
◇ **roll-out** *verb* to save the contents of main memory onto backing store
◇ **rollover** *noun* keyboard with a small temporary buffer so that it can still transmit correct data when several keys

are pressed at once; **key rollover** = use of a buffer between the keyboard and computer to provide rapid keystroke storage for fast typists
◇ **roll scroll** *verb* displayed text that moves up *or* down the computer screen one line at a time

ROM = READ ONLY MEMORY; **CD-ROM** *or* **compact disk-ROM** = compact disk-ROM small plastic disk that is used as a high capacity ROM device, data is stored in binary form as holes etched on the surface which are then read by a laser; **ROM cartridge** = software stored in a ROM mounted in a cartridge that can be easily plugged into a computer NOTE: there is no plural for ROM, and it is often used without the article: **the file is stored in ROM**
◇ **romware** *noun* software which is stored in ROM

root *noun* **(a)** starting node from which all paths branch in a data tree structure **(b)** fractional power of a number; **square root** = number raised to the power one half; *the square root of 25 is 5*

rotate *verb* to move data within a storage location in a circular manner
◇ **rotation** *noun* amount by which an object has been rotated; **bit rotation** *or* **rotate operation** = shifting a pattern of bits in a word to the left or right, the old last bit moving to the new first bit position; **matrix rotation** = swapping the rows with the columns in an array (equal to rotating by 90 degrees); *see also* SHIFT (CYCLIC)

round 1 *adjective* which goes in a circle; **round robin** = way of organizing the use of a computer by several users, who each use it for a time and then pass it on the next in turn **2** *verb* **to round down** = to approximate a number to a slightly lower one of lower precision; *we can round down 2.651 to 2.65;* **to round off** = to approximate a number to a slightly larger *or* smaller one of lower precision; *round off 23.456 to 23.46;* **round off errors** = inaccuracies in numbers due to rounding off; **to round up** = to approximate a number to a slightly larger one of lower precision; *we can round up 2.647 to 2.65*
◇ **rounding** *noun* **(a)** approximation of a number to a slightly larger one of lower precision; **rounding error** = error in a result caused by rounding off the number **(b)** giving graphics a smoother look; **character rounding** = making a displayed character more pleasant to look at (within the limits of pixel size) by making sharp corners and edges smooth

route *noun* path taken by a message between a transmitter and receiver in a network; *the route taken was not the most direct since a lot of nodes were busy*

◊ **routing** *noun* determining a suitable route for a message through a network; *there is a new way of routing data to the central computer;* routing overheads = actions that have to be taken when routing messages; *the information transfer rate is very much less once all routing overheads have been accommodated;* routing page = videotext page describing the routes to other pages; routing table = list of preferred choices for a route for a message

routine *noun* a number of instructions that perform a particular task, but are not a complete program; they are included as part of a program; *the routine copies the screen display onto a printer; the RETURN instruction at the end of the routine sends control back to the main program;* closed routine *or* closed subroutine = one section of code at a location, that is used by all calls to the routine; fall back routines = routines that are called *or* processes which are executed by a user when a machine *or* system has failed; floating-point routines = set of routines that allow floating-point numbers to be handled and processed; input routine = short section of code that accepts data from an external device, such as reading an entry from a keyboard; open routine *or* open subroutine = set of instructions in a routine, that are copied to whichever part of the program requires them; packing routine = program which packs data into a small storage area; *see also* CALL, RETURN

COMMENT: routines are usually called from a main program to perform a task, control is then returned to the part of the main program from which the routine was called once that task is complete

row *noun* (a) (i) line of printed *or* displayed characters; (ii) horizontal line on a punched card; *the figures are presented in rows, not in columns; each entry is separated by a row of dots* (b) horizontal set of data elements in an array *or* matrix

RPG = REPORT PROGRAM GENERATOR

RS-232C EIA approved standard used in serial data transmission, covering voltage and control signals

COMMENT: the RS232C has now been superceeded by the RS423 and RS422 interface standards, similar to the RS232, but allowing higher transmission rates

RTE = REAL TIME EXECUTION

RTS REQUEST TO SEND SIGNAL

rubber banding *see* ELASTIC BANDING

rubout *see* ERASE

rule *noun* set of conditions that describe a function; *the rule states that you wait for the clear signal before transmitting;* rule-based system = software that applies the rules and knowledge defined by experts in a particular field to a user's data to solve a problem

run 1 *noun* execution by a computer of a set of instructions *or* programs *or* procedures; *the next invoice run will be on Friday;* program run = executing (in correct order) the instructions in a program; run indicator = indicator bit *or* LED that shows that a computer is currently executing a program **2** *verb* to make a device work; *the computer has been running ten hours a day; do not interrupt the spelling checker while it is running; the new package runs on our PC;* parallel running = running old and new computer systems together to allow the new system to be checked before it becomes the only system used; run around = to fit text around an image on a printed page; run in = to operate a system at a lower capacity for a time in case of any faults

◊ **runaway** *noun* uncontrolled operation of a device *or* computer (due to a malfunction *or* error)

◊ **running head** *noun* title line of each page in a document

◊ **run on** *verb* to make text continue without a break; *the line can run on to the next without any space*

◊ **run-time** *or* **run-duration 1** *noun* (a) period of a time a program takes to run (b) time during which a computer is executing a program **2** *adjective* (operation) carried out only when a program is running; run-time error = fault only detected when a program is run *or* error made while a program is running; *see also* EXECUTION ERROR; run-time system = software that is required in main storage while a program is running (to execute instructions to peripherals, etc.)

R/W = READ/WRITE
◇ **R/W cycle** = READ/WRITE CYCLE sequence of events used to retrieve *or* store data
◇ **R/W head** = READ/WRITE HEAD electromagnetic device that allows data to

be read from *or* written to a storage medium

RX = RECEIVE, RECEIVER *the RXed signal needs to be amplified*

Ss

S100 bus *or* **S-100 bus** *noun* IEEE-696 standard bus, a popular 8 and 16 bit microcomputer bus using 100 lines and a 100-pin connector; *see also* BUS
NOTE: say "S one hundred bus"

safety net *noun* software *or* hardware device that protects the system *or* files from excessive damage in the event of a system crash; *if there is a power failure, we have a safety net in the form of a UPS*

salami technique *noun* computer fraud involving many separate small transactions that are difficult to detect and trace

SAM = SERIAL ACCESS MEMORY storage where a particular data item can only be accessed by reading through all the previous items in the list (as opposed to random access)

COMMENT: magnetic tape is a form of SAM; you have to go through the whole tape to access one item, while disks provide random access to stored data

sample 1 *noun* measurement of a signal at a point in time; *the sample at three seconds showed an increase;* **sample and hold circuit** = circuit that freezes an analog input signal for long enough for an A/D converter to produce a stable output **2** *verb* to obtain a number of measurements of a signal that can be used to provide information about the signal; **sampling interval** = time period between two consecutive samples; **sampling rate** = number of measurements of a signal recorded every second; *see also* ANALOG/DIGITAL CONVERSION, QUANTIZE

◊ **sampler** *noun* electronic circuit that takes many samples of a signal and stores them for future analysis

SAR = STORE ADDRESS REGISTER register within the CPU that contains the address of the next location to be accessed

satellite *noun* small system that is part of a larger system; **satellite computer** = computer doing various tasks under the control of another computer; **satellite terminal** = computer terminal that is outside the main network

COMMENT: in a network the floppy disk units are called 'satellites' and the hard disk unit the 'server'. In a star network each satellite is linked individually to a central server

saturation *noun* point where a material cannot be further magnetized; **saturation noise** = errors due to saturation of a magnetic storage medium; **saturation testing** = testing a communications network, by transmitting large quantities of data and messages over it

save *verb* to store data *or* a program on an auxiliary storage device; *this WP saves the text every 15 minutes in case of a fault; don't forget to save the file before switching off;* **save area** = temporary storage area of main memory, used for registers and control data

SBC = SINGLE BOARD COMPUTER computer whose main components such as processor, input/output and memory are all contained on one PCB

scalar *noun* variable that has a single value assigned to it; *a scalar has a single magnitude value, a vector has two or more positional values*

◊ **scale 1** *noun* ratio of two values; **large scale** *or* **small scale** = working with large *or* small amounts of data; **large scale integration (LSI)** = integrated circuit with 500 - 10,000 components; **medium scale integration (MSI)** = integrated circuit with 10 - 500 components; **small scale integration (SSI)** = integrated circuit with 1 - 10 components; **very large scale integration (VLSI)** = integrated circuit with 10,000 - 100,000 components **2** *verb* **to scale down** *or* **scale up** = to lower *or* increase in proportion

scan 1 *noun* examination of an image *or* object *or* list of items to obtain data; *the heat scan of the computer quickly showed* *which component was overheating; the scan revealed which records were now out of date;* **raster scan** = one sweep of the picture beam horizontally across the front of the CRT screen **2** *verb* to examine and produce produce data from the shape *or* state of an object *or* drawing *or* file *or* list of items; *he scanned the map for Teddington; the facsimile machine scans the picture and converts this to digital form before transmission; the machine scans at up to 300 dpi resolution;* **scan area** = section of an image read by a scanner; **scan length** = number of items in a file *or* list that are examined in a scan

◊ **scanner** *noun* device that scans; *a scanner reads the bar-code on the product label using a laser beam and photodiode;* **scanner memory** = memory area allocated to store images which have been scanned; **image scanner** = input device that converts documents *or* drawings *or* photographs into digitized machine-readable form; **optical scanner** = equipment that converts an image into electrical signals which can be stored in and displayed on a computer

COMMENT: a scanner can be a device using photoelectric cells as in an image digitizer, or a device that samples data from a process

scanning *noun* action of examining and producing data from the shape of an object *or* drawing; **scanning error** = error introduced while scanning an image; **scanning line** = path traced on a CRT screen by the picture beam; **scanning rate** = time taken to scan one line of a CRT image; **scanning resolution** = ability of a scanner to distinguish between small points (usual resolution is 300 dpi); **scanning software** = dedicated program that controls a scanner and allows certain operations (rotate *or* edit *or* store, etc.) to be performed on a scanned image; **scanning speed** = how fast a line *or* image is scanned; *throughput is 1.3 inches per second scanning speed; its scanning speed is 9.9 seconds for an 8.5inch by 11inch document; (of modem)* **auto-baud scanning** *or* **auto-baud sensing** = circuit that can automatically sense and select the correct baud rate for a line

COMMENT: a modem with auto-baud scanning can automatically sense which baud rate to operate on and switches automatically to that baud rate

QUOTE scanning time per page ranged from about 30 seconds to three minutes
PC Business World

scatter load *verb* to load sequential data into various (non-continuous) locations in memory; **scatter read** = to access and read sequential data stored in various (non-continuous) locations

scavenging *verb* to search through and access database material without permission

schedule *noun* order in which tasks are to be done *or* order in which CPU time will be allocated to processes in a multi-user system

◊ **scheduled circuits** *noun* telephone lines for data communications only

◊ **scheduler** *noun* program which organizes use of a CPU *or* of peripherals which are shared by several users

◊ **scheduling** *noun* method of working which allows several users to share the use of a CPU; **job scheduling** = arranging the order in which jobs are to be processed

schema *noun* graphical description of a process *or* database structure

◊ **schematic** *adjective & noun* (diagram) showing system components and how they are connected

SCR = SEQUENCE CONTROL REGISTER

scramble *verb* to code speech *or* data which is transmitted in such a way that it cannot be understood unless it is decoded

◊ **scrambler** *noun* device that codes a data stream into a pseudorandom form before transmission to eliminate any series of one's or zero's *or* alternate one's and zero's that would cause synchronization problems at the receiver

scratch 1 *noun* mark on a disk **2** *verb* to delete *or* move an area of memory to provide room for other data

◊ **scratch file** *or* **work file** *noun* work area which is being used for current work; **scratch tape** = magnetic tape used for a scratch file

◊ **scratchpad** *noun* workspace *or* area of high speed memory that is used for temporary storage of data currently in use

screen 1 *noun* **(a)** display device capable of showing a quantity of information, such as a CRT *or* VDU; *see also* READOUT; **screen border** = margin around text displayed on a screen; **screen buffer** = temporary storage area for characters *or* graphics before they are displayed; **screen dump** = outputting the text *or* graphics displayed on a screen to a printer; **screen editor** or **text editor** = software that allows the user to edit text on-screen, with one complete screen of information being displayed at a time; **screen format** = way in which a screen is laid out; **screen grab** = digitizing a single frame from a display or television; **screen memory** = in a memory-mapped screen, the area of memory that represents the whole screen, usually with one byte representing one or a number of pixels; **on-screen** = information displayed on a screen; *the dtp package offers on-screen font display;* **text screen** = area of a computer screen that has been set up to display text; **touch screen** = computer display that allows the user to control the cursor position by touching the screen **(b)** thing which protects; **magnetic screen** = metal screen to prevent stray magnetic fields affecting electronic components; *without the metal screen over the power supply unit, the computer just produced garbage* **2** *verb* **(a)** to protect something with a screen; *the PSU is screened against interference* **(b)** to select

◊ **screenful** *noun* complete frame of information displayed on a screen

> QUOTE the screen memory is, in fact a total of 4K in size, the first 2K hold the character codes, of which 1K is displayed. Scrolling brings the remaining area into view
> *Computing Today*

scroll *verb* to move displayed text vertically up or down the screen, one line or pixel at a time; **roll scroll** = displayed text that moves up or down the screen one line at a time; **smooth scroll** = text that is moved up a screen pixel by pixel rather than line by line, which gives a smoother movement; **scroll mode** = terminal mode that transmits every key press and displays what is received

scrub *verb* to wipe information off a disk or remove data from store; *scrub all files with the .BAK extension*

SCSI = SMALL COMPUTER SYSTEM INTERFACE

> QUOTE the system uses SCSI for connecting to the host and ESDI for interconnecting among drives within a multidrive system
> *Byte*

SD = SINGLE DENSITY (DISK)

SDLC = SYNCHRONOUS DATA LINK CONTROL

SDR = STORE DATA REGISTER register in a CPU which holds data before it is processed or moved to memory location

seal *verb* to close something tightly so that it cannot be opened; *the hard disk is in a sealed case*

search 1 *noun* process of looking for and identifying a character or word or section of data in a document or file; **chaining search** = searching a file of elements arranged as a chained list; **linear search** = search method which compares each item in a list with the search key until the correct entry is found (starting with the first item and working sequentially towards the end); **retrospective search** = search of documents on a certain subject since a certain date; **search key** = (i) word or phrase that is to be found in a text; (ii) field and other data used to select various records in a database; **search memory** = method of data retrieval that uses part of the data rather than an address to locate the data; **search and replace** = feature on some word processors that allows the user to find certain words or phrases, then replace them with another word or phrase; **global search and replace** = word-processor search and replace function covering a complete file or document **2** *verb* to look for an item of data

◊ **searching storage** *noun* method of data retrieval that uses part of the data rather than an address to locate the data

> QUOTE a linear search of 1,000 items takes 500 comparisons to find the target, and 1,000 to report that it isn't present. A binary search of the same set of items takes roughly ten divisions either to find or not to find the target
> *Personal Computer World*

second *adjective* (thing) which comes after the first; *we have two computers, the second one being used if the first is being repaired;* **second generation computers** = computer which used transistors instead of valves; **second-level addressing** = instruction that contains an address at which the operand is stored; **second sourcing** = granting a licence to another manufacturer to produce an electronic item or component when production capacity is not great enough to meet demand; **second user** or **second hand** = (old equipment) that has already been used and is be sold again

◊ **secondary** *adjective* second in importance or less important than the first; **secondary channel** = second channel containing control information transmitted at the same time as data; **secondary station** = temporary status of a station that is receiving data; **secondary storage =** any data storage medium (such as magnetic tape *or* floppy disk) that is not the main, high-speed computer storage (RAM)

COMMENT: this type of storage is usually of a higher capacity, lower cost and slower access time than main memory

section *noun* part of a main program that can be executed in its own right, without the rest of the main program being required

sector 1 *noun* smallest area on a magnetic disk that can be addressed by a computer **2** *verb* to divide a disk into a series of sectors; **(disk) sector formatting =** dividing a disk into a series of addressable sectors (a table of their addresses is also formed, allowing each sector to be accessed); **sectoring hole =** hole in the edge of a disk to indicate where the first sector is located; **hard-sectored =** disk with sector start locations described by holes *or* other physical marks on the disk, which are set when the disk is manufactured; **soft-sectored =** disk where sectors are described by an address and start code data written onto it when the disk is formatted; *see also* FORMAT

COMMENT: a disk is divided into many tracks, each of which is then divided into a number of sectors which can hold a certain number of bits

secure system *noun* system that cannot be accessed without authorization

◊ **secured** *adjective* (file) that is protected against accidental writing *or* deletion *or* against unauthorized access

◊ **security** *noun* being protected *or* being secret; *the system has been designed to assure the security of the stored data;* **security backup =** copy of a disk *or* tape *or* file kept in a safe place in case the working copy is lost *or* damaged; **security check =** identification of authorized users (by a password) before granting access

seek *verb* to try to find; **seek area =** section of memory that is to be searched for a particular item of data *or* a word; **seek time =** time taken by a read/write head to find the right track on a disk; *the new hard disk drive has a seek time of just 35mS*

segment 1 *noun* section of a main program that can be executed in its own right, without the rest of the main program being required **2** *verb* to divide a long program into shorter sections which can

then be called up when required; *see also* OVERLAY

QUOTE you can also write in smaller program segments. This simplifies debugging and testing
Personal Computer World

select *verb* to find and retrieve specific information from a database; **chip select (CS) =** single line on a chip that will enable it to function when a signal is present (often ICs do not function even when power is applied, until a CS signal is provided)

◊ **selectable** *adjective* which can be selected; **jumper-selectable =** circuit *or* device whose options can be selected by positioning various wire connections; **selectable attributes =** the function *or* attributes of a device which can be chosen by the user; **user-selectable =** which can be chosen or selected by the user; **this modem has user-selectable baud rates =** the receive and transmit baud rates of the modem can be chosen by the user, and are not preset

◊ **selection** *noun* action of selecting; *selection of information from a large database may take some time*

◊ **selective** *adjective* which chooses certain items; **selective dump =** display *or* printout of a selected area of memory; **selective sort =** sorting a section of data items into order

◊ **selector** *noun* mechanical device that allows a user to choose an option *or* function

self- *prefix* referring to oneself; **self-adapting system =** system that can change adapt itself to various tasks; **self-checking system =** system that carries out diagnostic tests on itself usually at switch on; **self-checking code =** character coding system that can detect an error *or* bad character but not correct it; **self-correcting codes =** character coding system that can detect and correct an error *or* bad character; **self-diagnostic =** computer that runs a series of diagnostic programs (usually when it is switched on) to ensure that it is all working correctly, often memory, peripherals and disk drives are tested; **self-documenting program =** computer program that provides the user with operating instructions as it runs; **self-learning =** (expert system) that adds each new piece of information or rule to its database, improving its knowledge, expertise and performance as it is used; **self-refreshing RAM =** dynamic RAM chip that has built in circuitry to generate refresh signals, allowing data to be retained when the power is off, using battery back-up; **self-relocating program =** program that can be loaded into any part of memory (that will modify its addresses depending on the program origin address); **self-resetting** or **self-restoring loop** = loop that returns any locations or registers accessed during its execution to the state they were in

semantics noun (i) part of language which deals with the meaning of words, parts of words or combinations of words; (ii) (in computing) meanings of words or symbols used in programs; **semantic error** = error due to use of an incorrect symbol within a program instruction

semaphore noun coordination of two jobs and appropriate handshaking to prevent lock-outs or other problems when both require a peripheral or function

semi- prefix meaning half or partly; **semi-processed data** = raw data which has had some processing carried out, such as sorting, recording, error detection, etc.

semicolon noun printed sign (;) which marks the end of a program line or statement in some languages (such as C and Pascal)

semicompiled adjective (object code) program converted from a source code program, but not containing the code for functions from libraries, etc., that were used in the source code

semiconductor noun material that has conductive properties between those of a conductor (such as a metal) and an insulator; **semiconductor device** = electronic component that is constructed on a small piece of semiconductor (the components on the device are constructed using patterns of insulator or conductor or semiconductor material whose properties can be changed by doping); **semiconductor memory** = storage using capacitors (dynamic memory) or latches and bistables (static memory) constructed as a semiconductor device to store bits of data

COMMENT: semiconductor material (such as silicon) is used as a base for manufacturing integrated circuits and other solid-state components, usually by depositing various types of doping substances on or into its surface

sender noun person who sends a message
◊ **send-only device** noun device such as a terminal which cannot receive data, only transmit it

sense verb to examine the state of a device or electronic component; *the condition of the switch was sensed by the program; this device senses the holes punched in a paper tape;* **auto-baud sensing** see SCANNING; **sense recovery time** = time that a RAM takes to switch from read to write mode; **sense switch** = switch on a computer front panel whose state can by examined by the computer
◊ **sensitive** adjective which can sense even small changes; *the computer is sensitive even to very slight changes in current*
◊ **sensitivity** noun being sensitive to something; *the scanner's sensitivity to small objects*
◊ **sensor** noun electronic device that produces an output dependent upon the condition or physical state of a process; see also TRANSDUCER *the sensor's output varies with temperature; the process is monitored by a bank of sensors;* **image sensor** = photoelectric device that produces a signal related to the amount of light falling on it

sentinel noun (i) marker or pointer to a special section of data; (ii) a flag that reports the status of a register after a mathematical or logical operation

separate 1 adjective not together; **separate channel signalling** = use of independent communications channel or bands in a multichannel system to send the control data and messages **2** verb to divide; **separated graphics** = displayed characters that do not take up the whole of a character matrix, resulting in spaces between them
◊ **separation** noun act of separating
◊ **separator** noun symbol used to distinguish parts of an instruction line in a program, such as command and argument; see also DELIMITER

septet noun word made up of seven bits

sequence noun number of items or data arranged as a logical, ordered list; *the sequence of names is arranged alphabetically; the program instructions are arranged in sequence according to line numbers;* **binary sequence** = series of binary digits; **control sequence** = (series of) codes containing a control character and various arguments, used to carry out a process or change mode in a device; **sequence check** = check to ensure that sorted data is in the correct order; **sequence control register (SCR)** or **sequence counter** or **sequence register** or **instruction address register** = CPU register that contains the address of the next instruction to be processed; **the logon sequence** = order in which user number, password and other authorization codes are to be entered when attempting to access a system

◇ **sequencer** *noun* section within a bit-slice microprocessor that contains the next microprogram address

◇ **sequential** *adjective* arranged in an ordered manner; **queued indexed sequential access method (QISAM)** = indexed sequential file that is read item by item into a buffer; **queued sequential access method (QSAM)** = queue of blocks waiting to be processed, retrieved using a sequential access method; **sequential batch processing** = completing one job in a batch before the next can be started; **sequential computer** = type of computer, for which each instruction must be completed before the next is started, and so cannot handle parallel processing; **sequential file** *or* **serial file** = stored file whose records are accessed sequentially; **sequential logic** = logical circuit whose output depends on the logic state of the previous inputs; *if the input sequence to the sequential logic circuit is 1101 the output will always be zero (0); compare with* COMBINATIONAL CIRCUIT; **sequential mode** = each instruction in a program is stored in consecutive locations; **sequential operation** = operations executed one after the other; **sequential processing** = data *or* instructions processed sequentially, in the same order as they are accessed; *see also* INDEXED; **sequential search** = each item in a list (starting at the beginning) is checked until the required one is found

◇ **sequentially** *adverb* (done) one after the other, in sequence

◇ **sequential access** *noun* method of retrieving data from a storage device by starting at the beginning of the medium (such as tape) and reading each record until the required data is found; **sequential access storage** = storage medium in which the data is accessed sequentially

COMMENT: a tape storage system uses sequential access, since the tape has to be played through until the section required is found. The access time of sequential access storage is dependent on the position in the file of the data, compared with random access that has the same access time for any piece of data in a list

serial *adjective* (data *or* instructions) ordered sequentially (one after the other) and not in parallel; **serial access** = one item of the data accessed by reading through all the data in a list until the correct one is found (as on a tape); **serial-access memory (SAM)** = storage where a

particular data item can only be accessed by reading all the previous items in the list (as opposed to random access); **serial adder** = addition circuit that acts on one digit at a time from a larger number; **serial computer** = computer system that has a single ALU and carries out instructions one at a time; *see also* SEQUENTIAL COMPUTER; **serial data transmission** = transmission of the separate bits that make up data words, one at a time down a single line; **serial file** = stored file whose records are accessed sequentially; **serial input/output (SIO)** *see* SERIAL TRANSMISSION; **serial input/serial output (SIPO)** *or* **serial to parallel converter** = device that can accept serial data and transmit parallel data; **serial input/serial output (SISO)** = *see* SERIAL TRANSMISSION; **serial interface** *or* **port** = circuit that converts parallel data in a computer to and from a serial form that allows serial data to be transmitted and received from other equipment (the most common form is the RS232C interface); *parallel connections are usually less trouble to set up and use than serial interfaces, but are usually limited to 20 feet in length;* **serial memory** = memory in which data is stored sequentially, only allowing sequential access; **serial operation** = device that acts on data in a sequential manner; **serial printer** = printer that prints characters one at a time; **serial processing** = data *or* instructions processed sequentially, in the same order as they are retrieved; **serial storage** = storage which only allows sequential access; **serial to parallel converter** = electronic device that converts data from a serial form to a parallel form; **serial transmission** *or* **serial input/output** = data transmitted one bit at a time (this is the normal method of transmission over long distances, since although slower it uses fewer lines and so is cheaper than parallel transmission); **word serial** = data words transmitted one after the other, along a parallel bus

◇ **serially** *adverb* one after the other *or* in a series; *their transmission rate is 64,000 bits per second through a parallel connection or 19,200 serially*

◇ **series** *noun* group of related items ordered sequentially; **series circuit** = circuit in which the components are connected serially

COMMENT: in a series circuit the same current flows through each component; in a parallel circuit the current flow is dependent upon the component impedance

server *noun* dedicated computer *or* peripheral that provides a function to a network; **file server** = small microcomputer and large backing storage device that is used for the management and storage of users' files in a network; **LAN server** = dedicated computer and backing storage used by terminals and operators in a LAN

COMMENT: in a network the hard disk machine is called the 'server' and the floppy disk units the 'satellites'. In a star network each satellite is linked individually to a central server

service *verb* to check *or* repair *or* maintain a system; *the disk drives were serviced yesterday and are working well;* **service bit** = transmitted bit that is used for control rather than data; **service contract** = agreement that an engineer will service equipment if it goes wrong; **service program** = useful program that is used for routine activities such as file searching, copying, sorting, debugging, etc.

session *noun* period of work; **session layer** = layer in the ISO/OSI standard model that makes the connection/disconnection between transmitter and receiver

set 1 *noun* number of related data items; **character set** = all the characters that can be displayed *or* printed; **set theory** = mathematics related to numerical sets **2** *verb* **(a)** (i) to make one variable equal to a value; (ii) to define a parameter value; *we set the right-hand margin at 80 characters;* **set breakpoints** = to define the position of breakpoints within a program being debugged **(b)** to give a bit the value of 1
◊ **set up** *verb* to initialize *or* define *or* start an application *or* system; *the new computer worked well as soon as the engineer had set it up;* **set-up option** = the choices available when setting up a system; **set-up time** = period of time between a signal to start an operation and the start

sexadecimal *see* HEXADECIMAL
◊ **sextet** *noun* byte made up of six bits

sf signalling = SINGLE FREQUENCY SIGNALLING

shadowmask *noun* sheet with holes placed just behind the front of a colour monitor screen to separate the three-colour picture beams
◊ **shadow memory** *or* **page** *noun* duplicate memory locations accessed by a special code; **shadow page table** =

conversion table that lists real memory locations with their equivalent shadow memory locations; *see also* VIRTUAL
◊ **shadow ROM** *noun* read-only shadow memory

shannon *noun* measure of the information content of a transmission
◊ **Shannon's Law** *noun* law defining the maximum information carrying capacity of a transmission line

COMMENT: Shannon's Law is defined as B lg(1 + S/N) where B = Bandwidth, lg is logarithm to the base two and S/N is Signal to Noise ratio

share *verb* to own *or* use something together with someone else; *the facility is shared by several independent companies;* **shared access** = computer *or* peripheral used by more than one person *or* system; *see also* TIME-SHARING SYSTEM, MULTI-USER; **shared bus** = one bus used (usually) for address and data transfer between the CPU and a peripheral; **shared file** = stored file that can be accessed by more than one user *or* system; **shared logic system** = one computer and backing storage device used by a number of people in a network for an application; **shared logic text processor** = word-processing available to a number of users of a shared logic system; **shared memory** = memory that can be accessed by more than one CPU; **shared resources system** = system where one peripheral *or* backing storage device *or* other resource is used by a number of users; **time-sharing** = computer system that allows several independent users to use it *or* be on-line at the same time
◊ **shareware** *noun* software that is available free to try, but if kept the user is expected to pay a fee to the writer (often confused with public domain software which is completely free)

sheet *noun* large piece of paper; **sheet feed** = paper feed system that puts single sheets of paper into a printer, one at a time; **sheet feed attachment** = device which can be attached to a printer to allow single sheets of paper to be fed in automatically

shell sort *noun* algorithm for sorting data items, in which items can be moved more than one position per sort action

shield 1 *noun* metal screen connected to earth, that prevents harmful voltages *or* interference reaching sensitive electronic equipment **2** *verb* to protect a signal *or* device from external interference *or* harmful voltages; **shielded cable** = cable made up of a conductive core surrounded by an insulator, then a conductive layer to protect the transmitted signal against interference

shift *verb* **(a)** to move a bit *or* word of data left or right by a certain amount (usually one bit); **arithmetic shift** = word *or* data moved one bit to the right *or* left inside a register, losing the bit shifted off the end; **cyclic shift** = rotation of bits in a word with the previous last bit inserted in the first bit position; **logical shift** = data movement to the left *or* right in a word, the bits falling outside the word boundary are discarded, the free positions are filled with zeros; **shift instruction** = computer command to shift the contents of a register to the left or right; **shift left** = left arithmetic shift of data in a word (the number is doubled for each left shift); *0110 left shifted once is 1100;* **shift register** = temporary storage into which data can be shifted; **shift right** = right arithmetic shift of data in a word (the number is halved for each right shift) **(b)** to change from one character set to another, allowing other characters (such as capitals) to be used; **shift character** = transmitted character code that indicates that the following code is to be shifted; **shift code** = method of increasing total possible bit combinations by using a number of bits to indicate is the following code is to be shifted

◊ **shift key** *noun* key on a keyboard that switches secondary functions for keys, such as another character set, by changing the output to upper case

short *adjective* not long; **short card** = add-on expansion board that is shorter than a standard size; **short haul modem** = modem used to transmit data over short distances (often within a building), usually without using a carrier

◊ **shorten** *verb* to make shorter; *we had to shorten the file to be able to save it on one floppy*

shut down *verb* to switch off and stop the functions of a machine *or* system

◊ **shut-off mechanism** *noun* device which stops a process in case of fault

COMMENT: most hard disks have an automatic shut-off mechanism to pull the head back from the read position when the power is turned off

sideways ROM *noun* software which allows selection of a particular memory bank *or* ROM device

sign 1 *noun* polarity of a number *or* signal (whether it is positive *or* negative); **sign and modulus** = way of representing numbers, where one bit shows if the number is positive *or* negative (usually 0 = positive, 1 = negative); **sign bit** *or* **sign indicator** = single bit that indicates if a binary number is positive *or* negative (usually 0 = positive, 1 = negative); **sign digit** = one digit that indicates if a number is positive *or* negative; **sign and magnitude** *or* **signed magnitude** = number representation in which the most significant bit indicates the sign of the number, the rest of the bits its value; **sign position** = digit *or* bit position that contains the sign bit *or* digit; **signed field** = storage field which can contain a number and a sign bit **2** *verb* to identify oneself to a computer using a personalized signature; **to sign off** = to logoff a system; **to sign on** = to logon to a system

signal 1 *noun* (i) generated analog *or* digital waveform used to carry information; (ii) short message used to carry control codes; *the signal received from the computer contained the answer;* **interrupt signal** = voltage pulse from a peripheral sent to the CPU requesting attention; **signal conditioning** = converting *or* translating a signal into a form that is accepted by a device; **signal conversion** = processing, changing or modulating a signal; **signal distance** = number of bit positions with different contents in two data words; *see also* HAMMING; **signal element** = smallest basic unit used when transmitting digital data; *the signal element in this system is a short voltage pulse, indicating a binary one; the signal elements for the radio transmission system are 10mS of 40KHz and 10mS of 60KHz for binary 0 and 1 respectively;* **signal processing** = processing of signals to extract the information contained; *the system is used by students doing research on signal processing techniques; the message was recovered by carrier signal processing* **2** *verb* to send a message to a computer; *signal to the network that we are busy*

◊ **signalling** *noun* (i) method used by a transmitter to warn a receiver that a message is to be sent; (ii) communication to the transmitter about the state of the receiver; **in band signalling** = use of a normal voice grade channel for data transmission

signature *noun* special authentication code, such as a password, which a user gives prior to access to a system *or* prior to the execution of a task (to prove identity)

signify *verb* to mean; *a carriage return code signifies the end of an input line*

◊ **significance** *noun* special meaning

◊ **significant** *adjective* which has a special meaning; **significant digit codes** *or* **faceted codes** = codes which indicate various details of an item, by assigning each one a value

silicon *noun* element with semiconductor properties, used in crystal form as a base for IC manufacture; **silicon chip** = small piece of silicon in and on the surface of which a complete circuit *or* logic function has been produced (by depositing other substances *or* by doping); **silicon disk** *or* **RAM disk** = section of RAM that is made to look and behave like a high speed disk drive; **Silicon Valley** = area in California where many US semiconductor device manufacturers are based; **silicon wafer** = thin slice of a pure silicon crystal, usually around 4 inches in diameter on which integrated circuits are produced (these are then cut out of the wafer to produce individual chips)

COMMENT: silicon is used in the electronics industry as a base material for integrated circuits. It is grown as a long crystal which is then sliced into wafers before being etched or treated, producing several hundred chips per wafer. Other materials, such as germanium or gallium arsenide, are also used as a base for ICs

SIMD = SINGLE INSTRUCTION STREAM MULTIPLE DATA STREAM

simple *adjective* not complicated, not difficult; **simple to use** = (machine *or* software) easy to use and operate

simplex *noun* data transmission in only one direction
NOTE: opposite is **duplex**

simplify *verb* to make something simpler; *function keys simplify program operation*

simulate *verb* to copy the behaviour of a system *or* device with another; *this software simulates the action of an aeroplane*

◊ **simulator** *noun* device that simulates another system; **flight simulator** = computer program which allows a user to pilot a plane, showing a realistic control panel and moving scenes (either as training programme *or* computer game)

◊ **simulation** *noun* operation where a computer is made to imitate a real life situation *or* a machine, and shows how

something works *or* will work in the future; *simulation techniques have reached a high degree of sophistication*

simultaneity *adjective* in which the CPU and the I/O sections of a computer can handle different data *or* tasks at the same time

simultaneous *adjective* which takes place at the same time as something else; **simultaneous processing** = two or more processes executed at the same time; **simultaneous transmission** = transmission of data *or* control codes in two directions at the same time NOTE: same as duplex

◊ **simultaneously** *adverb* at the same time

COMMENT: true simultaneous processing requires two processors, but can be imitated by switching rapidly between two tasks with a single processor

single *adjective* only one; **single address code** *or* **instruction** = machine code instruction that contains one operator and one address; **single address message** = message with a single destination; **single board computer (SBC)** = micro *or* mini computer whose components are all contained on a single printed circuit board; **single density disk (SD)** = standard magnetic disk and drive able to store data; **single frequency signalling** *or* **sf signalling** = use of various frequency signals to represent different control codes; **single function software** = applications program that can only be used for one kind of task; **single instruction stream multiple data stream (SIMD)** = architecture of a parallel computer that has a number of ALUs and data buses with one control unit; **single instruction stream single data stream (SISD)** = architecture of a serial computer, that has one ALU and data bus, with one control unit; **single key response** = software that requires only one key to be pressed (no CR required) to select an option; **single length precision** = number stored in one word; *compare with* DOUBLE, MULTIPLE LENGTH; **single length working** = using numbers that can be stored within a single word; **single line display** = small screen which displays a single line of characters at a time; **single operand instruction** see SINGLE ADDRESS INSTRUCTION; **single operation** = communications system that allows data to travel in only one direction at a time (controlled by codes S/O = send only, R/O = receive only, S/R = send or receive); *see also* SIMPLEX; **single pass operation** = software that produces the required result *or* carries out a task after one run; **single precision** = number stored in one word; **single sheet feed** = device attached to a printer to allow single sheets of paper to be used instead of continuous stationery; **single-sided disk (SSD)** = floppy disk that can only be used to store data on one side, because of the way it is manufactured *or* formatted; **single step** = to execute a program one instruction at a time; **single-strike ribbon** = printer ribbon which can only be used once; *compare* MULTI-STRIKE; **single-user system** = computer system which can only be used by a single user at a time (as opposed to a multi-user system)

sink *noun* receiving end of a communications line; **sink tree** = description in a routing table of all the paths in a network to a destination NOTE: the opposite of sink is **source**

SIO = SERIAL INPUT/OUTPUT

SIPO = SERIAL INPUT/PARALLEL OUTPUT

SISD = SINGLE INSTRUCTION STREAM SINGLE DATA STREAM

SISO = SERIAL INPUT/SERIAL OUTPUT

site *noun* place where something is based ◊ **site poll** *verb* to poll all the terminals *or* devices in a particular location *or* area; *see also* POLLING

sixteen-bit *adjective* (microcomputer system *or* CPU) that handles data in sixteen bit words, providing much faster operation than older eight bit systems

size 1 *noun* physical dimensions of an image *or* object *or* page; **screen size** = (i) number of characters a computer display can show horizontally and vertically; (ii) size of a monitor screen based on international paper sizes **2** *verb* to calculate the resources available, and those required to carry out a particular job

skeletal code *noun* program which is not complete, with the basic structure coded

skip *verb* to ignore an instruction in a sequence of instructions; *the printer skipped the next three lines of text;* **skip capability** = feature of certain word-processors to allow the user to jump backwards *or* forwards by a quantity of text in a document; **skip instruction** = null computer command which directs the CPU to the next instruction; **high-speed skip** = rapid movement of paper in a printer, ignoring the normal line advance

slashed zero *noun* a printed *or* written sign (∅) to distinguish a zero from the letter O

slave *noun* remote secondary computer *or* terminal controlled by a central computer; **bus slave** = data sink which receives data from a bus master; **slave cache** *or* **store** = section of high-speed memory which stores data that the CPU can access quickly; **slave processor** = dedicated processor that is controlled by a master processor; **slave terminal** = terminal controlled by a main computer *or* terminal; **slave tube** = second CRT display connected to another so that it shows exactly the same information

sleep *noun* system that is waiting for a signal (log-on) before doing anything; *see also* WAKE-UP

sleeve *noun* cover for a magnetic disk

slew *noun* rapid movement of paper in a printer, ignoring the normal line advance

slice *noun* section *or* piece of something; **bit-slice architecture** = construction of a large word size CPU by joining a number of smaller word size blocks; *the bit-slice design uses four four-bit word processors to make a sixteen-bit processor;* **time slice** = period of time allocated for a user *or* program *or* job within a multitasking system; amount of time allowed for a single task in a time-sharing system *or* in multiprogramming

slide *verb* to move smoothly across a surface; *the disk cover slides on and off easily*

slot 1 *noun* (a) long thin hole; *the system disk should be inserted into the left-hand slot on the front of the computer;* **expansion slot** = expansion connector available on a computer's backplane *or* motherboard, into which an expansion board can be plugged; *there are two free slots in the micro, you only need one for the add-on board* (b) **message slot** = number of bits that can hold a message which circulates round a ring network **2** *verb* to insert an object into a hole; *the disk slots into one of the floppy drive apertures*

SLSI = SUPER LARGE SCALE INTEGRATION

small *adjective* not large; **small scale integration (SSI)** = integrated circuit with 1 to 10 components

smart *adjective* intelligent; **smart card** = plastic card with a memory and microprocessor embedded in it, so that it can be used for direct money transfer *or* for identification of the user; *see also* PID; **smart terminal** *or* **intelligent terminal** = computer terminal that is able to process information

smog *noun* **electronic smog** = excessive stray electromagnetic fields and static electricity generated by large numbers of electronic equipment (this can damage equipment and a person's health)

smoke test *informal* casual test that indicates that the machine must be working if no smoke appears when it is switched on

SNA = SYSTEMS NETWORK ARCHITECTURE

snapshot *noun* (i) recording of all the states of a computer at a particular instant; (ii) storing in main memory the contents of a screen full of information at an instant; **snapshot dump** = printout of all the registers and a section of memory at a particular instant, used when debugging a program

SNOBOL = STRING ORIENTATED SYMBOLIC LANGUAGE high-level programming language that uses string processing methods

soak *verb* to run a program *or* device continuously for a period of time to make sure it functions correctly; *the device was soak-tested prior to delivery*

socket *noun* device with a set of holes, into which a plug fits; **female socket** = hole into which a pin *or* plug can be inserted to make an electrical connection

QUOTE the mouse and keyboard sockets are the same, and could lead to the kind of confusion that arose with the early PCs when the keyboard could be connected to the tape socket
PC User

soft *adjective* **(a)** (material) that loses its magnetic effects when removed from a magnetic field **(b)** (data) that is not permanently stored in hardware (soft usually refers to data stored on magnetic medium); **soft copy** = text listed on screen (as opposed to hard copy on paper); **soft error** = random error caused by software or data errors (this type of error is very difficult to trace and identify since it only appears under certain conditions); *compare with* HARD ERROR; **soft-fail** = system that is still partly operational even after a part of the system has failed; **soft hyphen** = hyphen which is inserted when a word is split at the end of a line, but is not present when the word is written normally; **soft keys** = keys which can be changed by means of a program; **soft keyboard** = keyboard where the functions of the keys can be changed by programs; **soft-reset** = instruction that terminates any program execution and returns the user to the monitor program *or* BIOS; *compare with* HARD RESET; **soft-sectored disk** = disk where the the sectors are described by an address and start code data written onto it when the disk is formatted; **soft zone** = text area to the left of the right margin in a word-processed document, where if a word does not fit completely, a hyphen is automatically inserted

software *noun* any program *or* group of programs which instructs the hardware on how it should perform, including operating systems, word processors and applications programs; **applications software** = programs which are used by the user to perform a certain task; **bundled software** = software which is included in the price of the system; **common software** = useful routines that can be used by any program; **network software** = software which is used to establish the link between a users' program and a network; **pirate software** = illegal copy of a software package; **system software** = programs which direct the basic functions, input-output control, etc., of a computer; **unbundled software** = software which is not included in the price of a system; **user-friendly software** = program that is easy for a non-expert to use and interact with; **software compatible** = computer that will load and run programs written for another computer; **software development** = processes required to produce working programs from an initial idea; **software documentation** = information, notes and diagrams that describe the function, use and operation of a piece of software; **software engineer** = person who can write working software to fit an application; **software engineering** = field of study covering all software-related subjects; **software house** = company which develops and sells computer programs; **software interrupt** = high priority program generated signal, requesting the use of the central processor; **software library** = number of specially written routines, stored in a library file which can be inserted into a program, saving time and effort; **software licence** = agreement between a user and a software house, giving details of the rights of the user to use *or* copy the software; **software life cycle** = period of time when a piece of software exists, from its initial design to the moment when it becomes out of date; **software maintenance** = carrying out updates and modifications to a software package to make sure the program is up to date; **software package** = complete set of programs (and the manual) that allow a certain task to be performed; **software piracy** = illegal copying of software for sale; **software quality assurance (SQA)** = making sure that software will perform as intended; **software reliability** = ability of a piece of software to perform the task required correctly; **software specification** = detailed information about a piece of software's abilities, functions and methods; **software system** = all the programs required for one or more tasks; **software tool** = program used in the development of other programs NOTE: no plural for **software;** for the plural say **pieces of software**

solid *adjective* **solid error** = error that is always present when certain equipment is used; **solid font printer** = printer which uses a whole character shape to print in one movement, such as a daisy wheel printer
◊ **solid-state** *adjective* referring to semiconductor devices; **solid-state device** = electronic device that operates by using the effects of electrical *or* magnetic signals in a solid semiconductor material; **solid-state memory device** = solid-state memory storage device (usually in the form of RAM or ROM chips)

solve *verb* to find the answer to a problem
◊ **solution** *noun* answer to a problem

son file *noun* latest working version of a file; *compare with* FATHER FILE, GRANDFATHER FILE

sophisticated *adjective* technically advanced; *a sophisticated desktop publishing program*
◊ **sophistication** *noun* being technically advanced; *the sophistication of the new package is remarkable*

sort *verb* to put data into order, according to a system, on the instructions of the user; *to sort addresses into alphabetical order; to sort orders according to account numbers;*

bubble sort = sorting method which repeatedly exchanges various pairs of data items until they are in order; **shell sort** = algorithm for sorting data items, in which items can be moved more than position per sort action; **sort/merge** = program which allows new files to be sorted and then merged in correct order into existing files; **tree selection sort** = rapid form of selection where the information from the first sort pass is used in the second pass to speed up selection
◊ **sortkey** *or* **sort field** *noun* field in a stored file that is used to sort the file; *the orders were sorted according to dates by assigning the date field as the sortkey*

source *noun* (a) point where a transmitted signal enters a network NOTE: opposite is **sink** (b) original *or* initial point; **source code** = set of codes written by the programmer which cannot be directly executed by the computer, but has to be translated into an object code program by a compiler *or* interpreter; **source deck** *or* **pack** = set of punched cards that contain the source code for a program; **source document** = form *or* document from which data is extracted prior to entering it into a database; **source editor** = software that allows the user to alter, delete or add instructions in a program source file; **source file** = program written in source language, which is then converted to machine code by a compiler; **source language** = programming language in which the source program is written; **source listing** = (i) listing of a text in its original form; (ii) listing of a source program; **source machine** = computer which can compile source code; *compare with* OBJECT MACHINE; **source program** = program, prior to translation, written in a programming language by a programmer
◊ **source language** *noun* (i) language in which a program is originally written in; (ii) language of a program prior to translation NOTE: opposite is **object** *or* **target language**

SP = STACK POINTER

space 1 *noun* gap (printed *or* displayed in text); **space character** = character code that prints a space; **space bar** = long bar at the bottom of a keyboard, which inserts a space into the text when pressed **2** *verb* to spread out text; *the line of characters was evenly spaced out across the page*
◊ **spacer** *noun* **intelligent spacer** = facility on a word-processing system used to prevent words from being hyphenated *or* separated at the wrong point

◊ **spacing** *noun* way in which spaces are inserted in a printed text; *the spacing on some lines is very uneven*

span *noun* set of allowed values between a maximum and minimum

spark printer *noun* thermal printer which produces characters on thermal paper by electric sparks

sparse array *noun* data matrix structure containing mainly zero *or* null entries

spec *informal* = SPECIFICATION; **high-spec** = high specification

special *adjective* which is different *or* not usual; **special character** = character which is not a normal one in a certain font (such as a certain accent *or* a symbol); **special purpose** = system designed for a specific *or* limited range of applications; **special sort** = extra printing character not in the standard font range

◊ **specialize** *verb* to study and be an expert in a subject; *he specializes in the design of CAD systems*

◊ **specialist** *noun* expert in a certain field of study; *you need a specialist programmer to help devise a new word-processing program*

specify *verb* to state clearly what is needed

◊ **specification** *noun* detailed information about what is to be supplied *or* about a job to be done; **to work to standard specifications** = to work to specifications which are accepted anywhere in the same industry; **the work is not up to specification** *or* **does not meet the customer's specifications** = the product was not manufactured in the way which was detailed in the specifications; **high specification** *or* **high spec** = high degree of accuracy *or* large number of features; *high spec cabling needs to be very carefully handled;* **program specification** = detailed information about a program's abilities, features and methods

specific address *noun* storage address that directly, without any modification, accesses a location *or* device

◊ **specific code** *noun* binary code which directly operates the central processing unit, using only absolute addresses and values; **specific coding** = program code that has been written so that it only uses absolute addresses and values

◊ **specificity** *noun* ratio of non-relevant entries not retrieved to the total number of non-relevant entries contained in a file, database or library

speech *noun* speaking *or* making words with the voice; **speech chip** = integrated circuit that generates sounds (usually phonemes) which when played together sound like human speech; **speech recognition** = analysing spoken words in such a way that a computer can recognize spoken words and commands; **speech synthesis** = production of spoken words by a speech synthesizer; **speech synthesizer** = device which takes data from a computer and outputs it as spoken words

QUOTE speech conveys information, and the primary task of computer speech processing is the transmission and reception of that information
Personal Computer World

speed *noun* time taken for a movement divided by the distance travelled; **speed of loop** = method of benchmarking a computer by measuring the number of loops executed in a certain time; **playback speed** = rate at which tape travels past a playback head

spellcheck *verb* to check the spelling in a text by comparing it with a dictionary held in the computer

◊ **spellchecker** *or* **spelling checker** *noun* dictionary of correctly spelled words, held in a computer, and used to check the spelling of a text; *the program will be upgraded with a word-processor and a spelling checker*

spike *noun* very short duration voltage pulse

spillage *noun* situation when too much data is being processed and cannot be contained in a buffer

spin *verb* to turn round fast; *the disk was spun by the drive; the disk drive motor spins at a constant velocity*
NOTE: spinning - span - spun

spindle *noun* object which grips and spins a disk in the centre hole

◊ **spindling** *noun* turning a disk by hand

splice *verb* to join two lengths of magnetic tape, forming a continuous length; **splicing tape** = non-magnetic tape which is applied to the back of the two ends of tape to be spliced

split screen *noun* system where more than one text file can appear on the screen at the same time (such as the text being worked on and another text from memory for comparison)

spool 1 *noun* reel on which a tape *or* printer ribbon is wound **2** *verb* to transfer data from a disk to a tape

◊ **spooler** *or* **spooling device** *noun* device which holds a tape and which receives information from a disk for storage

◊ **spooling** *noun* transferring data to a disk from which it can be printed at the normal speed of the printer, leaving the computer available to do something else

sporadic fault *noun* error that occurs occasionally

spreadsheet *noun* (i) program which allows calculations to be carried out on several columns of numbers; (ii) printout of calculations on wide computer stationary

sprite *noun* object which moves round the screen in computer graphics

sprocket *or* **sprocket wheel** *noun* wheel with teeth round it which fit into holes in continuous stationery *or* punched tape

◊ **sprocket feed** *noun* paper feed, where the printer pulls the paper by turning sprocket wheels which fit into a series of holes along each edge of the sheet; *see also* TRACTOR FEED

◊ **sprocket holes** *noun* series of small holes on each edge of continuous stationery, which allow the sheet to be pulled through the printer

SPX = SIMPLEX

SQA = SOFTWARE QUALITY ASSURANCE

SSD = SINGLE-SIDED DISK

SSI = SMALL SCALE INTEGRATION

stable *adjective* not moving *or* not changing; **stable state** = the state of a system when no external signals are applied

◊ **stability** *noun* being stable; **image stability** = ability of a display screen to provide a flicker-free picture

stack *noun* temporary storage for data, registers *or* tasks where items are added and retrieved from the same end of the list; *see also* LIFO; **pushdown stack** *or* **pushdown list** = method of storing data, where the last item stored is always at the same location, the rest of the list being pushed down by one address; **virtual memory stack** = temporary store for pages in a virtual memory system; **stack address** = location pointed to by the stack pointer; **stack base** = address of the origin *or* base of a stack; **stack job processor** = storing a number of jobs to be processed in a stack and automatically executing one after the other; **stack pointer (SP)** = address register containing the location of the most recently stored item of data *or* the location of the next item of data to be retrieved

stage *noun* one of several points in a process; *the text is ready for the printing stage; we are in the first stage of running in the new computer system*

◊ **staged** *adjective* carried out in stages, one after the other; **staged change-over** = change between an old and a new system in a series of stages

stand-alone *or* **standalone** *adjective & noun* (device *or* system) which can operate without the need of any other devices; *the workstations have been networked together rather than used as stand-alone systems;* **stand-alone system** = system that can operate independently; **stand-alone terminal** = computer terminal with a processor and memory which can be directly connected to a modem, without being a member of a network *or* cluster

standard *adjective* normal *or* usual; **standard document** *or* **standard form** *or* **standard paragraph** *or* **standard text** = normal printed document *or* form *or* paragraph which is used many times (with different names and addresses often inserted - as in a form letter); **standard function** = special feature included as normal in a computer system; **standard interface** = interface between two or more systems that conforms to pre-defined standards; **standard letter** = letter which is sent without any change to the main text, but being personalised by inserting the names and addresses of different people; **standard subroutine** = routine which carries out an often used function, such as keyboard input *or* screen display

◊ **standardize** *verb* to make a series of things conform to a standard; *the standardized control of transmission links*

◊ **standards** *plural noun* normal quality *or* normal conditions which are used to judge other things; **production standards** =

quality of production; **up to standard** = of an acceptable quality; *this batch of disks is not up to standard;* **standards converter** = device to convert received signals conforming to one standard into a different standard; **modem standards** = rules defining transmitting frequencies, etc., which allow different modems to communicate

COMMENT: modem standards are set by the CCITT in the UK, the Commonwealth and most of Europe, while the USA and part of South America use modem standards set by Bell

standby *noun* (device *or* program) which is ready for use in case of failure; **standby equipment** = secondary system identical to the main system, to be used if the main system breaks down; **cold standby** = backup system that will allow the equipment to continue running but with the loss of any volatile data; **hot standby** = backup equipment that is kept operational at all times in case of system failure

QUOTE before fault-tolerant systems, users had to rely on the cold standby, that is switching on a second machine when the first developed a fault; the alternative was the hot standby, where a second computer was kept running continuously
Computer News

star network *noun* network of several machines where each terminal *or* floppy disk unit *or* satellite is linked individually to a central hard disk machine *or* server; *compare* BUS NETWORK, RING NETWORK

◊ **star program** *noun* perfect program that runs (first time) with no errors *or* bugs

start *adjective* beginning *or* first part; **cold start** = switching on a computer *or* to run a program from its original start point; **start bit** *or* **element** = transmitted bit used (in asynchronous communications) to indicate the start of a character; **warm start** = restarting a program which has stopped, without losing any data; **start of header** = transmitted code indicating the start of header (address *or* destination) information for a following message; **start of text (SOT** *or* **STX)** = transmitted code indicating the end of control *or* address information and the start of the message NOTE: opposite is **stop bit**

state *noun* the way something is; **active state** = state in which an action can *or* does occur; **steady state** = circuit *or* device *or* program state in which no action is occurring but can accept an input

statement *noun* (i) expression used to convey an instruction *or* define a process; (ii) instruction in a source language which is translated into several machine code instructions; **conditional statement** = program instruction that will redirect program control according to the outcome of an event; **control statement** = (i) program instruction that directs a program (to another branch, etc.); (ii) program instruction that directs a CPU to provide controlling actions *or* controls the actions of the CPU; **directive statement** = program instruction used to control the language translator, compiler, etc.; **input statement** = computer programming command that waits for data entry from a port *or* keyboard; **multi-statement line** = line from a computer program that contains more than one instruction *or* statement; **narrative statement** = statement which set variables and allocates storage; **statement number** = number assigned (in a sequential way) to a series of instruction statements; *see also* LINE NUMBER

state-of-the-art *adjective* very modern *or* technically as advanced as possible

QUOTE the main PCB is decidedly non-state-of-the-art
Personal Computer World

static *adjective* (i) (data) which does not change with time; (ii) (system) that is not dynamic; **static dump** = printout of the state of a system when it has finished a process; **static memory** = non-volatile memory that does not require refreshing; **static RAM** = RAM which retains data for as long as the power supply is on, and where the data does not have to be refreshed; *compare with* DYNAMIC RAM; **static subroutine** = subroutine that uses no variables apart from the operand addresses

COMMENT: static RAM uses bistable devices such as flip-flops to store data; these take up more space on a chip than the capacititive storage method of dynamic RAM but do not require refreshing

station *noun* point in a network *or* communications system that contains devices to control the input and output of messages, allowing it to be used as a sink *or* source; **secondary station** = temporary status of the station that is receiving data; **workstation** = desk with computer, keyboard, monitor, printers, etc., where a person works

stationery *noun* office supplies for writing, especially paper, envelopes, labels,

etc.; **computer stationery** = paper specially made for use in a computer printer; **continuous stationery** = printer stationery which takes the form of a single long sheet; **preprinted stationery** = computer stationery (such as invoices) which is preprinted with the company heading and form layout onto which the details will be printed by the computer
NOTE: no plural

statistics *noun* (study of) facts in the form of figures
◊ **statistical** *adjective* based on statistics

status *noun* importance *or* position; **status bit** = single bit in a word used to provide information about the state *or* result of an operation; **status line** = line at the top *or* bottom of a screen which gives information about the task currently being worked on (number of lines, number of columns, filename, time, etc.); **status poll** = signal from a computer requesting information on the current status of a terminal; **status register** = register containing information on the status of a peripheral device; **program status word (PSW)** = word which contains a number of status bits, such as carry flag, zero flag, overflow bit, etc.

steady state *noun* circuit *or* device *or* program state in which no action is occurring but can accept an input

stencil *noun* **flowchart stencil** *or* **template** = plastic sheet with template symbols cut out, to allow flowcharts to be quickly and clearly drawn

step 1 *noun* a single unit; **single step** = executing a computer program one instruction at a time, used for debugging **2** *verb* to move forward *or* backwards by one unit; *we stepped forward through the file one record at a time*
◊ **stepper motor** *or* **stepping motor** *noun* motor which turns in small steps as instructed by a computer (used in printers, disk drives and robots)

stochastic model *noun* mathematical representation of a system that includes the effects of random actions

stock control program *noun* software designed to help manage stock in a business

stop *verb* not doing any action; **stop and wait protocol** = communications protocol in which the transmitter waits for a signal from the receiver that the message was correctly received before transmitting further data; **tab stop** = preset point along a line, where the printing head *or* cursor will stop for each tabulation command

◊ **stop bit** *or* **stop element** *noun* transmitted bit used in asynchronous communications to indicate the end of a character; **stop code** = instruction that temporarily stops a process to allow the user to enter data; **stop instruction** = computer programming instruction that stops program execution; **stop list** = list of words that are not to be used *or* are not significant for a file *or* library search; **stop time** = time taken for a spinning disk to come to a stop after it is no longer powered

storage *noun* memory *or* part of the computer system in which data *or* programs are kept for further use; **archive storage** = storage of data for a long period of time; **auxiliary storage** = any data storage medium (such as magnetic tape *or* disk) that is not the main, high speed memory; **dynamic storage** *or* **memory** = memory that requires its contents to be updated regularly; **external storage** = storage device which is located outside the main computer system but which can be accessed by the CPU; **information storage** = storing data in a form which allows it to be processed at a later date; **instruction storage** = section of memory that is used to store instructions; **intermediate storage** = temporary area of memory for items that are currently being processed; **mass storage system** = data storage that can hold more than one million million bits of data; **nonerasable storage** = storage medium that cannot be erased and re-used; **primary storage** = (i) small fast-access internal memory of a system which contains the program currently being executed; (ii) main internal memory of a system; **secondary storage** = any data storage medium (such as magnetic tape *or* floppy disk) that is not the main, high-speed computer storage; **static storage** = non-volatile memory that does not require refreshing; **temporary storage** = storage which is not permanent; **volatile storage** = memory *or* storage medium that loses data stored when the power supply is switched off; **storage allocation** = how memory is allocated for different uses, such as programs, variables, data, etc.; **storage capacity** = amount of space available for storage of data; **storage density** = number of bits that can be recorded per unit area of storage medium; **storage device** = any device that can store data and then allow it to retrieved when required; **storage disk** = disk used to store data **storage dump** =

printout of all the contents of an area of storage space; **storage media** = various materials which are able to store data; **storage tube** = special CRT used for computer graphics that retains an image on screen without the need for refresh actions; *see also* REFRESH

◊ **store 1** *noun* memory *or* part of the computer system in which data *or* programs are kept for further use; **store address register (SAR)** = register in a CPU that contains the address of the next location to be accessed; **store data register (SDR)** = register in a CPU which holds data before it is proceesed *or* moved to a memory location; **store location** *or* **cell** = unit in a computer system which can store information **2** *verb* to save data, which can then be used again as necessary; *storing a page of high resolution graphics can require 3Mb;* **store and forward** = communications system that stores a number of messages before retransmitting them; **stored program** = computer program that is stored in memory (if it is stored in dynamic RAM it will be lost when the machine is switched off, if stored on disk or tape (backing store) it will be permanently retained); **stored program signalling** = system of storing communications control signals on computer in the form of a program

COMMENT: storage devices include hard and floppy disk, RAM, punched paper tape and magnetic tape

straight-line coding *noun* program written to avoid the use of loops and branches, providing a faster execution time

stray *adjective* lost *or* wandering; (something) which has avoided being stopped; *the metal screen protects the CPU against stray electromagnetic effects from the PSU*

stream *noun* long flow of serial data; **job stream** = number of tasks arranged in order waiting to be processed in a batch system

◊ **streamer** *noun* **tape streamer** *or* **streaming tape drive** = (device containing a) continuous loop of tape, used as backing storage

QUOTE the product has 16Mb of memory, 45Mb of Winchester disk storage and 95Mb streaming tape storage
Minicomputer News

string *noun* any series of consecutive alphanumeric characters *or* words that are manipulated and treated as a single unit by the computer; **alphanumeric** *or* **character string** = storage allocated for a series of alphanumeric characters; **numeric string** = string which contains only numbers; **null** *or* **blank string** = string that contains nothing; **string area** = section of memory in which strings of alphanumeric characters are stored; **string concatenation** = linking a series of strings together; **string function** = program operation which can act on strings; **string length** = the number of characters in a string; **string name** = identification label assigned to a string; **string orientated symbolic language (SNOBOL)** = high-level programming language that uses string processing methods; **string variable** = variables used in a computer language that can contain alphanumeric characters as well as numbers

◊ **stringy floppy** *or* **tape streamer** *noun* continuous loop of tape, used for backing storage

strip 1 *noun* long thin piece of material; **strip window** = display which shows a single line of text; **magnetic strip** = layer of magnetic material on the surface of a plastic card, used for recording data **2** *verb* to remove the control data from a received message, leaving only the relevant information

strobe *verb* to send a pulse (usually on the selection line) of an electronic circuit; **address strobe** = signal indicating that a valid address is on the address bus; **data strobe** = signal indicating that valid data is on the data bus

structure 1 *noun* way in which something is organized *or* formed; **network structure** = data structure that allows each node to be connected to any of the others **2** *verb* to organize *or* to arrange in a certain way; *you first structure a document to meet your requirements and then fill in the blanks;* **structured design** = problem solved by a number of interconnected modules; **structured programming** = well-ordered and logical technique of assembling programs

STX = START OF TEXT

style sheet *noun* template that can be preformatted to generate automatically the style *or* layout of a document such a a manual, a book, a newsletter, etc.

stylus *noun* pen-like device that is used in computer graphics systems to dictate cursor position on the screen; *use the stylus to draw on the graphics tablet;* **stylus printer** *see* DOT MATRIX PRINTER

sub- *prefix* meaning less (important) than *or* lower than; **subaddress** = peripheral identification code, used to access one peripheral (this is then followed by address data to access a location within the peripheral's memory); **subclass** = number of data items related to one item in a master class

subdirectory *noun* directory of disk *or* tape contents contained within the main directory

QUOTE if you delete a file and then delete the subdirectory where it was located, you cannot restore the file because the directory does not exist
Personal Computer World

subprogram *noun* (i) subroutine in a program; (ii) program called up by a main program

subroutine *noun* section of a program which performs a required function and that can be called upon at any time from inside the main program; **closed** *or* **linked subroutine** = number of computer instructions in a program that can be called at any time, with a control being returned on completion to the next instruction after the call; **open subroutine** = code for a subroutine which is copied into memory whenever a call instruction is found; **static subroutine** = subroutine that uses no variables apart from the operand addresses; **two-level subroutine** = subroutine containing another subroutine; **subroutine call** = computer programming instruction that directs control to a subroutine

COMMENT: a subroutine is executed by a call instruction which directs the processor to its address; when finished it returns to the instruction after the call instruction in the main program

subscriber *noun* (i) person who has a telephone; (ii) person who pays for access to a service such as a BBS

subscript *noun* small character which is printed below the line of other characters; *see also* SUPERSCRIPT NOTE: used in chemical formulae: CO_2 **subscripted variable** = element in an array, which is identified by a subscript

◊ **subset** *noun* small set of data items which forms part of a another larger set

◊ **subsegment** *noun* small section of a segment

substitute *verb* to put something in the place of something else; **substitute character** = character that is displayed if a received character is not recognized NOTE: you substitute one thing **for** another

◊ **substitution** *noun* replacing something by something else; **substitution error** = error made by a scanner which mistakes one character *or* letter for another; **substitution table** = list of characters *or* codes that are to be inserted instead of received codes

subtraction *noun* taking one number away from another

◊ **subtrahend** *noun* in a subtraction operation, the number to be subtracted from the minuend

substrate *noun* base material on which an integrated circuit is constructed; *see also* INTEGRATED CIRCUIT

subsystem *noun* one smaller part of a large system

successive *adjective* which follow one after the other; *each successive operation adds further characters to the string*

suffix notation *noun* mathematical operations written in a logical way, so that the symbol appears after the numbers to be acted upon; *see also* POSTFIX NOTATION

suite of programs *noun* (i) group of programs which run one after the other; (ii) number of programs used for a particular task; *the word-processing system uses a suite of three programs, editor, spelling checker and printing controller*

sum *noun* total of a number of items added together

◊ **summation check** *noun* error detection check performed by adding together the characters received and comparing with the required total

super- *prefix* meaning very good *or* very powerful; **supercomputer** = very powerful mainframe computer used for high speed mathematical tasks

◊ **super large scale integration (SLSI)** *noun* integrated circuit with more than 100,000 components

superimpose *verb* to place something on top of something else

superior number *noun* superscript figure

superscript *noun* small character printed higher than the normal line of characters; *compare with* SUBSCRIPT
NOTE: used often in mathematics: 10^5 (say: ten to the power five)

supersede *verb* to take the place of something which is older *or* less useful; *the new program supersedes the earlier one, and is much faster*

supervise *verb* to watch carefully to see if work is well done; *the manufacture of circuit boards is very carefully supervised*
◇ **supervision** *noun* being supervised
◇ **supervisor** *noun* (i) person who makes sure that equipment is always working correctly; (ii) section of a computer operating system that regulates the use of peripherals and the operations undertaken by the CPU
◇ **supervisory** *adjective* as a supervisor; **supervisory program** *or* **executive program** = master program in a computer system that controls the execution of other programs; **supervisory sequence** = combination of control codes that perform a controlling function in a data communications network; **supervisory signal** = (i) signal that indicates if a circuit is busy; (ii) signal that provides an indication of the state of a device

supply 1 *noun* providing goods *or* products *or* services; *the electricity supply has failed; they signed a contract for the supply of computer stationery* 2 *verb* to provide something which is needed (for which someone will pay); *the computer was supplied by a recognized dealer; they have signed a contract to supply on-line information*
◇ **supplier** *noun* company which supplies; *a supplier of computer parts; a supplier of disk drives or a disk drive supplier; Japanese suppliers have set up warehouses in the country*

support *verb* to give help to *or* to help to run; *the main computer supports six workstations;* **support chip** = dedicated IC that works with a CPU, and carries out an additional function *or* a standard function very rapidly, so speeding up the processing time; *the maths support chip can be plugged in here*

suppress *verb* to remove; *the filter is used to suppress the noise due to static interference*
◇ **suppression** *noun* act of suppressing
◇ **suppressor** *noun* device which suppresses interference

surge *noun* sudden increase in electrical power in a system, due to a fault *or* noise *or* component failure; **surge protector** = electronic device that cuts off the power supply to sensitive equipment if it detects a power surge that could cause damage

COMMENT: power surges can burn out circuits before you have time to pull the plug; a surge protector between your computer and the wall outlet will help prevent damage

swap 1 *noun* = SWAPPING 2 *verb* to stop using one program, put it into store temporarily, run another program, and when that is finished, return to the first one
◇ **swapping** *or* **swap** *noun* system where a program is moved to backing storage while another program is being used

swim *noun* computer graphics that move slightly due to a faulty display unit

switch 1 *noun* (a) point in a computer program where control can be passed to one of a number of choices (b) mechanical *or* solid state device that can electrically connect *or* isolate two or more lines 2 *verb* to connect *or* disconnect two lines by activating a switch; **to switch on** = to start to provide power to a system by using a switch to connect the power supply lines to the circuit; **to switch off** = to disconnect the power supply to a device; **to switch over** = to start using an alternative device when the primary one becomes faulty; **switched network backup** = user's choice of a secondary route through a network if the first is busy
◇ **switching** *noun* constant update of connections between changing sinks and sources in a network; **switching centre** = point in a communications network where messages can be switched to and from the various lines and circuits that end there; **switching circuit** = electronic circuit that can direct messages from one line or circuit to another in a switching centre; **line switching** = communication line and circuit established on demand and held until no longer required

symbol *noun* sign *or* picture which represents something; *this language uses the symbol ? to represent the print command;* **logic symbol** = graphical symbol used to represent a type of logic function in a diagram; **symbol table** *or* **library** = list of labels *or* names in a compiler *or* assembler, which relate to their addresses in the machine code program

◊ **symbolic** *adjective* which acts as a symbol *or* which uses a symbol name *or* label; **symbolic address** = address represented by a symbol *or* name; **symbolic code** *or* **instruction** = instruction that is in mnemonic form rather than a binary number; **symbolic debugging** = debugger that allows symbolic representation of variables *or* locations; **symbolic language** = (i) any computer language where locations are represented by names; (ii) any language used to write source code; **symbolic logic** = study of reasoning and thought (formal logic); **symbolic name** = name used as a label for a variable *or* location; **symbolic programming** = writing a program in a source language

symmetric difference *noun* logical function whose output is true if either (of 2) inputs is true, and false if both inputs are the same

sync *noun* *informal* = SYNCHRONIZATION; **sync bit** = transmitted bit used to synchronize devices; **sync character** = transmitted character used to synchronize devices; **sync pulses** = transmitted pulses used to make sure that the receiver is synchronized with the transmitter; **the two devices are out of sync** = the two devices are not properly synchronized

◊ **synchronization** *noun* action of synchronizing two or more devices; **synchronization pulses** = transmitted pulses used to make sure that the receiver is synchronized with the transmitter

◊ **synchronize** *verb* to make sure that two or more devices *or* processes are coordinated in time or action

◊ **synchronizer** *noun* device that will perform a function when it receives a signal from another device

◊ **synchronous** *adjective* which runs in sync with something else (such as a main clock); **synchronous computer** = computer in which each action can only take place when a timing pulse arrives; **synchronous data link control (SDLC)** = protocol and rules used to define the way in which synchronous data is transmitted *or* received; **synchronous data network** = communications network in which all the actions throughout the network are controlled by a single timing signal; **synchronous idle character** = character transmitted by a DTE to ensure correct synchronization when no other character is being transmitted; **synchronous mode** = system mode in which operations and events are synchronized with a clock signal; **synchronous network** = network in which all the links are synchronized with a single timing signal; **synchronous system** = system in which all devices are synchronized to a main clock signal; **synchronous transmission** = transmission of data from one device to another, where both devices are controlled by the same clock, and the transmitted data is synchronized with the clock signal

syntactic error *noun* programming error in which the program statement does not follow the syntax of the language

syntax *noun* grammatical rules that apply to a programming language; **syntax analysis** = stage in compilation where statements are checked to see if they obey the rules of syntax; **syntax error** = programming error in which the program statement does not follow the syntax of the language

synthesis *noun* producing something artificially (from a number of smaller elements)

◊ **synthesize** *verb* to produce something artificially (from a number of smaller elements)

◊ **synthesizer** *noun* device which generates something (signals *or* sound *or* speech); **speech synthesizer** = device which generates sounds which are similar to the human voice

◊ **synthetic address** *noun* location used by a program that has been produced by instructions within the program; **synthetic language** = programming language in which the source program is written

QUOTE despite the fact that speech can now be synthesized with very acceptable quality, all it conveys is linguistic information
Personal Computer World

sysgen = SYSTEM GENERATION

system *noun* any group of hardware *or* software *or* peripherals, etc., which work together; **adaptive system** = system which is able to alter its responses and processes according to inputs *or* situations; **computer system** = central processor with storage and associated peripherals which make up a working computer; **information system** = computer system which provides information according to a user's requests; **interactive system** = system which provides an immediate response to the user's commands *or* programs *or* data; **operating system (op sys)** = basic software that controls the running of the hardware and the management of data files, without the user having to operate it; **secure system** = system that cannot be accessed without authorization; **system check** = running diagnostic routines to ensure that there are no problems; **system control panel** = main computer system control switches and status indicators; **system crash** = situation where the operating system stops working and has to be restarted; **system design** = identifying and investigating possible solutions to a problem, and deciding upon the most appropriate system to solve the problem; **system diagnostics** = tests, features and messages that help find hardware *or* software faults; **system disk** = disk which holds the system software; **system firmware** = basic operating system functions and routines in a ROM device; **system flowchart** = diagram that shows each step of the computer procedures needed in a system; **system generation** *or* **sysgen** = process of producing an optimum operating system for a particular task;

system library = stored files that hold the various parts of a computer's operating system; **system life cycle** = time when a system exists, between its initial design and its becoming out of date; **system log** = record of computer processor operations; **system security** = measures, such as password, priority protection, authorization codes, etc., designed to stop browsing and hackers; **system software** = software which makes applications run on hardware; **system specifications** = details of hardware and software required to perform certain tasks; **system support** = group of people that maintain and operate a system

◊ **systems analysis** *noun* (i) analysing a process *or* system to see if it could be more efficiently carried out by a computer; (ii) examining an existing system with the aim of improving *or* replacing it; **systems analyst** = person who undertakes system analysis; **systems program** = program which controls the way in which a computer system works; **systems programmer** = person who writes system software

QUOTE the core of an expert system is its database of rules

Personal Computer World

Tt

T junction *noun* connection at right angles with a main signal *or* power carrying cable

TAB = TABULATE

tab *verb* to tabulate *or* to arrange text in columns with the cursor automatically running from one column to the next in keyboarding; *the list was neatly lined up by tabbing to column 10 at the start of each new line;* **tab memory** = ability of a editing program (usually a word-processor) to store details about various tab settings; **tab rack** *or* **ruler line** = graduated scale, displayed on the screen, showing the position of tabulation columns; *the tab rack shows you the left and right margins;* **tab stops** = preset points along a line, where the printing head *or* cursor will stop for each tabulation command

◇ **tabbing** *noun* movement of the cursor in a word-processing program from one tab stop to the next; *tabbing can be done from inside the program;* **decimal tabbing** = adjusting a column of numbers so that the decimal points are aligned vertically

table *noun* list of data in columns and rows on a printed page *or* on the screen; **decision table** = list of all possible events *or* states that could happen and the actions taken (sometimes used instead of a flowchart); **lookup table** = collection of stored results that can be accessed very rapidly; *this is the value of the key pressed, use a lookup table to find its ASCII value;* **table lookup** = using one known value to select one entry in a table, providing a secondary value; **reference program table** = list produced by a compiler *or* system of the location, size and type of the variables, routines and macros within a program; **symbol table** = list of all the symbols that are accepted by a language *or* compiler and their object code translation

tablet *noun* **graphics tablet** = graphics pad *or* flat device that allows a user to input graphical information into a computer by drawing on its surface; *it is much easier to draw accurately with a tablet than with a mouse*

tabulate *verb* to arrange text in columns, with the cursor moving to each new column automatically as the text is keyboarded

◇ **tabular** *adjective* **in tabular form** = arranged in a table

◇ **tabulating** *noun* processing punched cards, such as a sorting operation

◇ **tabulation** *noun* (i) arrangement of a table of figures; (ii) moving a printing head *or* cursor a preset distance along a line; **tabulation markers** = symbols displayed to indicate the position of tabulation stops; **tabulation stops** = preset points along a line at which a printing head *or* cursor will stop for each tabulation command

◇ **tabulator** *noun* part of a typewriter *or* word-processor which automatically sets words *or* figures into columns

tactile *adjective* using the sense of touch; **tactile keyboard** = keyboard that provides some indication that a key has been pressed, such as a beep

tag *noun* **(a)** one section of a computer instruction **(b)** identifying characters attached to a file *or* item (of data); *each file has a three letter tag for rapid identification*

tail *noun* **(a)** data recognized as the end of a list of data **(b)** control code used to signal the end of a message

takedown *verb* to remove paper *or* disks *or* tape from a peripheral after one job and prepare it for the next; **takedown time** = amount of time required to takedown a peripheral ready for another job

take-up reel *noun* reel onto which magnetic tape is collected; *put the full reel on this spindle, and feed the tape into the take-up reel on the other spindle*

talk *verb* to speak *or* to communicate

QUOTE a variety of technologies exist which allow computers to talk to one another
Which PC?

tandem *noun* **working in tandem** = situation where two things are working together

tape *noun* long thin flat piece of material; **cassette tape** = tape stored on two small reels protected by a solid casing; *cassette tape is mainly used with home computers;* **(magnetic) tape** = narrow length of thin plastic coated with a magnetic material used to store signals magnetically; **master tape** = magnetic tape which contains all the vital operating system routines, loaded by the initial program loader once when the computer is switched on *or* hard reset; **(paper) tape** *or* **punched tape** = strip of paper on which information can be recorded in the form of punched holes; **streaming tape drive** = device containing a continuous loop of tape, used as backing store; **tape back-up** = to use (usually magnetic) tape as a medium for storing back-ups from faster main *or* secondary storage (such as RAM *or* hard disk); **tape cable** *or* **ribbon cable** = number of insulated conductors arranged next to each other forming a flat cable; **tape cartridge** = cassette box containing magnetic tape (on a reel); **tape cassette** = small box containing a reel of magnetic tape and a pickup reel; **tape code** = coding system used for punched data representation on paper tape; **tape deck** = device which plays back and records data onto magnetic tape; **tape drive** = mechanism which controls magnetic tape movement over the tape heads; *our new product has a 96Mb streaming tape drive;* **tape format** = way in which blocks of data, control codes and location data is stored on tape; **tape guide** = method by which the tape is correctly positioned over the tape head; *the tape is out of alignment because one of the tape guides has broken;* **tape head** = transducer that can read and write signals onto the surface of magnetic tape; **tape header** = identification information at the beginning of a tape; **tape label** = tape header and trailer containing information about the contents of a tape; **tape library** = (i) secure area for the storage of computer data tapes; (ii) series of computer tapes kept in store for reference; **tape loadpoint** = position on a magnetic tape at which reading should commence to load a file; **tape punch** = machine that punches holes into paper tape; **tape reader** = machine that reads punched holes in paper tape *or* signals on magnetic tape; **tape streamer** = continuous loop of tape used for backing storage; **tape to card converter** = device that reads data from magnetic tape and stores it on punched cards; **tape transmitter** = device that reads data from paper tape and transmits it to another point; **tape trailer** = identification information at the beginning of a tape; **tape transport** = method (in a magnetic tape recorder) by which the tape is moved smoothly from reel to reel over the magnetic heads

COMMENT: cassettes *or* reels of tape are easy to use and cheaper than disks, the cassette casing usually conforms to a standard size. They are less adaptable and only provide sequential access, usually being used for master copies *or* making back-ups

target *noun* goal which you aim to achieve; **target computer** = computer which software is to be run on (but not necessarily written on, e.g. using a cross-assembler); **target language** = language into which a language will be translated from its source language; *the target language for this PASCAL program is machine code*

◊ **target level** = interpretive processing mode for program execution; **target** *or* **run phase** = period of time during which the target program is run; **target program** = object program *or* computer program in object code form, produced by a compiler

QUOTE the target board is connected to the machine through the in-circuit emulator cable
Electronics & Wireless World

tariff *noun* charge incurred by a user of a communications *or* computer system; *there is a set tariff for logging on, then a rate for every minute of computer time used*

task *noun* job which is to carried out by a computer; **multitasking** = ability of a computer system to run two or more programs at the same time; *this operating system provides a multitasking environment, but not a multi-user one;* **task management** = system software that controls the use and allocation of resources to programs; **task queue** = temporary storage of jobs waiting to be processed

TAT = TURNAROUND TIME

TDS = TRANSACTION-DRIVEN SYSTEM computer system that will normally run batch processing tasks until interrupted by a new transaction, at which point it allocates resources to the new transaction

technical *adjective* referring to a particular machine *or* process; *the document gives all the technical details on the new computer*

◊ **technician** *noun* person who is specialized in industrial work; *the computer technicians installed the new system*

◊ **technique** *noun* skilled way of doing a job; *the company has developed a new technique for processing customers' disks; he has a special technique for answering complaints from users of the software*

technology *noun* applying scientific knowledge to industrial processes; **information technology (IT)** = technology involved in acquiring, storing, processing, and distributing information by electronic means (including radio, TV, telephone and computers); **new technology** = electronic instruments which have recently been developed; **the introduction of new technology** = putting new electronic equipment into a business *or* industry

◊ **technological** *adjective* referring to technology; **the technological revolution** = changing of industrial methods by introducing new technology

tele- *prefix* meaning long distance; **telecommunications** = technology of passing and receiving messages over a distance (as in radio, telephone, telegram, satellite broadcast, etc.)

◊ **teleinformatic services** *noun* any data only service, such as telex, facsimile, which uses telecommunications

telematics *noun* interaction of all data processing and communications devices (computers, networks, etc.)

telephone *noun* machine used for speaking to someone *or* communicating with another computer (using modems) over a long distance; **telephone as a data carrier** = using a modem to send binary data as sound signals over a telephone line

teleprinter *noun* device that is capable of sending and receiving data from a distant point by means of a telegraphic circuit, and printing out the message on a printer; *you can drive a teleprinter from this modified serial port;* **teleprinter interface** = terminal interface *or* hardware and software combination required to control the functions of a terminal; **teleprinter roll** = roll of paper onto which messages are printed

teleprocessing (TP) *noun* processing of data at a distance (as on a central computer from outside terminals)

telesoftware (TSW) *noun* software which is received from a viewdata *or* teletext service; *the telesoftware was downloaded yesterday*

teletext *noun* method of transmitting text and information with a normal television signal, usually as a serial bit stream that can be displayed using a special decoder

teletype (TTY) *noun* term used for teleprinter equipment

◊ **teletypewriter** *noun* keyboard and printer attached to a computer system which can input data either direct *or* by making punched paper tape

television (TV) *noun* device that can receive (modulated) video signals from a computer *or* broadcast signals with an aerial and display images on a CRT screen with sound; **television monitor** = device able to display signals from a computer without sound, but not broadcast signals (this is usually because there is no demodulator device which is needed for broadcast signals); **television receiver/monitor** = device able to act as a TV receiver *or* monitor; **television scan** = horizontal movement of the picture beam over the screen, producing one line of an image; **television tube** = CRT with electronic devices that provide the line by line horizontal and vertical scanning movement of the picture beam; *see also* CRT, RGB

template *noun* (i) plastic *or* metal sheet with cut-out symbols to help the drawing of flowcharts and circuit diagrams; (ii); *(in text processing)* standard text (such as a standard letter *or* invoice) into which specific details (company address *or* prices *or* quantities) can be added; **template command** = command that allows functions *or* other commands to be easily set; *a template paragraph command enables the user to specify the number of spaces each paragraph should be indented; see also* STANDARD, FORM LETTER

temporary storage *noun* storage which is not permanent; **temporary register** = register used for temporary storage for the results of an ALU operation

◊ **temporarily** *adverb* for a certain time *or* not permanently

ten's complement *noun* formed by adding one to the nine's complement of a decimal number

terminal 1 *noun* **(a)** device usually made up of a display unit and a keyboard which allows entry and display of information when on-line to a central computer system; **addressable terminal** = terminal that will only accept data if it has the correct address and identification data in the message header; *all the messages go to all the terminals since none are addressable terminals;* **applications terminal** = terminal (such as at a sales desk) which is specifically configured to carry out certain tasks; **dumb terminal** = peripheral that can only receive and transmit data, and is not capable of processing data; **central terminal** = terminal which controls communications between a central *or* host computer and remote terminals; **intelligent terminal** *or* **smart terminal** = computer terminal which contains a CPU and memory, allowing basic data processing to be carried out, usually with the facility to allow the user to program it independently of the host computer; *the new intelligent terminal has a built-in text editor;* **master terminal** = one terminal in a network that has priority over any other, used by the system manager to set-up the system *or* carry out privileged commands; *the system manager uses the master terminal to restart the system;* **remote terminal** = computer terminal connected to a distant computer system; **slave terminal** = terminal controlled by a main computer *or* terminal; **terminal area** = part of a printer circuit board at which edge connectors can be connected; **terminal character set** = range of characters available for a particular type of terminal, these might include graphics *or* customized characters; **terminal controller** = hardware device *or* IC that controls a terminal including data communications and display; **terminal identity** = unique code transmitted by a viewdata terminal to provide identification and authorization of a user; **terminal interface** = hardware and software combination required to control the functions of a terminal from a computer; *the network controller has 16 terminal interfaces; (slang)* **terminal junky (TJ)** = person (a hacker) who is obsessed by computers; *my son has turned into a real terminal junky;* **terminal keyboard** = standard QWERTY *or* special keyboard allowing input at a terminal **(b)** an electrical connection point **(c)** point in a network where a message can be transmitted *or* received; *see also* SOURCE, SINK

COMMENT: computer terminals can be intelligent, smart or dumb according to the inbuilt processing capabilities

2 *adjective* fatal *or* which cannot be repaired; *the computer has a terminal fault*

terminate *verb* to end
◊ **termination** *noun* ending *or* stopping; **abnormal termination** = unexpected stoppage of a program which is being run, caused by a fault *or* power failure
◊ **terminator** *or* **rogue value** *noun* item in a list of data, which indicates the end of a list

ternary *adjective* (number system) with three possible states

test 1 *noun* action carried out on a device *or* program to establish whether it is working correctly, and if not, which component *or* instruction is not working; **test bed** = (software) environment used to test programs; **test data** = data with known results prepared to allow a new program to be tested; **test equipment** = special equipment which tests hardware *or* software; *the engineer has special test equipment for this model;* **test numeric** = check to ensure that numerical information is numerical; **test run** = program run with test data to ensure that the software is working correctly; *a test run will soon show up any errors* **2** *verb* to carry out an examination of a device *or* program to see if it is working correctly; **saturation testing** = testing a communications network by transmitting large quantities of data and messages over it

text *noun* alphanumeric characters that convey information; **ragged text** = unjustified text, text with a ragged right margin; **start-of-text (SOT** *or* **STX)** = transmitted code indicating the end of control and address information and the start of the message; **text compression** = reducing the space required by a section of text, by using one code to represent more than one character, by removing spaces and punctuation marks, etc.; **text-editing facilities** = word-processing system that allows the user to add, delete, move, insert and correct sections of text; **text-editing function** = option in a program that provides text-editing facilities; *the program includes a built-in text-editing function;* **text editor** = piece of software that provides the user with text-editing facilities; *the text editor will only read files smaller than 64Kbytes long;* **text file** = stored file on a computer that contains text rather than digits *or* data; **text formatter** = program that arranges a text file according to preset rules, such as line width and page size; *people use the text formatter as a basic desktop publishing program;* **text management** =

facilities that allow text to be written, stored, retrieved, edited and printed; **text manipulation =** facilities that allow text editing, changing, inserting and deleting; **text processing =** word-processing *or* using a computer to keyboard, edit and output text, in the forms of letters, labels, etc.; **text register =** temporary computer storage register for text characters only; **text retrieval =** information retrieval system that allows the user to examine complete documents rather than just a reference to one; **text screen =** area of computer screen that has been set up to display text; **text-to-speech converter =** electronic device that uses a speech synthesizer to produce the spoken equivalent of a piece of text that has been entered

thermal *adjective* referring to heat; **thermal paper =** special paper whose coating turns black when heated, allowing characters to be printed by using a matrix of small heating elements; **thermal printer =** type of printer where the character is formed on thermal paper with a printhead containing a matrix of small heating elements

COMMENT: this type of printer is very quiet in operation since the printing head does not strike the paper

◊ **thermal transfer** *noun* method of printing where the ink is attached to the paper by heating; *a thermal transfer printer; colour ink-jet technology and thermal transfer technology compete with each other*

thick *adjective* with a large distance between two surfaces; **thick film =** miniature electronic circuit design in which miniature components are mounted on an insulating base, then connected as required

COMMENT: this provides a package that is larger but cheaper for short runs than chips

thimble printer *noun* computer printer using a printing head similar to a daisy wheel but shaped like a thimble

thin *adjective* with only a small distance between two surfaces; **thin film =** method of constructing integrated circuits by depositing in a vacuum very thin patterns of various materials onto a substrate to form the required interconnected components; *see also* CHIP, SUBSTRATE; **thin film memory =** high-speed access RAM device using a matrix of magnetic cells and a matrix of read/write heads to

access them; **thin window =** single line display window

third *adjective* coming after second; **third generation computers =** range of computers where integrated circuits were used instead of transistors; **third party =** company which supplies items *or* services for a system sold by one party (the seller) to another (the buyer)

COMMENT: a third party might supply computer maintenance *or* might write programs, etc.

QUOTE they expect third party developers to enhance the operating systems by adding their own libraries
PC Business World

thirty-two bit system *noun* microcomputer system *or* CPU that handles data in thirty-two bit words

thrashing *noun* computer program design fault that results in the CPU wasting time moving pages of data between main memory and backing store

thread *noun* program that consists of many independent smaller sections or beads; **threaded file =** file in which an entry will contain data and an address to the next entry that has the same data content (allowing rapid retrieval of all identical records); **threaded language =** programming language that allows many small sections of code to be written then used by a main program; **threaded tree =** structure in which each node contains a pointer to other nodes

three-address instruction *noun* instruction which contains the addresses of two operands and the location where the result is to be stored

◊ **three-dimensional** *or* **3D** *adjective* (image) which has three dimensions (width, breadth and depth), and therefore gives the impression of being solid

◊ **three input adder** *see* FULL ADDER

three-pin plug *noun* standard plug with three connections, to connect an electric device to the mains electricity supply

COMMENT: the three pins are for the live, neutral and earth connections

three state logic *noun* logic gate *or* IC that has three possible output states (rather than the usual two): logic high, logic low and high impedance

throughput *noun* rate of production by a machine *or* system, measured as total useful information processed in a set period of time; *for this machine throughput is 1.3 inches per second (ips) scanning speed;* **rated throughput** = maximum throughput of a device that will still meet original specifications

tilt and swivel *adjective* (monitor) which is mounted on a pivot so that it can be moved to point in the most convenient direction for the operator

time 1 *noun* period expressed in hours, minutes, seconds, etc.; **addition time** = time an adder takes to carry out an addition operation; **cycle time** = time between start and stop of an operation, especially between addressing a memory location and receiving the data; **queuing time** = period of time messages have to wait before they are processed *or* transmitted; **real time** = actions *or* processing time that is of the same order of magnitude as the problem to be solved (i.e. the processing time is within the same time as the problem to be solved, so that the result can influence the source of the data); **response time** = (i) time which passes between the user starting an action (by pressing a key) and the result appearing on the screen; (ii) speed with which a system responds to a stimulus; **stop time** = time taken for a spinning disk to come to rest after it is no longer powered; **time base** = (i) signal used as a basis for timing purposes; (ii) regular sawtooth signal used in an oscilloscope to sweep the beam across the screen; **time slice** = amount of time allowed for a single task in a time-sharing system *or* in multiprogramming; period of time allocated for a user *or* program *or* job within a multitasking system **2** *verb* to measure the time taken by an operation; **microprocessor timing** = correct selection of system clock frequency to allow for slower peripherals etc.; **network timing** = signals that correctly synchronize the transmission of data; **timing loop** = computer program loop that is repeated a number of times to produce a certain time delay; **timing master** = clock signal that synchronizes all the components in a system

◇ **timeout** *noun* (i) logoff procedure carried out if no data is entered on an on-line terminal; (ii) period of time reserved for an operation

◇ **timer** *noun* device which records the time taken for an operation to be completed

◇ **time-sharing** *noun* computer system that allows several independent users to use it *or* be on-line at the same time

COMMENT: in time-sharing, each user appears to be using the computer all the time, when in fact each is using the CPU for a short time slice only; the CPU processing one user for a short time then moving on to the next

title *noun* identification name given to a file *or* program *or* disk; **title of disk** = identification of a disk, referring to its contents

toggle *verb* to switch between two states; **toggle switch** = electrical switch that has only two positions

QUOTE the symbols can be toggled on or off the display
Micro Decision

token *noun* internal code which replaces a reserved word *or* program statement in a high-level language

toolbox *noun* box containing instruments needed to repair *or* maintain *or* install equipment

◇ **toolkit** *noun* series of functions which help a programmer write *or* debug programs

◇ **tools** *noun* set of utility programs (backup, format, etc.) in a computer system

top *noun* part which is the highest point of something; **top down programming** *or* **structured programming** = method of writing programs where a complete system is divided into simple blocks *or* tasks, each block unit is written and tested before proceeding with the next one; **top of stack** = the newest data item added to a stack

topology *noun* way in which the various elements in a network are interconnected; **network topology** = layout of machines in a network (such as a star network *or* a ring network *or* a bus network) which will determine what cabling and interfaces are needed and what possibilities the network can offer

total *noun* **hash total** = total of a number of hashed entries, used for error detection

touch *verb* to make contact with something with the fingers; **touch pad** = flat device that can sense where on its surface and when it is touched, used to control a cursor position *or* switch a device on or off;

touch screen = computer display that has a grid of infrared transmitters and receivers, positioned on either side of the screen used to control a cursor position (when a user wants to make a selection *or* move the cursor, he points to the screen, breaking two of the beams, which gives the position of his finger)

TP = TELEPROCESSING, TRANSACTION PROCESSING

TPI = TRACKS PER INCH

trace *noun* method of verifying that a program is functioning correctly, in which the current status and contents of the registers and variables used are displayed after each instruction step; **trace program** = diagnostic program that executes a program that is being debugged, one instruction at a time, displaying the states and registers; **trace trap** = selective breakpoint where a tracing program stops, allowing registers to be examined

track 1 *noun* one of a series of thin concentric rings on a magnetic disk *or* thin lines on a tape, which the read/write head accesses and along which the data is stored in separate sectors; **address track** = track on a magnetic disk containing the address of files, etc., stored on the other tracks; **track address** = location of a particular track on a magnetic disk; **tracks per inch (TPI)** = number of concentric data tracks on a disk surface per inch **2** *verb* to follow a path *or* track correctly; *the read head is not tracking the recorded track correctly*

COMMENT: the first track on a tape is along the edge and the tape may have up to nine different tracks on it, while a disk has many concentric tracks around the central hub; the track and sector addresses are set-up during formatting

trackball *noun* device used to move a cursor on-screen, which is controlled by turning a ball contained in a case

tractor feed *noun* method of feeding paper into a printer, where sprocket wheels on the printer connect with the sprocket holes on either edge of the paper to pull the paper through

QUOTE the printer is fairly standard with both tractor and cut sheet feed system
Which PC?

traffic *noun* term covering all the messages and other signals processed by a system; **traffic analysis** = study of the times, types and quantities of messages and signals being processed by a system; **traffic density** = number of messages and data transmitted over a network *or* system in a period of time; **traffic intensity** = ratio of messages entering a queue against those leaving the queue within a certain time; **incoming traffic** = data and messages received
NOTE: no plural

trail *noun* line followed by something; **audit trail** = recording details of the use made of a system by noting transactions carried out (used for checking on illegal use *or* malfunction)

◊ **trailer** *noun* final byte of a file containing control *or* file characteristics; **trailer record** = last record in a file containing control *or* file characteristics

transaction *noun* one single action which affects a database (a sale, a change of address, a new customer, etc.); **transaction-driven system (TDS)** = computer system that will normally run batch processing tasks until interrupted by a new transaction, at which point it allocates resources to the transaction; **transaction file** *or* **change file** *or* **detail file** *or* **movement file** = file containing recent changes *or* transactions to records which is then used to update a master file; **transaction processing (TP)** = interactive processing in which a user enters commands and data on a terminal which is linked to a central computer, with results being displayed on-screen; **transaction record** *or* **change record** = record containing new data which is to be used to update a master record

transceiver *noun* transmitter and receiver *or* device which can both transmit and receive signals (such as a terminal *or* modem)

transcribe *verb* to copy data from one backing storage unit *or* medium to another

transfer *verb* (a) to change command *or* control; *all processing activities have been transferred to the mainframe;* **conditional transfer** = programming instruction that provides a jump to a section of a program if a certain condition is met; **radial transfer** = data transfer between two peripherals *or* programs that are on different layers of a structured system (such as an OSI/ISO system); **transfer check** = check that a data transfer is correct according to a set of rules; **transfer command** = instruction that directs processor control from one part of a program to another; *see also* JUMP, CALL; **transfer control =** when a branch *or* jump instruction within a program is executed, control is transferred to another point in the program **(b)** to copy a section of memory to another location; **transfer rate =** speed at which data is transferred from backing store to main memory; **transfer time =** time taken to transfer data between devices *or* locations

transform *verb* to change something from one state to another

◊ **transformation** *noun* action of changing

◊ **transformational rules** *noun* set of rules that are applied to data that is to be transformed into coded form

transient *adjective* state *or* signal which is present for a short period of time; **power transient =** very short duration voltage pulse *or* spike; **transient suppressor =** device which suppresses voltage transients; **transient area =** section of memory for user programs and data; **transient error =** temporary error which occurs for a short period of time

transistor *noun* electronic semiconductor device which can control the current flow in a circuit (there are two main types of transistors: bipolar and unipolar); **bipolar** *or* **junction transistor (BJT) =** transistor constructed of three layers of alternating types of doped semiconductor (p-n-p or n-p-n), each layer has a terminal labelled emitter, base and collector, usually the base controls the current flow between emitter and collector; **field effect transistor (FET) =** electronic device that can act as a variable current flow control (an external signal varies the resistance of the device and current flow by changing the width of a conducting channel by means of a field. It has three terminals: source, gate and drain; **transistor-transistor logic (TTL) =** most common family of logic gates and high-speed transistor circuit design, in which the bipolar transistors are directly connected (usually collector to base) to provide the logic function; **unipolar transistor =** FIELD EFFECT TRANSISTOR

transition *noun* change from one state to another; **transition point =** point in a program *or* system where a transition occurs

translate *verb* to convert data from one form into another

◊ **translation tables** *or* **conversion tables** *noun* lookup tables *or* collection of stored results that can be accessed very rapidly by a process without the need to calculate each result when needed

◊ **translator (program)** *noun* program that translates a high level language program into another language (usually machine code); *see also* INTERPRETER,COMPILER

transmit *verb* to send information from one device to another, using any medium, such as radio, cable, wire link, etc.

◊ **transmission** *noun* sending of signals from one device to another; **neutral transmission =** (transmission) in which a voltage pulse and zero volts represent the binary digits 1 and 0; **parallel transmission =** number of data lines carrying all the bits of a data word simultaneously; **serial transmission =** data transmission one bit at a time (this is the normal method of transmission over longer distances, since although slower, it uses fewer lines and so is cheaper than parallel); **synchronous transmission =** transmission of data from one device to another, where both devices are controlled by the same clock, and the transmitted data is synchronized with the clock signal; **transmission channel =** physical connection between two points that allows data to be transmitted (such as a link between a CPU and a peripheral); **transmission errors =** errors due to noise on the line; **transmission media =** means by which data can be transmitted, such as radio, light, etc.; **transmission rate =** measure of the amount of data transmitted in a certain time; *their average transmission is 64,000 bits per second (bps) through a parallel connection or 19,200 bps through a serial connection*

◊ **transmissive disk** *noun* optical data storage disk in which the reading laser beam shines through the disk to a detector below; *compare with* REFLECTIVE DISK

◊ **transmitter (TX)** *noun* device that will take an input signal, process it (modulate *or* convert to sound, etc.) then transmit it by some medium (radio, light, etc.)

transparent *noun* computer program which is not obvious to the user *or* which cannot be seen by the user when it is running; **transparent interrupts =** mode in which, if an interrupt occurs, all program and machine states are saved, the interrupt is serviced and then the system is restored to its previous states; **transparent paging =** software that allows the user to access any memory location in a paged memory system as if it were not paged

transphasor *noun* optical transistor, that is constructed from a crystal which is able to switch a main beam of light according to a smaller input signal

> COMMENT: this is used in the latest research for an optical computer which could run at very high speeds, i.e., at the speed of light

transport *verb* to carry from one place to another; **transport layer** = layer in the ISO/OSI standard that checks and controls the quality of the connection; *see also* LAYER

◊ **transportable** *adjective* which can be carried; *a transportable computer is not as small as a portable or a laptop*

transputer *noun* single large very powerful chip containing a 32-bit microprocessor running at around 10 MIPS, that can be connected together to form a parallel processing system (running OCCAM)

trap *noun* device, software or hardware that will catch something, such as a variable, fault or value; **trace trap** = selective breakpoint where a tracing program stops, allowing registers to be examined

◊ **trapdoor** *noun* way of getting into a system to change data *or* browse *or* hack

tree *noun* **tree (structure)** = data structure system where each item of data is linked to several others by branches (as opposed to a line system where each item leads on to the next); **tree and branch network system** = system of networking where data is transmitted along a single output line, from which other lines branch out, forming a tree structure that feeds individual stations; **tree selection sort** = rapid form of selection where the information from the first sort pass is used in the second pass to speed up selection; **binary tree** = data system where each item of data *or* node has only two branches

triad *noun* (i) three elements *or* characters *or* bits; (ii) triangular shaped grouping of the red, green and blue colour phosphor spots at each pixel location on the screen of a colour RGB monitor

Trojan Horse *noun* program inserted into a system by a hacker that will perform a harmless function while copying information in a classified file into a file with a low priority, which the hacker can then access without the authorized user knowing

troubleshoot *verb* (i) to debug computer software; (ii) to locate and repair faults in hardware

◊ **troubleshooter** *noun* person who troubleshoots hardware *or* software

TRUE *noun* logical condition (representing binary one); *compare* FALSE

truncate *verb* **(a)** to cut short **(b)** to give an approximate value to a number by reducing it to a certain number of digits

◊ **truncation** *noun* removal of digits from a number so that it is a certain length; *3.5678 truncated to 3.56;* **truncation error** = error caused when a number is truncated

trunk *noun* bus *or* communication link consisting of wires *or* leads, which connect different parts of a hardware system

truth table *noun* method of defining a logic function as the output state for all possible inputs; **truth value** = two values (true *or* false, T *or* F, 1 *or* 0) used in Boolean algebra

TSW = TELESOFTWARE

TTL = TRANSISTOR-TRANSISTOR LOGIC most common family of logic gates and high-speed transistor circuit design in which the bipolar transistors are directly connected (usually collector to base); **TTL compatible** = MOS or other electronic circuits *or* components that can directly connect to and drive TTL circuits; **TTL logic** = use of TTL design and components to implement logic circuits and gates

TTY = TELETYPE

tune *verb* to set a system at its optimum point by careful adjustment; **to fine tune** = to adjust by small amounts the parameters of hardware *or* software to improve performance

Turing machine *noun* mathematical model of a device that could read and write data to a controllable tape storage while altering its internal states

◊ **Turing test** *noun* test to decide if a computer is "intelligent"

turn off *verb* to switch off *or* to disconnect the power supply to a machine; *turn off the power before unplugging the monitor*

◊ **turn on** *verb* to switch on *or* to connect the power supply to a machine

◇ **turnaround document** *noun* document which is printed out from a computer, sent to a user and returned by the user with new notes *or* information written on it, which can be read by a document reader

◇ **turnaround time (TAT)** *noun* **(a)** length of time it takes to switch data flow direction in a half duplex system **(b)** *US* time taken to activate a program and produce the result which the user has asked for

◇ **turnkey system** *noun* complete system which is designed to a customer's needs and is ready to use (to operate it, the user only has to switch it on or turn a key)

turtle *noun* device whose movement and position are controllable, which is used to draw graphics (with instructions in the computer language LOGO), either a device which works on a flat surface (floor turtle) *or* which draws on a VDU screen (screen turtle), used as a teaching aid; **turtle graphics** = graphic images created using a turtle and a series of commands; *the charts were prepared using turtle graphics*

two-address instruction *noun* instruction format containing the location of two operands, the result being stored in one of the operand locations; **two-plus-one instruction** = instruction containing the locations of two operands and an address for the result

◇ **two-dimensional** *adjective* which has two dimensions (that is, flat, with no depth); **two-dimensional array** = array which locates items both vertically and horizontally

◇ **two input adder** *see* HALF ADDER

◇ **two-level subroutine** *noun* subroutine containing another subroutine

◇ **two-part** *noun* paper (for computers *or* typewriters) with a top sheet for the original and a second sheet for a copy; *two-part invoices; two-part stationery*

◇ **two-pass assembler** *noun* assembler that converts an assembly language program into machine code in two passes - the first pass stores symbolic addresses, the second converts them to absolute addresses

two's complement *noun* formed by adding one to the one's complement of a binary number, often used to represent negative binary numbers

TX – TRANSMITTER

type *noun* definition of the processes *or* sorts of data which a variable in a computer can contain (this can be numbers, text only, etc.); **variable data type** = variable that can contain any sort of data, such as numerical, text, etc.; **string type** = variable that can contain alphanumeric characters only

Uu

UART = UNIVERSAL ASYNCHRONOUS RECEIVER/TRANSMITTER chip which converts asynchronous serial bit streams to a parallel form *or* parallel data to a serial bit stream; **UART controller** = circuit that uses a UART to convert (serial) data from a terminal into a parallel form, then transmits it over a network; *see also* USART

UBC = UNIVERSAL BLOCK CHANNEL

ULA = UNCOMMITTED LOGIC ARRAY chip containing a number of unconnected logic circuits and gates which can then be connected by a customer to provide a required function

ultra- *prefix* meaning very large *or* further than; **ultraviolet (UV) light** = electromagnetic radiation with wavelength just greater than the visible spectrum, from 200 to 4000 angstrom; **ultraviolet erasable PROM** = EPROM whose contents are erased by exposing to UV light

un- *prefix* meaning not; **unallowable digit** = illegal combination of bits in a word, according to predefined rules; **unauthorized** = which has not been authorized; *the use of a password is to prevent unauthorized access to the data*

unary operation *noun* computing operation on only one operand, such as the logical NOT operation

unattended operation *noun* system that can operate without the need for a person to supervise

◊ **unbundled software** *noun* software which is not included in the price of the equipment

◊ **unclocked** *adjective* electronic circuit *or* flip-flop that changes state as soon as an input changes, not with a clock signal

◊ **uncommitted logic array (ULA)** *noun* chip containing a number of unconnected logic circuits and gates which can then be connected by a customer to provide a required function; **uncommitted storage list**

= table of the areas of memory in a system that are free *or* have not been allocated

◊ **unconditional** *adjective* which does not depend on any condition being met; **unconditional branch** *or* **jump** *or* **transfer** = instruction which transfers control from one point in the program to another, without depending on any condition being met
NOTE: opposite is **CONDITIONAL**

underflow *noun* result of a numerical operation that is too small to be represented with the given accuracy of a computer

underline *or* **underscore 1** *noun* line drawn *or* printed under a piece of text **2** *verb* to print *or* write a line under a piece of text; **underlining** = word-processing command which underlines text

undertake *verb* to agree to do something; *he has undertaken to reprogram the whole system*
NOTE: **undertaking - undertaken - undertook**

undetected *adjective* which has not been detected; *the programming error was undetected for some time*

◊ **unedited** *adjective* which has not been edited

◊ **unformatted** *adjective* (disk) which has not been formatted; *it is impossible to copy to an unformatted disk; the cartridge drive provides 12.7Mbyte of unformatted storage*

uni- *prefix* meaning one *or* single

◊ **union** *noun* logical function that produces a true output if any input is true

◊ **unipolar** *adjective* (a) (transistor) that can act as a variable current flow control an external signal varies the resistance of the device; *see also* FET, TRANSISTOR (b) (transmission system) in which a positive voltage pulse and zero volts represents the binary bits 1 and 0; *compare with* POLAR; **unipolar signal** = signal that uses only positive voltage levels

uninterruptable power supply (UPS)
noun power supply that can continue to
provide a regulated supply to equipment
even after a mains power failure (using a
battery)

unique *adjective* which is different from
everything else; *each separate memory byte
has its own unique address*

unit *noun* **(a)** smallest element; **unit buffer**
= buffer that is one character long (NOTE:
usually used to mean that there are no buffering
facilities) **unit record** = single record of
information **(b)** single machine (possibly
with many different parts); **arithmetic and
logic unit (ALU)** = section of the CPU that
performs all the mathematical and logical
functions; **central processing unit (CPU)** =
group of circuits which perform the basic
functions of a computer, made up of three
main parts: the control unit, the arithmetic
and logic unit and the input/output unit;
control unit = section of the CPU that
selects and executes instructions; **desk top
unit** = computer *or* machine that will fit
onto a desk; **input/output unit** *or* **device** =
peripheral (such as a terminal in a
workstation) which can be used both for
inputting and outputting data to a
processor

universal *adjective* which applies
everywhere *or* which can be used
everywhere *or* used for a number of tasks;
**universal asynchronous receiver/transmitter
(UART)** = chip which converts an
asynchronous serial bit stream to a parallel
form *or* parallel data to a serial bit stream;
universal block channel (UBC) =
communications channel allowing high
speed transfer of blocks of data to and
from high speed peripherals; **universal
device** = (i) UART; (ii) USRT; (iii)
USART; **universal product code (UPC)** =
standard printed bar coding system used to
identify products in a shop (using a bar
code reader *or* at a EPOS); *see also* EAN;
universal programming = writing a
program that is not specific to one
machine, so that it can run on several
machines; **universal set** = complete set of
elements that conform to a set of rules; *the
universal set of prime numbers less than ten
and greater than two is 3,5,7;* **universal
synchronous asynchronous receiver-
transmitter (USART)** = chip that can be
instructed by a CPU to communicate with
asynchronous or synchronous bit streams
or data lines; **universal synchronous
receiver/transmitter (USRT)** = single
integrated circuit that can carry out all the
serial to parallel and interfacing operations

required between a computer and
transmission line

Unix *noun* popular operating system for
small micros and large mainframes

unjustified *adjective* (text) which has not
been justified; **unjustified tape** *or* **idiot tape**
= tape containing unformatted text, which
cannot be printed until formatting data
(such as justification, line width and page
size) has been added by a computer

unmodified instruction *noun* program
instruction which is directly processed
without modification to obtain the
operation to be performed

unmodulated *adjective* (signal) which has
not been modulated; *see also* BASE BAND

unpack *verb* to remove packed data from
storage and expand it to its former state;
this routine unpacks the archived file

unplug *verb* to take a plug out of a socket;
*do not move the system without unplugging
it; simply unplug the old drive and plug-in a
new one*

unprotected *adjective* (data) that can be
modified and is not protected by a security
measure; **unprotected field** = section of a
computer display that a user can modify

unrecoverable error *noun* computer
hardware *or* software error that causes a
program to crash

unsigned *adjective* (number system) that
does not represent negative numbers

unsorted *adjective* (data) which has not
been sorted; *it took four times as long to
search the unsorted file*

unwanted *adjective* which is not needed;
*use the global delete command to remove
large areas of unwanted text*

up *adverb* (of computer *or* program)
working *or* running; *they must have found
the fault - the computer is finally up and
running;* **up time** *or* **uptime** = time during
which a device is operational and error free
NOTE: opposite is **down**

UPC = UNIVERSAL PRODUCT CODE

update 1 *noun* (i) master file which has
been made up-to-date by adding new

material; (ii) printed information which is an up-to-date revision of earlier information; (iii) new version of a system which is sent to users of the existing system; **update file** *or* **transaction file** = file containing recent changes *or* transactions to records which is used to update the master file **2** *verb* to change *or* add to specific data in a master file so as to make the information up-to-date; *he has the original and updated documents on disks*

> QUOTE it means that any item of data stored in the system need be updated only once
> *Which PC?*

up/down counter *noun* electronic counter that can increment *or* decrement a counter with each input pulse

upgrade *verb* to make (a system) more powerful *or* more up-to-date by adding new equipment; *they can upgrade the printer; the single processor with 2Mbytes of memory can be upgraded to 4Mbytes; all three models have an on-site upgrade facility*

> QUOTE the cost of upgrading a PC to support CAD clearly depends on the peripheral devices added
> *PC Business World*

upkeep *noun* keeping data up-to-date; keeping devices in working order; *the upkeep of the files means reviewing them every six months*

upload *verb* to transfer data files *or* programs from a small computer to a main CPU; *the user can upload PC data to update mainframe applications* NOTE: the opposite is **download**
◊ **uploading** *noun* action of transferring files to a main CPU; *the image can be manipulated before uploading to the host computer*

UPS = UNINTERRUPTABLE POWER SUPPLY power supply that can continue to provide a regulated supply to equipment even after a mains power failure (using a battery)

upper case *noun* series of capital letters and other symbols on a typewriter *or* keyboard, which are accessed by pressing the shift key

uptime *noun* time when a computer is functioning correctly (as opposed to downtime)

upwards compatible *or* US **upward compatible** *adjective* (hardware *or*

software) designed to be compatible either with earlier models *or* with future models which have not yet been invented

usable *adjective* which can be used *or* which is available for use; *the PC has 512K of usable memory*

USART = UNIVERSAL SYNCHRONOUS ASYNCHRONOUS RECEIVER-TRANSMITTER chip that can be instructed by a CPU to communicate with asynchronous *or* synchronous bit streams or parallel data lines

USASCII *US* = USA STANDARD CODE FOR INFORMATION INTERCHANGE *see* ASCII

use 1 *noun* (a) way in which something can be used; *the printer has been in use for the last two hours; the use of the that file is restricted;* to make use of something = to use something (b) value; being useful; *what use is an extra disk drive? it's no use, I cannot find the error;* in use = already in operation; *sorry, the printer is already in use* **2** *verb* (a) to operate something; *if you use the computer for processing the labels, it will be much quicker; the computer is used too often by the sales staff* (b) to consume heat, light, etc.; *it's using too much electricity*
◊ **used** *adjective* which is not new; *special offer on used terminals*

user *noun* (i) person who uses a computer *or* machine *or* software; (ii) especially, a keyboard operator; **user area** = part of the memory which is available for the user, and does not contain the operating system; **user-definable** = feature *or* section of a program that a user can customize as required; *the style sheet contains 125 user-definable symbols;* **user-defined characters** = characters which are created by the user and added to the standard character set; **user documentation** = documentation provided with a program which helps the user run it; *using the package was easy with the excellent user documentation;* **user group** = association *or* club of users of a particular system *or* computer; *I found how to solve the problem by asking people at the user group meeting;* **user guide** = manual describing how to use a software package *or* system; **user ID** = unique identification code that allows a computer to recognize a user; *if you forget your user ID, you will not be able to logon;* **user interface** = hardware *or* software designed to make it easier for a user to communicate with the machine; **user-operated language** = high-level programming language that allows certain problems *or* procedures to be easily expressed; **user port =** socket which allows peripherals to be connected to a computer; **user's program =** computer software written by a user rather than a manufacturer; **user-selectable =** which can be chosen *or* selected by the user; *the video resolution of 640 by 300, 240 or 200 pixels is user-selectable*

◊ **user-friendly** *adjective* (language *or* system *or* program) that is easy to use and interact with; *it's such a user-friendly machine; compared with the previous version this one is very user-friendly*

QUOTE the user's guides are designed for people who have never seen a computer, but some sections have been spoiled by careless checking

PC User

QUOTE the first popular microcomputer to have a user-friendly interface built into its operating system

Micro Decision

USRT = UNIVERSAL SYNCHRONOUS RECEIVER/TRANSMITTER

utility (program) *noun* useful program that is concerned with such routine activities as file searching, copying files, file directories, sorting and debugging and various mathematical functions; *a lost file cannot be found without a file-recovery utility; on the disk is a utility for backing up a hard disk*

UV light = ULTRAVIOLET LIGHT

Vv

V = VOLTAGE

V & V = VERIFICATION AND VALIDATION

V format *noun* data organization, in which variable length records are stored with a header which contains their length

V series *noun* CCITT (UK-European) standards for data transmission using a modem
NOTE: **V.21 =** 300 baud transmit and receive, full duplex **V.22 =** 1200 baud transmit and receive, half duplex **V.22 BIS =** 1200 baud transmit and receive full duplex **V.23 =** 75 baud transmit, 1200 baud receive, half duplex

valid *adjective* correct, according to a set of rules; **valid memory address** = signal on control bus indicating that an address is available on the address bus
◊ **validate** *verb* to check that an input *or* data is correct according to a set of rules
◊ **validation** *noun* check performed to validate data
◊ **validity** *noun* correctness of an instruction *or* password; **validity check** = check that data *or* results are realistic

value *noun* what something is worth (either in money *or* as a quantity); **absolute value** = value of a number regardless of its sign; *the absolute value of -62.34 is 62.34;* **initial value** = starting point (usually zero) set when initializing variables at the beginning of a program

vapourware *noun informal* products which exist in name only

variable 1 *adjective* is able to change; **variable data** = data which can be modified, and is not write-protected; **variable length record** = record which can be of any length; **variable word length computer** = computer in which the number of bits which make up a word is variable, and varies according to the type of data **2** *noun* (computer program identifier for a) register *or* storage location which can contain any number *or* characters and which may vary during the program run;

global variable = number that can be accessed by any routine *or* structure in a program; **local variable** = number which can only be accessed by certain routines in a certain section of a computer program
◊ **vary** *verb* to change; *the clarity of the signal can vary with the power supply*

VDT *or* **VDU** = VISUAL DISPLAY TERMINAL, VISUAL DISPLAY UNIT terminal with a screen and a keyboard, on which text *or* graphics can be viewed and information entered

QUOTE it normally consists of a keyboard to input information and either a printing terminal or a VDU screen to display messages and results
Practical Computing
QUOTE a VDU is a device used with a computer that displays information in the form of characters and drawings on a screen
Electronics & Power

vector *noun* **(a)** address which directs a computer to a new memory location **(b)** coordinate that consists of a magnitude and direction; **vector graphics** *or* **vector image** *or* **vector scan** = computer drawing system that uses line length and direction from an origin to plot lines; **vector processor** = coprocessor that operates on one row or column of an array at a time
◊ **vectored interrupt** *noun* interrupt signal which directs the processor to a routine at a particular address

QUOTE the great advantage of the vector-scan display is that it requires little memory to store a picture
Electronics & Power

Veitch diagram *noun* graphical representation of a truth table

velocity *noun* speed; *the disk drive motor spins at a constant velocity*

Venn diagram *noun* graphical representation of the relationships between the states in a system *or* circuit

verify *verb* to check that data recorded *or* entered is correct

◊ **verification** *noun* checking that data has been keyboarded correctly *or* that data transferred from one medium to another has been transferred correctly; **keystroke verification** = check made on each key pressed to make sure it is valid for a particular application; **verification and validation (V & V)** = testing a system to check that it is functioning correctly and that it is suitable for the tasks intended

◊ **verifier** *noun* special device for verifying input data

version *noun* copy *or* program *or* statement which is slightly different from others; *the latest version of the software includes an improved graphics routine*

vertical *adjective* at right angles to the horizontal; **vertical blanking interval** *see* RASTER; **vertical format unit (VFU)** = part of the control system of a printer which governs the vertical format of the document to be printed (such as vertical spacing, page length); **vertical justification** = adjustment of the spacing between lines of text to fit a section of text into a page; **vertical parity check** = error detection test in which the bits of a word are added and compared with a correct total; **vertical redundancy check (VRC)** = (odd) parity check on each character of a block received, to detect any errors; **vertical scrolling** = displayed text that moves up or down the computer screen one line at a time; **vertical tab** = number of lines that should be skipped before printing starts again

◊ **vertically** *adverb* from top to bottom *or* going up and down at right angles to the horizontal; *the page has been justified vertically*

very large scale integration (VLSI) *noun* integrated circuit with 10,000 to 100,000 components

VFU = VERTICAL FORMAT UNIT

VHD = VERY HIGH DENSITY capacitance type video disk able to store very large quantities of data

via *preposition* going through something *or* using something to get to a destination; *the signals have reached us via satellite; you can download the data to the CPU via a modem*

video *noun* text *or* images *or* graphics viewed on television *or* a monitor; **video display** = device which can display text *or* graphical information, such as a CRT;

video game = game played on a computer, with action shown on a video display; **video interface chip** = chip that controls a video display allowing information stored in a computer (text, graphics) to be displayed; **video memory** *or* **video RAM (VRAM)** = high speed random access memory used to store computer-generated *or* digitized images; **video monitor** = device able to display, without sound, signals from a computer; *informal* **video signal** = signal which provides line picture information and synchronization pulses; **video scanner** = device which allows images of objects *or* pictures to be entered into a computer; *new video scanners are designed to scan three-dimensional objects;* **video terminal** = keyboard with a monitor

◊ **videotext** *or* **videotex** *noun* system for transmitting text and displaying it on a screen

COMMENT: this covers information transmitted either by TV signals (teletext) *or* by signals sent down telephone lines (viewdata)

view *verb* to look at something, especially something displayed on a screen; *the user has to pay a charge for viewing pages on a bulletin board*

◊ **viewdata** *noun* interactive system for transmitting text *or* graphics from a database to a user's terminal by telephone lines, providing facilities for information retrieval, transactions, education, games and recreation

COMMENT: the user calls up the page of information required, using the telephone and a modem, as opposed to teletext, where the pages of information are repeated one after the other automatically

virgin *adjective* (tape) that has not been recorded on before

virtual *adjective* feature *or* device which does not actually exist but which is simulated by a computer and can be used by a user as if it did exist; **virtual address** = an address referring to virtual storage; **virtual circuit** = link established between a source and sink (in a packet-switching network) for the duration of the call; **virtual disk** = section of RAM used with a short controlling program as if it were a fast disk storage system; **virtual machine** = simulated machine and its operations; **virtual memory** *or* **virtual storage (VS)** = large imaginary main memory made available by loading smaller pages from a backing store into the available main memory only as and when they are required; **virtual terminal** = ideal terminal specifications used as a model by a real terminal

virus *noun* short hidden routine that corrupts all data and files, which spreads from computer to computer when disks are exchanged

visible *adjective* which can be seen

visual *adjective* which can be seen *or* which is used by sight; **visual programming** = method of programming a computer by showing it or taking it through the processes of what it has to do rather than writing a series of instructions

◇ **visual display terminal (VDT)** *or* **visual display unit (VDU)** *noun* terminal with a screen and a keyboard, on which text *or* graphics can be viewed and information entered

VLSI = VERY LARGE SCALE INTEGRATION system with between 10,000 and 100,000 components on a single IC

voice *noun* sound of human speech; **voice answer back** = computerized response service using a synthesized voice to answer enquiries; **voice data entry** *or* **input** = input of information into a computer using a speech recognition system and the user's voice; **voice output** = production of sounds which sound like human speech, made as a result of voice synthesis; **voice recognition** = ability of a computer to recognize certain words in a human voice and provide a suitable response; **voice response** = VOICE OUTPUT; **voice synthesis** = reproduction of sounds similar to those of the human voice; **voice synthesizer** = device which generates sounds which are similar to the human voice

volatile memory *or* **volatile store** *or* **volatile dynamic storage** *noun* memory *or* storage medium which loses data stored in it when the power supply is switched off NOTE: opposite is **non-volatile memory**

◇ **volatility** *noun* number of records that are added *or* deleted from a computer system compared to the total number in store

volt *noun* SI unit of electrical potential, defined as voltage across a one ohm resistance when one amp is flowing

◇ **voltage** *noun* electromotive force expressed in volts; **voltage regulator** = device which provides a steady output voltage even if the input supply varies; **voltage transient** = spike of voltage that is caused by a time delay in two devices switching *or* by noise on the line

COMMENT: electricity supply can have peaks and troughs of current, depending on the users in the area. Fluctuations in voltage can affect computers; a voltage regulator will provide a steady supply of electricity

volume *noun* total space occupied by data in a storage system

VRAM = VIDEO RANDOM ACCESS MEMORY high speed random access memory used to store computer-generated *or* digitized images

VRC = VERTICAL REDUNDANCY CHECK (odd) parity check on each character of a block received, to detect any errors

VS = VIRTUAL STORAGE

Ww

wafer *noun* thin round slice of a large single crystal of silicon onto which hundreds of individual integrated circuits are constructed, before being cut into individual chips

◇ **wafer scale integration** *noun* one large chip, the size of a wafer, made up of smaller integrated circuits connected together (these are still in the research stage)

wait condition *or* **state** *noun* state where a processor is not active, but waiting for input from peripherals

◇ **wait loop** *noun* processor that repeats one loop of program until some action occurs

◇ **wait time** *noun* time delay between the moment when an instruction is given and the execution of the instruction *or* return of a result (such as the delay between a request for data and the data being transferred from memory)

◇ **waiting list** *noun see* QUEUE

◇ **waiting state** *noun* computer state, in which a program requires an input *or* signal before continuing execution

wake up *verb* to switch on *or* start *or* initiate; **wake up a system =** code entered at a remote terminal to indicate to the central computer that someone is trying to log-on at that location

walk through *verb* to examine each step of a piece of software

WAN = WIDE AREA NETWORK

wand *noun* bar code reader *or* optical device which is held in the hand to read bar codes on products in a store

warm standby *noun* secondary backup device that can be switched into action a short time after the main system fails; *compare with* COLD STANDBY, HOT STANDBY

◇ **warm start** *noun* restarting a programme which has stopped, but without losing any data; *compare* COLD START

◇ **warm up** *verb* to allow a machine to stand idle for a time after switching on, to reach the optimum operating conditions

> QUOTE warm-up time measures how long each printer takes to get ready to begin printing
> *Byte*

warn *verb* to say that something dangerous is about to happen; to say that there is a possible danger; *he warned the keyboarders that the system might become overloaded* NOTE: you warn someone **of** something, or **that** something may happen

◇ **warning** *noun* notice of possible danger; *to issue a warning; warning notices were put up around the high powered laser;* **warning light =** (small light) which lights up to show that something dangerous may happen; *when the warning light on the front panel comes on, switch off the system*

wash PROM *verb* to erase the data from a PROM

waste instruction *noun* instruction that does not carry out any action (except increasing the program counter to the location of next instruction)

Watt *noun* SI unit of measurement of electrical power, defined as power produced when one amp of current flows through a load that has one volt of voltage across it

wave *noun* signal motion that rises and falls periodically as it travels through a medium

◇ **waveform** *noun* shape of a wave; **waveform digitization =** conversion and storing a waveform in numerical form using an A/D converter

weighted bit *noun* each bit having a different value depending on its position in a word

◇ **weighting** *noun* sorting of users, programs or data by their importance or priority

well-behaved *noun* program that does not make any non-standard system calls, using only the standard BIOS input/output calls rather than directly addressing peripherals *or* memory

> COMMENT: if well-behaved, the software should work on all machines using the same operating system

wetware *noun US informal* the human brain *or* intelligence which writes software to be used with hardware

What-You-See-Is-All-You-Get (WYSIAYG) *noun* program where the output on screen cannot be printed out in any other form (that is, it cannot contain hidden print *or* formatting commands)

What-You-See-Is-What-You-Get (WYSIWYG) *noun* program where the output on the screen is exactly the same as the output on printout, including graphics and special fonts

while-loop *noun* conditional program instructions that carries out a loop while a condition is true

white *adjective & noun* the colour of snow; **white writer** = laser printer which directs its laser beam on the points that are not printed NOTE: the opposite is **black writer**

> COMMENT: with a white writer, the black areas are printed evenly but edges and borders are not so sharp

wide area network (WAN) *noun* network where the various terminals are far apart and linked by radio, satellite and cable; *compare with* LAN

> COMMENT: WANs use modems, radio and other long distance transmission methods; LANs use cables or optical fibre links

width *noun* size of something from edge to edge; **page width** *or* **line width** = number of characters across a page *or* line

wild card *noun* symbol that represents all files *or* names, used when searching for data; *a wild card can be used to find all files names beginning DIC*

WIMP = WINDOW, ICON, MOUSE, POINTERS description of an integrated software system that is entirely operated using windows, icons and a mouse controlled pointer; *see also* ENVIRONMENT

Winchester disk *or* **drive** *noun* compact high-capacity hard disk which is usually built into a computer system and cannot be removed; **removable Winchester** = small hard disk in a sealed unit, which can be detached from a computer when full *or* when not required

window 1 *noun* (i) reserved section of screen used to display special information, that can be selected and looked at at any time and which overwrites information already on the screen; (ii) part of a document currently displayed on a screen; (iii) area of memory *or* access to a storage device; *several remote stations are connected to the network and each has its own window onto the hard disk; the operating system will allow other programs to be displayed on-screen at the same time in different windows;* **active window** = area of the display screen where the operator is currently working; **command window** = area of the screen that always displays the range of commands available; *the command window is a single line at the bottom of the screen;* **edit window** = area of the screen in which the user can display and edit text *or* graphics; **text window** = window in a graphics system, where the text is held in a small space on the screen before being allocated to a final area; **window, icon, mouse, pointer (WIMP)** = description of an integrated software system that is entirely operated using windows, icons and a mouse controlled pointer **2** *verb* to set up a section of screen by defining the coordinates of its corners, that allows information to be temporarily displayed, overwriting previous information but without altering information in the workspace

◊ **windowing** *noun* (i) action of setting up a window to show information on the screen; (ii) displaying *or* accessing information via a window; *the network system uses the latest windowing techniques*

> QUOTE when an output window overlaps another, the interpreter does not save the contents of the obscured window
> *Personal Computer World*
> QUOTE windowing facilities make use of virtual screens as well as physical screens
> *Byte*
> QUOTE you can connect more satellites to the network, each having its own window onto the hard disk
> *PC Plus*
> QUOTE the network system uses the latest windowing techniques
> *Desktop Publishing*
> QUOTE the functions are integrated via a windowing system with pull-down menus used to select different operations
> *Byte*

wipe *verb* to clean data from a disk; *by reformatting you will wipe the disk clean*

wire 1 *noun* (a) thin metal conductor; **wire printer** = dot-matrix printer; **wire wrap** = simple method of electrically connecting component terminals together using thin insulated wire wrapped around each terminal which is then soldered into place, usually used for prototype systems **2** *verb* to install wiring; **wired** *or* **hardwired program computer** = computer with a program built into the hardware which cannot be changed; *see also* HARDWIRED

◊ **wiring** *noun* series of wires; *the wiring in the system had to be replaced*

WISC = WRITABLE INSTRUCTION SET COMPUTER CPU design that allows a programmer to add extra machine code instructions using microcode, to customize the instruction set

word *noun* (a) separate item of language, which is used with others to form speech *or* writing which can be understood; **words per minute (wpm** *or* **WPM)** = method of measuring the speed of a printer; **word break** = division of a word at the end of a line, where part of the word is left on one line with a hyphen, and the rest of the word is taken over to begin the next line; **word count** = number of words in a file *or* text; **word wrap** *or* **wraparound** = system in word processing where the operator does not have to indicate the line endings, but can keyboard continuously, leaving the program to insert word breaks and to continue the text on the next line (b) separate item of data on a computer, formed of a group of bits, stored in a single location in a memory; **word length** = length of a computer word, counted as the number of bits; **word mark** = symbol indicating the start of a word in a variable word length machine; **word serial** = data words transmitted along a parallel bus one after the other; **word time** = time taken to transfer a word from one memory area *or* device to another

◊ **word-process** *verb* to edit, store and manipulate text using a computer; *it is quite easy to read word-processed files*

◊ **word-processing (WP)** *noun* using a computer to keyboard, edit, and output text, in the form of letters, labels, address lists, etc.; *load the word-processing program before you start keyboarding;* **word-processing bureau** = office which specializes in word-processing for other companies NOTE: no plural

◊ **word-processor** *noun* (a) small computer *or* typewriter with a computer in it, used for word-processing text and documents (b) word-processing package *or* program for a computer which allows the editing and manipulation and output of text, such as letters, labels, address lists, etc.

work 1 *noun* things done using the hands *or* brain; **work area** = memory space which is being used by an operator; **work disk** = disk on which current work is stored; **work file** *or* **scratch file** temporary work area which is being used for current work; **working store** *or* **scratch pad** = area of high-speed memory used for temporary storage of data in current use NOTE: no plural **2** *verb* to function; *the computer system has never worked properly since it was installed*

◊ **working** *adjective* (something) which is operating correctly

◊ **workload** *noun* amount of work which a person *or* computer has to do; *he has difficulty in dealing with his heavy workload*

◊ **workspace** *noun* space on memory, which is available for use *or* is being used currently by an operator

◊ **workstation** *noun* place where a computer user works, with a terminal, VDU, printer, modem, etc.; *the system includes five workstations linked together in a ring network; the archive storage has a total capacity of 1200 Mb between seven workstations*

QUOTE an image processing workstation must provide three basic facilities: the means to digitize, display and manipulate the image data
Byte

WORM = WRITE ONCE READ MANY times memory

WP = WORD-PROCESSING

WPM *or* **wpm** = WORDS PER MINUTE

wraparound *or* **word wrap** *noun* system in word-processing where the operator does not have to indicate the line endings, but can keyboard continuously, leaving the program to insert word breaks and to continue the text on the next line; **horizontal wraparound** = movement of a cursor on a computer display from the end of one line to the beginning of the next

write *verb* (a) to put words *or* figures on to paper; *she wrote a letter of complaint to the manager; the telephone number is written at the bottom of the notepaper* (b) to put text *or* data onto a disk *or* tape; *access time is the time taken to read from or write to a location in memory;* **write head** = transducer that can write data onto a magnetic medium; **write once, read many times memory (WORM)** = optical disk storage system that allows one writing action but many reading actions in its life; **writing pad** = special device which allows a computer to read in handwritten characters which have been written onto a special pad; *see* OCR; **write time** = time between requesting data transfer to a storage location and it being written NOTE: you write data **to** a file. Note also: writing - wrote - has written

◇ **writable instruction set computer (WISC)** *noun* CPU design that allows a programmer to add extra machine code instructions using microcode, to customize the instruction set

◇ **write-permit ring** *noun* ring on a reel of magnetic tape which allows the tape to be overwritten *or* erased

◇ **write protect** *verb* to make it impossible to write to a floppy disk *or* tape by moving a special write-protect tab; **write-protect tab** = tab on a floppy disk which if moved, prevents any writing to *or* erasing from the disk

◇ **writer** *noun see* BLACK, WHITE

◇ **writing** *noun* something which has been written
NOTE: no plural

WYSIAYG = WHAT YOU SEE IS ALL YOU GET

WYSIWYG = WHAT YOU SEE IS WHAT YOU GET

Xx

X = EXTENSION

X-axis *noun* horizontal axis of a graph
◇ **X-coordinate** *noun* horizontal axis position coordinate
◇ **X direction** *noun* movement horizontally
◇ **X distance** *noun* distance along an X-axis from an origin

xerographic printer printer (such as a photocopier) where charged ink is attracted to areas of a charged picture

x punch *noun* card punch for column 11, often used to represent a negative number

X-series *noun* recommendations for data communications over public data networks

X-Y *noun* coordinates for drawing a graph, where X is the vertical and Y the horizontal value; **X-Y plotter** = device for drawing lines on paper between given coordinates

Yy

Y-axis *noun* vertical axis of a graph
◇ **Y-coordinate** *noun* vertical axis position coordinate
◇ **Y-direction** *noun* vertical movement

Y-distance *noun* distance along an Y-axis from an origin

yoke *noun* **deflection yoke** = magnetic coils around a TV tube used to control the position of the picture beam

y punch *noun* card punch for column 12 (often used to indicate a positive number)

Zz

Z = IMPEDANCE

zap *verb* to wipe off all data currently in the workspace; *he pressed CONTROL Z and zapped all the text*

z-axis *noun* axis for depth in a three-dimensional graph *or* plot

zero 1 *noun* (i) the digit 0; (ii) equivalent of logical off or false state; *the code for international calls is zero one zero (010);* **jump on zero** = conditional jump executed if a flag *or* register is zero; **zero compression** *or* **zero suppression** = shortening of a file by the removal of unnecessary zeros; **zero flag** = indicator that the contents of a register *or* result is zero; *the jump on zero instruction tests the zero flag;* **zero-level address** *or* **immediate address** = instruction in which the address is the operand **2** *verb* to erase *or* clear a file; **to zero a device** = to erase the contents of a programmable device; **to zero fill** = to fill a section of memory with zero values

◇ **zero insertion force (ZIF)** *noun* chip socket that has movable connection terminals, allowing the chip to be inserted with no force, then a small lever is turned to grip the legs of the chip

zone *noun* region *or* part of a screen defined for specialized printing; **hot zone** = text area to the left of the right margin in a word-processed document, if a word does not fit completely into the line, a hyphen is automatically inserted

zoom *verb* to enlarge an area of text (to make it easier to work on)

◇ **zooming** *noun* enlarging an area of text *or* graphics; *variable zooming from 25% to 400% of actual size*

QUOTE there are many options to allow you to zoom into an area for precision work

Electronics & Wireless World

QUOTE any window can be zoomed to full-screen size by pressing the F-5 function key

Byte

COMPUTER AND PERIPHERALS

SINGLE BUS COMPUTER

MAR: Memory Address Register
MDR: Memory Data Register
ALU: Arithmetic and Logic Unit
ACC: Accumulator
IR: Instruction Register

MULTI-USER COMPUTER SYSTEM

Architecture of a multi-user computer system

hardware:
the base of the system, including the CPU and
memory
kernel:
routines used by every hardware operation
(access restricted to privileged users)
operating system:
system software used by all users (access
restricted to privil e ged users)
applications:
a user can select applications such as a compiler
or word-processing software

VIRTUAL MEMORY SYSTEM

To provide a 4Mbyte virtual memory space using a 4Mbyte backing store and 32Kbytes of main memory, with 4Kbyte pages:

user RAM
paged RAM
Memory Management Unit
Operating System
BIOS

Diagram components: 4Mbyte backing store — CPU — memory management — RAM

HANDSHAKING

Signals ensuring correct timing for data transfer between two communicating devices.

RS232 SIGNALS

Standard 25-pin connector

Pin	Description	Name
1	frame ground	FG
2	transmit data to equipment	TxD
3	receive data from equipment	RxD
4	request to send	RTS
5	clear to send	CTS
6	data set ready	DSR
7	signal ground	SG
8	data carrier detect	DCD
9	positive DC test voltage	+V
10	negative DC test voltage	−V
11	equalizer mode	QM
12	secondary DCD	(S)DCD
13	secondary clear to send	(S)CTS
14	secondary transmit data	(S)TxD
15	transmitter clock	TxC
16	secondary receive data	(S)RD
17	receiver clock	RxC
18	not used	
19	secondary RTS	(S)RTS
20	data terminal ready	DTR
21	signal quality detect	SQ
22	ring indicator	RI
23	data rate selector	
24	external transmitter clock	(TC)
25	not used	

PROGRAMMING LANGUAGES

The following demonstrates the differences in programming languages for a similar function, an input, n, is requested (the number of entries in the list) then a loop asking for the next entry and comparing it with the current biggest number is repeated n times, the biggest entry is then printed out.

ALGOL

```
begin    integer n,x,q;
         q:=0;
         read n;
         for i:=1 step 1 until n do
         begin
         B:        read x;
                   if x>00 then
                   goto A;
                   if x>q then
                       q:=x;
                   goto B;
         A:        print q;
         end;
end
```

BASIC

```
5 BIG=0
10 INPUT"How many numbers ";N
20 FOR I=1 TO N
30 INPUT X
40 IF X=0 THEN GOTO 100
50 IF X>BIG THEN BIG=X
60 NEXT I
100 PRINT BIG
110 END
```

C

```c
main()
{
        int n,i,x,big;
        scanf(%d,&n);
        (for(i = 0; i < n; i++)
        {
                scanf("%d",&x);
                if (x > big)
                        big=x;
        }
        printf("%d",big);
}
```

FORTRAN

```fortran
        INTEGER BIG
        BIG=0
        READ,N
        DO 2 I=1,N
        READ,X
   2    IF (X.GT.BIG)BIG=X
        PRINT,BIG
        STOP
        END
```

PASCAL

```pascal
program bignum(input,output);
var n,i,x,big : integer;
begin
        big := 0;
        read (n);
        for i:=1 to n do;
        begin
                read(x);
                if x > big then big:=x
        end;
        write(big)
end
```

ASCII IN DECIMAL, HEXADECIMAL

dec.	HEX	CHAR	dec.	HEX	CHAR	dec.	HEX	CHAR	dec.	HEX	CHAR
0	00	NUL	32	20	SP	64	40	@	96	60	
1	01	SOH	33	21	!	65	41	A	97	61	a
2	02	STX	34	22	"	66	42	B	98	62	b
3	03	ETX	35	23	#	67	43	C	99	63	c
4	04	EOT	36	24	$	68	44	D	100	64	d
5	05	ENQ	37	25	%	69	45	E	101	65	e
6	06	ACK	38	26	&	70	46	F	102	66	f
7	07	BEL	39	27	'	71	47	G	103	67	g
8	08	BS	40	28	(	72	48	H	104	68	h
9	09	HT	41	29	)	73	49	I	105	69	i
10	0A	LF	42	2A	*	74	4A	J	106	6A	j
11	0B	VT	43	2B	+	75	4B	K	107	6B	k
12	0C	FF	44	2C	,	76	4C	L	108	6C	l
13	0D	CR	45	2D	-	77	4D	M	109	6D	m
14	0E	SO	46	2E	.	78	4E	N	110	6E	n
15	0F	SI	47	2F	/	79	4F	O	111	6F	o
16	10	DLE	48	30	0	80	50	P	112	70	p
17	11	DC1	49	31	1	81	51	Q	113	71	q
18	12	DC2	50	32	2	82	52	R	114	72	r
19	13	DC3	51	33	3	83	53	S	115	73	s
20	14	DC4	52	34	4	84	54	T	116	74	t
21	15	NAK	53	35	5	85	55	U	117	75	u
22	16	SYN	54	36	3	86	56	V	118	76	v
23	17	ETB	55	37	7	87	57	W	119	77	w
24	18	CAN	56	38	8	88	58	X	120	78	x
25	19	EM	57	39	9	89	59	Y	121	79	y
26	1A	SUB	58	3A	:	90	5A	Z	122	7A	z
27	1B	ESC	59	3B	;	91	5B	[	123	7B	{
28	1C	FS	60	3C	<	92	5C	\	124	7C	¦
29	1D	GS	61	3D	=	93	5D	]	125	7D	}
30	1E	RS	62	3E	>	94	5E	↑	126	7E	~
31	1F	US	63	3F	?	95	5F	_	127	7F	DEL

THE ASCII SYMBOLS

NUL	Null	DLE	Data Link Escape
SOH	Start of Heading	DC	Device Control
STX	Start of Text	NAK	Negative Acknowledge
ETX	End of Text	SYN	Synchronous Idle
EOT	End of Transmission	ETB	End of Transmission Block
ENQ	Enquiry	CAN	Cancel
ACK	Acknowledge	EM	End of Medium
BEL	Bell	SUB	Substitute
BS	Backspace	ESC	Escape
HT	Horizontal Tabulation	FS	File Separator
LF	Line Feed	GS	Group Separator
VT	Vertical Tabulation	RS	Record Separator
FF	Form Feed	US	Unit Separator
CR	Carriage Return	SP	Space (Blank)
SO	Shift Out	DEL	Delete
SI	Shift In		

EBCDIC code

bits 0, 1, 2, 3

bits 4,5,6,7	0	1	2	3	4	5	6	7	8	9	10	11	12	13	14	15
0	NUL	DLE			SP	&	—									0
1	SOH	DC₁					/		a	j			A	J		1
2	STX	DC₂	SYN						b	k	s		B	K	S	2
3	ETX	DC₃							c	l	t		C	L	T	3
4									d	m	u		D	M	U	4
5	HT	NL	LF						e	n	v		E	N	V	5
6	LC	BS	ETB						f	o	w		F	O	W	6
7	DEL		ESC	EOT					g	p	x		G	P	X	7
8									h	q	y		H	Q	Y	8
9									i	r	z		I	R	Z	9
10	RPT				¢	!		:								
11	VT				.	$	,	#								
12	FF	IFS		DC₄	<	★	%	@								
13	CR	IGS	ENQ	NAK	(	)	|	'								
14		IRS	ACK		+	;	>	=								
15			BEL		|	¬	?	"								